Life's 'ANSWER'

A LIFE CHANGING MESSAGE OF ASSURANCE AND CHALLENGE

By Richard Broadhurst

authorHOUSE®

AuthorHouse™ UK Ltd.
500 Avebury Boulevard
Central Milton Keynes, MK9 2BE
www.authorhouse.co.uk
Phone: 08001974150

Published by AuthorHouse 8/21/2012

ISBN: 978-1-4772-1436-7 (sc)

Many thanks to my wife Jean for her patience over the years whilst this book was being written and compiled.

I would also like to thank Beryl and John Trundle for their help on this long project, Beryl for her work on the computer, and John for proof reading the text.

INTRODUCTION

This book is divided into two parts, and each part is written in a different style with different content as outlined below.

Part One is entitled 'Life's ANSWER'.

This book has been written for those who want to find the answer for a fulfilled worthwhile life, want to get the best out of life or make a new start in life. This quest includes those who are thinking that there must be more to life than their present experience, and also applies to those who are looking for a satisfying purpose in life with positive hope and security. It addresses those basic questions that most people would like to ask, but hesitate to do so for various reasons.

To realize these aspirations a series of progressive steps are set out that lead to achieving the desired result and provide an opportunity to achieve these goals whatever their past or present lifestyle or circumstances, and as these questions affect us all the solution applies to all.

TABLE OF CONTENTS

PART ONE
Life's ANSWER

PART ONE

LIFE'S ANSWER

SEARCHING FOR LIFE'S ANSWER

Everybody needs a reason to get up in the morning, they need a driving force or motive within themselves to spur and encourage them every day. Ultimately people are looking for some form of gain, adventure, fulfilment, enjoyment or challenge.

The types of force or motive that drive people are many and varied and would include: getting enough money and/or food to live for themselves or their family; finding a job; keeping a job; finding somewhere to live; keeping healthy; recovering their health; finding a happy and lasting relationship; having a family of their own; finding a fulfilling purpose in life; finding acceptance and love; knowing enjoyment and happiness; finding contentment, satisfaction and peace; seeking fame and fortune; making money; to achieve high academic or job status; solving problems; knowing an assured peace with God; etc., etc.

Some, however, do not seem to have any strong motivations in life, but are content to live life as it comes along and try to make the best of it.

Another aspect of life that affects people's motivation is the circumstances in which they are born. Some start life in comfortable circumstances, others in poor surroundings, some able bodied, others disabled, some having higher mental faculties than others.

The consequences of these varied motivations and circumstances on people may, or may not, help them to find a fulfilling worthwhile life, so it is necessary to look at the spiritual aspects of life to find an answer. However, before this topic is looked at from a spiritual point of view it is essential to cover the wider view of circumstances that surround us by also considering the issues of security and hope that affect us all.

Looking for security in an insecure world

We know that life has its uncertainties and insecurities, but in recent days a number of disturbing facts have made the world increasingly insecure. The effects of this on people's lives is shown in a general unrest, disillusionment, loss of hope, and has caused many to feel powerless, unfulfilled and some consider life is pointless. The effect on others causes them to seek a more lasting purpose and fulfilment for their lives, whilst some who have fulfilled their material and/or spiritual goals still feel there's something missing in their lives – a void they cannot fill.

All the above situations have motivated and positively compelled the author to address these most important issues. In response to this challenge the reader is offered assured hope and spiritual security through acting on the truths stated in these pages. So please read on.

Over recent years we have seen the world around us changing at an ever faster rate with increasing frequency of wars, and these have been accompanied with changes in the methods of dispute from direct confrontation of armies to the use of sniper tactics and suicide bombers employing surprise, through individual people and small terrorist groups. This makes it increasingly difficult to create even small safe havens for anybody.

Worldwide changes are also being experienced on the morality front where many of the once generally accepted standards of behaviour, often emanating from religions, have been bypassed as old-fashioned and irrelevant to a 'modern' age. Moral frameworks have either been allowed to decay or have been attacked and replaced by personal codes that say: "If it pleases you, do it." This and similar selfish codes of behaviour have resulted in huge increases in crime, corruption and a general disregard for the law and authority, which have brought in their wake much distress, disillusionment and dissatisfaction, and all this has left lawmakers and authorities not knowing the answers to the root of these problems which have affected all sectors of society.

Whilst all the above has been happening there has been enormous developments in technology, especially in the means of communication. One aspect of this has meant, however, that more and more people are better informed of how those in wealthier parts of the world live and what they have and this has caused a further discontentment, resulting in a greater movement of people from all parts of the world seeking to improve their lot. This movement has caused, and will seem to continue to cause, a disturbance and a challenge to family values, religious beliefs, customs and traditions to themselves and those they move near to.

These changes in circumstances will unsettle many and cause doubts, fears, conflicts with others and raise questions within themselves in a quest for truth and satisfaction, and many in the end will consider that everything is relative as there is no absolute fundamental truth, so just get the biggest slice of the cake you can by whatever means.

With all the above situations in mind it is quite understandable that people are beginning to search, but don't know where to look, for a worthwhile purpose in life that will provide an inner peace and fulfilment that gives hope and security. Also, the consequences of these events is that many face a future with little or no hope causing some to take desperate measures to improve their circumstances, whilst others despondently accept their lot in life. It follows, therefore, that the most urgent need is to offer people positive, solidly founded hope, which should be the birthright of everyone.

This scene of disturbance and unrest provides the setting for a challenge and an opportunity for the presentation of a personal solution for these problems through Christianity, which claims to have the answer to the deep needs of all people, whoever they are, whatever their background and wherever they come from. Unfortunately, the very mention of Christianity can bring such responses as: "I've heard it all before and am not interested", "I know nothing about it, but I'm quite satisfied with my present lifestyle, my religion, or no religion"; "It's irrelevant to a 'modern' world"; "I consider myself a Christian because I follow it as my religion as best I can". However, what people have heard about Christianity, and what causes them to make these kind of statements is based on many things including: a total ignorance of true Christian teaching and practice; bad examples of the lives of people who call themselves 'Christian'; accepting partially true statements about Christianity; accepting distorted teaching; or teaching that has no biblical foundation; etc.

Others may well say: "It's teaching will only cramp my lifestyle"; or "Hasn't Christianity been responsible for wars in the past, so how can it offer solutions?" etc.

The above responses are quite understandable in the light of what people have been told about Christianity from those who are prejudiced or sometimes ill informed. Also in history books, for example, in what has been portrayed as the wars of the, so called, 'Christian Crusades', were not in fact enacted by 'Christians', but by religious people who waged war on those of other religions in the name of 'Christianity'. In fact these people are shown to be in error because in the Christian's Book, the Bible, Jesus Christ never asked his followers to fight or kill to defend the Faith, or to increase the number of believers, but rather, to turn the other cheek, to love their enemies, to care for the sick and the poor, and that their 'war' was with the demonic spirits through prayer. In addition He asked them to teach and preach the truth in an attitude of love, and also to pray for healing.

The topics of conflicts and persecutions that have arisen from religions will be referred to again later.

From a historical point of view, as far as England was concerned, it was only the separation of church from state that has enabled Christianity to shake off most of it's sometimes violent, corrupt and un-Christ like character of the past. So today's Christian Church, whilst seemingly fragmented with a number of denominations, on closer inspection one finds that the majority of these are quite similar in what they believe and have a common foundation of biblical truth. The denominational differences stemming from varying emphasises of teaching, forms of worship and/or traditions. This means that some searching may be required to discover the 'best' church in your area. To those, therefore, who are in any way looking for answers to the basic issues raised here, and also to a range of other related issues that concern us all, then all that follows will help.

Finding security, purpose and hope

To meet the need of finding answers to the many vitally important questions relating to the meaning of life, spiritual security, fulfilling purpose and lasting hope in an increasingly insecure and confused world, it is not easy to know where to start, except to begin this quest with the basic challenge of asking people what they believe about God, - does He exist? - Are there many gods? In fact does it matter what people believe? Or indeed, whether or not a person believes in any Supreme Being or system of belief, so do these matters have any relevance today?

To begin this search for answers let us start by showing where they are not found, and progress to where they are found.

Formal Religion - No Answer

Firstly it is necessary to address a common misunderstanding that exists, by stating that the answer to these most important questions is not to be found in any formal religion. To explain this challenging statement it is essential to know how formal religion is defined.

Those who follow a religion in a formal manner can be described as people who sincerely submit to its teaching and modify their lifestyle in accordance with it, and this often entails conforming to a number of associated traditions. Also, this kind of religion would not claim to personally know their God, or gods.

Sadly, the majority of religious people in the world would fall into this category of following a religion formally.

World history, past and present, show only too clearly that formal religions have been, and still are, responsible a large proportion of wars and conflicts. Also they are responsible for a great many injustices towards, and the persecution of, those who follow a different formal religion, or no religion. One of the effects of this is to cause people to live in fear of expressing what they really believe when it is at variance to the beliefs of others around them.

Most religions offer a kind of security, but this comes at a price of living by set rules enforced with the fear that if broken, punishment will be meted out through those in authority in that religion.

All the above considerations clearly show that formal religions, whilst they may have many good aspects such as providing an ordered society, a sense of kinship and acceptance, they fail to give the person a lasting hope or the spiritual security of an assured eternal life that is coupled with a change of heart and motives that wants to please God and bless others. The reason for this failure is because formal religion lacks the power to change the person's character in the positive way described above.

This important topic of formal religion is referred to later in more detail under the headings of, 'Formal Religion' and 'Formal religion links with family or nationality'.

Towards an Answer

Throughout history it is plain to see that matters of belief related to a God or gods have always been of concern to most people of all ages. The reason for this being that they considered that what they believed and how they lived would affect their life here and their eternal destiny.

To begin with we are surrounded by many Faiths and systems of belief all making certain claims, so we are faced with choices.

In these pages we are considering the claims of the Christian Faith and how it is personally validated through scriptural evidence and borne out by life changing experiences. Also, in these pages various checklists are provided to help someone assess the true worth of their Faith.

To continue this search for the truth in these important matters, the issue of getting the best out of life is addressed next.

Getting Life's Best

Everyone wants to get the best out of life and this book points the way in which this can be achieved through Christianity, and provides a detailed inquiry into the subject.

The inquiry begins here by looking briefly at the ambitions, circumstances and purposes that people have in life.

Ambitions - Most people have ambitions of some sort, and want to get the best out of life. People generally have a mixture of material and spiritual goals, and mostly it would seem are material. The limitation with all materialistic goals is that they only last for the length of a person's life and at the end their assets, if they have any, are shared out. Also, the person that dies leaves behind a family, a good, or not so good reputation and perhaps a notable set of achievements. The problem with materialism, or any other doctrinal 'ism', or just seeking wealth for its own sake, is that they do not provide the lasting satisfaction or meet the deep down spiritual need that we all have.

Some aspire towards more spiritual goals in life, for example, to become teachers, nurses, doctors, pastors, priests, or those who care for animals or the environment etc. Whatever goals a person has in life, however, it still leaves many asking such questions as: what is life all about?; how can I get the best out of life?; can one ever be assured of receiving eternal salvation? (and some would say: 'if such a thing exists'). In these pages the fundamentals relating to such questions are addressed and answered.

Circumstances - It may seem to many people that life is random concerning what sort of circumstances they were born into – good, not so good, poor, or desperate, and they respond to those circumstances as best they can without considering whether of not there is any particular plan or purpose behind them. Then, as they grow up they begin to see that there are those who have, and those who don't have. The *have's* seek to enjoy to the full all they have been given and the *have-not's* respond generally either by struggling to improve their lot or despondently accepting their situation, having little or no hope of seeing things get better.

Purposes - So what's it all about, this life? Where does a person begin to look to find an answer? With these questions in mind let us review a list of purposes in life that people commonly have, such as:

- to enjoy a loving, long lasting relationship;
- to belong and feel secure in a loving family;
- to get married, have children, friends and enough money to enjoy and have a long life;
- to enjoy a long life with good health;
- to get a good education that enables them to get a satisfying job;
- to attain high office in a chosen profession;
- to attain a position of power and influence over others;
- to become very wealthy at an early age;

- to dedicate one's life to serve or care for others;
- to provide practical help to the poor and disadvantaged;
- to endeavour to provide comfortable and secure surroundings for yourself and others;
- to follow a religious Faith in the hope that it will provide eternal salvation;
- to seek to protect the environment for future generations; etc, etc, or any combination of the above.

It follows that many of the above aims are honourable in themselves and provide a level of fulfilment and contentment. However, there is an overarching purpose that can be sought and found, one that embodies many of the above but has at its core a foundational drive and desire that enhances life and provides positive hope through tough times, and finally an assurance of a place in heaven at death.

The above considerations now provide the lead into the next topic, headed 'Religion or Living Faith?' which is perhaps, not the most obvious place people would look to discover *the overarching purpose* that is referred to above, but if one is serious about wanting answers to this life and beyond, then please read on.

LOOKING IN THE RIGHT PLACE

Religion or Living Faith?

A dictionary definition of 'Religion' is stated as "a system of belief in a superhuman controlling power, especially in a personal God or gods entitled to obedience and worship".

The word 'religion' in the Bible is used only a few times and it generally signifies 'religion' in its external aspect and further stresses that it must not only have words, but have practical expression in serving others and endeavouring with God's help, to live pleasing to Him, our creator, and bless others. In practice often Religion gets mixed up with traditions and customs, with the danger that this can blur the distinction between the words and requirements of God and those of man. Again, for the sake of clarity, let us consider a dictionary definition of 'tradition', which is stated as "a custom, opinion or belief handed down to posterity, especially orally or by practice".

Although many traditions and customs are helpful and acceptable in themselves, they should never cause people to be dependant on them as a means of obtaining what can only come from God.

The generally preferred name when referring to the 'Christian Religion' is the term 'Christian Faith', which no doubt derives from the need to avoid the dangers mentioned above.

In reality it can be stated that any religion, including Christianity, that is followed through acknowledging certain beliefs and practicing a set of rules such as: adhering to its teaching; serving activities; preaching for conversions; teaching the faith; praying; attending services and adopting an appropriate lifestyle, but does not have as its foundation a personal relationship with God, should be classified as a 'formal religion', or following a religion in a formal manner.

At this point it is necessary to explain how adopting a 'formal religion' will prove to be an unsatisfactory and misleading route to follow.

Formal Religion

Those who practice a 'Formal Religion', or those who follow a religion in a formal manner can be defined as those who follow rules, codes of behaviour, customs and ceremonies that relate to any religious or Faith group, including Christianity, but do not have a personal interactive relationship with the author or originator of that Religion or Faith. Also, these formally religious people commonly rely on obedience to scriptures, laws or customs to earn salvation or acceptance to obtain a better future life. By contrast, however, in true Christianity salvation cannot be earned but can only be received as a free gift.

In 'Formal Religion' man seeks God, to find Him, appease Him, gain His favour and gifts etc. However, in the Christian Faith God seeks us in a variety of ways and wants us to come to know Him, receive His love and become empowered to live for Him.

Formally religious people can be utterly sincere, zealous, and their motives honourable, but sadly they will not find a spiritual life that connects them into a source of power to change their character for the better and for the benefit of others, or be able to break an enslaving damaging addiction or lifestyle. In fact, these people may be able to achieve great areas of control in their lives and achieve great things through their endeavours, but their lack of a personal relationship with the central God of their Religion/ Faith means that their Religion is lifeless, and this is explained by the fact that formal religions provide the rules/laws for living a certain type of lifestyle, but they cannot provide the inner power to change a person's character for the better, as stated above.

The danger of adopting a formal religion can be outlined as providing: a false sense of security and hope; also a false view of thinking that utter sincerity and deep conviction are sufficient and right to justify any actions they take, even if they are harmful to others. A biblical example of this was the Pharisees in the Bible's New Testament; they followed the Jewish

Faith with great zeal and sincerity, and yet were responsible for the death of the Lord Jesus Christ.

However, there is good news and positive hope for those who want to find and know the security of a living Faith, one that connects into God's vast resources of power, so please read on.

Formal religion links with family or nationality

Concerning family or nationality everybody accepts that they had no choice or control over where they were born, into what family, tribe, nation, circumstances-rich or poor etc., - they were just a helpless baby. With this choice factor in mind, it is a common fact of life that many are born into families that have strong links with formal religions and traditions, and as they grow up it is assumed that they will follow the religion of their family. However, when that person becomes an adult they may want to choose another religion, or no religion, but if they exercise this choice they often have to suffer being disowned by their family and/or wider family or tribe, and in many cases face persecution or death. Thus people in this situation are denied a free, without penalty, choice, whether they know it or not, and so must be prepared to pay the 'price' for a different choice.

The family involved in this situation normally considers that the family member has brought disgrace on the family and the wider family, and thereby justifies any action that they take against the family member.

In stark contrast to this if Christians move away from their Faith they are generally prayed for and gently encouraged through loving concern to return, but no threats are applied.

Living Faith

As can be seen from the above statement following a formal religion only changes the person's *external* words and actions, but when someone forms a personal relationship with the living God, the Lord Jesus Christ, a process is started that changes the *internal* character, aims and motives of the person for the benefit of all. It is this personal relationship that is a truly unique aspect of Christianity, and is the channel by which a person receives the power and motivation of love to live pleasing to God, and to know with positive assurance that they have eternal salvation. In addition, this relationship provides: the life purpose; the joy; the security; the sense of belonging; the inner peace; and the lasting hope that people are looking for.

Also, a further unmatched feature that comes from this relationship is that the above qualities of life are not related to the person's circumstances or well-being.

As explained in the Bible, and in this book, God wants us to know Him, love and obey Him, and to walk in unity and friendship with Him and others, and it is through this personal relationship that the Christian Faith becomes a Living Faith because God becomes the One who motivates the heart to want to follow, love and serve Him and others.

It has also been said that a another characteristic unique to the Christian Faith is 'grace', i.e. God's unconditional love for all people, and He, having done all that was required to bring that relationship about waits for us to respond to Him.

Religion -A Historical Aspect

Many people today question the relevance and/or value of following any particular religion. It is hoped, however, that this book will help people to see and experience that a true Faith does exist that is relevant, gives positive purpose and hope, is of great value, and has extremely important consequences for this life and eternity.

Sadly the history of those holding to various religions is one littered with much confusion, erroneous unfounded beliefs and myths, often coupled with utter sincerity, harsh judgements, and dogmatic intolerant ungracious attitudes. The consequences of all this has led to misunderstandings, conflicts and wars. In addition, there are those who have been, and still are seeking to forcefully convert others to their system of belief. However, in the Christian Faith it clearly states that when people make a commitment to God to become a Christian it is only through the operation of their own free will and conviction. It is an individual and very personal decision, and cannot be forced on anyone against their will and cannot come about through natural birth.

Another very sad and serious fact to consider is that there are many millions of people in the world who are sincerely practising their religion without being sure of receiving eternal salvation, and this is often linked to believing that they must fulfil certain conditions to obtain it. This frequently entails living a life of anxiety and self-effort to achieve definite goals without the assurance and peace of mind that they have met the targets or been accepted. Alternatively people can sincerely believe that they have met all the required conditions for eternal salvation and not be aware that they are living in a false sense of security. Another choice that many make is to live wholly or mainly to serve their own interests and put all thoughts aside of being accountable to any God or gods, and are unconcerned about the consequences this may, or may not, have.

The issues raised here are serious and should be the concern of everybody, which supports the case that every person should be afforded the right to question their own faith or that of others.

Hope Offered

It is good to note that the Christian Faith addresses the above and many other issues relating to life now and the situation after death, and the approach used here to answer these concerns is initially to: explain what the Christian Faith is not; unravel the problems associated with it; and then, to define the true claims of the Faith.

Hence, in the Christian Faith, salvation is not obtained by doing good works, fulfilling certain conditions, achieving specified goals, taking part in particular religious ceremonies or rituals, or the wearing of prescribed clothes, going on specified pilgrimages, attending particular buildings for worship or saying formal prayers, but is only entered into through a confession of sin to God and accepting The Lord Jesus Christ as the sinless Son of God, who died to pay the penalty for our sin once and for all. This demonstrated how much He loved us, and still loves us, and further declares that nobody else was, or is, able to procure our salvation because He was the only One who was able to pay the price, as He alone was sinless. This is Good News indeed, and will be more fully explained later.

The issue of 'good works' is of course relevant in the Christian Faith, and they should be seen after the person has known a conversion experience, and indeed, has the proof of character change that it has taken place.

There are many aspects associated with religions of all types where essential truth has been overlaid with secondary issues and unhelpful organisational structures that have prevented many from seeing these truths. One such aspect is when religions are institutionalised which sometimes means that they become integrated with a nation state. So when these events occur a hierarchy of status positions is created, and down the ages this has opened the way for corruption by many power-loving people, also, when a religion is built into the state people can sometimes be denied a choice of faith. In a state-faith situation it is often the case that those who choose another faith are regarded as betraying the family and the state and will suffer as a consequence.

It can be said that the Christian Church is partially institutionalised with a hierarchical structure, but with a large proportion having only minimum structures sufficient to allow them to function. However, this does not detract from the fact that it is fundamentally different from all other Religions as revealed by the following concise statement where Religion has been described as, *"Man's search for God"*, therefore, there are many religions. By contrast, the Christian Faith is about, *"God's search for man"*, - this makes it unique.

From earliest times special buildings for the worship of God or gods have been built at much cost of time, money and dedication. Indeed, in the Bible we see the development of firstly a special tent for worship constructed according to God's detailed instructions, followed in later times by a Temple designed by God according to His requirements.

Temple worship continued until the death of the Lord Jesus Christ, and at this time the first believers, known as Christians, were persecuted, so they met in houses. This move from 'dedicated' worship buildings to houses has widened over the years to include cathedrals, stadiums, renovated factories and warehouses, cinemas, halls and schools, as well as church buildings.

This change to meeting in a variety of buildings has evolved from teaching initially given to the early Christians, and later incorporated into the Bible, that a group of Christian believers was to be known as 'THE CHURCH'. Hence, it follows that 'THE CHURCH' can meet together for worship in any convenient place. This development has demonstrated that whilst many Christians seek to have their own buildings to worship in, they are not dependant on them in an institutionalised way.

In the Christian Faith idols of any type are considered an abomination to God as seen in the few, (of many), biblical Scriptures references given below:

Please note: A list of the abbreviations for the Books of the Bible is given at the back of the book.

People are warned not to turn to idols or make gods of any type of idol for themselves – see Lev: 19:4
Those who worship images will be put to shame – see Ps: 97:6-7
Idols are lifeless – see Ps: 135:15-18

In the Bible (Acts 17:22-25) it says that Paul went to Athens and he observed that the people were very religious, and said he even found an altar with the inscription "TO AN UNKNOWN GOD". He then proclaimed to the people about the God who made the world and everything in it is the Lord of heaven and earth and does not live in temples built by hands.

People turned from idols to the true God – see 1Thess:1:9-10

The Lord Jesus Christ warned people not to teach the rules and traditions of men as a substitute for the teachings of the Scriptures, as shown in the Bible passage (Mk 7:7-9) below:

"They worship me in vain; their teachings are but rules taught by men.' You have let go of the commands of God and are holding on to the traditions of men."

And he said to them: "You have a fine way of setting aside the commands of God in order to observe your own traditions!"

The Good News is that our unique God, as revealed in the Bible, is not only living, but is eternal and hence, is not just God of the past, but also God of the present and the future and He has provided us with clear direction for living and the power required to live a life that is pleasing to Him. He is also the One who can provide us with all that is necessary for this life and eternity. His provision includes God's Word, the Bible, which not only reveals the character of God but also provides the essential foundation of truth through which, and with God's help we can receive guidance, assurance and a sure hope for this life and eternity.

He has given us positive promises for now and eternity to those who trust Him alone for the forgiveness of sin and the free gift of salvation.

<u>Note:</u> The meaning of the word 'sin' is explained later.

HISTORY AND SOLUTIONS

Misunderstandings and Apologies

In history much blood has been shed in wars and disputes in the name of 'religion', and some of these have been in the name of Christianity. This is not only sad but also highly regrettable because whilst arms can be used to defend oppressed and defenceless peoples, Christ never asked His followers to take up arms to defend the Christian Faith. He did, however, ask them to contend for the Faith with prayer, living lives that please Him and serve others. He also asked us to proclaim the truths of the Faith in an attitude of love. It follows, therefore, that any war fought for the Christian Faith was done in the name of a lifeless religion, and not really in the name of true Christianity, because it says in the Bible "For we do not wrestle (or contend) against flesh and blood, but against principalities, against powers, against the rulers of the darkness of this age, against spiritual hosts of wickedness in the heavenly places"- Eph 6:12.

The result of past wars and disputes has led to misunderstandings and mistrust of Christians and Christianity and this has lasted for many years, and in some cases centuries. These events have made it much harder, therefore, for people of other Faiths to put aside prejudices that have understandably built up, and been passed on down the generations. Even when Christians seek to live out their life according to Biblical standards, which is only possible by God's power and grace, sometimes this is seen as a threat and a challenge to others leading to discord and their persecution, despite the acts of love and care they have shown towards others outside the Faith.

Another area of misunderstanding and confusion concerns what people consider to be 'Christian' or 'a Christian', for example, some consider 'The West' is Christian, some think that Great Britain is 'Christian', others think that if you are born here or go to church that makes you a 'Christian'. The truth is, however, that a person is only truly a Christian when they come into a personal relationship with The Lord Jesus Christ, the Son of the living God. Also, regarding Great Britain as Christian could only have been considered (to be 'Christian') to a limited extent in the past due to the fact that many of its laws and customs were based on biblical laws and principles, and the same would apply to the term 'The West'

So, if biased attitudes are put aside so that people can objectively and sincerely consider the claims made for the true Christian Faith then they will find it worthwhile. To this end, it is the sincere hope of the author that this book will help people to approach the Christian Faith with an open mind and come to know for themselves the love, forgiveness and new life that God is waiting to give them, and to welcome them into His eternal kingdom. As people venture on this personal journey of faith they will be helped as they consider the aspects of God's character, and the sacrifice He has made for them, as revealed in the book.

Claims made for the Christian Faith

The claims as summarised below can be used as a standard against which other Religions/Faiths can be compared.

The Initial Personal Claims

Among these claims a true Christian should be able to say that they: have a personal relationship with God; have the power, purpose and joy to live the Christian life; have experienced forgiveness and acceptance and are assured of their eternal salvation

The General Claims

1) The Creator and Redeemer God is the one and only God as revealed in the Bible and He is living, supernatural, eternal, absolutely unique, all powerful, our creator and the creator of the universe.
2) God is holy, absolutely pure.
3) He has demonstrated in the past and still proves in the present day that He is: loving, gracious, forgiving, empowering, unique, and gives true just judgement over all peoples and will pass final judgement on each person.

4) Anyone can meet with God directly through prayer at any time and in any place – no intermediary or priest is required.
5) Personal eternal salvation is offered together with the power to live a full life that is pleasing to God and fulfilling to the person.
6) Provides a clear purpose in life.
7) Provides a fellowship of love, acceptance and family through other Christians and the church.
8) Provides a gathering of Believers where people can participate in worship, and in sharing their lives and can also receive teaching and help, all in a family atmosphere – which gives acceptance, and the sense of belonging.
9) Provides the Bible - the living Word of God through which He speaks and guides believers through life.
10) The Bible states the conditions on which we obtain eternal salvation, and consequently, the way in which we will be judged.

Characteristics of the Christian Faith and its Historical Roots

The Christian Faith has its historical roots in the early Hebrew Nation and has embraced the Scriptural truths about God and His chosen people as revealed and recorded through its' prophets. These Scriptures are known collectively as the 'Old Testament' (O.T.) portion of the Bible.

The story of the Lord Jesus Christ was prophesied in the O.T. and detailed in the 'New Testament' (N.T.) portion of the Bible. The teaching for Christians is given in both O.T. and N.T.

A few hundred years after the last of the O.T. prophets had died Jesus Christ was born. His birth was miraculous as He was born through a virgin (Mary), and the O.T. prophets foretold this. However, the Hebrew people did not accept that He was the long awaited and promised Messiah - The Christ, God's Anointed One, but His sinless life, His redemptive death, His victorious resurrection and His fulfilment of O.T. Scriptures have proved beyond any doubt that He was and is 'The Christ' - God's Only Son.

This rejection of Christ by the Hebrew people opened the way for anyone, (including Jews), who repented and believed in Him as God's Son to be forgiven and accepted by Him and to become His new 'People' - Christians.

In O.T. times forgiveness for sins committed was obtained through the sacrifice of unblemished animals (often lambs), but this method was superseded once and for all time when the perfect sinless Son of God, the Lord Jesus Christ, died on a Roman cross to pay the penalty for the sin of the whole world which was the price demanded by a Holy God. This act of sacrificial love has thus provided the means whereby believers have eternal salvation and He alone as God's sinless Son, is the only One through whom people can obtain forgiveness of sin and receive an empowered new life with a new start (Acts 4:12).

When He died He paid the penalty for the sin of the whole world, but He waits for people to personally accept that they are guilty of sin, and that His sacrifice was for them, and this course of sincere action opens the way to receive personal forgiveness and new life.

Note: The meaning of the word 'sin' is explained later.

People's Basic Needs

An experienced traveller and writer has made the following astute observation from his many worldwide travels concerning the basic needs of the human race, and has stated that many people around the world were searching for: love, a sense of belonging, belief in a faith, and a means of salvation. All these needs and far more are met in God through the Christian Faith.

THE 'GOOD NEWS'

To meet the above basic human needs, and much more, God has revealed Himself over 5000 years ago through the Jewish people as proclaimed in the Hebrew Scriptures (the Old Testament) of the Bible, and has shown a fuller revelation of His character in the person of the Lord Jesus Christ in the New Testament portion of the Bible. The coming of the Lord Jesus Christ 2000 years ago has provided open access for all peoples to have enlightened and fulfilled lives with positive hope for the present, and for eternity. Our God is unique in Himself, and in His attitude of sacrificial love, which He demonstrated to us by the Lord Jesus Christ dying for us, His creation. Not only has He shown us the character of God through the life, death, and resurrection of the Lord Jesus Christ, but has provided us with a unique Guidebook, the Bible. This Book has proved to be God's authoritative and empowered Word from its inception to the present day, and has clearly demonstrated throughout its history that it is well able to defend itself.

The unique features of God's character are shown and defined by the biblical Scriptures quoted in this book, and paramount in His character of love is that He is always seeking us, wanting to have friendship and fellowship with us, and is passionately concerned about our present welfare and eternal well being. His objectives are that we come to know Him; know the joy of fulfilling His will and becoming more like Him; and these are pursued by Him with an eternal perspective in mind for our lives and destiny. Such is His love and grace towards us that He wants us to share with Him abundant everlasting life, and avoid eternal punishment.

The love of Jesus Christ was demonstrated through the ultimate sacrifice of dying on a cross for us, and when He died He paid the penalty for the sin of the whole world, but He waits for people to personally accept that they are guilty of sin (as explained under the heading 'Conversion'), and repent of it. Acknowledging this fact and taking this action, opens the way to receive personal forgiveness, a new and empowered life, and eternal life. These actions from God on our behalf are at the centre of what is known as 'The Good News' - or 'The Gospel'.

The Lord Jesus Christ whilst on earth was someone who showed a personal interest in people, and He has not changed because He still wishes to be in direct contact with us, and this does not require an intermediary because our God is a loving relational God and earnestly desires us to know Him personally, and hence, has purchased our personal salvation through being crucified for us. However, in our 'natural' state we are estranged from Him and a miraculous interaction needs to take place between God and us, enabling us to come to know Him personally, and this divine process is known as 'Christian Conversion'.

The Steps to Become a Christian

Christian Conversion

The key distinguishing feature of the Christian Faith is that it operates through God's miraculous power and grace (undeserved love), and this requires from the person a humble, thankful and repentant response.

The first thing to understand is that a person cannot be born a Christian, and no one is acceptable or unacceptable based on whether their parents or family were Christians or not. Another common misunderstanding is that a person can become a Christian through doing good deeds; unfortunately this is not the way.

The fact is, that each person must always have a direct meeting with God – initially through recognition of the deity of the Lord Jesus Christ as God's Son, coupled with confession and repentance, as explained below.

The process of Christian conversion starts in a personal way when a person first becomes aware of a need before God – a need to be forgiven for ignoring God's love as demonstrated through Jesus dying as a sacrifice for them – a need to know God's forgiveness for living just to please themselves, – a need for a new start in life, – a need to know God personally. Becoming aware of these needs are indications of God's Spirit interacting with our spirit, when He is speaking to them and endeavouring to draw them to Himself in a love bond of salvation.

When people fail to keep God's laws, ignore them, or just want to please themselves how they live, then they are showing a rebellious attitude towards God, their creator. This attitude is referred to as 'sin' in the Bible. Sin is defined as lawlessness in the Bible (1Jn 3:4), and refers to the failure of people to keep God's moral laws. The Scriptures further reveal that this failure to keep God's laws and prefer to live their lives to please themselves is due to an inborn weakness in all people, so all are guilty. Furthermore, God has always demanded a blood sacrifice to pay the penalty for the person's guilt.

In the times before Christ came the Hebrew people were required to sacrifice an unblemished lamb to cover their personal sin, but the good news is, that when the Lord Jesus Christ came He paid the ultimate blood sacrifice by dying on the cross, and He was the only One who was able to pay the penalty for sin for all mankind because He alone was sinless.

When people recognise the need for their sin to be forgiven and their guilt to be removed, and they respond by confessing and turning away from their sin, ask for forgiveness and thank God that the Lord Jesus Christ, God's Son, has paid for their sin too, then, when these steps are taken a transaction takes place between God and the person. This response is known as Christian Conversion, and is also known as 'being born again', or 'being saved' and so the person begins a new empowered life – as explained later.

If a person has made this commitment to God with a sincere and humble attitude, and a repentant spirit, then He responds by cleansing them from sin and the guilt of sin of their past life, and empowers them through the gift of the Person of His Holy Spirit that He gives to dwell within them, enabling them to start living a new life as they submit themselves to God.

When people submit to God they must understand that He does not wish to dominate and control them like puppets, but invites them to submit to Him as a loving Father, and their relationship to Him becomes that of His sons and daughters. It should be borne in mind that submission to God is not weakness, but wisdom.

This person has now become a Christian, and starts to live a new life in God's family.

So it can be said that unless a person accepts the 'Bad News' of the need before a Holy God to be forgiven and cleansed, then they are not in a position to appreciate or receive the 'Good News' of God's forgiveness and an empowered new life.

The Bible teaches that as far as God is concerned a penalty must be paid for sin, so either because the person cannot pay and then they suffer eternally for it, or they accept the penalty already paid for them through Christ's death on the cross on their behalf. It follows, therefore, that there are only two types of people in the world – the unforgiven sinner, and the forgiven sinner.

There are many passages of Scripture that contain the conditions that have to be met for people to obtain personal salvation, and two are given below:

"For God so loved the world that he gave his one and only Son, that whoever believes in him shall not perish but have eternal life. For God did not send his Son into the world to condemn the world, but to save the world through him. Whoever believes in him is not condemned, but whoever does not believe stands condemned already because he has not believed in the name of God's one and only Son."Jn 3:16-18

The Bible also states that:" if you confess with your mouth, "Jesus is Lord," and believe in your heart that God raised him from the dead, you will be saved" And will receive the gift of Holy Spirit. See Rom 10:9-13

From the above passages of Scripture we can see there are three basic conditions to be met by us to achieve personal salvation, namely: repentance, belief, confession and thanking Him for dying for us and paying our penalty. These elements or conditions are outlined below, and further reference is made to them in Sections E1 and E2 of the book.

It is to be noted that in the process of salvation the person receives forgiveness of sin, and the gift of the Person of the Holy Spirit to dwell within them providing the power to live for God.

Repentance and Confession to God

In Christian terms repentance refers to a personal change of mind, regretting one's past lifestyle, seeking God's forgiveness for the fact that we have lived to please ourselves and ignored His claims on our lives', and confess that we need His power to start and continue a new life. Part of this process is recognising and accepting that God's Word, the Bible, is true and that we can rely on what it says, and be confident that we have received His forgiveness and salvation when we understand that The Lord Jesus Christ, the sinless Son of God, is the One alone who has made these things possible by dying to pay the price of our sin. Hence, this relates to what we truly believe concerning Him as outlined below:

Belief:

Personal salvation centres around what we believe concerning The Lord Jesus Christ, and the basic essential beliefs for someone seeking to come to God in repentance and faith is that they will initially acknowledge that He is God Almighty their only Saviour and Redeemer, and will go on to accept that:

- He is the eternal Son of God,
- He is part of the Godhead of Father, Son and Holy Spirit,
- He is Holy, All knowing and All-powerful,
- He is the Creator of heaven and earth,
- He came from heaven to earth and was made man through a virgin birth by Mary,
- He was sinless, yet was crucified for the sin (rebellion) of His creation - mankind,
- He died, was buried and on the third day rose again in accordance with scripture,
- He procured personal salvation, through His death and resurrection, for all who repent and believe on Him - become Christians,
- He will return to earth to judge the living and the dead,
- He sent the Person of the Holy Spirit to empower and guide Christians,
- He created The Church - the company of Christians.

Confession before others

There are two aspects of confession: one informal and the other formal.

The informal aspect relates to our everyday conversations where we share openly about our Faith in a natural way, as opportunities occur and then confine ourselves to answering only the point in question. Any further talk about the Faith should generally be by 'invitation only' from the other person(s). The words of confession should be spoken in an attitude of humility, and backed up by appropriate actions and lifestyle.

The formal aspect of our confession relates to a public declaration of our Faith by giving a word of testimony, or being baptised by immersion in a public place before a number of people.

Whilst baptism is not part of the process of personal salvation it is closely linked to it, and there is much evidence for this given in the Scriptures, particularly in the book of the Acts of the Apostles. The baptism referred to was by immersion in water, and according to Scripture is required of every Believer as an act of obedience to witness that they have become a Christian. It is not an optional extra. Baptism has been described 'as an outward sign of an inner faith' in the Lord Jesus Christ and that the person has committed their life to Him. Thus, the act of baptism in the company of witnesses can be considered as the formal aspect of confession.

Baptism is further likened to the death and burial of the old life when we go under the water, and rising to a new life as we come out of the water, and relates to Christ's death, burial and resurrection as shown by the following Scripture:

"We were therefore buried with him through baptism into death in order that, just as Christ was raised from the dead through the glory of the Father, we too may live a new life. If we have been united with him like this in his death, we will certainly also be united with him in his resurrection." Rom 6:4-5

As our personal salvation is based on the supernatural actions and grace of God and His interaction with us through His Spirit, it follows that He has not required us to do anything to earn our salvation, because it cannot be earned - see the following passage of Scripture:

"For it is by grace (God's unmerited favour) you have been saved, through faith— and this not from yourselves, it is the gift of God-- not by works, so that no-one can boast." Eph 2:8-9

It is after we have become Christians that God expects us to live for Him, serve Him and other people, and all this must come out of the love God gives us and not out of a sense of duty or self-will.

How to respond to God to become a Christian is further explained in the 'E4' Section of the book under the heading, "Becoming a Christian", and other related aspects are headed: Evidence for those who claim to be Christians; Scriptural Evidence; and, Opportunity and Freedom Offered.

The Final Step to Becoming a Christian

We have clear guidance from the Bible regarding this life-changing step as outlined below:

Jesus answered, "I am the way and the truth and the life. No-one comes to the Father except through me" Jn 14:6

"For God so loved the world that he gave his one and only Son, that whoever believes in him shall not perish but have eternal life". Jn 3:16

"All the prophets testify about him that everyone who believes in him receives forgiveness of sins through his name". Acts 10:43

Using the authority of God's Word, The Bible, we can see the conditions that are laid down for becoming a Christian, namely, we need to recognise that our present lifestyle is lived for ourselves and others, but not God. The situation where God is not at the centre of our lives' is in fact a rejection of Him and is our chief sin. If therefore, we have reached this point then we need to continue on to the next steps as outlined below:

- repent of our sin, (change one's mind towards God - regretting our previous lifestyle that meant that we just lived to please ourselves),
- ask for forgiveness,
- believe on the Lord Jesus Christ as God's Son - the one who has paid the penalty for our sin,
- thank Him for what He has done for us,
- make a confession of our faith in the Lord Jesus Christ to others,
- thank Him for the gift of His Holy Spirit who He has given to live in us.

When we are prepared to take these steps with sincerity, humility and with a repentant spirit, then we need to pray to God in the way indicated above, or use a prayer like the one given below.

There is no exact set of words to make this commitment, but remember, whatever words we use God does not only hear the expression of our lips but He reads the attitude of our hearts.

Lord Jesus Christ,
I know you died on the cross for my sin and
I want you to be the Lord of my life; now and forever.
Please forgive me for the way I have sinned against you by leaving you out of my life and living only as I wanted.
I submit my life to you and thank you for paying the penalty for my sin.
Thank you Lord for your forgiveness that I don't deserve, and for the person of your Holy Spirit to live in me.
With your help I will seek to love and obey you as Lord of my life.

<u>Now</u> – tell someone what you have done – see the Scripture below. And if you have prayed this, or a similar prayer containing the above essential truths with sincerity, then, based not on your feelings, but on the authority of the Bible you can state with confidence that:

God has saved you - see the Scripture below;

"That if you confess with your mouth, "Jesus is Lord," and believe in your heart that God raised him from the dead, you will be saved.

For it is with your heart that you believe and are justified, and it is with your mouth that you confess and are saved.

As the Scripture says, "Anyone who trusts in him will never be put to shame."

For there is no difference between Jew and Gentile--the same Lord is Lord of all and richly blesses all who call on him, for, "Everyone who calls on the name of the Lord will be saved." Rom 10:9-13

He has made you into a new person with a fresh start - see the Scripture below;

"So from now on we regard no-one from a worldly point of view. Though we once regarded Christ in this way, we do so no longer. Therefore, if anyone is in Christ, he is a new creation; the old has gone, the new has come." 2Cor 5:16-17

He has started a personal relationship with us, He knows us and we are just beginning to know Him - see the Scripture below;

"I am the good shepherd; I know my sheep and my sheep know me-- just as the Father knows me and I know the Father--and I lay down my life for the sheep." Jn 10:14-15

Evidence for those who claim to be Christians

After this 'conversion' experience has taken place the person's character begins to change little by little, to make them more and more like the character of The Lord Jesus Christ. Some of these miraculous changes are outlined below - given in no particular order.

- They want others to know and experience what they have received from God - acceptance into God's Kingdom, forgiveness of sin, cleansing from guilt, joy, fellowship with God and other believers, a purpose in living and the power to live a new life.
- They want to share God's love with others.
- They want to worship and praise God.
- They want to pray - to commune with their Father in heaven, and hear what He has to say to them.
- They want to read His Word the Bible.
- They want to meet together with other Christians to enjoy one another's friendship and fellowship.
- They want to live pleasing to God - finding and fulfilling His will for their lives resulting in the fruit of God's Spirit being seen by positive changes in attitude and lifestyle - see Gal 5:22-24.
- They want to receive from God whatever spiritual gifts He has for them, and use these to bring honour to Him and benefit to others.

From the above list it can be seen that the motivation for living the Christian life is not out of a sense of duty or fear, but out of a response of love for God and the change He has brought about in their lives enabled by His power.

Note:

The extent to which the above changes take place will depend on a number of factors including: the person's walk of faith and obedience to the will of God. As the Christian matures more of the above changes will be realised.

It will be observed that none of the above characteristics are 'natural' but supernatural, and hence, it is not within our power or ability to effect these changes in attitude or lifestyle, nor can we take credit for them. We can only thank God for His love, grace and help for others and us.

From the list given above it should be evident that God is *not* concerned with our *OUTWARD APPEARANCE* and *ACTS OF DEVOTION* because He looks behind our appearance and actions at our *INNER LIVES* –our attitude to God and others, our aims and motives in life, and our lifestyle. He does this because it is these factors that indicate who we truly worship, and who comes first in our lives. It is, therefore, when these inner aspects of a person's life start to change in a way that pleases God and benefits others that the beginnings of a relationship with the living Christ has begun, as explained under the heading 'The steps to becoming a Christian'.

Scriptural Evidence

The Lord Jesus Christ supplies further supporting evidence when He said:

"By their fruit you will recognise them. Do people pick grapes from thorn bushes, or figs from thistles? Likewise every good tree bears good fruit, but a bad tree bears bad fruit."

Mat 7:16-17

Also in 2Cor 5:17 it states that those who have submitted their lives' to the Lord Jesus Christ have become "a new creation"-- "Therefore, if anyone is in Christ, he is a new creation; the old has gone, the new has come!". In a further passage of Scripture written by St Paul to the Galatians he says that 'the fruit of the Spirit is love, joy, peace, patience, kindness, goodness, faithfulness, gentleness and self-control. Against such things there is no law', and 'Those who belong to Christ Jesus have crucified the sinful nature'. See Gal 5:22-24

The above statements can be used to show the extent to which miraculous changes in attitude and lifestyle have taken place. This will be observed by changes in attitude towards others and God. There will be increased love, care and concern for the welfare of others, Christians and non-believers, resulting in practical action for their benefit. There will also be a desire to live in a way that is pleasing to God, coupled with wanting to worship and serve Him. This can be summed up in the words of Scripture where it states that we become "a new creation" as given in 2Cor 5:17 above.

Opportunity and Freedom Offered

Another aspect of the 'Good News' is that we are all equal in God's sight, all basically sinful and in need of His salvation, and therefore, when we are called by God we have an opportunity of accepting or rejecting His offer of salvation, forgiveness and a fresh start in life. Also, the offer is such that it does not matter where a person was born, or into what family they were born, rich or poor, privileged or under privileged, fit or disabled or what were the religious beliefs of the person's parents, their tribe, race or nationality.

Our gracious God wants us to know Him, love Him and walk with Him in freedom and joy.

When we become Christians He provides freedom from the power of sin, and freedom from religious customs, practices and rituals devised by man - not ordained by God. In consequence, God has not placed any of the following conditions on us either as a means to attain personal salvation or to gain merit or approval and therefore, He has <u>not</u> requested us to:

- worship Him in a particular type of building;
- contact Him through an intermediary e.g. a priest;
- work for our personal salvation;
- fulfil any particular attainment (other than to obey Him and seek to fulfil His will for our lives) or ascetic lifestyle;
- worship any other person or thing besides Him;
- use icons, idols or statues of any kind;

- partake in elaborate ceremonies or processions;
- wear any special type of clothes;
- change or mutilate our body in any way;
- take up arms to defend the Bible or the Christian Faith;
- pray at any particular time, or frequency, day or night;
- pray using any particular form of words, except that we should include the model prayer that the Lord Jesus Christ gave us in Mat 6:5-13 – its frequency is not indicated.

Nobody is required to fulfil the above conditions because they could be relied on as a way of earning salvation or merit, but it must always be remembered that good works of any kind cannot earn salvation – it must be received through faith in the sacrifice of Christ for our sin, as a free gift, or not received at all. It follows, therefore, that a person cannot be born physically into the Christian Faith.

Hence, a person does *NOT* become a Christian by:

- Being born into a Christian family – NO, it is personal decision;
- Being born into a 'Christian' country – e.g. born in a garage does not make the person a car;
- Doing good deeds – NO, they come after;
- Following religious laws or traditions;
- Becoming a priest or holding any clerical position;
- Having a position of privilege or poverty;
- Enduring self-sacrifice or suffering;

The above information has been included to avoid any misunderstanding and to encourage the reader to continue to read on to discover the truth about being a Christian with the assurance that God '*wants all men to be saved and to come to a knowledge of the truth*', as it states in the Bible.

<u>A few supporting Scriptures:</u>
When a person has taken this step of faith they will:

- know the truth –see Jn 8:32-36
- be set free from sin - see Rom 6:16-18
- need to stand firm so that they are not enslaved again –see Gal 5:1

Having read through this whole topic headed "Religion or Living Faith" it should leave you to ask yourself one very important question: "am I just following a formal Religion, no Religion, or do I know the Living God and have a Living Faith and hence, am enjoying a useful and satisfying life here and looking forward to an assured, wonderful and everlasting future"?

In conclusion, any type of religion that is just a set of rules and regulations which seeks to please/appease a Deity where the ability and motivation to follow these codes is only provided through ardent desire, personal convictions, customs, traditions, family pressures, sincerity or fear etc, then, it is not a ***living*** faith, but a ***formal religion.*** Also, when Christianity is followed as a set of rules or codes, then again, it is not a ***living*** faith, but a ***formal religion.*** However, when a person has a true Christian conversion experience, then they are changed 'within themselves' by God and are thus empowered and want to live for God. So whereas people following a ***formal religion*** are driven by many factors including traditions and fear etc., the truly converted Christian is motivated by love for God and others through a changed heart. This 'heart' change starts at conversion and should continue to develop throughout life, but the progress of change is determined by that person's obedience to God.

Another important and unique factor for the person who has come into this living faith in Christ is to know that whilst all the resources of God are made available to them through their relationship with Him, they must learn to trust and rely on Him to meet their needs.

When Christian's sin by going their own way instead of God's through disobedience, failing to trust or rely on Him, then they should not blame God because His resources are always available. The good news is that through confession and repentance the person can be forgiven and restored to fellowship with God.

To help confirm whether or not you are a Christian, then speak to a mature Christian.

The next important step is to join a Church.

God's Offer comes with a Condition

God's offer of being accepted by Him, knowing Him and receiving the gift of eternal life comes with the conditions of us recognising that there are first the matters of belief and repentance to be accepted and acted on by us. Many people would respond to this by saying: "what do I need to believe? and what do I need to repent about?" Basically we need to believe that Jesus Christ was and is God's Son and that He died on the cross to pay the penalty for the sin of the world, and that includes our sin.

The sin, of all people, is the fact of just living to please themselves without reference to God. Some erroneously thinking that following a religious code of rules will be acceptable to God. In the Scripture Rom 3:23 it states that we are all sinners in God's sight, and the solution to this problem is addressed in the Scripture 2Pet 3:9 (given below) by calling us to repent (to change our mind and direction of life), because this Scripture, among others, clearly shows us that God does not want anyone to perish. So in His kindness He warns us not to show contempt for His kindness, tolerance and patience, otherwise we are left only waiting for His judgment, (see Rom 2:4-5)

The death of the Lord Jesus Christ for the sin of all mankind provided the way to escape condemnation by people believing on Him as stated in the Scripture Jn 3:16-18 (given below).

True belief, however, is not just in the head, but starts with the action of repentance.

The Bible further states that He was the only one who could pay this penalty for sin because He alone was sinless. It is, therefore, everyone's responsibility to recognise the unparalleled sacrifice, the depth of mercy and the undeserved love shown by God and respond accordingly.

He also warns people who through their actions or inactions ignore the gracious call and offer of salvation by God who waits to grant them forgiveness and entry into His Kingdom. These are people who are presuming that their good works and kindly deeds will somehow be acceptable to God and give them a place in heaven, sadly however, they are mistaken. That is because firstly He wants to know us and have a Father/child relationship with us, and this comes about through us recognising

Him as our creator God, confessing our failure of keeping Him out of a central place in our lives, and then thanking Him for dying to purchase our eternal salvation. The fact of God knowing us and we knowing Him is the very essence of being a true believer, a Christian, as borne out by the words of Jesus in Jn 10:14 given below.

Regarding our good works and kindly deeds, it's not that He does not want to see them, He welcomes them, but does not accept them as a means of earning eternal salvation, because it cannot be earned as stated in the Scripture Eph 2:8-9 given below.

It is clearly shown in the Scriptures that God does not want anyone to perish, (see 2Pet 3:9 below), but calls us to repent (to change our mind), and He warns us not to show contempt for His kindness, tolerance and patience, otherwise we are left only waiting for His judgment, (see Rom 2:4-5 below). Many people would respond to the statement above by saying: "what do I need to repent about"? The fact is, that when men and women just live to please themselves, without reference to God their creator, they are classified by Him as sinners and as He says in His Word the Bible in Rom 3:23, that we are ALL sinners, and all, therefore, in need of forgiveness and salvation.

God's solution to this situation was to send His Son, the Lord Jesus Christ, to die on a cross to pay the penalty for the sin of all mankind, thus providing the way to escape condemnation by repenting and believing as stated in the Scripture Jn 3:16-18 (given below). The Bible states that He was the only one who could pay this penalty for sin because He alone was sinless. It is, therefore, everyone's responsibility to recognise the unparalleled sacrifice, the depth of mercy and the undeserved love shown by God and respond accordingly.

He warns people who are sexually immoral, thieves, drunkards, slanderers or swindlers, that they will not inherit the Kingdom of God, (see 1Cor 6:9-11). However, there is hope here because this text says: "and that is what some of you were", and that through repentance, mentioned in 2Pet 3:9, they were washed from sin (rejection of Him), sanctified and justified.

The process of salvation is more fully explained in Section E4.

"For God so loved the world that he gave his one and only Son, that whoever believes in him shall not perish but have eternal life. For God did not send his Son into the world to condemn the world, but to save the world through him. Whoever believes in him is not condemned, but whoever does not believe stands condemned already because he has not believed in the name of God's one and only Son." Jn 3:16-18

Note the word '*perish*'

In verse 16 above this word is associated with God's Judgment and has great significance.

W.E.Vine refers to the word '*perish*' in the Greek and states: "The idea is not extinction but ruin, loss, not of being, but of well-being".

Jesus said: (in Jn 10:14)

"I am the good shepherd; I know my sheep and my sheep know me-"

People are warned not to show contempt for the riches of God's kindness, tolerance and patience, because his kindness is meant to lead people to repentance – see Rom 2:4-5. Also they are reminded that everybody has sinned and that they are justified freely by his grace (unmerited favour) through the redemption that came by Jesus Christ – see Rom 3:23-24

We are reminded in the scripture (Eph 2:8-9) that it is by God's grace that we are saved through faith as a gift from him, and he does not want anyone to perish, but everyone to come to repentance. – see 2Pet 3:9

A Brief Outline of the Christian Faith

The Unique Faith.

Unique to the Christian Faith is the fact that people connect and have a relationship with the Living Loving God who seeks after them.

Salvation.

Unique to the Christian Faith is that eternal salvation cannot be earned, but it can be freely accepted as a gift through repentance and trusting in the sufficiency of the sacrifice of Jesus Christ to cover our sin.

The Church.

Unique to the Christian Faith, the church is designed to provide a double set of family relationships, one with God and his people, and the other with our natural family, to fulfil every persons need to be accepted and belong.

Joining a Church

It is important that you tell a Christian that you have prayed a prayer like the one given above (under the heading "Becoming a Christian) and then seek to join a Church as soon as possible. You will soon discover, however, that there are many different types of Churches with a wide variety of names, so a few recommendations are set out as guide lines below.

Firstly, if you have a Christian friend you could find out about their Church. Whether you have a Christian friend or not you should join a local Church, but only after you have seen what they provide. Certain things to look for would include: a friendly welcome and acceptance; a teaching programme for new Christians e.g. an Alpha Course; Bible-based teaching; a place that has prayer meetings; a place with the possibility of developing Christian friends; a place where you can grow as a Christian and go on to serve God in some way; and a Church that has a missionary outlook both local and overseas.

A note of caution

Be wary of joining any Church where the leader or leaders demand absolute allegiance to them, and/or claim that they alone have the whole 'Truth' and the final say when interpreting the Bible.

Finding out more about Christianity

To those who wish to find out more about Christianity there are a number of avenues open to you including the following:

i) Read the Bible.
ii) Read Part 2 of this book "Christianity Defined" as it provides a detailed explanation of the main elements of the Faith – for further information please see the 'Introduction'.
iii) Read books from a Christian Bookshop, selected with guidance from someone in (iv) or (v) below.

iv) Speak to a Christian who you know and respect.
v) Speak to a Christian minister or Church leader who is well respected.
vi) Go on to an Alpha course.
vii) Listen to Christian Radio or Christian TV programmes, usually found on satellite TV, again, selected with guidance.
viii) For those who want to know more why not chat now at www.Groundwire.org.uk - they are available 24/7

CONCLUSION

The Ultimate Faith – Its Summary

The Christian message is unique in that it relates to a Living God who:

- Has the grace to forgive and give people a new start in life;
- Has the power to transform and empower lives for the good of themselves and others;
- Listens to and answers prayers;
- Loves us and wants us to know Him and walk this life with Him;
- Provides a purpose in life that does not fade with the years; *
- Provides hope in an often-hopeless world;
- Has paid the penalty for our sin for all who change their minds and trust in Him and these he gives eternal life and accepts them into His family;
- Offers all the above to all peoples.

So what more can anyone want for this life and the next?

*That purpose is found and fulfilled when they listen to and obey God's voice and thus live to please Him. Also this purpose is God's purpose tailored to you.

The Ultimate Aim

It is the sincere desire of the author that this book will act to bring help, new spiritual life, encouragement and enlightenment of biblical truth to the non-Christian, the seeker after truth, and the Christian alike. Also in this pursuit for truth I earnestly wish people to see that the Bible is the most precious source of God's wisdom, love, grace, forgiveness and direction for life, and the sure hope of eternal life that is offered to all people.

For those of another Faith, no faith, or those who are unclear about these matters, the author also hopes that the reader will find all the help they need in this book to experience the reality of a living, loving relationship with God.

If, however, you have not accepted the Christian Faith because you're not convinced about the evidence, the importance or the relevance of the issues presented, or you're fearful about the consequences etc., then please consider the destiny that we all are travelling towards, as outlined under the following heading.

The Ultimate Destiny

Given below are the steps of a typical life's journey that everybody has:

- Born into a set of circumstances over which you have neither choice or control;
- WHAT THEN? Has family or no family upbringing, with or without love;
- WHAT THEN? Has none, some or much schooling;
- WHAT THEN? Hears, or does not hear, about a religious Faith;
- WHAT THEN? Accepts or rejects that Faith;
- WHAT THEN? Achieves none or some skills or qualifications;
- WHAT THEN? Tries or gets desired job/money/place to live;
- WHAT THEN? Tries or gets desired personal relationship;
- WHAT THEN? Enjoys a good or not so good life;
- WHAT THEN? Has health problems or an accident;
- WHAT THEN? Thinks about what will happen when they die;
- WHAT THEN? Thinks about their destiny, could it be Heaven or Hell?
- WHAT THEN? Considers what determines their destiny?

Through some or all of these stages of life one becomes aware that God is speaking to us in various ways. This is because He loves us and longs that we may enjoy the very best in life, and to achieve this has gradually been trying to help us to understand that it is only through repentance and trusting in the Lord Jesus Christ that provides forgiveness and assurance of entrance into heaven.

Let us remember that God's heart has been revealed to us through the Bible when it says: "God wants all men to be saved and to come to a knowledge of the truth".

THE PRIESTHOOD OF ALL BELIEVERS

This Apostolic Doctrine is outlined below:
Some Scriptures that relate to this doctrine:

1Pet 2:4-10, Rom 12:5-8, Rom 15:14, 1Cor 12:7-11, 1Cor 14:26-40, Eph 5:19, Col 3:16, Jas 5:14-16, 1Pet 4:10, Rev 1:6.

In the book "Expository Dictionary of Bible Words" by W.E. Vine he refers to the Scripture 1Pet 2:4-10 and states regarding the word 'priesthood' in the original Greek is "HIERATEUMA" and says this: "denotes a priesthood, a body of priests, consisting of all believers, the whole church (not a special order from among them), called "a holy priesthood," 1Pet 2:5; "a royal priesthood," ver.9; the former term is associated with offering spiritual sacrifices, the latter with the royal dignity of showing forth the Lord's excellencies."

Peter pictures the Church as a building constructed of living stones with Christ as the Chief Cornerstone and this represents the congregation as a company of priests of royal lineage with Christ as the great King High Priest when they meet together.

In the above Scriptures there is a common theme of participation by believers in the congregation making contributions as led by God's Holy Spirit (1Cor 14:26-40), with a caution given in verse 40 that "everything should be done in a fitting and orderly manner." This 'order,' however, should be God's order that may not necessarily be ours, so this calls for people being sensitive to the leading of the Holy Spirit.

With reference to the other Scriptures:

- Rom 12:5-8 – refers to believers as "one body" having and using different gifts for the 'body'.
- Rom 15:14 – calls believers to "instruct one another."
- 1Cor 12:7-11 – states that: "to each one the manifestation of the Spirit is given for the common good."
- Eph 5:19 – refers to believers speaking and singing to one another.
- Col 3:16 – calls believers to: "teach and admonish one another with all wisdom."
- Jas 5:14-16 – this Scripture invites the sick person to call the elders of the Church to pray over them and anoint them with oil. It also calls believers to: "confess your sins to each other and pray for each other."
- 1Pet 4:10 – calls believers to use their gifts to serve others.
- Rev 1:6 – refers to believers as: "a kingdom of priests."

Practical Outworking.

This teaching is stating that each Church member has an opportunity to be a participant in a Church service, through: choosing hymns/songs, giving a Bible reading, praying, giving a short word of testimony, and using gifts of the Holy Spirit as they sense His leading. This participation should be by general invitation and its practice will be determined by the size of the congregation.

For a congregation of say over two hundred people it would not perhaps, be practical due to the difficulty of hearing the contributions from different parts of a building and therefore, may well only be carried out in the house groups or cell groups of the Church.

For a congregation of say less than two hundred people an opportunity can be provided for any who wish to participate by sharing what they believe God has said to them. This practice could also be adopted in the Church's house groups or cell groups. However, there is one special case where the above practice is modified, that is, when a person feels they have received a directional prophetic word. In this case they should share it first with an elder, and the word would be 'weighed or considered' by the elders, and if they discern it to be a word from the Lord for the congregation it would be given to the Church.

Many Churches adopt this method of handling the above forms of participation.

PART TWO

Christianity Defined

Note: Each Section contains:
Biblical Definitions;
Notes and Quotations;
Biblical Texts & Text References.

The Character of God and His Provision for us

PART TWO

CHRISTIANITY DEFINED

This part of the book provides the essential teaching and characteristics of the Faith, to help people understand it, and for those who have made a Christian commitment it provides the material to aid maturity.

The approach used is by grouping related topics together in Sections that are presented under headings of 'Biblical Definitions', Notes and Quotations', and Biblical Texts and Text References'.

It uses the Bible as its basis of divine authority and shows the powerful, positive and transforming effect the God of the Bible has on the lives of true believers.

The writing format adopted provides sufficient explanation to give a clear understanding of the subject matter, and relies on the biblical Scriptures to support the narrative, and the way the subject matter is presented and illustrated will enable those with no background or previous interest in matters of Faith, to understand it. Also a sufficient number of written biblical Scriptures have been quoted to enable those without a Bible or access to one, to follow it, and for those with a Bible many extra Scripture text references have been given.

It should be noted that this part of the book is not written as a Bible commentary, but as a Handbook that engages the reader to respond to the important matters being considered.

It includes among its multiple subjects an outline history and composition of the Bible.

A

PRAISE AND WORSHIP

Biblical Definitions

Worship

It is an inbuilt characteristic in people that they desire someone or something to worship, to adore or pay homage to. This is borne out by history up to the present day, and is seen in the formation of many religions or religious type of systems of living throughout the world. Even when a previously unknown tribe is found, the explorer discovers that they worship some type of god in the form of idols, sun, moon, trees, animals etc.

One of the key reasons why this book has been written and compiled is to meet this basic need that people have in the most fulfilling way possible. This is done by pointing people to the God of the Bible, the Christian's God, and the whole approach to the subject starts through introducing them to this God. To reveal His character and worth and so provide the basis and reason for people to worship Him, appreciate what He has done for them and so come to believe on Him, know and love Him.

From this introduction to the subject let us begin this most worthwhile of all quest's by coming to appreciate, then to know and worship the unique God of the Bible. People will then discover the true source and power of a new life, a life of assured hope, and an eternal life.

Now let us look at the various definitions and expressions of worship that are provided below.

In W.E. Vine's 'Expository Dictionary of Bible Words' it states that the worship of God is nowhere defined in the biblical Scriptures, but is broadly regarded as the direct acknowledgement of God, of His nature, attributes, ways and claims. However, a number of words are used to help us understand such as the Greek word 'Proskuneo' which is to make obeisance to; do reverence to God; to come towards to kiss like a subject bowing down to kiss the King's hand, to demonstrate a giving of devotion and honour.

Other biblical words relate to the giving of willing service to God. The giving of devotion and honour is demonstrated by walking upright before God in justice, love and humility (Mic 6:8).

Worship is also expressed by living in obedience and presenting ourselves to God, body, soul and spirit as a living sacrifice (Rom 12:1-2). In Genesis 22:1-18 it says that because Abraham obeyed God and was prepared to sacrifice his only son, God declared that He would make his descendants as numerous as the stars in the sky, and through them bless all nations on earth. From this story of Abraham a broad aspect of worship is demonstrated through a lifestyle lived with faith in God and sacrificial giving coupled with obedience to God.

The following passage of Scripture shows us the attitude we should have in worship:

28 Therefore, since we are receiving a kingdom that cannot be shaken, let us be thankful, and so worship God acceptably with reverence and awe,
29 for our "God is a consuming fire."

Heb 12:28-29

Also in Jn 4:23-24 it says we should worship Him "in spirit and in truth".

L.O.Richards in his book: "Expository Dictionary of Bible Words" also states with reference to the word '*proskyneo*' (or '*proskuneo*'): "Although worship is a matter of the heart and an expression of one's inner relationship with God, it may also be a public expression of a corporate relationship with God (Jn 12:20; Acts 8:27; 24:11).

To Worship – "GK 'proskuneo' means- do obeisance to, prostrate oneself, do reverence to. The basic meaning of *proskuneo,* in the opinion of most scholars, is to kiss. Among the Greeks the verb is a technical term for the adoration of the gods, meaning to fall down, prostrate oneself, adore on one's knees. Probably it came to have this meaning because in order to kiss the earth (i.e. the earth deity) or the image of a god, one had to cast oneself on the ground. (see 2Chron. 20:18)"

The above statement is taken from the 'Dictionary of New Testament Theology Vol.2' Editor-Colin Brown.

The Open Bible – New King James Version gives the following definitions for the word 'worship':

"*shachah* – the verb, translated "worship," and meaning "bow down," is *shachah.* A person bows down before a superior or a monarch to show respect (Gen 23:7; Ruth 2:10; 1Kg 1:31). People bowed before God in worship as Moses did on Mt. Sinai when God came to inscribe the tablets (Ex 34:8). - - - - - - - - - ."

"*proskuneo.* - Noun used to designate the act of obeisance, which involves falling down or bowing before kings, deities, or masters and kissing their feet, the hem of their garment, or the ground. *Proskuneo* can be translated as "to (fall down and) worship," "to do obeisance to," "to prostrate oneself before," "to do reverence to." In the NT *proskuneo* is used for the reverence of a slave towards his master(Mat 18:26). Cornelius toward Peter (Acts 10:25), but it is used especially with reference to the worship of God (Matt 4:10; 1Cor 14:25; Rev 7:11), of Jesus as Messianic King (Mat 2:2, 8, 11), and the Risen Lord (Mat 28:9, 17). - - - - - - - - -."

Another example of 'bowing down' in worship is found in Job 1:20-22, and his action here shows complete submission to God, and as the whole story of Job shows that for a long period of time it cost him a great deal, but in the end he was greatly blessed.

It has been said that "worship that costs nothing is worth nothing" -see 2Sam 24:24 and Mk 14:3-9. The quality of our service for God is a key expression of our worship and this needs to be matched by our daily living for God for it to have value.

William Temple, a former Archbishop of Canterbury, said:

To worship is: To quicken the conscience by the holiness of God
To feed the mind with the truth of God
To purge the imagination by the beauty of God
To open the heart to the love of God

Our whole lives are meant to be an expression of worship, and hence 'praise' is one part of worship as it is part of life. Key parts of worship are expressed by time spent in adoration in His presence, and living a lifestyle that reflects that of a devoted loving disciple in every part of our lives, and so use all the time He has given us to reveal something of the nature and effect of our God to those around us.

No part of our life is secular but it is all spiritual and hence, all activities and attitudes will reflect our submission to, and our worship of, God.

The word 'worship' comes from the Anglo-Saxon word 'weothscipe' meaning to give worth to something. To-day the word 'worship' is generally taken to mean to give worth to something or someone.

It is recommended that there should be an acknowledgement of God at the outset of a worship service by addressing Him in worship and praise and then progress towards our response to Him. If this general approach is adopted it provides a right focus to consider first His character, attributes and supernatural actions, as this gives us the substance on which to decide our response to Him.

Praise

The meaning of the Biblical words for 'Praise' express it as commendation given to God in respect of His character and actions (Vine - Expository Dictionary), and other words also include commendation in respect of His glory and grace.

In a time of praise we have an opportunity to express our thanks to God in recognition of His attributes of character and His acts of love, grace and mercy. We can also acknowledge with gratitude His greatness, majesty, uniqueness and holiness, and One that has all wisdom and knowledge and is absolute truth, always acts in purity, righteousness and all-knowing just judgement. Also we acknowledge Him as being God Almighty, the creator of heaven and earth.

In 'praise' we lift His name above all others. Throughout the Bible there are a variety of ways in which praise is expressed and these include: the voice in word, in singing and in shouting - and include physical expressions such as raising hands, clapping, kneeling, standing and laying prostrate - these should be the free expression of the individual believer at that time reflecting feelings varying from joy to earnest acknowledgements of sadness with tears of repentance.

Praise comes out of our worship, and its value directly relates to the quality and obedience of our worshipful lives'. Praising God whilst remaining in an unforgiven state towards God or another person is just singing, and is unacceptable to Him.

The Psalmist e.g. in Ps 41, praised God not because He spares us pain and anguish, but because He is with us in them, for our growth and His glory.

There are many varied expressions of praise in the Bible as shown by the small sample of Scriptures given below:

In Ps 43:3-4 it states that we should praise God 'with joy and delight and with the harp'

In Col 3:15-17 it invites people to 'sing psalms, hymns and spiritual songs with gratitude in your hearts to God.' And through the Lord Jesus to give thanks 'to God the Father through him.'

In the Bible a wide range of musical instruments were used, and therefore, in principle, a wide range of updated instruments can be used to-day as long as they serve the purpose of aiding sung expressions of praise to God.

PRAISE AND WORSHIP

Notes and Quotations

In the Scripture Phil 2:8-11 we see the Lord Jesus Christ given the highest place and a name that is above every name, and therefore, all people should bow the knee to Him and acknowledge Him as Lord. This claim is supported by other Scriptures, and in particular, Isa 45:22-24 and Rom 14:11.

Selwyn Hughes has made a number of statements concerning worship in his "Every Day with Jesus" Notes, and the following are a few that the writer has come across:

"Let us focus on what the Bible has to say on praise and worship. An appropriate reading from Scripture is an essential prerequisite to divine worship. Such a passage is one that states who God is, not just what He does, - see Ps 48:1-14."

"Worship is adoring God not so much for what He does, but for who He is. Let us focus some of the attributes of God, such as His love, holiness, righteousness, power, grace, and so on. And as I meditate the fire burns and my soul soars in adoration of God."

"We cannot expect to enter into worship on the Lord's Day if worship has not flowed from our hearts over the preceding six days. Corporate worship must never be a substitute for individual worship."

"If God does not occupy the throne of our hearts, the central point of our being, then we can quickly idolise ourselves. "Self-centredness," said William Law, "is the root, branches, and tree of all the evils of the human race." We cannot worship God when the god who is at the centre of our hearts is 'I'."

"True worship removes God from His throne in a temple and places Him on the throne of the human heart, where His life and power and holiness can be brought to bear upon every aspect of our inner nature and character."

"Worship is giving God his rightful due. It is enjoying God, as the old theologians put it. To worship God and not to enjoy Him is impossible."

In Jn 4:23 Jesus says: "Yet a time is coming and has now come when the true worshippers will worship the Father in spirit and truth, for they are the kind of worshippers the Father seeks." Thus, worship requires honest reality, truth and repentance.

The act of 'worship' should indicate the attitude of the heart and a posture of the body. It begins in the spiritual but also affects the physical. e.g. Jews rock backwards and forwards when they pray. Postures in the Bible include: lying face down; kneeling in God's presence; and standing with uplifted hands.

"Praise is thanking God for the things He has done, is doing, and is going to do."

Selwyn Hughes

A. W. Tozer said: "Praise," is thanking God for what He does; and "worship," is adoring Him for who He is."

He also stated: "If you will not worship God seven days a week you will not worship Him on one day a week."

Selwyn Hughes points out in his "Every Day with Jesus" Notes with reference to the word 'worship' that: "Our English word has evolved from the Anglo Saxon *weorthscipe* which means "to give worth to something." Worship is worth-ship – giving to someone the honour or worth that is due to them."

Singing spiritual songs in not worship, but according to the attitude of the heart can lead to worship. – See Ps 148.

Also, true worship involves sacrifice. Sacrificing thoughts about ourselves, about time and our possessions – see Gen 22;4-13 and Heb 13:15-16

"An idol is anything that takes the place of God in our lives, (the first place), and is the main focus of our love, time, and attention. Idols introduce a divided loyalty.

Selwyn Hughes

<u>Note:</u> In Neh. 8:5-12 we observe that worship was preceded by: reading the Word of God, and blessing the Lord with the people lifting up their hands, and this led to the people bowing their heads and worshipping with their faces to the ground, followed by weeping due to confession of sin, and ending in joy.

<u>Note:</u> An essential factor in the quality aspect of a person's 'worship' is related to the measure of obedience to God that is reflected in their lifestyle, in thought, word and deed. Submitting their lives willingly, sacrificially and continually to God. When people are endeavouring to live this type of lifestyle then there is meaning and reality in the act of divine worship.

In Ex 7:16 Moses, prompted by God says to Pharaoh: "Let my people go that they may worship (RSV 'serve') me." See also Ex 3:18; 8:1; 9:1; 10:3; 1Sam 1:25-28. In these, and similar passages on worship there is reference to 'sacrifice' but no reference to 'singing'. In 1Cor 14:25; Rev 4:10; 11:16; 19:10; 22:8 there is reference 'falling down to worship' but, again, no reference to 'singing'. However, there is reference to 'singing' associated with other forms of declaration of worship in many Scriptures such as: 1Chron 16:23-30; 2Chron 29:25-28; Ps 95:1-6; 96:1-6; 100:1-2; Mat 14:33; Jn 9:38; and in Rev 5:8-9 where the elders '*fell down before the Lamb'*. If one considers the Scriptures: Jn 12:20; Acts 8:27; 24:11, we see reference to people 'going somewhere to *worship*', but it does not say what this entailed.

In view of the above Scriptures it might be a wise exercise for many Churches to consider adopting a wider range of expression of, or types of declaration in, worship, in addition to singing.

<u>A note of caution:</u>
Whilst a worship leader, worship group or choir may enhance a person's praise or worship of God it can also become a substitute for it, and in such a case the person can be 'carried along' with the music etc. When this happens they are in danger of their worship not being a true reflection of their personal Christian life.

<u>Note:</u> In Ex. 20:25 and Josh. 8:31 it refers to the fact that an altar should not be built from hewn stones, as man's workmanship on them would defile them. This could be a warning to us that we should not display *"man's workmanship"* in a worship service, e.g. any person(s), self aggrandisement in any way, that could distract our attention away from Him whom we have come to worship.

Jamie Buckingham has made the following comment concerning Exodus 20:25 in his book "A way through the wilderness"- "Bricks and hewn stones are made to conform. There is never any variation allowed. All are made to fit exactly into a designated place, with little or no irregularity or originality allowed or needed".

This person made two statements on worship as given below:
"True worship is inner health made audible".
"In the process of worship God communicates His presence to us, and that communication takes place when we worship Him in spirit and truth", See Jn 4:23-24

Author unknown

Martin Luther said: "A dairymaid can milk cows to the glory of God." The secret of true worship is doing everything 'as unto the Lord'. An extract from "The Word for Today" Notes by Bob Gass

Worship is focusing on the greatness, the glory and the supreme worth of God and responding to Him in adoration and awe.

Selwyn Hughes

When we truly worship God we are submitting to His will, accepting the fact that His will is best.

A line in a Christian song says:"The reason I live is to worship you". This statement is true in the broad sense that the worship, the adoration of God is when we, His creation begin to reflect something of His characteristics, i.e. His love, compassion and godly morals in our everyday lives in our thoughts, words and actions. It follows, therefore, that when Christians come together to worship and praise God, if their lives are not reflecting some of the above characteristics then their songs and actions will not be acceptable to God.

Note: Ways in which worship and praise are expressed in the Bible:

Worship -bowing down to Him in adoration, submission of our will, obedient to His leading, living a lifestyle that willingly puts His objectives for our lives first e.g. seeking to take on the characteristics of God such as love, joy, peace, etc. as portrayed in Gal. 5:22-26.

Thanking Him for who He is, as expressed in His moral and non-moral attributes (as given in this book). Approaching Him with an attitude of humility, awe, intimacy and adoration.

Praise - giving thanks for what He has done for the whole of mankind and for us individually, and this is expressed in a number of ways including: spoken words, singing with or without instruments, raising hands, dancing, shouting, clapping.

To have meaning these expressions must come from people with thankful hearts, who have responded to God in repentance and have experienced something of the grace of God in their lives.

The following verse in Ps 34:3 is given below in three Bible Versions and a comment on it to consider given under the verse.

- Glorify the LORD with me: let us exalt his name together. (NIV)
- O magnify the LORD with me, and let us exalt his name together! (RSV and NKJV)

It is worth noting the words 'Glorify' and 'Magnify' above, as they refer to the same exhortation of the Lord, where glorify means to make glorious, and relates to giving honour and magnificence. Also, in the sense of 'making much of' in the above setting the word magnify is used.

As a further point of interest the word 'magnify' in this context of 'The Lord God' as we magnify, or look more closely at, everything associated with Him, His character, creation and deeds we see only more and more magnificence, perfection and beauty, whereas the closer we look at man's character and deeds we see more and more imperfections and undesirable features.

In the book "Praise" by Psalmody International, it explains many aspects of praise, and two useful statements are shown below:

"Praise to God without fellowship is religion. It is empty, meaningless and a hindrance to true Christianity. Praise is a particularly transforming exercise since the Scripture infers that God is personally drawn to it."

"Hallelujah – A spontaneous outcry of one who is excited about God."

'Praise', without faithful living is just 'singing'.

Praise – is a sacrifice that costs, whatever the circumstances. See Heb 13:15-16

God is to be praised not because He spares us pain and anguish, but because He is with us in them for our growth and His glory.

<u>Note:</u> Worship involves giving: see the story of Abraham's offering up of His son Isaac in Genesis: 22, also look at the following biblical references:

But the king replied to Araunah, "No, I insist on paying you for it. I will not sacrifice to the LORD my God burnt offerings that cost me nothing." So David bought the threshing-floor and the oxen and paid fifty shekels of silver for them. See 2Sam 24:24

In 2Cor 9:7 it says:

7 Each man should give what he has decided in his heart to give, not reluctantly or under compulsion, for God loves a cheerful giver.

It has been said that "Whatever you worship will mould you".

Graham Kendrick has stated that "Worship that depends on externals (e.g. a certain style, format, music or place) for existence is not real worship at all. True worship is what you have when the externals are taken away,"

"True worship happens when we are taken up with God, and this requires the burning up of pretence."

The very foundation of our worship emanates from our daily walk with God. See Heb 12:28-29.

A motive for praise is expressed in Acts 3:6-8 due to a lame man being miraculously healed, and in Lk 7:47-48 due to a woman being forgiven her sins.

So we need to recognise the immensity of what God has done for us – then we will praise more as we ought.

It has been said that "Whatever you worship will mould you."

Graham Kendrick has stated that "Worship that depends on externals (e.g. a certain style, format, music or place) for its existence is not real worship at all. True worship is what you have when the externals are taken away."

True worship depends [illegible] are walking with God and [illegible] pure the burning [illegible]

The very foundation of our worship emanates from our daily walk with God. See Heb 12:28-29.

A [illegible] Acts [illegible] 18 [illegible]

[illegible]

PRAISE AND EXALTATION BY DR S. M. LOCKRIDGE - "MY KING IS"

The Bible says my King is a seven-way King:
He's the King of the Jews - that's a racial King.
He's the King of Israel - that's a national King.
He's the King of Righteousness.
He's the King of Ages.
He's the King of Heaven.
He's the King of Glory.
He's the King of Kings and He's the Lord of Lords.
That's my King.
...Well, I wonder, do you know Him?
David said, "The heavens declare the glory of God and the firmament showeth His handiwork."
My King is a sovereign King - no means of measure can define His limitless love.
No farseeing telescope can bring into visibility the coastline of His shoreless supplies.
No barrier can hinder Him from pouring out His blessings.
He's enduringly strong.
He's entirely sincere.
He's eternally steadfast.
He's immortally graceful.
He's imperially powerful.
He's impartially merciful.
...Do you know Him?
He's the greatest phenomenon that has ever crossed the horizon of this world.
He's God's Son.

He's the sinner's Saviour.
He's the centrepiece of civilisation.
He stands in the solitude of Himself.
He's august and He's unique.
He's unparalleled, He's unprecedented.
He's the loftiest idea in literature.
He's the highest personality in philosophy.
He is the supreme problem in higher criticism.
He's the fundamental doctrine of true theology.
He's the core and necessity for for spiritual religion.
He's the miracle of the age,yes, He is.
He's the superlative of everything good that you choose to call Him.
He's the only one qualified to be an all sufficient Saviour.
...I wonder if you know Him today?
He supplies the strength for the weak.
He's available for the tempted and the tried.
He sympathises and He saves.
He strengthens and sustains.
He guards and He guides.
He heals the sick.
He cleanses the lepers.
He forgives sinners.
He discharges debtors.
He delivers the captives.
He defends the feeble.
He blesses the young.
He serves the unfortunate.
He regards the aged.
He rewards the diligent and
He beautifies the meek.
...I wonder if you know Him?
Well this is my King.
He is the King.
He is the key to knowledge.
He's the wellspring of wisdom.
He's the doorway of deliverance.
He's the pathway of peace.
He's the roadway of righteousness.

He's the highway of holiness.
He's the gateway of glory.
...Do you know Him?
Well, His office is manifold.
His promise is sure.
His life is matchless.
His goodness is limitless.
His mercy is everlasting.
His love never changes.
His word is enough.
His grace is sufficient.
His reign is righteous and
His yoke is easy and
His burden is light.
I wish I could describe Him to you.
But He's indescribable - Yea ! Yea ! Yea !
He's indescribable - Yes He is ! He's God.
He's indescribable.
He's incomprehensible.
He's invincible.
He's irresistible.
Well, you can't get Him out of your mind.
You can't get Him off your hand.
You can't outlive Him and
You can't live without Him.
Well the Pharisees couldn't stand Him, but they found out they couldn't stop Him.
Pilate couldn't find any fault in Him.
The witnesses couldn't get their testimonies to agree.
Herod couldn't kill Him.
Death couldn't handle Him.
The grave couldn't hold Him - Yea !
That's my King.
That's my King ! - Yea !
And thine is the Kingdom and the power and the glory forever and ever and ever and ever.
How long is that?
And ever and ever.

And when you get through all the forevers, then Amen !
GOOD GOD ALMIGHTY ! AMEN ! AMEN !

The Psalmist in Ps 3 and Ps 41 praised God in difficult times and this is an example to follow. We then are not praising Him because He spares us pain and anguish, but because He is with us in them, for our growth and His glory.

2 Praise the LORD, O my soul, and forget not all his benefits— Ps 103:2 Comment has been made on this Scripture in a booklet called "Praise" from a series of booklets named the "Life Style Series", in which it states:

- "Let your judgement bless Him by making decisions in accordance with His Word.
- Let your imagination bless Him by thinking pure thoughts.
- Let your affections bless Him by loving what He loves.
- Let your desires bless Him by seeking after His glory.
- Let your memory bless Him by not forgetting all His benefits.
- Let your thoughts bless Him by meditating on His Word.
- Let your hope bless Him by looking for and longing for His glory to be revealed.
- Let your words bless Him by your speech.
- Let your actions bless Him by your integrity.
- Let everything that is within you bless His Holy name."

Also in the above mentioned booklet called "Praise" it makes under the heading 'The Catalyst for Praise', the following comment:

"A catalyst is something that causes a reaction to take place between two or more chemical components. The significance of a catalyst is that its presence causes a change or reaction without the catalyst being changed or used up in the reaction. God's Word is the necessary catalyst for praise to take place in a Christian's life." Without this catalyst of God's Word in us, there is little hope of us reacting to God in genuine praise. God has created us in this way.

PRAISE AND WORSHIP

Biblical Texts & Text References

Worship

It states in Ps 22:27-28 that; "all the families of the nations will bow down before him"

Also in Isa 45:22-24 people are invited to 'turn to Him (God) and be saved, because there is no other, and every knee will bow to Him.'

1 Therefore, I urge you, brothers, in view of God's mercy, to offer your bodies as living sacrifices, holy and pleasing to God—this is your spiritual act of worship.
2 Do not conform any longer to the pattern of this world, but be transformed by the renewing of your mind. Then you will be able to test and approve what God's will is—his good, pleasing and perfect will.

Rom 12:1-2

Additional Scripture references

Gen 23:7, Ex 3:18; 8:1; 20:22-26: 33:9-11, Josh 8:30-31, 1Sam 1:25-28, 2Sam 24:24, 1Kg 1:31, 1Chron 21:24-26, 2Chron 20:18-19, Neh 9:1-3, Job 1:20-22, Ps 22:27-31; 29:1-2; 33:1-9; 34:8; 48:1-3; 66:8-12; 89:8-9; 118:14-15 ; 146:1-10, Isa 29:13, Mat 4:10; 28:8-9 & 16-17, Mk 14:3-9, Jn 4:23-24, 12:20; Acts 8:27; 24:10-11, Rom 14:9-11, 1Cor14:24-25, Gal 5:22-26, Phil 3:3; 4:18, 1Tim 6:14-16, Heb 12:28-29; Rev 5:8-9; 7:11-12; 15:2-4

Worship and Praise

1 *A psalm. For giving thanks.* Shout for joy to the LORD, all the earth.

2 Worship the LORD with gladness; come before him with joyful songs.

Ps 100:1-2

Praise

In Ps103:1-4 people are reminded to praise the Lord, not forgetting all his benefits, and that he is the one 'who forgives all your sins and heals all your diseases, who redeems your life from the pit and crowns you with love and compassion'.

15 Through Jesus, therefore, let us continually offer to God a sacrifice of praise--the fruit of lips that confess his name.
16 And do not forget to do good and to share with others, for with such sacrifices God is pleased.

Heb 13:15-16

Additional Scripture references

Ps 47:5-9; 96:1-6; 105:1-5; 119:12-14 & 171-172; 145:1-3 & 8-13

Worship Postures

Falling down – see Josh 5:13-15
Kneeling – see 1Kgs 8:54
Bowing low and falling prostrate – see 1Chron 29:20
Bowing low and lifting up hands – see Neh 8:6
Tearing robe, shaving head and falling down – see Job 1:20-21

B

GOD'S CHARACTER

The whole subject of God's character is so vast that any attempt to describe it, even partially, seems an impossible task. However, an introduction to the subject has been devised in this Section by dividing His Character into two parts, namely, 'His Moral Attributes', and 'His Non-Moral Attributes', and supporting these aspects with written Biblical texts that will speak for themselves. In addition, Biblical definitions and quotations have been provided in each Section to help further appreciate and understand the meaning of the topics.

The written Scriptures quoted are not claimed to be complete on any topic but are given as an introduction to the boundless subject matter, and additional text references are given to provide further support.

'His Moral Attributes' are referred to in Section B1 and these have been summarised under the following headings:

His Love - as revealed in the Old Testament Scriptures.
His Love - as revealed in the New Testament Scriptures.
His Grace - His unmerited favour.
His Goodness.
His Forgiveness and Reconciliation.
His Fatherhood.
His Truth, Purity, Sinlessness and Incorruptibility.
His Holiness, Righteousness and Justice.
His Judgment and Mercy.

'His Non-Moral Attributes' are referred to in Section B2 and these have been summarised under the following headings:

His Infinity, Eternity and Uniqueness.

His Self-Existence, Immortality and Omnipresence.
His Wisdom and Omniscience.
His Sovereignty and Omnipotence.
His Perfection and Immutability.
His Immensity.
One and Only God in the Unity of the Godhead - The Trinity.
His Absolute Supernatural Creative and Healing Power in the Old Testament.
His Absolute Supernatural Creative and Healing Power in the New Testament.

B1

GOD'S CHARACTER

-HIS MORAL ATTRIBUTES-

Biblical Definitions

God's Character – His Moral Attributes

It is important for the reader to endeavour to understand something of the foundational nature of the attributes of God who claims to be our creator and the One who has a close interest in our welfare and eternal salvation. So let us begin this quest by considering the most significant qualities that people are looking for in life, is to be loved, valued and accepted, and these qualities are offered to all people through the God of the Bible. So it is a distinct advantage for people to know this God and to recognise that He is unique as shown by the perfect quality of His moral attributes as outlined below:

His love is without measure and pre-conditions as shown in the life of the Lord Jesus Christ, in that He was prepared to die to make forgiveness, hope and salvation available to all peoples and is also presently sympathetic to our feelings and weaknesses – see Heb 4:14-16;

His grace - His unmerited favour, is shown to us in His words when it says that all spoke well of Him and were amazed at the gracious words He spoke, - see Lk 4:22;

His grace is also shown towards us all, the undeserving, in His attitude and actions in that whilst He was God He did not exalt Himself but acted with humility and in the interests of others, - see Phil 2:5-11;

His fatherhood is shown to us by the way He cares and provides for us, and disciplines us for our good, - see Heb 12:7-11;

His truth is absolute, trustworthy and reveals true facts and conditions of people's hearts and motives, and so provides the standard against which all else can be judged and sound laws based;

He is all-knowing, all-seeing, all-wise and perfectly holy God and alone is able to act in perfect justice, righteousness, judgment and mercy.

These attributes are more fully reviewed under the next heading below.

Index of Sub-Headings

The biblical Scriptures given under these headings are to be considered as a brief summary of supporting evidence, and reveal the unparalleled claims made for God. An additional listing of Scripture Texts and Text references is given later in the B1 Text Section.

His Love.
His Grace - His unmerited favour.
His Goodness.
His Forgiveness and Reconciliation.
His Fatherhood.
His Truth, Purity, Sinlessness and Incorruptibility.
His Holiness, Righteousness and Justice.
His Judgment and Mercy.

His Love

His love is without measure and pre-conditions as shown in the life of the Lord Jesus Christ, also He "is touched by the feelings of our weaknesses" Heb 4:14-15 – see below:

14 Therefore, since we have a great high priest who has gone through the heavens, Jesus the Son of God, let us hold firmly to the faith we profess.
15 For we do not have a high priest who is unable to sympathise with our weaknesses, but we have one who has been tempted in every way, just as we are—yet was without sin.

The love of the Lord Jesus Christ was demonstrated to the full when He died for the sin of all mankind and paid the price of redemption for all who would trust and thank Him for dying for their sin, - see the Scriptures below:

16 "For God so loved the world that he gave his one and only Son, that whoever believes in him shall not perish but have eternal life.
17 For God did not send his Son into the world to condemn the world, but to save the world through him.
18 Whoever believes in him is not condemned, but whoever does not believe stands condemned already because he has not believed in the name of God's one and only Son.

Jn 3:16-18

It states in Rom 5:8-9 that God has demonstrated his love for us in that 'While we were still sinners, Christ died for us. See Rom 5:8-9

The two principal Greek words used in the New Testament of the Bible are *'agapao'* and *'phileo'*.

'agapao' is unconditional love - the type of love that is not requiring any response in love or gratitude from us for it to be given. Such is God's love towards the human race.

'phileo' is the love expressed between people in friendship.

Both of these words are used in the passage John 21:15-17 given below:

15 When they had finished eating, Jesus said to Simon Peter, "Simon son of John, do you truly love (agapao) me more than these?" "Yes, Lord," he said, "you know that I love (phileo) you." Jesus said, "Feed my lambs."
16 Again Jesus said, "Simon son of John, do you truly love (agapao) me?" He answered, "Yes, Lord, you know that I love (phileo) you." Jesus said, "Take care of my sheep."
17 The third time he said to him, "Simon son of John, do you love (phileo) me?" Peter was hurt because Jesus asked him the third time, "Do you love me?" He said, "Lord, you know all things; you know that I love (phileo) you." Jesus said, "Feed my sheep.

<u>His Love - as revealed in Old Testament Scriptures:</u>
Text Isa 38:17 is shown below and see Ps 25:7; Ps 52:8

17 Surely it was for my benefit that I suffered such anguish. In your love you kept me from the pit of destruction; you have put all my sins behind your back.

<u>His Love - as revealed in New Testament Scriptures:</u>
Text Mat 9:35-36 is shown below, and see Mat 14:14; Rom 5:8

35 Jesus went through all the towns and villages, teaching in their synagogues, preaching the good news of the kingdom and healing every disease and sickness.
36 When he saw the crowds, he had compassion on them, because they were harassed and helpless, like sheep without a shepherd.

<u>His Grace – His unmerited favour</u>
This describes God's undeserved favour towards us, e.g. God not only pardons undeserving sinners, but welcomes them into His Kingdom. The word 'sinner' refers to the condition of the whole of mankind who inherently fall short of God's standards and rebel against His benevolent rule over us. See the following Scriptures:

Old Testament text Ps 86:15; is shown below

15 But you, O Lord, are a compassionate and gracious God, slow to anger, abounding in love and faithfulness.

New Testament text Eph 2:8-9 is shown below, and see Lk 4:22

8 For it is by grace you have been saved, through faith—and this not from yourselves, it is the gift of God—
9 not by works, so that no-one can boast.

<u>We are no longer under 'THE LAW' as given to Moses, because 'THE LAW' was fulfilled (not abolished) in Christ, see the following typical Scriptures:</u> Mat 5:17 and Rom 10:4.

<u>His Goodness</u>
God's attitude towards His creation has always been good and His goodness is sustained because He does not change (Heb 13:8). Note the Scriptures below range over the time span from the Old Testament to the New Testament.

Old Testament text Gen 1:31 is shown below, and see: Ps 31:19

31 God saw all that he had made, and it was very good. And there was evening, and there was morning—the sixth day.

New Testament text Jn 10:11 is shown below, and see Jas 1:17

11 "I am the good shepherd. The good shepherd lays down his life for the sheep

His Forgiveness and Reconciliation

His Forgiveness

God's forgiveness has a unique quality in that He does not just forget our sins, but chooses to remember them no more, which means they are gone and will not be brought back and held against us in the future, see the Scriptures below:

Old Testament text Isa 43:25 is shown below, and see 2Chron 7:14; Ps 103:2-4

25 "I, even I, am he who blots out your transgressions, for my own sake, and remembers your sins no more.

New Testament text 1Jn 1:8-9 is shown below.

8 If we claim to be without sin, we deceive ourselves and the truth is not in us.
9 If we confess our sins, he is faithful and just and will forgive us our sins and purify us from all unrighteousness.

As L.O. Richards states; "The NT relates forgiveness to Jesus, specifically to his sacrificial death. The basis on which God can forgive sin and remain righteous has been provided by Jesus' sacrifice of Himself as atonement, in that ultimate sacrifice to which OT offerings merely pointed. As Hebrews puts it, "By one sacrifice he has made perfect forever those who are being made holy" (10:14)."

His Forgiveness and Reconciliation

Reconciliation

Old Testament text Ps 23:3 it says 'he restores my soul. He guides me in paths of Righteousness'. Also see Ps 147:3 and Isa 53:5

New Testament text 2Cor 5:17-19 states 'if anyone is in Christ, he is a new creation; the old has gone, the new has come!' Also see Jn 10:10

His Fatherhood

The Lord wants to be a true Father to all who trust in Him, and hence, His love includes His care and the tough love aspect which embraces discipline for our good and relates to His purpose for us to be mature, and all this is coupled with promises as seen in the Scripture below:

Old testament text Pro 3:11-12 is shown below, and see Isa 9:6

11 My son, do not despise the LORD's discipline and do not resent his rebuke,
12 because the LORD disciplines those he loves, as a father the son he delights in.

New Testament text 2Cor 6:18 is shown below, and see Heb 12:7-11

18 "I will be a Father to you, and you will be my sons and daughters, says the Lord Almighty."

His Truth, Purity, Sinlessness and Incorruptibility.

His Truth

All TRUTH is in JESUS CHRIST "Surely you heard of him and were taught in him in accordance with the truth that is in Jesus." Eph 4:21 The whole substance of TRUTH is IN, and emanates FROM, JESUS CHRIST.

Text Jn 1:17 is shown below, and see Prov 30:5; Jn 14:617

17 For the law was given through Moses; grace and truth came through Jesus Christ.

His Purity, Sinlessness and Incorruptibility

Texts Ps 119:151 and Heb 7:26-27 are shown below, and see 1Pet 2:22-23; 1Jn 3:3

151 Your righteousness is everlasting and your law is true.
26 Such a high priest meets our need—one who is holy, blameless, pure, set apart from sinners, exalted above the heavens.
27 Unlike the other high priests, he does not need to offer sacrifices day after day, first for his own sins, and then for the sins of the people. He sacrificed for their sins once for all when he offered himself.

His Holiness, Righteousness and Justice.

Holiness

In the Scriptures the word *holiness* signifies (a) a separation to God, and (b) the conduct of those so separated. (Vine).

Scriptures relating to (a):

Text 2Cor 6:16-18 is shown below, and see 1Cor 1:30; 2Thess 2:13-14

16 What agreement is there between the temple of God and idols? For we are the temple of the living God. As God has said: "I will live with them and walk among them, and I will be their God, and they will be my people."
17 "Therefore come out from them and be separate, says the Lord. Touch no unclean thing, and I will receive you."
18 "I will be a Father to you, and you will be my sons and daughters, says the Lord Almighty."

Scriptures relating to (b):

Text 1Thess 4:3-5 is shown below, and see 1Pet 1:15-16

3 It is God's will that you should be sanctified: that you should avoid sexual immorality;
4 that each of you should learn to control his own body in a way that is holy and honourable,
5 not in passionate lust like the heathen, who do not know God;

His Holiness

Text Ps 111:9 is shown below, and see Ps 103:1; 1Pet 1:15-16

9 He provided redemption for his people; he ordained his covenant for ever—holy and awesome is his name.

<u>His Righteousness</u>

Text Ps 145:17 is shown below, and see Ezr 9:15; Rom 3:21-22; 1Pet 3:18

17 The LORD is righteous in all his ways and loving towards all he has made.

<u>Justice</u>

Text Deut 32:3-4 is shown below, and see Isa 9:7; 2Thess 1:6; 1Jn 1:9

3 I will proclaim the name of the LORD. Oh, praise the greatness of our God!
4 He is the Rock, his works are perfect, and all his ways are just. A faithful God who does no wrong, upright and just is he.

<u>His Judgment and Mercy.</u>

<u>His Judgment - See Book Part 1 and Section E4</u>

Texts Mat 12:41 and Jn 3:16-18 are shown below, and see Ps 89:14; Rom 2:4-5

41 The men of Nineveh will stand up at the judgment with this generation and condemn it; for they repented at the preaching of Jonah, and now one greater than Jonah is here.
16 "For God so loved the world that he gave his one and only Son, that whoever believes in him shall not <u>perish</u> but have eternal life.
17 For God did not send his Son into the world to condemn the world, but to save the world through him.
18 Whoever believes in him is not condemned, but whoever does not believe stands condemned already because he has not believed in the name of God's one and only Son.

<u>Note the word *'perish'*</u>

In verse 16 above this word is associated with God's Judgment and has great significance. W.E.Vine refers to the word *'perish'* in the Greek and states: "The idea is not extinction but ruin, loss, not of being, but of well-being". Please note also 'we must all appear before the judgment seat of Christ'-see 2Cor 5:10-11 and Heb 9:27-28

His Mercy

Text Eph 2:4-5 is shown below, and see 1Chron 21:13; Ps 32:5; Jas 2:12-13

4 But because of his great love for us, God, who is rich in mercy,
5 made us alive with Christ even when we were dead in transgressions—it is by grace you have been saved.

GOD'S CHARACTER

-HIS MORAL ATTRIBUTES-

Notes and Quotations

Love

Someone has said "God loves us as we are, but loves us too much to leave us as we are".

Love

Someone has said "Love is the power that moves us towards another without expecting a reward".

God's Love

"God loves us wholeheartedly, unconditionally, and continually" Alex Buchanan

God's Love

Someone has commented on the story of the Prodigal (recklessly wasteful) Son (Luke 15) by saying "By taking 'half' of his father's goods was like wishing his father dead, but when the son, now destitute, decides to return home the father 'ran' to meet him, - and this was not Middle East culture for the older man to 'run', but to "walk' with dignity. Hence, this reveals something of God's love towards us when we return to Him in repentance".

Compassion

Someone has stated that: Compassion is expressed by tears + action.

<u>Grace</u>
Selwyn Hughes in EDWJ Notes has stated "Grace is a characteristic of God which is exercised only towards those who are seen as having a special relationship with Him".

Arthur W. Pink says: "Grace is the sole source from which flows the goodwill, love and salvation of God into His chosen people. "Grace cannot be bought, earned, deserved, or merited. If it could, it would cease to be Grace. Grace flows down as pure charity, falling on the unlovable and making it lovely". Amazing !

<u>Justice and Mercy</u>
When dealing with people, some are all mercy and no justice and others are all justice and no mercy – but God requires both. The first is weak, the other harsh, but each of these ways of dealing with people are unbalanced. See Ps 101:1

<u>Grace and Mercy</u>
Someone has said "Grace is getting what we don't deserve" and "Mercy is not getting what we deserve".

<u>Grace and Truth</u>
Grace and Truth is a couplet that should not be separated – see Jn 1:14-17 and Eph 4:15

All grace (or love) and no truth is misleading, giving a false sense of security.

All truth and no love is harsh and off-putting.

So 'speaking the truth in a loving manner' should be the method adopted.

<u>Truth</u>
Know one should teach as doctrine the precepts, or rules, of men – see Mk 7:6-8

<u>Grace</u>
Someone has said "Grace is the strength God gives us to obey His commands".

Mercy
Charles Haddon Spurgeon said: "If we look for mercy in that day, we must show mercy in this day." From "The Christian Book of Lists" by Randy Petersen.

Mercy and Justice is a couplet that should never be broken. – See Ps 101:1

When dealing with others –some are all mercy and no justice and others are all justice and no mercy. But God requires both. The one is soft and the other harsh, but each needs balancing with the other.

Truth
In Jn 14:6 Jesus said "I am the way and the truth and the life." So we can say that All TRUTH is in Jesus. His exclusive claim is that all TRUTH comes from Him.

Truth
For biblical truth to be effective someone has said:

"Truth that addresses the mind must penetrate the heart to motivate the will".

Holiness
Biblical scholars said that there are more references to God's holiness in the Bible than to any other aspect of His character.

Those who came into direct contact with His moral majesty and purity were overwhelmed as is shown for example in the passage Isa 6:1-5.

Recognition of and submission to His holiness are the divine prerequisites for admission to the inner heart of God and the most important requirements for knowing Him and fulfilling His Will for us, and is also the most important qualification for learning from Him.

14. Make every effort to live in peace with all men and to be holy; without holiness no-one will see the Lord.

Heb 12:14

"The most damnable and pernicious heresy that ever plagued the mind of man was the idea that somehow he could make himself good enough to deserve to live with an All-Holy God".

Martin Luther

See Rom 3:22-23 "22 This righteousness from God comes through faith in Jesus Christ to all who believe. There is no difference, for all have sinned and fall short of the glory of God,"

10 The fear of the LORD is the beginning of wisdom; all who follow his precepts have good understanding. To him belongs eternal praise.

Ps 111:10

The above verse and other passages like Ps 99 show that we should be overawed by His holiness. Hence, all Christian activities should be rooted in this 'fear'. The word 'fear' meaning to 'revere' Him. It is considered that we are not likely to be much affected by the Doctrines of love and grace unless we are first aware of His holiness.

In 1Pet 1:13-16 people are asked to: prepare their minds for action; be self-controlled, obedient and just as he who called you is holy, so be holy in all you do.

Note:

Concerning 'Holiness' – God alone is holy – see the following Scripture:

4 "Who will not fear you, O Lord, and bring glory to your name? For you alone are holy. All nations will come and worship before you, for your righteous acts have been revealed."

Rev 15:4

Goodness

Concerning 'Goodness' – God alone is good –as described in the following Scriptures:

Ps 27:13, and Lk 18:19

Judgment

Bob Gass in his "The Word for Today" Notes states: '... each of us must ...account ...for what we do' (Rom 14:12 CEV), '....Everything is ... bare before ...him to whom we must give account' (Heb 4:13 NIV).' He goes on to say:"it sounds more like cause for panic than reassurance, does it not? So why is it a reason for rejoicing? The answer is found in Rom 2:16. Listen: 'God will judge men's secrets through Jesus Christ ... (NIV)." He goes on to say: "Jesus is the filter through which God sees and judges you. Listen: 'Those ...in Christ are not judged guilty' (Rom 8:1 NCV)".

on to say, there is even more [illegible] cause for panic than [illegible] us [illegible] does it
not? So why is that a reason for rejoicing? The answer is found in [illegible]
[illegible] God will judge men's secrets through Jesus Christ [illegible] (NIV) [illegible] He
[illegible] Jesus is the filter through which God sees and judges [illegible]
[illegible] Those in Christ [illegible] not judged [illegible]

GOD'S CHARACTER

-HIS MORAL ATTRIBUTES-

Biblical Texts & Text References

See the supporting biblical texts given below that outline the above qualities:

Index of Sub-Headings

His Love - as revealed in the Old Testament Scriptures:

8 The LORD is gracious and compassionate, slow to anger and rich in love.
9 The LORD is good to all; he has compassion on all he has made.

Ps 145:8-9

3 He heals the broken-hearted and binds up their wounds.

Ps 147:3

Additional Scripture references:

Ps 34:18-19; 103:13-14; 147:10-11, Isa 61:1-3, Jer 33:10-11, Hos 3:1; 11:1-4; Zeph 3:17

His Love - as revealed in the New Testament Scriptures:

In 1Jn 4:16 speaking to believers it says' we know and rely on the love God has for us. God is love'.

Additional Scripture references:

Jn 14:21; 15:13; 17:22-23, Rom 2:4; 5:8; 8:37-39, 2Cor 5:14-15, Eph 3:17-19, Phil 2:5-11, 2Thess 3:5; Heb 7:25; 12:3-7, 1Jn 4:19; Jude 21

His Grace - His unmerited favour

It says in Lk 4:2 that 'All spoke well of him and were amazed at the gracious words that came from his lips'.

Additional Scripture references

Gen 21:1, 1Sam 2:21, 2Kg 13:23, 2Chron 30:9, Ezra 7:9, Neh 2:8, Ps 86:15; Jer 33:14, Joel 2:13, Jn 1:16-17; Rom 3:19-24; 5:17, 1Cor 9:6-8; 15:9-10, 2Cor 1:12; 6:1-2; 8:9; 12:7-9, Gal ; Eph 2:6-9; 2:19-21, Eph 1:7-8; 2:6-9; 3:1-3; 6:23-24, 1Tim 2:1, Heb 4:16; 13:8; 13:20-21; 1Pet 5:5-6

His Goodness

It says in 2 Pet 1:3 speaking to believers that 'His divine power has given us everything we need for life and Godliness', and that called us out of his goodness.

Additional Scripture references:

Ex 33:19; 34:5-7, 2Chron 6:41, Neh 9:35, Ps 27:13; 31:19; 86:17; 109 :21; 142:7, 145:7-9; Isa 25:89; 61:1-3, Jer 33:10-11, Mat 4:23; 7:7-11, Lk 7:21-23; 8:1, Jn 10:11-14, Heb 12:22-29, 1Jn 4:7-8

His Forgiveness and Reconciliation

Forgiveness

46 He told them, "This is what is written: The Christ will suffer and rise from the dead on the third day,
47 and repentance and forgiveness of sins will be preached in his name to all nations, beginning at Jerusalem.

Lk 24:46-47

Additional Scripture references:

Ps 130:3-4; Isa 53:5-7, Mic 7:18-19; Mat 26:28, Mk 1:4, Lk 5:24, Acts 10:43, Eph 1:7, Col 1:13-14, Heb 10:14-18; 1Jn 1:9

Reconciliation

It states in Rom 5:9-11 speaking to believers that they have 'been justified by his blood', saved from God's wrath through him! and have 'now received reconciliation'.

Additional Scripture references:

Jer 33:7-8; Joel 2:25, Zech 3:1-4, 2Cor 5:17-19, Eph 2:14-16, Col 1:19-20, Heb 8:10-12

His Fatherhood

In Ps 68:5-6 it says that God is 'A father to the fatherless, a defender of widows'.

Additional Scripture references:

Deut 1:30-31, Jn 16:26-27, Rom 1:6-7; 8:15-16, 1Cor 1:3, 2Cor 1:2-4; 6:17-18, Gal 4:4-6, Eph 5:19-20, Col 1:12-14; 2Thess 2:16-17, Heb 5:5, Jas 1:16-17, 1Pet 1:3-4, 1Jn 1:3-4; 3:1

His Truth, Purity, Sinlessness and Incorruptibility

His Truth

In Eph 4:21 it refers to the truth that is in Jesus.

Additional Scripture references:

Ps 12:5-6; 19:7-8, Prov 1:29-31; 30:5, Jn 14:5-6; 18:36-38; Jas 1:17-18

His Purity, Sinlessness and Incorruptibility

14 Therefore, since we have a great high priest who has gone through the heavens, Jesus the Son of God, let us hold firmly to the faith we profess.

15 For we do not have a high priest who is unable to sympathise with our weaknesses, but we have one who has been tempted in every way, just as we are--yet was without sin.

Heb 4:14-15

Additional Scripture references:

Ps 92:14-15; 119:142-144, Lk 23:46-47, Jn 1:14-17 ; 2Cor 5:20-21, Tit 2:13-14, 1Pet 2:21-22, 1Jn 1:5-7; 3:3-5

His Holiness, Righteousness and Justice

His Holiness

13 Your ways, O God, are holy. What god is so great as our God?
14 You are the God who performs miracles; you display your power among the peoples.

Ps 77:13-14

Additional Scripture references:
Lev 11:45, Josh 24:19-21, 1Chron 16:10, Ps 99:1-5; 145:17-19, Isa 6:1-5; 17:7; 30:15-18; 40:25-26; 52:10, Ezek 20:39-41; 36:22-23, 39:7; Hab 2:18-20, Rom 1:1-4, Heb 7:26-28, Rev 4:8; 15:4.

His Righteousness and Justice

In Isa 5:16 it refers to the LORD Almighty being exalted by his justice and will show his righteousness

Additional Scripture references:
Job 37:23; Ps 9:16; 11:7; 36:5-6; 111:9-10; 145:17-21, Prov 21:12-15, Lam 1:18, Isa 30:18; 42:1-4, Acts 7:52, Rom 3:22-26, 1Jn 2:1-2.

His Judgment and Mercy

His Judgment

22 Moreover, the Father judges no-one, but has entrusted all judgment to the Son,

Jn 5:22

Additional Scripture references:
Gen 19:24-29, Neh 9:29-31, Ps 9:16-17; 11:6-7; 58:11; 92:6-8; 96:9-13, Isa 65:11-14; 66:22-24, Ezek 16:49-50, Dan 12:1-3, Mal 3:5-6, Mat 3:11-12; 13:41-43; 18:1-7; 23:13; 25:31-34 & 41-46, Mk 9:42-43, Lk 16:19-31, Jn 5:22-29; 8:16, Acts 17:29-31, Rom 1:20-2:4; 2:13-16; 11:33-34; 14:10-12, 1Cor 6:9-11, Gal 5:19-21, Eph 5:3-6, 2Thess 1:8-9; 2:9-12, 1Tim 4:1-4, Heb 10:26-31; 10:35-39; 13:4-6, 1Pet 4:17-18, 2Pet 2:4-9; 3:3-9, Rev 14:9-11.

His Mercy

35 But love your enemies, do good to them, and lend to them without expecting to get anything back. Then your reward will be great, and

you will be sons of the Most High, because he is kind to the ungrateful
and wicked.
36 Be merciful, just as your Father is merciful.

Lk 6:35-36

Additional Scripture references:

Deut 4:30-31, Ps 78:36-38, Isa 1:26-28, Jer 3:12-13, Dan 9:8-10, Rom 8:1-3; 11:21-22, 1Tim 1:12-14; Heb 2:16-18, Jas 3:16-17, 2Pet 3:9-11

B2

GOD'S CHARACTER

HIS NON-MORAL ATTRIBUTES

Biblical Definitions

God's Character - His Non-Moral Attributes

Surely what most people are looking for in life is to have the security of living in the warmth and protection of a loving Father figure, a Supreme Being, who is all knowing so cannot be deceived and whose true justice and judgement is never blurred or compromised. Also, Someone whose power to act with perfect wisdom is never found wanting, and whose supernatural creative and healing power has been demonstrated over all time. Well, it is this Supreme Being whose attributes we are further considering and this is the God of the Bible.

So to complete the overview of the attributes of God, it is necessary to consider His non-moral attributes. All these attributes should cause everyone to consider them in awe that such a mighty, majestic, perfect and immense God not only is the creator of all, but is the ONE who always shows such love and consideration for the relative frailty of us, His creation, bearing in mind that He sees the 'big picture' and knows the beginning and the end of all people and events. He also knows of the problems that are caused by man and those that He allows according to His compassion, wisdom, foreknowledge and purposes.

To enable the reader to discover more of the true nature of God these attributes are more fully reviewed under the next heading below.

Index of Sub-Headings

The biblical Scriptures given under these headings are to be considered as a brief summary of supporting evidence, and reveal the unparalleled claims made for God. An additional listing of Scripture Texts and Text references is given later in the B2 Text Section.

His Infinity, Eternity and Uniqueness.
His Self-Existence, Immortality and Omnipresence.
His Wisdom and Omniscience.
His Sovereignty and Omnipotence.
His Perfection and Immutability.
His Immensity.
One and Only God in the Unity of the Godhead - The Trinity.
His Absolute Supernatural Creative and Healing Power in the Old Testament.
His Absolute Supernatural Creative and Healing Power in the New Testament

His Infinity, Eternity and Uniqueness

These qualities apply in absolute and exclusive terms to God as revealed in the Bible.

He is not confined to the limits of time and space. His existence is from eternity past to eternity future.

Please see the following summary of supporting biblical Scriptures given here, and the additional listing given later in this Section.

In Ecc3;14-15 it states that God: will endure for ever, and will call the past to account.

Also in 1Tim 1:17 in speaking about God it states that he is:" eternal, immortal, invisible, the only God".

Additional Scripture references

Job 11:7-9; 26:7-11, Ps 93:1-2, Mat 16:16; 1Tim 4:7-10; Heb 1:10-12, 2Pet 3:8

His Self-Existence, Immortality and Omnipresence

These claims mean that God, as revealed in the Bible, has no beginning, no end, and is present everywhere at the same time. Also, He is not bounded by space and time.

Please see the following summary of supporting biblical Scriptures given here, and the additional listing given later in this Section.

In Ps 90:2 it states that:" from everlasting to everlasting you are God".

In Col 1:17 referring to the Lord Jesus Christ, it states:" He is before all things, and in him all things hold together".

<u>Additional Scripture references</u>
Isa 41:1-4, Mic 5:2, Jn 1:1-3; 8:56-58; Phil 2:6-11

<u>God is a Spirit as shown by the Scriptures given below:</u>

In Ps 139:7-8 it asks questions concerning God's Spirit saying 'Where can I go from your Spirit? Where can I flee from your presence? And wherever we go he is there.

9 You, however, are controlled not by the sinful nature but by the Spirit, if the Spirit of God lives in you. And if anyone does not have the Spirit of Christ, he does not belong to Christ.

Rom 8:9

<u>Additional Scripture references</u>
Gen 1:1-2, Ezek 37:14, Joel 2:28-29; Jn 4:24, 1Cor 2:11, 2Cor 3:17-18

<u>His Wisdom and Omniscience</u>

God's wisdom is infinite and He is the fount of all knowledge and hence, knows everything.

No seemingly new thought or invention is new to God.

Please see the following summary of supporting biblical Scriptures given here, and the additional listing given later in this Section.

In Ex 3:19-20 it states that after all the wonders that God will perform among the Egyptians that Pharaoh will let the Jewish people go from Egypt.

In Isa 40:28 it states that: "The LORD is the everlasting God, the Creator of the ends of the earth. He will not grow tired or weary, and his understanding no-one can fathom.

10 His intent was that now, through the church, the manifold wisdom of God should be made known to the rulers and authorities in the heavenly realms,
11 according to his eternal purpose which he accomplished in Christ Jesus our Lord.

Eph 3:10-11

Additional Scripture references

Gen 18:18-19, Ex 3:19-20, Ps 104:24, Jer 10:12, Mat 6:3-4, Rom 11:33-36, 1Jn 3:19-20

His Sovereignty and Omnipotence

With God nothing is impossible, and the only constraint on His actions is that which He puts on Himself out of love, grace and timing to fulfil His purposes.

Please see the following summary of supporting biblical Scriptures given here, and the additional listing given later in this Section.

1 In the beginning God created the heavens and the earth.

Gen 1:1

With reference to the Lord Jesus Christ it states in Col 1:15-17 that:" He is the image of the invisible God, the firstborn over all creation. For by him all things were created: things in heaven and on earth, visible and invisible, whether thrones or powers or rulers or authorities; all things were created by him and for him". It also says that he is before all things and that he holds all things together.

Additional Scripture references

Gen 17:1, Ps 33:9-11; 96:10, Lk 1:35-37, Rom 1:20; 3:20, 1Cor 15;24-25; Jude 24-25

His Perfection and Immutability

God's character is one of absolute perfection and this is linked to the fact that He is unchangeable in nature and purpose. He has no need to change because He is, and always was, perfect.

Please see the following summary of supporting biblical Scriptures given here, and the additional listing given later in this Section.

Jesus Christ does not change, and is the same for ever - see Heb 13:8

10 The LORD foils the plans of the nations; he thwarts the purposes of the peoples.
11 But the plans of the LORD stand firm for ever, the purposes of his heart through all generations.

Ps 33:10-11

Additional Scripture references

Num 23:19, Deut 32:4, 1Sam 15:29, Ps 19:7-9; 102:27, Isa 14:24, Mal 3:6, Heb 2;10; 4:15; 6:17-18, Jas 1:17

His Immensity

The span He covers is limitless and reaches beyond every corner of the vast immeasurable universe.

Please see the following summary of supporting biblical Scriptures given here, and the additional listing given later in this Section.

('God Almighty' in Heb. is EL SHADDAI meaning "the God of the mountains", or alternatively translated "God the enough"; enough for all powers, circumstances or situations.)

24 Can anyone hide in secret places so that I cannot see him?" declares the LORD. "Do not I fill heaven and earth?" declares the LORD.

Jer 23:24

Additional Scripture references

Gen 17:1, 1Kg 8:27-28, 1Chron 29:10-11, Job 11:7-9, Ps 8:3-4; 145:3, Isa 66:1, Eph 4:10, 2Pet 3:8

One and only God in the unity of the Godhead - The Trinity

In the Scriptures we see all three Persons of the Godhead referred to and identified as God the Father, God the Son and God the Holy Spirit. We also see many Scriptures that show their unified and close relationship. Although there remains a mystery about this whole concept of a triune Godhead, it is reassuring to know that there is much evidence given in the Scriptures to support it.

A few Scriptures that indicate something of the nature of these interrelationships and of their activities, with brief comments, are given below.

There is also an additional listing of supporting biblical Scriptures given later in this Section.

Please see the following summary of supporting biblical Scriptures given here, and Note the use of 'US' and 'OUR' in the act of creation.

26 Then God said, "Let us make man in our image, in our likeness, and let them rule over the fish of the sea and the birds of the air, over the livestock, over all the earth, and over all the creatures that move along the ground."

Gen 1:26

Note the use of 'US' as they confuse and prevent people from achieving their pride driven plans.

7 Come, let us go down and confuse their language so they will not understand each other."
8 So the LORD scattered them from there over all the earth, and they stopped building the city.
9 That is why it was called Babel— because there the LORD confused the language of the whole world. From there the LORD scattered them over the face of the whole earth.

Gen 11:7-9

In Isa 43:10-11 we see here the claim that He is God alone, there is no other.

Here it mentions all the Persons of the Trinity and indicates the unity between them.

19 Therefore go and make disciples of all nations, baptising them in the name of the Father and of the Son and of the Holy Spirit,

Mat 28:19

The Lord Jesus Christ speaks here of the other two members of the Trinity, and refers to the activity of the Holy Spirit. – See Jn 14:15-17

Here we see something of the relationship between Father and Son, and that He includes those who trust in Him in that relationship. See Jn 20:17

The apostle Paul refers here to believers having access through Jesus Christ to the Father by the Holy Spirit, and so reveals the unity of purpose of the Godhead. See Eph 2:18

Here we see the Deity and humanity of the Lord Jesus Christ.

9 For in Christ all the fulness of the Deity lives in bodily form,
10 and you have been given fulness in Christ, who is the Head over every power and authority.

Col 2:9-10

<u>Additional Scripture references</u>
Isa 42:1, Joel 2:28-29, Jn 10:29-30; 15:26, 1Pet 1:1-2

His absolute supernatural creative and healing power in the O.T.

To fully show the proof for God's power in the above ways is an immense task as the quantity of evidence is so vast, so please see the Scriptures below just as an introduction to this topic.

Although God has such absolute power it is mostly used in a positive creative way for the benefit of mankind, and yet sometimes it is used in a destructive way as a warning, but throughout the Scriptures we see that it is God's heart to want to forgive, restore and empower erring people.

Please see the following summary of supporting biblical Scriptures given here and the additional listing given later in this Section.

In Gen 1:1-3 is seen the very beginning of the creation of the heavens and the earth.

27 So God created man in his own image, in the image of God he created him; male and female he created them.

Gen 1:27

He created all the plants,trees, animals and birds – see Gen 1:29-31

17 But the LORD provided a great fish to swallow Jonah, and Jonah was inside the fish three days and three nights. See Jon 1:17-2:2 & 10

Additional Scripture references

Gen 7:17-24; Ex 14:21-22, Josh 10:12-13, 2Kg 5:1-3 & 13-14, Jer 10:12-13; Dan 3:21-27

His absolute supernatural creative and healing power in the N.T.

In the Scriptures we have ample evidence of God's unlimited power and this is demonstrated by the magnificence of His creative, healing and restorative abilities, including physical healing, demonic deliverance, spiritual conversion and regeneration.

Many of the words commonly used in the N.T. for healing are given the meaning of 'being made whole'. In the ministry of the Lord Jesus Christ sick people were 'made whole'. He had a wider concern than just physical healing, and this included the person's emotional, mental and spiritual health.

Please see the following summary of supporting biblical Scriptures given here, and the additional listing given later in this Section.

The two Scriptures below state that Jesus Christ, the Son of God, is the creator of the universe.

15 He is the image of the invisible God, the firstborn over all creation.
16 For by him all things were created: things in heaven and on earth, visible and invisible, whether thrones or powers or rulers or authorities; all things were created by him and for him.
17 He is before all things, and in him all things hold together.

Col 1:15-17

1 In the past God spoke to our forefathers through the prophets at many times and in various ways,
2 but in these last days he has spoken to us by his Son, whom he appointed heir of all things, and through whom he made the universe.

Heb 1:1-2

Additional Scripture references

Mat 1;18-20; 12:9-13, 15:28-31; Lk 4;33-36; 8:27-35, Jn 1:1-3, Acts 3:1-8; Acts 16:24-34, 2Cor 5:17-19; Heb 1:10-12

GOD'S CHARACTER

- HIS NON-MORAL ATTRIBUTES-

Notes and Quotations

A summary of God's non-moral attributes, particularly showing His miraculous power, is given below under the title 'Our Miraculous God'.

Our Miraculous God

God is referred to as everlasting and the Creator of the ends of the earth. See Isa 40:28.

In a prophetic statement if says he will be referred to a "Wonderful Counsellor, Mighty God, Everlasting Father, Prince of Peace." See Isa 9:6

In 1Tim 1:17 God is referred to as: King eternal, immortal, invisible, the only God.

His creative and healing power is shown in Lk 8:26-36 when a demon possessed man is delivered and healed.

He demonstrated His miraculous power – See Lk 7:11-16

He possesses all wisdom and knowledge - "Christ, in whom are hidden all the treasures of wisdom and knowledge." See Col 2:2b-3

God's supernatural character is demonstrated throughout the whole Bible by a vast amount and variety of miraculous events, in fact a hallmark of the character of God in the Bible is the miraculous as outlined below:

- from creation to the cross

- from the flood to the feeding of the five thousand
- from the giving of the commandments to the glory of His transfiguration
- from the crossing of the Red Sea to the ceasing of the wind on the lake
- from the fall of Jericho to the failure of the furnace for Daniel's friends
- from the writing on the wall to Paul's Damascus Road revelation
- from the speaking of an ass to the speaking of dumb people
- from manna from Heaven to the manifestation of the Holy Spirit
- from angelic visitations to prophetic messages given in visions
- from Daniel's rescue from lions to Jesus' resurrection
- from wisdom given to Solomon to the wonders of healing the sick
- from the regurgitation of Jonah to raising the dead

The character of God does not change, - see Heb 13:8 "Jesus Christ the same, yesterday, today and forever".

In Mat 21:23 the chief priests and elders questioned the authority of Jesus, but His credentials were seen in changed lives, not just words, - see Mat 11:2-5 below:

2 When John heard in prison what Christ was doing, he sent his disciples
3 to ask him, "Are you the one who was to come, or should we expect someone else?"
4 Jesus replied, "Go back and report to John what you hear and see:
5 The blind receive sight, the lame walk, those who have leprosy are cured, the deaf hear, the dead are raised, and the good news is preached to the poor.

In the above Scripture we see that His authority was demonstrated through the powerful effect His words had, and thus His words were life-giving, enlightening, empowering, challenging and encouraging, and also in the Scripture below we see His words contain eternal life for those who believe on Him:

16 "For God so loved the world that he gave his one and only Son, that whoever believes in him shall not perish but have eternal life.

Jn 3:16

God Almighty

"The term 'God - the Enough' is a working equivalent of the Hebrew name for God - El-Shaddai - ". Quote from Selwyn Hughes in his 'Every Day With Jesus' Notes.

This name for God is used in many places in Scripture including Gen. 17:1 and indicates that He is always 'Enough' and has more than 'Enough':

- grace for any human condition,
- provision for every circumstance,
- wisdom and power for any situation in time or eternity.

"The Greek word for 'ALMIGHTY' signifies the unmatched Greatness of God, who has power over all humankind and every competing authority" (Eph 1:19-21). - L.O. Richards.

In these days we live in a culture that no longer takes seriously the idea of a weighty God but rather celebrates a God who cooperates with our agenda - and that is bad and misleading as illustrated by Dr Larry Crabb below.

A quotation with a warning given by Dr Larry Crabb - "There is no weighty (Mighty) God to fall before (in these days), only a cooperative God to celebrate".

See two typical Scriptures given below:

120My flesh trembles in fear of you; I stand in awe of your laws.

Ps 119:120

See also Jer 2:19 that refers to punishment to backsliders, those who forsake the Lord.

Our confessed weakness – the opportunity for Christ's POWER to be demonstrated and this is shown by the apostle Paul when he relates that

God said to him, "My grace is sufficient for you, for my power is made perfect in weakness. "See 2Cor 12:9

One of the meanings for the word 'POWER' in the above passage, and many other passages of Scripture is the ability to perform the miraculous.

Quotes from Selwyn Hughes in his 'Every Day With Jesus' Notes.

"'Jesus' divinity was part of His very nature. In Him the supernatural was natural".

and "Jesus gives God a face".

God's Self Existence

In Jamie Buckingham's book "A Way Through the Wilderness" he says: "At the burning bush, He told Moses He was not only EL SHADDAI (God Almighty), the God of Abraham, Isaac and Jacob; He went ahead to say He was *'ehyeh asher ehyeh'* - 'I AM THAT I AM'. At this point, God declared He was more than the essence of being, which is the root of 'I AM'. He said He was the cause of being - underived existence coupled with an independent and uncontrolled will". A little later in the book he states that the name of God was originally YHWH. and he then adds, "This was translated out in the later renderings as JEHOVAH - the self-existent God. This name, YAHWEH or JEHOVAH, has its roots in *ehyeh* - underived existence".

Healing

When the Lord Jesus Christ was involved with needy people it is to be noted that He asked them what they wanted from Him, and He did not impose His will on them. - see the following Scriptures:

A blind man named Bartimaeus is healed by Jesus –see Mk 10:46-52

In Jn 5:5-9 Jesus encounters a man by a pool who has been an invalid for thirty-eight years, and Jesus asked him, "Do you want to get well?" and the man replies," I have no-one to help me into the pool" Then Jesus said to him, "Get up! Pick up your mat and walk.". The man did this and was immediately cured.

The Trinity

L.O. Richards in his book "Expository Dictionary of Bible Words" under the heading 'The Holy Spirit in the NT.' states: "The Greek word for "spirit," *pneuma,* with the adjective "holy," identifies the Third Person of the Trinity in the NT. The clearest expression of this is found in Mat 28:19, where Jesus gives the Great Commission's baptismal formula. Believers are to be baptized in the name of the Father, the Son, and the holy Spirit."

An illustration of 'The Trinity'

Someone has provided the following example to illustrate 'The Trinity'.

If we consider the substance of water, we know that it can exist in three forms: as a solid (ice); as a liquid; and as a vapour (steam). However, all three forms are in fact one substance. In a simple basic way the analogy of water can be compared with 'The Godhead' that is one divine 'substance' that exists in three Persons: The Father, the Son and The Holy Spirit, - and these three Persons are referred to as 'The Trinity'.

GOD'S CHARACTER

-HIS NON-MORAL ATTRIBUTES -

Biblical Texts & Text References

Index of Sub-Headings

His Infinity, Eternity, and Uniqueness.

6 For to us a child is born, to us a son is given, and the government will be on his shoulders. And he will be called Wonderful Counsellor, Mighty God, Everlasting Father, Prince of Peace.

Isa 9:6

Additional Scripture references:

Gen 17:1-19; 35:10-13, 1Chron 29:10-12, Job 38:3-6, Ps 90:2; 95:3-6; 104:1-5; 119:142, Isa 9:6; 40:12-14, Jn 1:1-3; 1:14-18, Rom 1:1-4; 11:33-36; 16:26-27, Col 2:9-10; Heb 13:8; 1Pet 1:20-21, Rev 15:2-4

His Self - Existence, Immortality and Omnipresence

30 At the resurrection people will neither marry nor be given in marriage; they will be like the angels in heaven.

31 But about the resurrection of the dead--have you not read what God said to you,
32 `I am the God of Abraham, the God of Isaac, and the God of Jacob'? He is not the God of the dead but of the living."

Mat 22:30-32

Additional Scripture references:
Ex 3:13-15; Ps 90:1-2, Isa 40:28, Jn 1:1; 3:16-18;, Col 1:17-20; 1Tim 6:13-16

His Wisdom and Omniscience

25 For the foolishness of God is wiser than man's wisdom, and the weakness of God is stronger than man's strength.

1Cor 1:25

Additional Scripture references:
Job 37:16, Ps 33;10-12; 92:5; 94:10-11; 139:1-4, 147:4-5; Isa 16:7; 55:6-9, Dan 2:47 Mat 9:3-4; 12:24-25, Mk 2:8, Lk 11:16-17, Jn 8:31-32; 14:5-6, 1Cor 2:9-11; Col 2:2-3; Heb 4:13

His Sovereignty and Omnipotence

In Mat 24:36-39 Jesus relates to the time of Noah when the flood came as a surprise to all the people who died, and says that this is how it will be at the coming of the Son of Man.

9 For in Christ all the fulness of the Deity lives in bodily form,
10 and you have been given fulness in Christ, who is the Head over every power and authority.

Col 2:9-10

Additional Scripture references:
Gen 6:13-14; 7:6-7:& 17-18; 8:1-6; 17:1-2; 19 :24-25, Ex 12 :19 ; 15:7-11, Deut 5:24-27; 9:25-26; 11:2-4, 2Sam 7 :18-22, 1Chron 16 :28-31 ; 29:10-12, 2Chron 32 :6-8, Job 12 :13-15; 38:4-9; 42:1-2, Ps 8 :1; 47 :7-9; 45:4-6; 68:19-20; 71 :4-6; 93:1-2; 96 :10 ; 99 :1-3; 104:5-9, Prov 3 :19-20, Isa 28 :16-17; 40:10-11; 54 :9-10, Jer 32:16-18; & 27; Dan 4 :17 ; 9 :3-4, Joel 2:28-32, Mat 8:8, Lk 7 :11-16 ; 17:27-30; 22 :67-70, Jn 15 :1-5, Acts 2:22; 4:12; 4:23-24, 2Cor 8 :9, Eph 1:19-21; Phil 2 :5-11, Col 2 :13-15, 2Thess:1:8-10, 1Tim 1:15-16, 2Pet 3 :3-8; 1:16-17; 1Jn 3:8

His Perfection and Immutability

27 Unlike the other high priests, he does not need to offer sacrifices day after day, first for his own sins, and then for the sins of the people. He sacrificed for their sins once for all when he offered himself.

28 For the law appoints as high priests men who are weak; but the oath, which came after the law, appointed the Son, who has been made perfect for ever.

Heb 7:27-28

See also 2Sam 22:31-32, Mal 3:6

His Immensity (having boundless limits)

28 Do you not know? Have you not heard? The LORD is the everlasting God, the Creator of the ends of the earth. He will not grow tired or weary, and his understanding no-one can fathom.

Isa 40:28

Additional Scripture references

Ex 15:6-7, Deut 3:24, 2Chron 2;5-6; 6:18, Job 38:10, Ps 150:1-2; Ezek 38:23, Mat 12 :41-42, Lk 9 :43-44, 1Jn 3:19-20; 4:4

One and Only God in the Unity of the Godhead - The Trinity

16 As soon as Jesus was baptised, he went up out of the water. At that moment heaven was opened, and he saw the Spirit of God descending like a dove and lighting on him.

17 And a voice from heaven said, "This is my Son, whom I love; with him I am well pleased."

Mat 3:16-17

In Phil 2:9-11 it refers to God saying that Jesus' name is above every name and that every knee on earth and in heaven shall bow to him, and that every tongue shall confess that Jesus Christ is Lord, to the glory of God the Father

Additional Scripture references:

Gen 3:21-22; Ex 15:9-11, Deut 4:33-39 ; 34:9, Ps 86:9-10; 95:1-3, Isa 6:8; 44:6-8; 54:5, Jer 10:10-15, Mk 12:28-29, Jn 5:44; 14;9-11; 15:21; 15:24-

26; 17:4-5 & 20-23, Acts 2:31-33, 1Cor 8:4-6, 2Cor 13:14, Rom 3:28-30, 1Tim 1:17; 2 :5-6, Jas 2:18-20, 1Pet 1:1-3, 1Jn 4:13-16, Jude 24-25

His Absolute Supernatural Creative and Healing Power in the O.T.

20 And God said, "Let the water teem with living creatures, and let birds fly above the earth across the expanse of the sky."
21 So God created the great creatures of the sea and every living and moving thing with which the water teems, according to their kinds, and every winged bird according to its kind. And God saw that it was good.
22 God blessed them and said, "Be fruitful and increase in number and fill the water in the seas, and let the birds increase on the earth."

Gen 1:20-22

Additional Scripture references:

Gen 2;18-23; 21:1-5, Ex 15:23-26, 2Kg 20:1-6, 2Chron 16:11-12, Job 42:1-2, Ps 33:6-9; 41:1-4; 90:1-2; 96:4-7; 102:25-27; 103:1-4; 104:5-9; 121:1-2, Prov 3:5-8; 4:20-22, Isa 42;5; 61:1-3; 65 17-18; 66:1-2, Jer 17:14; 32:17-20, Dan 6:16-22, Jon 2:7-10; 4:6-7

His Absolute Supernatural Creative and Healing Power in the N.T.

21 At that very time Jesus cured many who had diseases, sicknesses and evil spirits, and gave sight to many who were blind.
22 So he replied to the messengers, "Go back and report to John what you have seen and heard: The blind receive sight, the lame walk, those who have leprosy are cured, the deaf hear, the dead are raised, and the good news is preached to the poor.

Lk 7:21-22

Words that refer to Jesus in Jn 1:3, where it states that all things were made through him.

Additional Scripture references:

Mat 8:8-10 & 13; Mk 8;5-9; 10:46-52, Lk 4:17-19; 17:12-19, Jn 1:10-12; 2:7-11; 4:47-53; 5:5-9, Acts 3:3-16; 4:24-25; 10:37-38; 16:16-18; 17:26-27; 28:7-9, 1Cor 12:7-9, 2Cor 5:17-18, Col 1:15-17; 2:13-14, Heb 2:9-10; 11:3; Jas 5:13-15, 2Pet 3:3-6

C1

THE LORD JESUS CHRIST

- HIS ADVENT AND LIFE -

Biblical Definitions

Index of Sub-Headings

The Incarnation of Christ - His Virgin Birth

This world-changing and miraculous event was foretold by Hebrew prophets hundreds of years before it happened, and they also said where it was to take place – in Bethlehem, a small village in Israel. What makes this even more remarkable is that these prophets lived at very different times.

The prophetic statements they made also gave much detail about the unblemished character He was to have, His compassion for the poor and the hope and salvation He was to offer, and also the rejection and suffering He was to endure. The statements also include many titles that were to refer to Him including: Mighty God; Everlasting Father; and Prince of Peace.

These prophetic statements are recorded in the Bible, and some of these Scriptures are given in this and other Sections.

The virgin birth of Jesus Christ relates to the fact that He is part of the Triune Godhead, and for a period of thirty plus years was embodied in human form. Christ being conceived through Mary by the Holy Spirit brought about this miraculous event. This fact forms a substantial part and foundation of the Good News and joy of the Gospel that was initiated at that time, and is supported by many Scriptures including the following:

10 But the angel said to them, "Do not be afraid. I bring you good news of great joy that will be for all the people.
11 Today in the town of David a Saviour has been born to you; he is Christ the Lord.

Lk 2:10-11

5 Therefore, <u>when Christ came into the world,</u> he said: "Sacrifice and offering you did not desire, but <u>a body you prepared for me;</u>

Heb 10:5

In Lk 1:30-35 the angel returns to Mary saying she had found favour with God and that she would give birth to a son whom she should name Jesus, and that he would be called the Son of the Most High, the Son of God and that his kingdom will never end.

<u>This momentous and history changing event was foretold hundreds of years before by Old Testament prophets and a few of these Scriptures are given below:</u>

1 The LORD had said to Abram, "Leave your country, your people and your father's household and go to the land I will show you.
2 "I will make you into a great nation and I will bless you; I will make your name great, and you will be a blessing.
3 I will bless those who bless you, and whoever curses you I will curse; and all peoples on earth will be blessed through you."

Gen 12:1-3

It was prophesied through the Isaiah that the Lord "will give you a sign: The virgin will be with child and will give birth to a son, and will call him Immanuel". See Isa:7:14

Again in the book of Isaiah it was prophesied that this Son to be born "will be called Wonderful Counsellor, Mighty God, Everlasting Father, Prince of Peace", and that he would establish a kingdom of justice and righteousness lasting for ever. See Isa 9:6-7

2 "But you, Bethlehem Ephrathah, though you are small among the clans of Judah, out of you will come for me one who will be ruler over Israel, whose origins are from of old, from ancient times."

Mic 5:2

The Purpose of His Coming - See also the C1 Biblical Text Section

These purposes were, and still are, extremely important for all mankind as His coming has brought life, hope, the possibility of forgiveness and eternal life. A fuller description of these purposes are outlined below with the Scriptures that support these statements.

An outline of the purposes is given below;

-*To bring us life - life to the full.* See Jn 10:10
-*To lay down His life for us.* See Jn 10:14-15
-*To seek and save the lost.* See Lk 19:10

Please see the texts referred to for the following headings:

- *To save those who believe on Him, and give them eternal life.* See Jn 3:16-18
- *To testify to the truth.* See Jn 18:37

To show His love to us and enable us to live through Him. See 1Jn 4:8-10
"He sent his one and only Son into the world that we might live through him."
and *To separate the true Christians from the false.* See Mat 25:31-46
To give the false eternal punishment, and the true eternal life. See Mat 25:46
To enable the dead to arise, - to be judged according to the life they have lived. See Jn 5:26-30, 1Thess 4:16-17
"To destroy the devil's work." See 1Jn 3:8

His Advent - Prophesied in the O.T. and Fulfilled in the N.T.

In Isa 7:14 it says that the Lord will provide a sign saying that a 'virgin will be with child and will give birth to a son, and will call him Immanuel.'

This scripture was fulfilled by God sending an angel to Mary, a virgin in Israel, saying that she would give birth to a son who is to be called Jesus, the Son of the Most High.

Also the scripture Isa 11:1-2 & 10 refers to the one who is to come from the line of Jesse (David's line) and the Spirit of the Lord will rest on him, a Spirit of wisdom, counsel and power, and this scripture is linked to Rom 15:12 where it also states that the Gentiles will hope in him.

His Life - Prophesied in the O.T. and Fulfilled in the N.T.

Abraham was told by the Lord (Gen 12;1-3) to leave his country and go to a land that God would show him, and that he would make him into a great nation. This was fulfilled, and that through Abraham all the people of the earth would be blessed – see Acts 3:24-25.

Further linked scriptures are given below:

Ps 16;10 linked to Acts 2;27
Ps 22:17 & 34:20 linked to Jn 19:33
Ps 22;18 linked to Mat 27;35-36
Isa 53:7 linked to Mk 15;4-5
Isa 53:9 linked to 1Pet 2:22-23
Zech 9;9 linked to Mat 21:4-5
Zech 12:10 linked to Jn 19;33-37

The Life of Christ

The Lord Jesus Christ is addressed by over one hundred different names and titles in the Bible due to His multi-faceted character covering His many roles. This supports His wide and absolutely unique position in history because as creator of all things He was and is before all things.

When He confined Himself to the limitations of human flesh, as a man, He showed us His humanity, humility, and sinlessness, and coupled these qualities with His deity and His power over death, and yet His willingness to submit to death to pay for the guilt of our sin. This action revealed His grace toward mankind so that He could make eternal salvation available to us all.

The following Scriptures reveal something of His purpose and compassionate heart.

1 The Spirit of the Sovereign LORD is on me, because the LORD has anointed me to preach good news to the poor. He has sent me to bind up the broken-hearted, to proclaim freedom for the captives and release from darkness for the prisoners,

2 to proclaim the year of the LORD's favour and the day of vengeance of our God, to comfort all who mourn,

Isa 61:1-2

<u>*Linked to*</u>

17 The scroll of the prophet Isaiah was handed to him. Unrolling it, he found the place where it is written:

18 "The Spirit of the Lord is on me, because he has anointed me to preach good news to the poor. He has sent me to proclaim freedom for the prisoners and recovery of sight for the blind, to release the oppressed,

19 to proclaim the year of the Lord's favour."

Lk 4:17-19

The texts given later in this Section provide only an introduction to the vast quantity of Scriptures that apply to the life of the Lord Jesus Christ, and also see Sections C2 – C7 for the many aspects of His character and work.

2 [illegible] the year of the LORD's favour and the day of vengeance of our God, to comfort all who mourn,

Is 61:1-2

Luke 4

17 The [illegible] of the prophet Isaiah was [illegible]. [illegible] it, He found the place where it is written:

18 "The [illegible] of the Lord is on me, because He has anointed me to preach good news to the poor. He has sent me to proclaim freedom for the prisoners and recovery of sight for the blind, to release the oppressed,

19 to proclaim the year of the Lord's favor."

[illegible]

THE LORD JESUS CHRIST

- HIS ADVENT AND LIFE -

Notes and Quotations

The Lord Jesus Christ is unique in every way - in position, power, holiness, grace, goodness and in His eternal provision for mankind.

The biblical claim is that He is part of the one and only God, The Triune God Almighty, and that there is no other God. These and other characteristics are given and supported in Sections B, C and D of the book.

What other 'God' do we have such solid proof of in the past, and such evidence for in the present? - To whom can we compare Him? - Who else do we have proof of a divine miraculous birth, a sinless life, one who has had so many prophecies fulfilled about Him, having the power to perform miracles (mostly used to heal people), showing love and grace for people and dying for all mankind to make eternal life available?

The Scriptures given below reveal God, as the only God, and the Lord Jesus Christ as part of the Godhead.

10 "You are my witnesses," declares the LORD, "and my servant whom I have chosen, so that you may know and believe me and understand that I am he. Before me no god was formed, nor will there be one after me.
11 I, even I, am the LORD, and apart from me there is no saviour.

Isa 43:10-11

The truth of who Jesus was, was revealed to Simon Peter when he said, "You are the Christ, the Son of the living God." and Jesus responded by saying "this was not revealed to you by man, but by my Father in heaven". See Mat 16:15-17

9 For in Christ all the fulness of the Deity lives in bodily form,
10 and you have been given fulness in Christ, who is the Head over every power and authority.

Col 2:9-10

The following is an extract from John Gill's book "A Body of Doctrinal Divinity" concerning the incarnation of Christ:

> "The incarnation of Christ is a most extraordinary and amazing affair; it is wonderful indeed, that the eternal Son of God should become man; that he should be born of a pure virgin, without any concern of man in it; that this should be brought about by the power of the Holy Ghost, in a way unseen, imperceptible and unknown, signified by his overshadowing; and all this in order to effect the most wonderful work that ever was done in the world, the redemption and salvation of men: it is a most mysterious thing, incomprehensible by men, and not to be accounted for upon the principles of natural reason; and is only to be believed and embraced upon the credit of divine revelation, to which it solely belongs."

<u>Why the Lord Jesus Christ came to earth</u>

There are many reasons why He came including, to seek and save the lost and to be the saviour of all who believe and trust in Him as shown by the following Scriptures Isa 61:1-2, Lk 1:68, Lk 4:18-21, Lk 19:10, Jn 3:17, Jn 4:42, Jn 12:47, 1Tim 1:15, 1Tim 2:3-4, 1Tim 4:9-10, Tit 3:4-5, 1Jn 4:14.

THE LORD JESUS CHRIST

- HIS ADVENT AND LIFE -

Biblical Texts & Text References

Index of Sub-Headings

The Purpose of His Coming.
His Advent.
His Life.

The Purpose of His Coming

In Isa 61:1-2 it states that he was sent "to preach good news to the poor. He has sent me to bind up the broken-hearted, to proclaim freedom for the captives and release from darkness for the prisoners".

In Lk 19:10 Jesus speaking about himself says: "For the Son of Man came to seek and to save what was lost."

He came as a light into the world and for the salvation of people, and out of His love for all mankind he sent His only Son as an atoning sacrifice for our sins- see Jn 12:46-47 and 1Jn 4:9-10

Additional Scripture references:

Lk 4:18-24, Jn 3:16-18; 4:41-42; 17:4-5, 2Cor 5:18-21; 8:9, 1 Thess 4:16-17, 1Tim 1:15; Tit 3:4-6, 1Jn 3:8; 4:14-15

His Advent

The story of the miraculous virgin birth of Christ is told in Mat 1:18-23

Further details of the story are found in Lk 2:10-14 where among other things it refers to the appearance of an angel who says:" "Glory to God in the highest, and on earth peace to men on whom his favour rests".

Additional Scripture references:
Mat 2:1-2, Lk 1:31-35; 2:25-32, Jn 1:10-14, 3:13; Rom 8:3, Gal 4:4-5; Heb 2:9-17, 1Jn 3:5

His Life

The following prophecy concerning the promised Christ to be born as a child was given hundreds of years before He came, and is shown in the scripture Isa 9:6-7

During His time here on earth He carried out many miracles mostly concerning with healing the sick because he had a heart of compassion for them, a typical example of this is shown in Mat 8:14-17

He also could read people's minds and forgive their sins – see Mat 9:1-7

In the scripture below we see God has spoken through His Son Jesus Christ:

1 In the past God spoke to our forefathers through the prophets at many times and in various ways,
2 but in these last days he has spoken to us by his Son, whom he appointed heir of all things, and through whom he made the universe.
3 The Son is the radiance of God's glory and the exact representation of his being, sustaining all things by his powerful word. After he had provided purification for sins, he sat down at the right hand of the Majesty in heaven.

Heb 1:1-3

Additional Scripture references:
Mat 8:23-27; 11:18-20; 23:1-3; 23:27-33, 28:6-9; Mk 1:23-27; 2:5-11; 6:1-4, 16:11-16; Lk 1:30-33; 2:25-32; 2:41-52; 4:38-39; 7:13-16; 9:18-22; 9:46-48; 24:33-38, Jn 1:1-4; 1:29-30; 1:40-41; 4:21-26; 6:35-40; 6:66-69; 9:1-7; 9:35-38; 10:7-11; 10:27-30; 11:25-27; 14:5-9; 14:18-20; 17:4-5; 20:10-17, Acts 9:1-6; 10:37-40, 1Cor 1:22-24; 15:3-7, Eph 5:1-2, 1Tim 2;5-6; 3:16; 6:13-16, Heb 3:1-3; 4:14-15; 10:1-7; 12:2, 1 Jn 2:1-2, Rev 22:16

C2

THE LORD JESUS CHRIST

-HIS HUMANITY AND DEITY-

Biblical Definitions

His Humanity and Deity

The concept of the person of the Lord Jesus Christ being one person, and yet being both human and divine is difficult, and some people have emphasised one side of His nature to the neglect of the other. But it is essential that a balance is struck here as the Scriptures provide clear evidence to support both sides of His nature as described below.

His humanity shows His connection with us and as one who is aware of our failures and frailties, yet He is sinless, whilst His deity and humanity together provides us with a more tangible view of what God is like. Also it is through His divine nature that we can receive forgiveness, hope, new life and eternal life etc.

The doctrine of these two natures in one person (Christ) is commonly accepted in the Christian Church, not because it fully understands the mystery, but because the mystery is revealed by the Word of God - the Bible.

The Biblical proof for the Deity of Christ is shown in both the Old and New Testaments, and these are given in Section C2 Texts.

The following quotations are taken from the book "Systematic Theology". by Louis Berkhof;

Concerning the scriptural proof for the real humanity of Christ he writes: "Men have sometimes forgotten the human Christ in their reverence for the divine. It is very important to maintain the reality and integrity of the humanity of Jesus by admitting His human development and human limitations. The splendor of His deity should be stressed to the extent of obscuring His real humanity. Jesus called Himself man, and is so called by others, Jn 8:40, Acts 2:22, Rom 5:15, 1Cor 15:21". Also, a little later he states: "The Bible clearly indicates that Jesus possessed the essential elements of human nature, that is, a material body and a rational soul, Mat 26:26,28,38; Luke 23:46: 24:39: John 11:33: Heb 2:14". Please see further supporting material in Section C2 Texts.

His Humanity

The humanity of the Lord Jesus Christ is clearly demonstrated in the New Testament and prophesied in the Old Testament with a vast array of human feelings, emotions, reactions, actions, words and thoughts. These range from all the common bodily needs of a human being and being subject to the frailties of tiredness, anger, grief, weeping, being troubled, being tempted, knowing pain and suffering. He was also subject to the discipline of obeying His Father, and praying to Him. Also as part of the normal human condition He demonstrated love and compassion for others and experienced joy.

There are a great many Scriptures that refer to the humanity of Christ, a few are given below and others are given in C2 Texts.

Scriptures referring to the humanity of Christ

A record of the genealogy of Jesus Christ the son of David, the son of Abraham is given in Mat 1:1-17

4 But when the time had fully come, God sent his Son, born of a woman, born under law,

Gal 4:4

In Phil 2:6-9 it states that Christ is "in very nature God" but he took on "the very nature of a servant, being made in human likeness" and "humbled himself and became obedient to death—even death on a cross!" This action resulted in him being exalted and given a name above every name.

5 For there is one God and one mediator between God and men, the man Christ Jesus,

1Tim 2:5

<u>His Deity</u>

The following comments are based on the writings of John Gill's book "A Body of Doctrinal Divinity" where he relates to Christ's deity.

The Son of God is shown to be a divine person distinct from The Father, and The Holy Spirit.

This statement is further clarified when we consider that The Father is a person, and it refers to the Son as "the express image of his person, and upholding all things by the word of his power, when he had by himself purged our sins, sat down on the right hand of the Majesty on high;" (Heb 1:3 A.V.), and this Scripture reveals that He must also be a divine person, the Son of God, and truly God.

He also explains that 'the express image' could not be referring to the human nature of the Son, because the Father never had 'human nature', so the Son could not be 'the image' of the Father in that respect.

The words of the above Scripture are slightly different in the version of the Scriptures used in this book (the N.I.V.) which states: "The Son is the radiance of God's glory and the exact representation of his being, sustaining all things by his powerful word. After he had provided purification for sins, he sat down at the right hand of the Majesty in heaven."

Another distinguishing feature of the Son shown as a separate personality from the Father is the fact that the Son offered Himself as a sacrifice for the sin of mankind and so became their Redeemer and Saviour. These are the personal acts of a distinct person, and they also show both His human and divine nature.

Two typical Scriptures that support the above facts are given below:

10 For if, when we were God's enemies, we were reconciled to him through the death of his Son, how much more, having been reconciled, shall we be saved through his life!

11 Not only is this so, but we also rejoice in God through our Lord Jesus Christ, through whom we have now received reconciliation.

Rom 5:10-11

14 How much more, then, will the blood of Christ, who through the eternal Spirit offered himself unblemished to God, cleanse our consciences from acts that lead to death, so that we may serve the living God!

Heb 9:14

Further considerations in this topic by John Gill relate to Scriptures where the Lord Jesus Christ is referred to as God, as in Heb 1:8 where it states: "But about the Son he says, "Your throne, O God, will last for ever and ever, - - -". There are many Scriptures where Christ is referred to in this way as shown below:

28 I came from the Father and entered the world; now I am leaving the world and going back to the Father."
29 Then Jesus' disciples said, "Now you are speaking clearly and without figures of speech.

Jn 16:28-29

4 But when the time had fully come, God sent his Son, born of a woman, born under law,
5 to redeem those under law, that we might receive the full rights of sons.

Gal 4:4-5

Another important reference to His Deity is the Scripture Col 1:15-20 –refer to Section B2 Biblical Definitions

For further Scriptures that relate to the humanity and deity of Christ, please see the biblical Texts in this Section.

THE LORD JESUS CHRIST

-HIS HUMANITY AND DEITY-

Notes and Quotations

His Humanity

The humanity of the person of Christ is revealed in a great many ways through actions and attitudes in the new Testament and is referred to in a number of Old Testament Scriptures.

He showed great compassion for the poor and those who were sick and healed them, but also had words of warning for the proud and those with hypocritical attitudes.

His teaching carried authority because His words were supported by accompanying deeds and also provided hope and an eternal future to those who believed Him.

Proof texts relating to His humanity are given in C2 Texts.

His Deity

Concerning His deity, again, we see this comprehensively demonstrated in the New Testament and prophesied in the Old Testament, with miraculous power, discernment and wisdom all tempered with grace. He has shown Himself to be God Almighty and as such was responsible for a wide variety of miracles, which according to the Scriptures, establishes the following, that:

1. He now sits on a throne interceding for us and will be the final judge of people and nations.

2. He has the authority and power to save people from the penalty of their sins and the grace to grant them eternal salvation.

3. All aspects of His miraculous birth, His character, and the type of death He was going to have were all prophetically foretold more than a thousand years before.

4. He showed the character and power of God in the vast amount and variety of miracles He performed, and these were not for self-aggrandisement, but, for the benefit of others.

5. He is revealed as the creator of all things in heaven and on earth, and they were created for Him.

6. He is positioned as the head of all Christian believers - the Church.

All of these statements are summed up in the Bible passage Col 2:9 “For in Christ all the fulness of the Deity lives in bodily form”.

Proof texts relating to His deity are given in C2 Texts.

-THE LORD JESUS CHRIST-

-HIS HUMANITY AND DEITY-

Biblical Texts & Text References

Index of Sub-Headings

Scripture Proofs for the Deity of Christ - O.T. linked to N.T.

The prophetic words below were given to David and were said by Christ as He dying on the cross as shown in Mk 15:33-34

1 A psalm of David. My God, my God, why have you forsaken me? Why are you so far from saving me, so far from the words of my groaning?

Ps 22:1

Other linked scriptures

Ps 2:6-12 linked to Heb 1:5-8
Isa 7:14 linked to Mat 1:21-23
Isa 9:6-7 linked to Jn 3:16-17
Isa 40;3 linked to Mk 1:2-3
Isa 53:5-6 linked to 1Pet 2:24-25
Mic 5:2 linked to Mat 2:5-6
Zech 13:7 linked to Mat 26:30-31

Additional Biblical Texts - His Deity

1 The beginning of the gospel about Jesus Christ, the Son of God.

Mk 1:1

In Col 2:9-10 it states that:"in Christ all the fulness of the Deity lives in bodily form".

Additional Scripture references:
Ps 45:6-7, Mat 5:17-18; 7:21; 9:2-6; 10:32-33; 11:1-6; 11:27; 27:50-54, Mk 1;9-11; 8:38, Lk 22:67-70, Jn 1:1-3 & 14; 3:35-36; 5:17-18; 8:23-28; 13:1-3; 17:4-5; 20:30-31, Rom 1:7; 5:10, 14;10-12; 1Cor 1:1-3, 2Cor 5:10, Eph 5:1-2, Phil 2:5-11, 1Tim 3:16; Heb 9:14 1Jn 4:35-36

Scripture Proofs for the Humanity of Christ

1 Then Jesus was led by the Spirit into the desert to be tempted by the devil.
2 After fasting for forty days and forty nights, he was hungry.

Mat 4:1-2

24 Without warning, a furious storm came up on the lake, so that the waves swept over the boat. But Jesus was sleeping.
25 The disciples went and woke him, saying, "Lord, save us! We're going to drown!"

Mat 8:24-25

He appeared in a body. See 1Tim 3:16
He was angry and deeply distressed-see Mk 3:5
He showed love-see - Mk 10:21
In anguish his sweat was like drops of blood – see Lk 22:44
Seeing a woman weep caused him to be deeply moved in spirit and troubled – See Jn 11;33-36

After some time on the cross the soldiers found that Jesus was already dead, and blood and water flowed out when they pierced his side – see Jn 19:33-34

Additional Scripture references:
Ps 22:1, Isa 7:13-15, 9:6; 53:1-4; Mat 9:36; 26:12; 26:26-28 & 38; 27:50; 27:59-60, Mk 1:35, Lk 1:31; 2:46; 23:46, 24:39-40; Jn 1:14; 4:6-9; 8:40; 14:30, Acts 2:22-23, Rom 5:15, 1Cor 15:20-21, 2Cor 5:21, Heb 2:10 & 14-18; 5:7-8; 9:14; 12:2-3, 1Pet 2:21-22; 4:1, 1Jn 3:5; 4:2-3

C3

THE LORD JESUS CHRIST

- HIS LOVE, GRACE AND GOODNESS -

Biblical Definitions

His Love - Also see Section B1

The word 'love' means many different things to people, so it is very important that it is clearly defined, especially as it is such a fundamental human emotion. Love embraces the thoughts and actions that strongly desire the best for the person that is the object of our love, coupled with a strong desire for togetherness of heart, mind and action. When this love is between a man and a woman it ideally results in the commitment of marriage and sexual union. By contrast lust, sometimes confused with love, is a selfish sexual desire of one person who wants to impose their will over another person.

In the English language there is only one word for love to cover a range of different expressions of affection, however, in the original Greek New Testament part of the Bible it is defined by a few different words with different meanings and applications as given below.

The two principal Greek words used in the Bible for love are *'agapao'* and *'phileo'*.

'agapao' is unconditional love - the type of love that is not requiring any response in love or gratitude from us for it to be given. Such is God's love towards the human race.

'phileo' is the love expressed between people in friendship.

Both of these words are used in the passage John 21:15-17 given below:

Brief extracts from L.O.Richards's book "Expository Dictionary of Bible Words" on these two words for love are given below:

"Love is the grandest theme of Scripture. It is a divine motivation. It moved God to reach out to the lost; and it enables the lost to look up in response, as well as to reach out to others. What the Bible says about love cannot help but enrich our lives.

His love was shown to many people in all kinds of need, physical and spiritual as illustrated in the C3 Texts.

<u>The Greek words for love.</u>
Only two of the three common Greek words for love are found in the N.T. -
'philos': friendship as a sharing of experiences, and
'agape': friendship as loving fellowship."

Some claim a notable distinction is seen between the use of the two above words in the Greek N.T. narrative of Jn 21:15-17 as shown below, where Jesus asks Peter three times "do you love me", and He uses *'agape'* on the first two occasions and the third time uses *'philos'*, but Peter only answers by using *'philos'* on each occasion.

15 When they had finished eating, Jesus said to Simon Peter, "Simon son of John, do you truly love me more than these?" "Yes, Lord," he said, "you know that I love you." Jesus said, "Feed my lambs."
16 Again Jesus said, "Simon son of John, do you truly love me?" He answered, "Yes, Lord, you know that I love you." Jesus said, "Take care of my sheep."
17 The third time he said to him, "Simon son of John, do you love me?" Peter was hurt because Jesus asked him the third time, "Do you love me?" He said, "Lord, you know all things; you know that I love you." Jesus said, "Feed my sheep.
Jn 21:15-17

<u>His Grace - Also see Section B1</u>
The true meaning of the word 'grace' is often misunderstood, so its biblical definition is given below by stating that 'grace' has been defined as:

"God's unmerited favour".

"God's goodness towards those who deserve only punishment" – From the book: "Bible Doctrine" by Wayne Grudem.

W.E. Vine refers to 'grace' as "Divine favour", and comments further by laying "stress on its freeness and universality, its spontaneous character, as in the case of God's redemptive mercy, and the pleasure or joy He designs for the recipient".

L.O. Richards states: "In the Greek language 'grace' is *'charis'*. It means "a gracious favour or benefit bestowed", and again he comments "Jesus shows that God stoops to help the undeserving and pardons the helpless sinner e.g. Mat 11:28 - 12:13: 18:21-34: 20:1-16: Lk7:36-50: 15".

The following are extracts from John Gill's book "A Body of Doctrinal Divinity":

<u>Of The Grace Of God</u>
"This attribute may be considered, both as it is in God himself, and as displayed in acts towards his creatures; as in himself, it is himself; it is his nature and essence; he is "Grace" itself, most amiable and lovely; hence so often called "gracious" in Scripture: it is a character expressive of the amiableness and loveliness of his nature: and thus he was before he had, and would have been for ever the same if he never had displayed his grace towards any of his creatures. And this appears from the loveliness of Christ, the image of the Father, the express image of his person; who, to them that believe, is exceeding precious, and altogether lovely; when they behold his glory, as the only begotten of the Father; the fulness of grace in him, - - - - - - - - - - - .

The grace of God may be considered as displayed in acts of goodness towards his creatures, especially men (mankind); and is no other than his free favour and good will to men (mankind); it is no other than love unmerited and undeserved, exercising and communicating itself to them in a free and generous manner; which they are altogether unworthy of. There are many things called grace, and the grace of God, because they flow from his grace, and are the effects of it; as the gospel, #2Co 6:1 Ga 5:4 #Tit 2:11 gifts for preaching the gospel, #Ro 12:6 Eph 3:7,8 the blessings of grace, as justification, adoption, &c. #Ps 84:11 2Ti 1:9 in each of the graces of the Spirit in regeneration, as faith, hope, love, &c. #2Co 9:8 Ga 2:9 but then these are to be distinguished from grace in God; as the Giver and the gift, the Fountain and the streams, the Cause and the effect."

For other examples of His grace see the C3 Texts.

His Goodness - Also see Section B1

This word is described here as meaning the goodness that comes from God with no ulterior motive other than to impart goodness out of a free will and desire to shower this favour on us whether we know, deserve, appreciate or understand it. It is, therefore, profitable for all to understand and rejoice in the fact of God's goodness – His goodwill and kindly feeling towards us.

So let us now look at what the Bible and Bible commentators have to say about this attribute.

W.E.Vine states: "The Greek word *'asathos'* describes that which, being good in its character or constitution, is beneficial in its effect". He comments further by saying "God is essentially, absolutely and consummately good, Mat 19:17, Mk 10:18, Lk 18:19".

The following are extracts from John Gill's book "A Body of Doctrinal Divinity":

Of The Goodness Of God.

"Having treated of the love, grace, mercy, and longsuffering of God, it will be proper to take some notice of his "goodness", from whence they all proceed; for that God loves any of his creatures, in the manner he does, bestows favours upon them, shows mercy to them, and bears much with them, is owing to the goodness of his nature. Hence one of his names and titles by which he is described and made known, is, that of Good; "thou, Lord, art good", #Ps 86:5 and in many other places; when God proclaimed his name before Moses, this was one part of it, "abundant in goodness", #Ex 34:6. Philo says *{1}*, God is the name of goodness. And our English word God seems to be a contraction of the word "Good"; or, however, is the same with the German "Gott" and "Godt"; which came, as it is thought *{2}*, from the Arabic word "Gada", which so signified; so that the German and English name of the divine Being, in common use, is taken from the attribute of his goodness. The name the heathens give to their supreme deity, is "optimus" {3}, the "best"; he being not only good, as they supposed, and better than others, but the best of beings. Our Jehovah, the true God, is superlatively good; good in the highest degree, good beyond all conception and expression.

1. Goodness is essential to God; without which he would not be God; he, is by nature good.

2. Goodness only belongs to God; he is solely good; "There is none good but one; that is, God"; is the assertion of Christ, #Mt 19:17 which is to be understood not to the exclusion of the Son, and Spirit of God, who are, with the Father, the one God; and so equally good: but with respect to creatures, who are not of themselves inderivatively and independently good; this is only true of God. Whatever goodness is in creatures, it is all from him, who made them good originally; or put into them, or bestowed upon them, what goodness they have: what goodness there is in the elect angels, who never sinned; what goodness was in Adam, in a state of innocence; what goodness is in any good man, who partakes of the grace of God, or is or will be in the saints in heaven, is all from God; every good and perfect gift comes from him; nor have creatures anything but what they receive from him; he is the source and fountain of all, and therefore all goodness, originally, ultimately, and solely, is to be referred to God."

For other examples of His goodness see the C3 Texts.

THE LORD JESUS CHRIST

- HIS LOVE, GRACE AND GOODNESS -

Notes and Quotations

Love

"God loves us wholeheartedly, unconditionally and continually". Alex Buchanan

Henry Drummond (1852-1897) a gifted evangelist who assisted Dwight L. Moody during his revival campaigns said that love is the greatest thing in the world. And from our point of view love is the greatest thing in God. Without love His justice would cut us off; His holiness would put us out of His sight; and His power would destroy us. Love is the one hope of sinners, and our great concern should be to discover God's love to us.

Some of the unsurpassable qualities of God's love have been well defined by the hymn writer (unknown):

"His love no end nor measure knows,
No change can turn its course,
Eternally the same it flows
From one eternal source."

God's love is unconditional – we neither deserve it, or do not deserve it. We cannot say: "the Lord will love me because - - - - -", or; "the Lord will not love me because - - - - -". See Jn 15:9; 1Jn 4:19.

In 1Cor 13:8 it states that: "Love never fails." This the quality and strategy in a relationship that God says and has demonstrated that 'never fails'.

Grace

Someone has said that - "*grace* is the strength God gives us to obey His commands".

Another person has said - "*grace* can be seen as God's love in action".

W.E. Vine defined it like this: "Grace, the divine quality of grace, is goodwill, favourable regard, extravagant loving-kindness and friendly disposition from which the kindly act proceeds"

Grace and Mercy - Author unknown.
Mercy - We don't get what we do deserve.
Grace - We do get what we don't deserve.

L.O. Richards states: "Grace" is a dominant N.T. theme. Salvation is by grace, not works (Rom 11:6; Eph 2:5). Grace releases us from the dominion of sin, for believers are "*not under law, but under grace*" (Rom 6:14). N.T. letters begin and conclude with the wish that grace will be with the readers, and the N.T. closes with these words: "*The grace of the Lord Jesus be with God's people. Amen*" (Rev 22:21).

Selwyn Hughes in his "Every Day with Jesus" Notes, records: "A wise person had written this in a Bible I was given as a child: "Dependence plus discipline equals dependable disciples."

There is a great emphasis on grace in the Christian life, but grace must be permeated with discipline."

Love that goes *upward* is worship
Love that goes *outward* is affection
Love that *stoops* is grace.

Author unknown

Philip Yancey in his book "WHAT'S SO AMAZING ABOUT GRACE" writes: "Grace means there is nothing we can do to make God love us more. And grace means there is nothing we can do to make God love us less."

The writer reminds us of a murderer and adulterer who gained a reputation as the greatest king of the Old Testament, a '*man* after God's own heart.'

And of a Church being led by a disciple who cursed and swore that he had never known Jesus. And of a missionary being recruited from the ranks of those who tortured Christians, who became the greatest Christian missionary history has known. He then states: "If God can love that kind of person, maybe, just maybe, he can love the likes of me."

Paul, who had persevered through much suffering and many difficulties in his Christian life asked God for some relief in his situation and He answered by saying: "My grace is sufficient for you, for my power is made perfect in weakness." Paul accepted this response from God and said: "Therefore I will boast all the more gladly about my weaknesses, so that Christ's power may rest on me."(2Cor 12:9).

It is good to know that in every situation we can find the grace we need through coming to God in prayer when we're in need. for the Scripture says: "Let us then approach the throne of grace with confidence, so that we may receive mercy and find grace to help us in our time of need."(Heb 4:16).

In the Scripture from John 1:14 given below we see that Jesus Christ was '*full of grace and truth*'. Sadly, however, Christians are sometimes more gracious than truthful, and sometimes more truthful than gracious.

14 The Word became flesh and made his dwelling among us. We have seen his glory, the glory of the One and Only, who came from the Father, full of grace and truth.
15 John testifies concerning him. He cries out, saying, "This was he of whom I said, 'He who comes after me has surpassed me because he was before me.'"
16 From the fulness of his grace we have all received one blessing after another.
17 For the law was given through Moses; grace and truth came through Jesus Christ.

Jn 1:14-17

Bob Gass in his "The Word for Today" Notes refers to 1Pet 5:12 and states: "God's *grace* is what gets us through rough times."

He quotes: "My grace [my sustaining care] is sufficient for thee . . . ."

(2Cor 12:9). And adds: "*Grace* is what enables you to love an abusive mate; keep waiting for a prodigal to come back; endure prolonged illness; live with little yet give much; overcome disappointments; and forgive repeated offences. Grace takes you beyond your natural ability by *forcing* you to rely on God's strength alone."

Bob Gass also refers to Phil 1:2 and says in another one of his notes, that God's grace enables Christians to do God's bidding in difficult circumstances when he states: "How could Paul maintain his joy through beatings, betrayals, shipwrecks and imprisonment? Because God told him, 'My grace is enough; it's all you need. My strength comes into its own in your weakness' (2 Cor 12:9 TM). Grace will enable you to pastor a difficult church; care for an ageing loved one who requires much time and patience; pray and never let go of a prodigal son or daughter; and keep your faith strong in the face of overwhelming odds". And he adds: "When does grace come? When you need it most".

Legalism and Grace

For many years in churches and denominations there has been much evidence of legalism, and this has been used as a strategy for holding God's people together by providing unity and control through the observance of common rules and regulations. In more recent days, however, there has been a challenge to that method of 'regulating' the lives of God's people through the renewed emphasis on God's grace and love toward them coupled with a renewed importance being placed on the leading and activity of the Holy Spirit.

In consideration of the above statements a balance must be struck in all these areas in the lives of Christians between: accepting the authority of church leaders; the membership rules of a church; the self-discipline required to live an effective Christian life; living in the good of God's grace and love as revealed through the Bible; and being obedient to the leading of God's Holy Spirit.

George Verwer has said,"Grace without discipline can often lead to disgrace. Grace does not lay aside basic biblical commandments, but rather brings them into balance and the right priority."

Some effects of God's Grace

the grace of God was upon him. (Jesus) Lk 2:40 - This caused Him to reach to all in need, meet their needs and make the ultimate sacrifice. he saw the evidence of *the grace of God- See* Acts 11:23

Paul ....urged them to continue in *the grace of God.*- See Acts 13:43

those who *by grace* had believed.- Acts 18:27

For sin shall not be your master, because you are not under law, but under grace. See Rom 6:14

The Lord said "My grace is sufficient for you, for my power is made perfect in weakness." Showing that we need to trust in Him and not ourselves. See 2Cor 12:9

it is *by grace* you have been saved.- Eph 2:5

by grace you have been saved, through faith------ it is the gift of God--Eph 2:8

It is good for our hearts to be strengthened *by grace,* not by ceremonial foods, See Heb 13:9

Goodness/Kindness

Mark Twain said, 'Kindness is the language which the deaf can hear and the blind can see.' This statement was taken from 'The Word for Today' Notes by Bob Gass, and he refers to Lk 6:28.

S[illegible]

the [illegible] and was [illegible] (Luke 2:40) [illegible]
to all [illegible] their needs and [illegible] the ultimate [illegible]
The evidence of the grace of God [illegible]

[illegible] urged them to continue in the grace of God [illegible] Acts 13:43

those who believed had been [illegible] Acts 18:27

[illegible]

[illegible]

[illegible] you [illegible]

[illegible] have been [illegible]

[illegible]

[illegible]

THE LORD JESUS CHRIST

- HIS LOVE, GRACE AND GOODNESS -

Biblical Texts & Text References

His Love

In Mat 9:35-36 and in many other N.T. passages of Scripture His love is demonstrated through preaching the good news of the kingdom and healing many people of their diseases.

16 "For God so loved the world that he gave his one and only Son, that whoever believes in him shall not perish but have eternal life.
17 For God did not send his Son into the world to condemn the world, but to save the world through him.

Jn 3:16-17

In Rom 5:8-9 it states that God demonstrates his own love for us in this: While we were still sinners, Christ died for us. He also justified and saved us from God's wrath.

Additional Scripture references:

Mat 14:14; 15:30-31; 20:32-34, Mk 1:40-42, Lk 7:12-15; Jn 11:33-36; 13:1-5; 13:34-35; 15:9-13; 17:24, Rom 8:38-39, 2Cor 5:14-15, Gal 2:20, Eph 2:4-5; 5:1-2; 6:23, Tit 3:4-7 1Jn 4;9-10 & 15-16

His Grace

In Lk 2:40 it says that He was: "was filled with wisdom, and the grace of God was upon him.

11 For the grace of God that brings salvation has appeared to all men.

Tit 2:11

Additional Scripture references:
Mat 12:13, Lk 7:36-50, Jn 1:14-17, Acts 11:23; 15:10-11, Rom 5:1-2; 5:20-21; 6:14-15, 12:6; 2Cor 8:9; 9:8, Gal 5:4; Eph 2:4-8, 2Tim 1:8-9; Heb 4:15-16; 12:15

His Goodness

In Ps 86:5 it refers to God as forgiving and good, abounding in love to all who call to Him.

Speaking about the Lord Jesus Christ in Jn 10:11 it refers to him as 'The good shepherd lays down his life for the sheep'.

38 how God anointed Jesus of Nazareth with the Holy Spirit and power, and how he went around doing good and healing all who were under the power of the devil, because God was with him.

Acts 10:38

Additional Scripture references:
Ex 34:6; Mat 7:11, 19;17; Lk 7:22; 11:9-13, Rom 2:3-4 Jas 1:17

C4

THE LORD JESUS CHRIST

- HIS CROSS, RESURRECTION AND ASCENSION -

Biblical Definitions

His Cross

The act of crucifixion, apart from being a very cruel and barbaric form of killing somebody, was also considered a degrading type of death, reserved for those who had committed heinous crimes or opposed the rulers of the day. However, it was plain for all to see that Jesus Christ did not fit either of these categories, hence, His death by this method was totally unjust, but it was foretold in the O.T. Scriptures (see Ps 22:15-18, Isa 53:7-12, Zech 12:10 in C4 Texts), and Christ Himself told His followers how He was to die (see Mat 16:21 and Lk 24:25-27 in C4 Texts). So, we see that He submitted Himself to this death because He knew this was the only way to procure forgiveness and eternal salvation for mankind who were to believe on Him.

The manner of the death of the Lord Jesus Christ, by crucifixion, shows us His amazing humility and condescension especially in view of the fact that He was the Son of God. He submitted to the law and suffered an ignoble, slow and painful death, which was also considered a shameful way to die. Suffering in this way only added to the tragic injustice He had already been subjected to.

He had shown that He had taken upon Himself the "nature of a servant"; had been obedient to God the Father, and was "obedient to death", and even scorned the shame of the cross, as the following Scriptures reveal: See Phil 2:6-8 and Heb 12:2-3.

<u>Statements by John Gill from his book "A Body of Doctrinal Divinity."</u>

The effects of the sufferings and death of Christ, or the things procured thereby, are many. As,

a. The redemption of his people from sin, from Satan, from the curse and condemnation of the law, and from wrath to come; which is through his blood, his sufferings, and death: he gave his flesh for the life of the world of his elect; and gave his life a ransom for them; and being made perfect through sufferings, became the author of salvation to them, #Eph 1:7 Joh 6:51 #Mt 20:28 Heb 2:10, 5:9.
b. Reconciliation, which is by the death of Christ; and peace, which is made by his blood; even a complete atonement for sin; which is obtained through Christ's being a propitiation for it, which he is, through his blood; that is, his sufferings and death, #Ro 3:25, 5:10 Col 1:20.
c. Pardon of sin; which is a branch of redemption, through the blood of Christ, which was shed for the remission of sin; and without shedding of blood there is no remission, #Eph 1:7 #Mt 26:28 Heb 9:22.
d. Justification, which is sometimes ascribed to the blood of Christ; that is, to his sufferings and death; the consequence of which is, deliverance, and security from wrath to come, #Ro 5:9.
e. In short, the complete salvation of all God's elect: Christ came to gather together the children of God that were scattered abroad, by dying for them to seek and to save that which was lost; even to save all his people from their sins, by finishing transgression, making an end of sin, making reconciliation for iniquity, and bringing in everlasting righteousness; and by obtaining an entire conquest over all enemies, sin, Satan, and death, and hell, #Joh 11:51,52 Mt 1:21 Da 9:24.
f. In all which the glory of God is great; the glory of his mercy, grace, and goodness; the glory of his wisdom, truth, and faithfulness; the glory of his power, and the glory of his justice and holiness.

His Resurrection

The fact of the resurrection of the Lord Jesus Christ is a hallmark and essential belief of Christians. His resurrection was not only unique but foundational to the Christian Faith, as observed by the following:

A divine work which only God could do - see the Scriptures below;

15 "You killed the author of life, but God raised him from the dead. We are witnesses of this.

Acts 3:15

8 Remember Jesus Christ, raised from the dead, descended from David. This is my gospel,

2Tim 2:8

A glorious work because it brought glory to God and eternal hope to mankind - see the Scriptures Acts 23:6 and 1Pet 1:3-4

A miraculous work because it showed the greatness of the power of God - see the Scriptures Rom 6:9 and 1Jn 3:8

A triumphant work showing God's power over Satan and the powers of evil - see the Scriptures Rom 1:3-4 and 1Cor 15:20-22

A work that brought proclamation of the Good News - see the Scriptures below;

2 "They were greatly disturbed because the apostles were teaching the people and proclaiming in Jesus the resurrection of the dead "

Acts 4:2

A work that generated faith as it caused people to believe on Him - see the Scripture Jn 2:22

His Ascension - Evidence

The fact of the ascension of Christ is well attested in Scripture and provides an assured future for all those who trust Him for salvation as outlined below.

His ascension was hinted at by Christ himself when he said to his disciples

"What if you see the Son of Man ascend to where he was before!"(Jn 6:62), and on other occasions He said "I came from the Father and entered the world; now I am leaving the world and going back to the Father." (Jn 16:28), (Jn 20:16-17).

Paul in Eph 4:8-10 refers to 'His ascension' when he quotes from Ps 68:18.

In 1Cor 15:3-8 it refers to; the fact that: Christ died for our sins according to the Scriptures; he was buried; he was raised on the third day according to the Scriptures; he appeared to Peter, and then to the Twelve; he appeared to more than five hundred of the brothers at the same time, most of whom are still living, though some have fallen asleep. It also says that he appeared to James, all the apostles and then to Paul.

Again, the apostle Peter testified to a large crowd:

32 "God has raised this Jesus to life, and we are all witnesses of the fact."

Acts 2:32

<u>His Ascension - Purpose</u>

There are many Scriptures that show the purpose for His ascension and return to God the Father was planned from the beginning as part of God's overall plan for the glorification of Jesus Christ the Son of God and the redemption and eternal salvation of those who would believe on Him as the following Scriptures show: (Note the underlined purposes.)

It states in Jn 14 1-3 that;" <u>I am going there to prepare a place for you</u>".

3 The Son is the radiance of God's glory and the exact representation of his being, sustaining all things by his powerful word. <u>After he had provided purification for sins, he sat down at the right hand of the Majesty in heaven.</u>

Heb 1:3

9 But we see Jesus, who was made a little lower than the angels, <u>now crowned with glory and honour because he suffered death, so that by the grace of God he might taste death for everyone.</u>

10 <u>In bringing many sons to glory, it was fitting that God</u>, for whom and

> through whom everything exists, should make the author of their salvation perfect through suffering.
>
> Heb 2:9-10

In Heb 7:24-25 it states that:" Jesus lives for ever, he has a permanent priesthood, therefore he is able to save completely those who come to God through him

THE LORD JESUS CHRIST

- HIS CROSS, RESURRECTION AND ASCENSION -

Notes and Quotations

His Cross

The sufferings of the Lord Jesus Christ prior to and at His crucifixion were submitted to willingly for the sake of providing a way of salvation for all those who were to believe on Him.

The event of His trial and suffering were foretold in Ps 2:2 where it states "the rulers gather together against the LORD and against his Anointed One."

This suffering was also foretold in Isa 50:5-6 where it says He would be subjected to a beating on His back, mocking and spitting in His face, yet in spite of this it says "he did not open his mouth" Isa 53:7, and other accounts can be seen in Isa 53 and Ps 22:15-18.

In Isa 53:12 it states that he "was numbered with the transgressors"- which relates to the fact that he was crucified between two thieves as though he was likewise guilty.

In Isa 53:9 it says "he was assigned a grave with the wicked, and with the rich in his death" - and this fits the facts of the thieves being the wicked, and that he was buried in the sepulchre of Joseph of Arimathea who was a rich man - see Mat 27:57-60, Mk 15:43, Lk 23:51, Jn 19:38.

Bob Gass in his "The Word for Today" Notes referring to Jesus' death, states: "it fulfilled 29 different prophecies", and goes on to quote the following Bible references: Ps 22:16 & 18, Isa 53:5, & Amos 8:9.

His Resurrection

In Jn 10:17-18 it states that Christ had authority to lay down his life and to take it up again. This is the ultimate authority of God.

In Ps 16:10 it says "because you will not abandon me to the grave, nor will you let your Holy One see decay." and this same Scripture is quoted by the Apostle Peter in Acts 2:25-27, and again by the Apostle Paul in Acts 13:34-37, further emphasising that Christ was the one who was not left in the grave, nor did he see decay.

In Phil 2:6-10 it describes Christ's change of state from one of humility to one of exaltation - when resurrected, - see also 1Pet 1:21.

His Ascension

In the Scriptures we see there were many witnesses who saw Him after His resurrection - see Mat 28:11-15, Lk 24:1-8, & 30-31 Jn 20:11-17, 1Cor 15:3-8 and many others.

There were also many people who saw Him ascend, had a vision of the ascended Christ or heard His voice, - see Acts 1:10-11, Acts 2:32, Acts 7:55-56, Acts 26:13-15, 1Tim 3:16 and many others.

C4

THE LORD JESUS CHRIST

- HIS CROSS, RESURRECTION AND ASCENSION -

Biblical Texts & Text References

His Cross

In Ps 22:15-18 spoken prophetically it describes Jesus' death on the cross, and refers to piercing his hands and feet, his bones could be counted and the casting of lots for his clothing.

Another prophetic Scripture in Zech 12:10 where it says;" They will look on me, the one they have pierced, and they will mourn for him as one mourns for an only child".

21 From that time on Jesus began to explain to his disciples that he must go to Jerusalem and suffer many things at the hands of the elders, chief priests and teachers of the law, and that he must be killed and on the third day be raised to life.

Mat 16:21

24 And they crucified him. Dividing up his clothes, they cast lots to see what each would get.
25 It was the third hour when they crucified him.
26 The written notice of the charge against him read: THE KING OF THE JEWS.

Mk 15:24-26

Additional Scripture references:

Ps 2:2, Isa 53:7-12; Mat 27:57-60, Mk 15:21-26, Lk 24:25-27, Jn 6:51; 11:51-52 ; 19:17-20 & 38, Rom 5 :9, 1Cor 1:17-18, Phil 2:5-11, Col 1:19-20; 2:13-15, Heb 2:9-15; 9:13-14 & 22; 10:11-14, 1Pet 2:22-25, 1Jn 1:7; 4:9-10

His Resurrection

In Lk 24:44-46 Jesus said:" Everything must be fulfilled that is written about me in the Law of Moses, the Prophets and the Psalms." And that he would suffer and rise from the dead on the third day.

17 The reason my Father loves me is that I lay down my life— only to take it up again.
18 No-one takes it from me, but I lay it down of my own accord. I have authority to lay it down and authority to take it up again. This command I received from my Father."

Jn 10:17-18

In Acts 2:31-32 it states;" God has raised this Jesus to life, and we are all witnesses of the fact".

Additional Scripture references:

Mat 27:53-54, Jn 11:23-26, Acts 2:25-27; 4:33, Rom 6;3-5; 1Cor 15:20-24, 2Cor 13:4, Phil 2:5-10, 1Pet 1:3-4 & 21

His Ascension

28 I came from the Father and entered the world; now I am leaving the world and going back to the Father."
29 Then Jesus' disciples said, "Now you are speaking clearly and without figures of speech.

Jn 16:28-29

Additional Scripture references:

Mat 28:11-15; Jn 1:50-51; 7:33, 20:16-17; Acts 7:54-56; 26:13-15; Eph 4:8-10

C5

THE LORD JESUS CHRIST

- HIS WORK OF JUSTIFICATION, REDEMPTION & RECONCILIATION -

Biblical Definitions

Justification

For a person to know that they have not only been forgiven for committing serious mistakes in their life, but that they are now considered not to have made those mistakes (or sins) is in essence the biblical meaning for the one who is 'justified'. It is this amazing situation and life condition that the person, who believes and trusts in the finished work of Christ on the cross for their sin, enjoys.

The topics of justification, redemption and reconciliation are further explored very ably by John Gill D.D. in his book "A Body of Doctrinal Divinity" and the following statements are extracts from it.

The book goes into great detail concerning every subject he refers to, so the passages given below are to be taken as introductory statements to the subject:

"Pardon of sin, and justification from it, are very closely connected; the one follows upon the other; according to the position of them in some passages of Scripture, pardon is first, and justification next; as in Acts 13:38-39 & 26:18 "given below:

38 "Therefore, my brothers, I want you to know that through Jesus the forgiveness of sins is proclaimed to you.
39 Through him everyone who believes is justified from everything you could not be.
justified from by the law of Moses

Acts 13:38-39

He also states:

"God only can and does forgive sin, it is his prerogative - so it is God that justifies the sinner - and justifies both Jews and Gentiles, who believe in Christ "- see Rom 3:29-30

Justification is given freely by his grace - see the Scriptures Ps 51:1, Rom 3:24,

Eph 1:7, Tit 3:7. These scriptures reveal a number of truths associated with justification, such as the need to recognise first of all that everybody has 'sinned and fall short of the glory of God' and that it is received by God's grace (undeserved love) made possible through Christ's sacrificial death .

This justification also provides hope of eternal life, and to be saved from God's wrath

"The same persons that are pardoned are justified, and the same that are justified are pardoned; to whom God imputes the righteousness of Christ, to their justification, to them he gives the remission of sin; and to whom he does not impute sin, but forgives it, he imputes righteousness without works," - see Rom 4:6-8.

"Justification is a pronouncing persons righteous, as if they had never sinned" -see Rom 5:1

Redemption

"Our English word Redemption, is from the Latin tongue, and signifies, buying again; and several words in the Greek language, of the New Testament, are used in the affair of our Redemption, which signify the obtaining of something by paying a proper price for it; sometimes the simple verb αγοραζω, to "buy", is used: so the redeemed are said to be "bought unto God" by the blood of Christ; and to be "bought" from the earth; and to be "bought" from among men; and to be "bought" with a price; that is, with the price of Christ's blood, see - Rev 5:9, 14:3-4, 1Cor

6:20, hence the church of God is said to be purchased with it, - see Acts 20:28."

28 Keep watch over yourselves and all the flock of which the Holy Spirit has made you overseers. Be shepherds of the church of God, which he bought with his own blood.

Acts 20:28

Regarding the subject of 'Redemption' John Gill has made a number of key statements, and in one of these he points out that a man in debt is liable to be arrested and put in prison where he must stay until the debt is discharged by himself or another. He states that debts are like sins, where the debtor is like a sinner who is guilty of many sins and has no way of making recompense for them, he has nothing to pay off the debt with. In this situation John Gill affirms that man cannot meet the demands of God's justice, and hence, is due for punishment according to God's law, and the only One who can pay that debt for the sin of disobedience, and bring him deliverance and release is Christ.

The Lord Jesus Christ paid this debt of sin for all mankind when He died on the cross, and the Scripture states that He: "cancelled the written code, with its regulations, that was against us" (Col 2:13-14). This indeed is good news.

Another picture used is that of ransoming people out of slavery by Christ paying a ransom price for them, thus bringing about the God's redemption of people. As John Gill states: "They are in a state of slavery, out of which they cannot deliver themselves; Christ is the one who buys them back; his life and blood are the ransom price he has paid for them. They are called the ransomed of the Lord, for he has delivered them from their present bondage, and their future ruin and destruction.

This redemption by Christ saves people from a just punishment for their sin (Tit 2:14); and that they are no longer under condemnation, but are justified in God's sight (Rom 8:1 & 33)."

Those who come into this debt free state, who are delivered from the guilt and the just punishment for sin, are those who believe on the Lord Jesus Christ as the only One who can redeem them, confess their sin (of living for themselves and ignoring God's redemptive love claim on them), and then thank Him for dying for them and bringing them deliverance.

<u>Reconciliation</u>

Another short extract from a very detailed statement by John Gill is given below:

"Men are not only enemies internally, and externally to God, but there is an enmity on the part of God to them; there is a law enmity, or an enmity declared in the law against them; they are declared by the law of God as enemies; traitors, and rebels to him; and as such God's elect were considered, when Christ died to make reconciliation for them; for it is said, "while they were sinners Christ died for them, and when they were enemies they were reconciled to God, the death of his Son", #Ro 5:8,10."

When we live for ourselves and ignore the gracious and rightful claims of the Lord Jesus Christ on our lives', we commit the most serious sin possible of rejecting the claims of God's Son, and this makes us enemies of God and only Christ's death on the cross could bring about a reconciliation between God and man as the following Scriptures show;

17 Therefore, if anyone is in Christ, he is a new creation; the old has gone, the new has come!
18 All this is from God, who reconciled us to himself through Christ and gave us the ministry of reconciliation:
19 that God was reconciling the world to himself in Christ, not counting men's sins against them. And he has committed to us the message of reconciliation.

2Cor 5:17-19

See also Eph 12-16

Wayne Grudem in his book "Bible Doctrine" states, with reference to 'Reconciliation' that:

"To overcome our separation from God, we needed someone to provide reconciliation and thereby bring us back into fellowship with God. Paul says that God "through Christ reconciled us to himself and gave us the ministry of reconciliation; that is, in Christ God was reconciling the world to himself" (2Cor 5:18-19)."

THE LORD JESUS CHRIST

- HIS WORK OF JUSTIFICATION, REDEMPTION & RECONCILIATION -

Notes and Quotations

Justification

Many people have used a phrase to explain the word 'justification' as follows; Justification - "just as if I'd never sinned".

Redemptive Love

It was normal custom with genealogies to list the male line only, but in Matthew chapter 1 four women are mentioned, and two of these are commented on here as we particularly see God's redemptive love and grace at work.

One of these women, Ruth, is listed in Ruth 4:18-22 and in Mat.1 (as shown below), which is unusual considering that she was non-Jewish, and her remarkable story is told in the book of Ruth in the O.T. of the Bible. She, a widow, married Boaz, became the great-grandmother of King David, and very remarkably, was included in the lineage that led to the birth of the Lord Jesus Christ.

Also, in the Matthew chapter 1 genealogy, we note that Rahab the prostitute, and mother of Boaz, is included in the lineage of the Lord Jesus Christ, (see Ru 4:20-22) and so again we see God's redemptive love and grace expressed through these stories.

To see this genealogy refer to Mat 1:1-6

THE LORD JESUS CHRIST

HIS WORK OF JUSTIFICATION, REDEMPTION AND RECONCILIATION

THE LORD JESUS CHRIST

- HIS WORK OF JUSTIFICATION, REDEMPTION & RECONCILIATION -

Biblical Texts & Text References

Justification

Man is not justified by observing the law, but by faith in Jesus Christ. See Gal 2:16

9 That if you confess with your mouth, "Jesus is Lord," and believe in your heart that God raised him from the dead, you will be saved.
10 For it is with your heart that you believe and are justified, and it is with your mouth that you confess and are saved.

Rom 10:9-10

Additional Scripture references

Ps 51:1-4, Mat 26:27-28, Rom 3:20-28; 4:1-8; 4:25; 5:1-2, 5:6-10; 5:15-18, 1Cor 6:9-11; Gal 3:9-11, Tit 3:4-7

Redemption

In Rom 3:22-24 it says that righteousness from God comes through faith in Jesus Christ to all who believe, and it further states that all have sinned and are justified freely by his grace through the redemption achieved by Christ's death.

13 Christ redeemed us from the curse of the law by becoming a curse for us, for it is written: "Cursed is everyone who is hung on a tree."
14 He redeemed us in order that the blessing given to Abraham might come to the Gentiles through Christ Jesus, so that by faith we might receive the promise of the Spirit.

Gal 3:13-14

Additional Scripture references

Ru 4:18, Job 19:25-26, Ps 34:21-22; 78:35; 103:2-4, Isa 41:13-14; 47:4; 54:5, Mat 1:3-6, Lk 21:27-28, Rom 8:1 & 33, 1Cor 1:30; 6:19-20, Gal 4:4-7, Col 1:13-14, Tit 2:12-14; Heb 9:12-14, 1Pet 1:18-19, Rev 5:9

Reconciliation

21 Once you were alienated from God and were enemies in your minds because of your evil behaviour.

22 But now he has reconciled you by Christ's physical body through death to present you holy in his sight, without blemish and free from accusation.

Col 1:21-22

C6

THE LORD JESUS CHRIST

- HIS KINGSHIP & KINGDOM -

Biblical Definitions

Jesus the King

Many of the images that come to mind when we think of a king is someone who rules harshly and metes out severe punishments on those he disagrees with, or challenge his authority or throne. This view of a king is far removed from the character and actions of 'Jesus the King', because whilst He has absolute authority He only uses it as a last resort, as shown by His willingness to humble Himself and suffer death on a cross to procure the forgiveness and eternal salvation for all who will truly believe and trust in Him for these things.

Whilst here on earth He showed compassion for the distressed and the sick and met their needs. Also He challenged the proud, the wealthy and the actions and attitudes of religious people who said one thing but did something different.

At all times He acted with grace and patience and endeavoured to win the hearts of people rather than bring condemnation on them.

The above statement is just a brief introduction to the wonderful character of Jesus Christ, so please read on to discover more.

Many of the images that come to mind when we think of a king is someone who rules harshly and metes out severe punishments on those he disagrees with, or challenge his authority or throne. This view of a king is far removed from the character and actions of 'Jesus the King', because whilst He has absolute authority He only uses it as a last resort, as shown by His willingness to humble Himself and suffer death on a cross to procure the forgiveness and eternal salvation for all who will truly believe and trust in Him for these things.

Whilst here on earth He showed compassion for the distressed and the sick and met their needs. Also He challenged the proud, the wealthy and the actions and attitudes of religious people who said one thing but did something different.

At all times He acted with grace and patience and endeavoured to win the hearts of people rather than bring condemnation on them.

The above statement is just a brief introduction to the wonderful character of Jesus Christ, so please read on to discover more.

Given below are a few extracts from the book "Expository Dictionary of Bible Words" by Lawrence O. Richards where he refers to 'Jesus the King' and 'Kingdom' as follows:

"Jesus the King. After carefully tracing Jesus' genealogy, the introduction to Matthew's Gospel quotes or alludes to many O.T. passages. His purpose is to demonstrate that Jesus of Nazareth truly was Israel's promised Davidic King, the Messiah (Mat 1:1-2:6).

In the Gospels, "king" is most often used of Jesus in the context of his trial and crucifixion. The very words "King of the Jews" were inscribed on the plaque attached to his cross (Mat 27:37; Mk 15:26; Lk 23:38; Jn 19:19,21)."

His Kingship

In the Scripture Isa 9:6-7 (in C6 Texts), we see a prophecy of the birth of the Lord Jesus Christ and His kingly characteristics, and this is followed (in C6 Texts) by the Scripture Mat 1:1-6 & 15-18 that gives His genealogy.

His kingship was seen in the way in which he exerted control and authority whilst on earth. He was fully aware of all that was happening around him and he knew what was going to take place, and hence, things were never out of control. There are many examples to illustrate this in the Bible and just a few are listed below:

Four men brought a paralysed man to Jesus, who said to him "Son your sins forgiven" and teachers of the law were there who were thinking, "He's blaspheming! Who can forgive sins but God alone? Jesus questioned them why they were thinking these things and then healed the man. - see Mk 2:1-12.

Jesus was in a boat with his disciples when a storm blew up - He spoke to the waves and the sea became calm - see Mk 4:35-41

Just before the crucifixion of Jesus he said to his disciples that they would fall away on account of him and Peter would deny him three times before the cock crows in the morning, and this all came true - see Mat 26:31-35 & 69-75.

Jesus always knew the type of death he would die, that he would rise from the dead and explained it to his disciples long before it happened - see Mat 16:21-23.

Jesus knew all about the 'End Times' and told them to his disciples - see Mat 24.

Further characteristics of his Kingship are seen in his gracious acts, unlimited love, profound wisdom, sacrificial life, speaking the truth in love, and his authority with healing people and casting out demons.

His Kingdom

The Kingdom of God does not have earthly boundaries, but spiritual ones, where those inside have a relationship with the King, but those outside it do not.

Other people have defined God's Kingdom as: 'a realm where Jesus Christ exerts control and authority'.

Lawrence .O. Richards refers to this subject under a number of headings including the following: 'Kingdom in the OT'; Kingdom in the NT'; 'The gospel of the kingdom'.

He defines the 'Kingdom in the OT' as: "best expressed by the idea of reign or sovereignty." And refers to Ps 103:19 and Ps 145:11-13.

He refers to the 'Kingdom in the NT' as: "rather than being a place, is a realm in which God is in control."

Concerning 'The gospel of the kingdom' he states: "When it was time for Jesus to begin his public ministry" and refers to Mat 4:17; 4:23; 12:28, Mk1:15 and Lk 11:20.

The Characteristics of His Kingdom

The following Scriptures reveal some of the characteristics and development of the kingdom Jesus was referring to;

In Jn 18:36 Jesus said "My kingdom is not of this world", so we see that he was not talking about an earthly kingdom but a kingdom in the spiritual realm.

During Jesus' ministry he said "The kingdom of God is near" or "at hand" - Mk 1:14-15. It had not yet come about, but it was near. It was coming soon, and Jesus in Mk 9:1 said "some who are standing here will not taste death before they see the kingdom of God come with power". This statement is repeated in Lk 9:27.

In Acts 1:1-8 Jesus is speaking about the kingdom of God and sending the gift (as promised) of the Holy Spirit. Again, he tells them they will receive power when the Holy Spirit comes on them. All this was fulfilled soon afterwards on the day of Pentecost (Acts 2), and thus, the spiritual kingdom of God commenced at this time.

Paul went about preaching the kingdom - Acts 20:25.

It states in Rom 14:17-18 that the kingdom of God is a matter "of righteousness, peace and joy in the Holy Spirit". It also states in Col 1:12-13 that believers have been qualified to share in the inheritance of the saints(believers) in the kingdom, and have been brought into (or, translated into) the kingdom of God's Son. This is all part of the Good News, the Gospel, "because it is the power of God for the salvation of everyone who believes" - Rom 1:16.

The Lord Jesus Christ asked us to pray (In the Lord's Prayer – Mat 6:5-15) "Thy kingdom come", well, it has come, and he is waiting for the time when all who are going to come into his kingdom, have come.

The Scriptures also give a warning that some people will not inherit the kingdom of God, and the reasons are given – 1Cor 6:9-10; 15:50; Gal 5:21; Eph 5:5.

In the Scripture Isa 9:6-7 (in C6 Texts), we see a prophecy of the birth of the Lord Jesus Christ and His kingly characteristics, and this is followed (in C6 Texts) by the Scripture Mat 1:1-6 & 15-18 that gives His genealogy.

His kingship was seen in the way in which he exerted control and authority whilst on earth. He was fully aware of all that was happening around him and he knew what was going to take place, and hence, things were never out of control. There are many examples to illustrate this in the Bible and just a few are listed below:

Four men brought a paralysed man to Jesus, who said to him "Son your sins forgiven" and teachers of the law were there who were thinking, "He's blaspheming! Who can forgive sins but God alone? Jesus questioned them why they were thinking these things and then healed the man. - see Mk 2:1-12.

Jesus was in a boat with his disciples when a storm blew up - He spoke to the waves and the sea became calm - see Mk 4:35-41

Just before the crucifixion of Jesus he said to his disciples that they would fall away on account of him and Peter would deny him three times before the cock crows in the morning, and this all came true - see Mat 26:31-35 & 69-75.

Jesus always knew the type of death he would die, that he would rise from the dead and explained it to his disciples long before it happened - see Mat 16:21-23.

Jesus knew all about the 'End Times' and told them to his disciples - see Mat 24.

Further characteristics of his Kingship are seen in his gracious acts, unlimited love, profound wisdom, sacrificial life, speaking the truth in love, and his authority with healing people and casting out demons.

The Scriptures also give a warning that some people will not inherit the kingdom of God, and the reasons are given (1Cor 6:9-10; 15:50; Gal 5:21; Eph 5:5).

[illegible]

THE LORD JESUS CHRIST

- HIS KINGSHIP & KINGDOM -

Notes and Quotations

Someone has said "The kingdom of God is the reign of God in the hearts of men".

In the 'United Christian Broadcasters' (UCB) 'The Word for Today' daily devotional notes of 19 May 1998 by Bob Gass, states "Any time the will of God is done in your life, the Kingdom of God has come. When you adopt His values, live by His standards and obey His commandments, the prayer of Jesus is answered, "Thy will be done on earth, as it is in heaven". An illustration given in the above notes says that each person belongs to the kingdom whose values they share.

The Thompson Chain Reference Bible quotes conditions for entry into the kingdom of God, as follows; humility (Mat 5:3), new birth (Jn 3:3), faith and love (Jas 2:5), sympathetic service (Mat 25:34-35), endurance (Acts 14:22), perseverance (Lk 9:62).

Jamie Buckingham in his book "Parables" states; "God has many ways of teaching us.

Jesus taught by example. Men looked at how He lived and decided to walk that way also.

He also taught by precept. By that I mean He often spoke directly to people. We might even call it preaching. But His favourite way of teaching was through the use of the parable. He loved to tell stories - stories with spiritual meanings".

In this book he also refers to Jesus as "the master storyteller".

Lawrence O. Richards in his "Expository Dictionary of Bible Words" states; "The Beatitudes describe the values of a person living a kingdom lifestyle (Mat 5:3-12)."

He goes on to give an interpretation of the parables in Mat 13 as outlined below:

The sower. :3-9, - 18-23	Individuals respond differently to the gospel invitation.
The wheat/tares. :24-30, - 36-43	The kingdom's citizens are among the men of the world, growing together till God's harvest-time.
The mustard seed. :31-32	The kingdom begins in insignificance; its greatness comes as a surprise
The leaven. grows:33	The kingdom is implanted in a different "raw material" and to fill the whole personality with righteousness.
The hidden treasure. :44	The hidden kingdom is for individual "purchase".
The priceless pearl. :45-46	The kingdom demands abandonment of all other values.

Kingdom and Church

In an endeavour to distinguish between 'The Kingdom of God' and 'The Church', the writer sees these in the following ways:

The Kingdom of God is seen through the godly actions and gracious attitudes shown by those who acknowledge Jesus Christ as Lord and leader of their lives, or as it has been expressed by others as, 'a realm where Jesus Christ exerts control and authority'; and the Church as the local and universal groups of believers in the Lord Jesus Christ, where each group functions under some form of leadership.

THE LORD JESUS CHRIST

- HIS KINGSHIP & KINGDOM -

Biblical Texts & Text References

His Kingship

21 From that time on Jesus began to explain to his disciples that he must go to Jerusalem and suffer many things at the hands of the elders, chief priests and teachers of the law, and that he must be killed and on the third day be raised to life.

Mat 16:21

19 Pilate had a notice prepared and fastened to the cross. It read: JESUS OF NAZARETH, THE KING OF THE JEWS.

Jn 19:19

Additional Scripture references:

Isa 9:6-7; Mat 1:1-6 & 15-18; 16:21-23; 24:1-51; 26:31-35 & 69-75; 27:37, Mk 2:1-12, 4:35-41; Lk 1:32-33, Jn 19:19-21

His Kingdom

In Mat 4:23 it says that:" Jesus went throughout Galilee, teaching in their synagogues, preaching the good news of the kingdom, and healing".

Jesus said "the kingdom of God is within you2 – see Lk 17:20-21

5 For of this you can be sure: No immoral, impure or greedy person—such a man is an idolater—has any inheritance in the kingdom of Christ and of God.

Eph 5:5

Additional Scripture references

Ps 145:10-13, Mat 3:1-3; 4:17; 5:3; 6:5-15; 9:35; 12:28; 18 :1-4 ; 19:23-24; 25:34-35; 26:27-29, Mk 1:14-15; Lk 9:62, 12:31-34, Jn 3:3-5; 18:36, Acts 1 :1-8 ; 14 :22 ; 20:25, Rom 14:17-18; 1Cor 4:20; 6:9-11; 15 :50, Gal 5:19-21, Eph 2:19-22, Col 1:12-13, Heb 12:26-28, Jas 2:5, Rev 1:4-6

Parables of the Kingdom - Also see Section E4 and C6 Notes

See Mat 13:1-52 for a group of parables.
See also Mat 13:3-9 & 18-23

C7

THE LORD JESUS CHRIST

-HIS SECOND COMING-

Biblical Definitions

His Second Coming

Throughout the times of the whole Bible there have been miraculous events foretold and recorded, with some leaving evidence of having taken place, e.g. the flood, the coming of Jesus Christ and the setting of the calendar from His birth, and the return of the Jewish nation to the land of Israel.

There are yet more supernatural events foretold in the Bible, and a very significant and world changing one will be the Second Coming of the Lord Jesus Christ to this earth. This event is referred to in many biblical Scriptures, and it will burst unexpectedly on most people as He comes to take His followers out of this world. This momentous happening has been a positive source of hope and joyful expectation to true believers for two thousand years, because He will return triumphantly to this earth for His own people, so whilst it will be a joyful day for them and those believers who had died before them, Conversely, it will be an unbelievably bad day for those who have ignored or rejected Him in their lives, because they can only look forward to judgement, - see the Scriptures below:

15 According to the Lord's own word, we tell you that we who are still alive, who are left till the coming of the Lord, will certainly not precede those who have fallen asleep.
16 For the Lord himself will come down from heaven, with a loud command, with the voice of the archangel and with the trumpet call of God, and the dead in Christ will rise first.
17 After that, we who are still alive and are left will be caught up together

with them in the clouds to meet the Lord in the air. And so we will be
with the Lord for ever.
18 Therefore encourage each other with these words.

1Thess 4:15-18

There is a warning given in 2Thess 1:8-10 that when he Returns he will punish those who do not know God and do not obey the gospel of our Lord Jesus.

Events prior to His Return

In the Bible there are many references not only to the Return of the Lord Jesus Christ, but also to the conditions and events that will occur prior to His Return.

Prior to His Return we can expect many things to happen and some of these are listed below, in no particular order;

Note: Most of the biblical texts referred to below are given in the C7 Notes and Quotations.

-There will be much Godlessness, lawlessness and religion that lacks God's power and favour.
See 2Tim 3:1-5

- There will be demonic activity coupled with religious practices rejected by God.
See 1Tim 4:1-3

- It will be a significant time of wars, earthquakes and famines.
See Mat 24:6-8, Mk 13:7-8

- During these testing times many Christians will be persecuted and some will abandon the Faith.
See Mat 24:9-13, 1Tim 4:1

- The Gospel will have been preached to all nations.
See Mat 24:14 Mk 13:10

- Many will be seeking to bring the truth of the Gospel into disrepute.
See 2Pet 2:1-3, Jude 17-18

- Many false 'Christ's' and spiritual leaders will arise.
See Mat 24:3-5

The manner of His Return

There are many Scriptures that relate to the way He will Return and the surrounding events, and an outline of these is given below, in no particular order;
See Mat 16:27-28, 1Cor 15:22-28, 1Thess 4:13-18, 2Thess 2:1-4

He will come suddenly and unexpectedly to many.
See 1Thess 4:15 - 5:3

Every eye shall see Him.
See Rev 1:7

He will return as judge.
See Mat 25:31-46, 2Cor 5:10, 2Tim 4:1

- Christians who are alive at the time of His Return will meet the Lord in the air.
See 1Thess 4:17

- He will expose the motives of peoples' hearts.
See 1Cor 4:5

- He will punish those who do not know Him, and those who have not obeyed the Gospel.
See 2Thess 1:6-10

Warnings regarding His Return

God desires people to enter into eternal life rather than eternal punishment, see the Scripture below:

> 9 The Lord is not slow in keeping his promise, as some understand slowness. He is patient with you, not wanting anyone to perish, but everyone to come to repentance. 2Pet 3:9

There are adequate warnings given in the Bible regarding His Return, and some of the Scriptures that relate to this are given below:

Mat 24:43-46, Mk 8:38, Lk 17:26-30, Heb 9:27-28.

THE LORD JESUS CHRIST

- HIS SECOND COMING -

Notes and Quotations

Lawrence O. Richards in his book "Expository Dictionary of Bible Words" states;

"The most wonderful truth for believers is that Jesus will come in person for them. In the resurrection, we will be transformed, enabled at last to share fully in joyful fellowship with God forever.

For unbelievers, Jesus' appearing will constitute a jarring intervention. All mankind's values and hopes, settled as they are on the narrow confines of this life, will be exposed as empty and meaningless."

Given below is a verse of a hymn that reminds us of the situation before our Lord's Return:

Our Lord is now rejected,
And by the world disowned,
By the many still neglected,
And by the few enthroned;
But soon He'll come in glory!
The hour is drawing nigh,
For the crowning day is coming
By - and - By.

Writer unknown

Eschatology - The doctrine of the LAST THINGS

Every religion stands or falls on this doctrine, e.g. Last Things are First Things. It is the END that makes the WAY worthwhile. It is better to bump along to a festival in a model T Ford than glide smoothly to a funeral in a Rolls Royce.

Many Faiths are vague in this area, but in the Christian Faith we have positive assurance and clear promises as shown below by a few of the many Scriptures that relate to this topic:

4 For everything that was written in the past was written to teach us, so that through endurance and the encouragement of the Scriptures we might have hope.

Rom 15:4

Note the word 'But' in verse 20 that changes the situation and provides positive hope.

17 And if Christ has not been raised, your faith is futile; you are still in your sins.
18 Then those also who have fallen asleep in Christ are lost.
19 If only for this life we have hope in Christ, we are to be pitied more than all men.
20 But Christ has indeed been raised from the dead, the firstfruits of those who have fallen asleep.

1Cor 15:17-20

Note:

Please read the additional texts in Section C7 Texts, and especially the texts 1Thess 4:13-5:3. & 2Tim 2:10-12

THE LORD JESUS CHRIST

- HIS SECOND COMING -

Biblical Texts & Text References

Events prior to His Return

3 As Jesus was sitting on the Mount of Olives, the disciples came to him privately. "Tell us," they said, "when will this happen, and what will be the sign of your coming and of the end of the age?"
4 Jesus answered: "Watch out that no-one deceives you.
5 For many will come in my name, claiming, 'I am the Christ,' and will deceive many.

Mat 24:3-5

In Mk 13:7-10 it refers to a time of wars, earthquakes and famines, and these will be thee beginning of birth-pains. Followers of Christ are warned to be on their guard and will suffer persecution, and the gospel will be preached to all nations.

In 2Tim 3:1-5 it describes the terrible times and dreadful attitudes of people before the Lord's Return e.g. people will be lovers of themselves, lovers of money, boastful, proud, abusive, disobedient to their parents, ungrateful, unholy without love, unforgiving, slanderous, without self-control, brutal, not lovers of the good, treacherous, rash, conceited, lovers of pleasure rather than lovers of God

Additional Scripture references

Mat 24:3-14; 29-31, 1Tim 4:1-3; 2Pet 2:1-3; Jude 17-18

The manner of His Return

When He Returns he will gather all nations before him and will separate the people one from another as a shepherd separates the sheep from the goats, and those who have trusted in Him for salvation (the sheep) will go into the kingdom prepared for them, but the others will go, into the eternal fire prepared for the devil and his angels. See Mat 25:31-34, 41, & 46

24 Then the end will come, when he hands over the kingdom to God the Father after he has destroyed all dominion, authority and power.
25 For he must reign until he has put all his enemies under his feet.
26 The last enemy to be destroyed is death.

1Cor 15:24-26

10 For we must all appear before the judgment seat of Christ, that each one may receive what is due to him for the things done while in the body, whether good or bad.

2Cor 5:10

In Rev 1:7-8 it says:" he is coming with the clouds, and every eye will see him", and that all the peoples of the earth will mourn because of him.

Additional Scripture references
Mat 16:27-28, Acts 1:10-11, 1Cor 4:5; 15:22-28, Col 3:4, 1Thess 4:13-5:3; 2Thess 2:1-4, 2Tim 4:1-3, 1Jn 3:2, Jude 14-18

Warnings regarding His Return
38 If anyone is ashamed of me and my words in this adulterous and sinful generation, the Son of Man will be ashamed of him when he comes in his Father's glory with the holy angels."

Mk 8:38

Jesus gave words of warning in Lk 17:26-30 that when he Returns things would happening just like they were in the days of Noah, when people were eating, drinking, marrying and being given in marriage up to the day Noah entered the ark. Then the flood came and destroyed them all.

Those who do not know God and do not obey the gospel of our Lord Jesus will be punished with everlasting destruction and shut out from the presence of the Lord, See 2Thess 1:8-10

Additional Scripture references
Mat 24:43-46; Heb 9:27-28

D1

GOD'S PROVISION

- THE BIBLE -

Biblical Definitions

Introduction to the Bible

Many religious Faiths refer to their 'Scriptures' which they trust implicitly, but a reader of the Bible will soon discover it is very different to other Scriptures for a number of reasons. To begin with, the way in which it was written was an amazing and miraculous story. This is because it had approximately forty writers and they covered a 1500 to 1600 year span of time, and yet unknowingly their writings would hundreds of years later be placed side by side and made into a book with one consecutive story having a vast interlocking unity and cohesion.

This book the Bible, is not only for priests and people with special training to read but for anyone to read. Another special feature about the book the reader will discover, is that it has a power to speak directly to them, which derives from the fact that it radiates divine authority. It is for this reason that the policy of some other Faiths dissuades their followers from reading it.

Historical Outline of the Bible

The following outline of the Bible has been compiled from statements by biblical scholars that relate to this topic. The complete set of books which make up the Old Testament (O,T.) and New Testament (N.T.) is referred to as the Bible.

The Bible derives it's authority neither from ecclesiastical statements nor from any human authority. The Bible is said to be self-authenticating, radiating its divine authority itself, and it is by the inward testimony of the Holy Spirit that a person perceives, and accepts as truth.

When the Books that make up the Bible were considered to be the very 'Word of God' they were referred to as the 'Canon of Scripture'. The term 'Canon' is used to denote a list of books which the church acknowledges as inspired and authoritative Scripture, established as a standard for faith and practice. Hence we have the Canon of the Old Testament (39 Books), and the Canon of the New Testament (27 Books).

The Books of the O,T. like those of the N.T. were inspired, 'God breathed'. But the Holy Spirit worked also in the hearts of God's people so that they came to accept these Books as the Word of God, and submitted to their divine authority. The church councils did not give the Books their divine authority, but simply recognised that they had it and exercised it.

The Hebrew Bible consists of the same 39 Books as that of the O.T. of the Christian Bible, however, apart from the first seven Books, they are placed in a different order.

The Books of the Bible

The listing of the Books of the Christian Bible is shown below together with their type and abbreviation (as used in this book).

The Canon of the Old Testament

Book Name	Type	Abbreviation
Genesis	L * *Refer to Books in	Gen
Exodus	L * the Pentateuch	Ex
Leviticus	L *	Lev
Numbers	L *	Num
Deuteronomy	L *	Deut
Jushua	H	Josh
Judges	H	Jud
Ruth	W	Ru
Samuel (1 & 2)	H	1Sam & 2Sam
Kings (1 & 2)	H	1Kg & 2Kg
Chronicles (1 & 2)	H	1Chron & 2Chron
Ezra	H	Ezr

Nehemiah	H	Neh
Esther	H	Est
Job	W	Job
Psalms	W	Ps
Proverbs	W	Prov
Ecclesiastes	W	Ecc
Song of Solomon	W	Ss
Isaiah	P	Isa
Jeremiah	P	Jer
Lamentations	W	Lam
Ezekiel	P	Ezek
Daniel	H	Dan
Hosea	P	Hos
Joel	P	Joel
Amos	P	Am
Obadiah	P	Ob
Jonah	P	Jon
Micah	P	Mic
Nahum	P	Nah
Habakkuk	P	Hab
Zephaniah	P	Zep
Haggai	P	Hag
Zechariah	P	Zec
Malachi	P	Mal

Key to the Type of Book

L - The Law

P - Prophets

W - Wisdom Writings

H - Historical

The Canon of the New Testament

Book Name	Type	Abbreviation

Matthew	G	Mat
Mark	G	Mk
Luke	G	Lk
John	CE	Jn
Acts of the Apostles	CE	Acts
Romans	PE	Rom
1Corinthians	PE	1Cor
2Corinthians	PE	2Cor
Galatians	PE	Gal
Ephesians	PE	Eph
Philippians	PE	Phil
Colossians	PE	Col
1Thessalonians	PE	1Thess
2Thessalonians	PE	2Thess
1Timothy	PE	1Tim
2Timothy	PE	2Tim
Titus	PE	Tit
Philemon	PE	Phm
Hebrews	CE	Heb
James	CE	Jas
1Peter	CE	1Pet
2Peter	CE	2Pet
1John	CE	1Jn
2John	CE	2Jn
3John	CE	3Jn
Jude	CE	Jude
Revelation	CE	Rev

Key to the Type of Book

G - Gospel

PE - Pauline Epistle

CE - 'Catholic' Epistle or General Epistle - apart from 2 & 3John they are addressed to a wider audience.

It is considered that when the N.T. Books were coming into being the O.T. Books existed as a completed collection to which divine authority was already given.

In the N.T. the O.T. is repeatedly referred to as '*the Scriptures*' (Mat 26:54, Jn 5:39, Acts 17:2 etc.), indicating that the O.T. was a well known collection of writings, forming a unity.

The unity of the O.T. with the N.T. is authenticated by the vast amount of cross-referencing that occurs between them.

In the N.T. we find the Lord Jesus Christ referring to the O.T. Scriptures and also acknowledging that His coming, birth, life and death were all foretold in them and that He would fulfil all the Scriptures that pertained to Him.

The apostolic church was not without Scripture, and looked for its doctrine to the O.T. As the apostles died their disciples upheld the apostolic doctrines and used their writings, and in the 4th century AD we see the fixation of the N.T. Canon within the limits to which we are accustomed to-day.

The Protestant English Bible

The story of the Protestant English Bible is a long and interesting one, but the objective here is to provide an outline that includes key points as given below. To this end information has been extracted from the book "Word Abiding" by Colin Clair.

One of the outstanding early translators of the Scriptures was Jerome, who was the most learned scholar of his time and he was called upon by the Bishop of Rome to produce an authorized Latin version of the Bible to replace the confusing variety of texts already in circulation. Jerome spent much of his life on the work, which was begun in the year 382 and not completed until 405.

His translation was at first received with bitter opposition and it was some two centuries before the old Latin version yielded to the Vulgate, as Jerome's text is called.

Augustine landed on the Kent coast in A.D. 597 and possibly brought the Latin Vulgate version of Jerome with him. This was, however, of little use to the Saxon people of whom few could read outside of the monasteries.

Several centuries past with only the educated clergy being able to read the Scriptures, however, there were missionaries who toured the land and proclaimed the Word orally and many were converted to Christianity through their teaching coupled with the example of their moral and devoted lives.

Bede, a monk at Jarrow, born about AD 674, became the Bishop of Hexham. He was a man of great ability who devoted his life to writing and instructing the young monks. He finished translating the Gospel of St. John into the Saxon language in AD 735 just before he died.

The Gospels were translated into Anglo-Saxon by a priest named Aldred in about the middle of the tenth century. After this, there is little evidence of further translations until we come to the 14th century, and during this period Norman French supplanted English as the language of the educated classes.

The next notable figure to appear on the scene was John Wycliffe, the first of the English Reformers, who won great repute as a scholar, and in 1360 was Master of Balliol College, Oxford. He resigned his mastership and accepted a living in Lutterworth, Leicestershire, in 1374. He attacked abuses in the church and went on to attack the constitution, initially using Latin, and then issued tracts in English. He sent out preachers to preach his doctrines of grace, with a clear message that it was the right of every man to study the Scriptures for himself and this required that the common man should have "Goddis Lawe" in his own tongue. So Wycliffe and his supporters set to work to translate the Bible into English, and this was completed in 1382. It was then revised by John Purvey, curate to Wycliffe, in 1388, and this revised version was widely read until it was superseded by printed versions in the 16th century. The great defect of the Wycliffe version of the Bible was that it was itself a translation of a translation. A direct translation from the original Hebrew and Greek was not made until 150 years later. However, before this time Bibles had been printed in German, Italian, Dutch, French, Danish, Russian, Bohemian and Spanish.

The reason for the delay for the Bible to be printed in English because it was prohibited by laws passed in 1408 and 1414 from translating the text of Scripture into English, and transgression of these laws held severe penalties.

A man who was to challenge these laws was William Tyndale who was born in Gloucestershire about 1490, and from his early years was determined to see the Bible translated into English so that people could read it for themselves, because he realized that religion had become merely a thing of outward form and lacked the spiritual life it should have. Opposition to his views from local priests drove him to Little Sodbury, and he made his way to London in 1523, but it was soon made clear to him that it was not possible to translate the Scriptures here so he went to Hamburg in Germany where the Reformation had established itself, and where there were printers willing to undertake the printing of his work. He never returned to England.

Due to the secrecy of his work and to avoid detection he moved from place to place around the Continent, and besides Hamburg was at Cologne, Worms and Antwerp.

He translated the New Testament first, aided by his secretary William Roye and this version was printed in 1526, This New Testament was different from those that preceded it in that, it was translated directly from the original Greek. Copies were secretly shipped to England, but when discovered were attacked by the ecclesiastical authorities and many were burnt. However, such was the thirst for the Word of God among the people that they were earnestly sought and bought by many.

Tyndale brought out a revised edition in 1534, in which he was assisted by a Cambridge scholar, John Fryth. Tyndale also translated the Pentateuch from the original Hebrew and the Book of Jonah, but he was prevented from translating the complete Bible as he was kidnapped in 1535, imprisoned for 18 months in the castle at Vilvorde where he was strangled and burnt at the stake. This was a sad end to a devoted man with such a high and noble purpose of bringing the Word of God to the English people, but he had won the battle for the Bible to be translated into the vernacular. The way was now open and many other translations of the Bible followed, encouraged by people like Thomas Cranmer the new Archbishop of Canterbury.

The success of Tyndale's English translation of the New Testament can be judged by the fact that nine-tenths of the Authorized Version of the New Testament remains as he wrote it.

Opposition to the sale of English Bibles continued for many years and in 1539 the statute, known as the Six Articles, re-imposed on England the leading doctrines of the Roman Catholic faith, and in 1543 an Act for the advancement of true religion prohibited women, artificers, apprentices, journeymen, serving men under the degree of yeomen, husbandmen and labourers from reading the Bible. The statute of 1539 caused many partisans of reform to leave the country, and this exodus was added to as a result of the persecutions during the reign of Queen Mary. Many of these people fled from France to Geneva due to the Inquisition which had started.

Despite all these difficulties Bibles continued to be published, and the list given below shows some of the Bibles published after Tyndale's work:

1537	The Matthew Bible by John Rogers? (Thomas Matthew).
1538	Parallel English-Latin N.T. (Vulgate) by Coverdale.
1539	The Great Bible by Coverdale for Thomas Cromwell.
1557	Geneva N.T. by William Wittington.
1560	Geneva Bible by various - including Wittington.
1611	Authorized King James Bible by fifty-four translators.
1885	Revised Version of Bible by British and American companies.
1901	American Standard Edition by American scholars.
1963	New American Standard Bible by Evangelical scholars.
1962-71	The Living Bible by K.N. Taylor.
1976	Good News Bible by American Bible Society.
1979	New International Version of Bible by Evangelical scholars.
1982	New King James version of Bible by Thomas Nelson.
1989	New Revised Standard Version of Bible by Oxford University Press.

1996 New Living Bible by Tyndale Press.
2002 The Message by Navigators.
2002 English Standard Version of Bible by Harper Collins.

From the above outline of the story of the Bible we can see the time, effort and great price, which has been paid to bring us the Bible in our own language, let us value it, use it and live by it, as it is the Word of God to us.

Important Observations

The writers of the Psalms had many positive things to say about God's Word, see - Ps 119:7-10, 119:8-16, 119:18 & 130.

The O.T. prophets like Isaiah and Amos received, recorded and spoke out God's Word, see – Isa 1:1-4, 1:10-11, 40:8, 55:10-11, Amos 8:1-6, 8:11-12.

God's Word is flawless and should not be added to, or subtracted from, see – Deut 4:2, Prov 30:5-6, Rev 22:18-19.

It says it is 'God-breathed', living and active, see – 2Tim 3:16, Heb 4:12.

It states that God's Word lives and endures for ever, see – 1Pet 1:23-25.

The words recorded by God's prophets were not theirs, but were given to them by God's Holy Spirit and carried His authority, see – 2Pet 1:19-21.

We need to listen to God's Word and obey it, see – Jas 1:21-22.

Note: All the above Scriptures are shown in Section D1 Texts.

[illegible] New Living [illegible] by Tyndale Press
2002 [illegible] by [illegible]
2002 English Standard Version of Bible by Harper Collins

[illegible] the above outline of the story of the Bible we can see the [illegible] and great price which has been paid to bring us [illegible] our language [illegible] and [illegible] it as the Word of God [illegible]

Important [illegible]
The writers of the Bible [illegible] many [illegible] things [illegible] about [illegible]
[illegible]

[illegible]

[illegible]

[illegible]

[illegible]

[illegible]

We need to [illegible]

[illegible] Texts

GOD'S PROVISION

- THE BIBLE -

<u>Notes and Quotations</u>

The unique power of the 'Word of God', the Bible, is revealed in the Scripture below:

12 For the word of God is living and active. Sharper than any double-edged sword, it penetrates even to dividing soul and spirit, joints and marrow; it judges the thoughts and attitudes of the heart.

Heb 4:12

Quotations concerning the Bible as the Word of God from unknown sources:

"The purpose of the Bible is to introduce us to the author."

"The purpose of the Bible is not to INFORM, but to TRANSFORM (lives)," – see Rom 12:1-2, 2Cor 3:18. The word 'transform' in Rom 12:2 refers to changing into another life form, a continuous process of inward change in the person effected by God's Holy Spirit.

"The more you feed on the Word of God, the hungrier you become."

"A text taken out of its context quickly becomes a pretext."

"If we do not <u>Heed</u> the Word of God, we will not <u>Hear</u> the Word of God and so will experience famine of the Word."- see Deut 8:3, Isa 1:1-4 & 10-11, Hos 5, Amos 8:1-6 & 11-12, Mat 4:4, 2Tim 3:16.

Quotations concerning the Bible as the Word of God from known sources:

Charles Haddon Spurgeon: "Nobody ever outgrows Scripture; the Book widens and deepens with the years." and again he said: "The Bible is like a lion, it needs no defence; let it out of its cage, and it will defend itself."

A.W. Tozer:"I did not go through the Book. The Book went through me."

F.F.Bruce: "The Bible was never intended to be a book for scholars and specialists only. From the beginning it was intended to be everybody's book, and that is what it continues to be."

Abraham Lincoln: "This great Book is the best gift God has given to man. But for it we could not know right from wrong."

D.L.Moody: "The Bible was not given to increase our knowledge, but to change our lives." An extract from "The Word for Today" Notes by Bob Gass.

"Either your situation is subject to the Word, or the Word is subject to your situation." -----By Bob Gass

"Your Bible is more than just a doctrinal guidebook; it generates life, creates faith, produces change, frightens the devil, causes miracles, heals hurts, builds character, transforms circumstances, imparts joy, overcomes adversity, defeats temptation, infuses hope, releases power, cleanses our minds, brings things into being, and guarantees our future forever." – From "The Word for Today" Notes by Bob Gass.

In 2Cor 3:14-16 it states that a veil lies over the eyes of all unbelievers so that they cannot understand the Scriptures, "But whenever anyone turns to the Lord, the veil is taken away."

The study of the Bible without acting on what it says produces pride and judgmental attitudes. Jas 1:22-25

"My conscience has been taken captive by the word of God, and to go against it is neither right nor safe" 1Tim 1:19, 1Tim 4:2

Martin Luther

The quotation given below is an extract from the SASRA "Ready" magazine Volume 1997-2002 No 13 Jan-June 2001

THE BIBLE

"This Book contains The mind of God, the state of man, the way of Salvation, the doom of Sinners, and the happiness of Believers.

Its doctrines are holy, its precepts are binding, its histories are true, and its decisions are immutable.

Read it to be wise, believe it to be safe, and practise it to be holy.

It contains light to direct you, food to support you, and comfort to cheer you.

It is the traveller's map, the pilgrim's staff, the pilot's compass, the soldier's sword, and the Christian's charter.

Here Paradise is restored, Heaven opened, and the gates of Hell disclosed.

Christ is its grand subject, our good its design, and the glory of God its end.

It should fill the memory, rule the heart, and guide the feet.

Read it slowly, frequently, and prayerfully; it is a mine of wealth, a paradise of glory, and a river of pleasure.

It is given you in life, will be opened at the Judgement, and be remembered for ever.

It involves the highest responsibility, will reward the greatest labour, and condemn all who trifle with its sacred contents."

All Knowing God - Speaking about the Lord Jesus Christ in Col 2:3 it says,

"in whom are hidden all the treasures of wisdom and knowledge".

Regarding this statement, Selwyn Hughes makes the following comment: "This is HIDDEN TRUTH for us to discover, to seek out through Bible study and waiting on Him. The Holy Spirit, as part of the Godhead, will guide us into ALL TRUTH- Jn 16:13."

Augustine, concerning John's Gospel said, "While it is easily read by all and offers itself to all in most plain words and in lowliest style, yet it demands the closest study of those who have the power of applying themselves".

Below is a plan for reading the Bible by Dr E Stanley Jones called "The Seven R's"

1. Relax – If you go stamping through the woods in a hurry, you will see little. But sit still and the squirrels will come down the tree, the birds will draw near, and nature will be alive in every twig and flower.

2. Recall – Ask questions like this as you read: Who is writing? To whom? For what purpose? What is he saying? How does it apply to me? How shall I put it into practice?

3. Rehearse – If you find something that speaks directly to your condition then turn it over and over in your mind.

4. Retain – When a verse of Scripture strikes you, plan to retain it – commit it to memory.

5. Rejoice – Reading the Bible is a tryst with God. Keep in mind the written word is designed to lead you into a deeper relationship with the living Word. So enjoy your devotional time with the Scriptures.

6. Realign – As you read the Word keep realigning your life with what you read.

7. Release – When something thrills you in your Bible reading, pass it on. Share its truth with someone. The repetition will help the retention, for we will always remember what we shared.

The above Bible reading plan was recorded in Selwyn Hughes's "Every Day with Jesus" Notes.

Bob Gass points out in his "The Word for Today" Notes that all Christians need:

Spiritual protection by " . . . . . the washing of water by the Word" (Eph 5:26), and Jesus said, "Now ye are clean through the Word" (Jn 15:3).

<u>Concerning the O.T. Book of Proverbs: - Author of the following quotations unknown.</u>
The purpose of this book is to put Godliness into working clothes as it addresses our lifestyle at home, in business and society.

Proverbs provide practical wisdom for all aspects of life, and wisdom for making decisions - see Mat 7:24-27.

'Knowledge' is what we know, and
'Wisdom' is the right application of what we know.

<u>A Test for all Sacred Scriptures</u>
The sacred Scriptures of any Faith must always be able to withstand criticism over hundreds or thousands of years, because the 'TRUTH' they are said to be proclaiming can only be attested as 'TRUE' with time without being defended by man. The Bible has been thoroughly tested in this way, is standing firmly today, its truth has not been undermined, and is the world's bestseller.

There are warnings given in the Bible that the words of the Bible should not be added to or subtracted from, - see Prov 30:5-6, Rev 22:18-19.

<u>The '*Word*' of God</u>
There are two principal 'words' used in the Greek New Testament for the '*Word* ' of God, namely; 'LOGOS' and 'RHEMA', and they are worthy of study to determine their use and application.

L.O. Richards states: "Two words are commonly found where the NIV and the NASB read "word." One is *rhema,* which typically focuses attention on a specific word or utterance. In contrast, *logos* is a broad term, sometimes including the entire Christian message and often used in technical theological senses.

Rhema occurs seventy times in the N.T. --(the Refs. are given).

The significance of *rhema* can be illustrated by its first occurrence. Challenged by Satan in the wilderness, Jesus responded that man is to live by "every *rhema* that comes from the mouth of God" (Mat 4:4). In the context He then proceeds to counter Satan's temptations by applying very specific words from Scripture to each situation that Satan creates. --------

Logos occurs over three hundred times in the N.T. and is often used in common-place ways, with meanings such as "speech," "report," "discourse," "subject matter." But often the use of *logos* has great theological significance. The "word" is the active, powerful presence of God, through which He works His will in history. --------The word that Jesus spoke was the word of transforming power. By His word the sick were made whole (Mat 8:8; Lk 7:7) and demons driven out (Mat 8:16)."

<u>How to Study the Bible – By Randy Petersen ("The Christian Book of Lists")</u>

1 With a regenerate mind (1Cor 2:14
2 With a willing mind (Jn 7:17)
3 With an obedient mind (Jas 1:21-22)
4 With a teachable mind (Mat 11:25)
5 In awe of God's holiness (Ex 3:5)
6 In awe of God's holiness (Ex 3:5)
7 Remembering it is God's Word (1Thess 2:13)

<u>Principles of Inductive Bible Study - By Randy Petersen ("The Christian Book of Lists")</u>

1 Observe the whole.
2 Observe each part.
3 Summarise the whole.
4 Ask: What does it say?
5 Ask: What does it mean?
6 Ask: What does it mean to me?

GOD'S PROVISION

- THE BIBLE -

Biblical Texts & Text References

The Bible

In Isa 40:8 it says that;" the word of our God stands for ever."

4 Jesus answered, "It is written: `Man does not live on bread alone, but on every word that comes from the mouth of God.'"

Mat 4:4

In Mat 5:17-18 Jesus says that he had not come to abolish the Law or the Prophets; but to fulfil them.

16 All Scripture is God-breathed and is useful for teaching, rebuking, correcting and training in righteousness,
17 that the man of God may be thoroughly equipped for every good work.

2Tim 3:16-17

The word of God judges the thoughts and attitudes of the heart. See Heb 4:12

Additional Scripture references

Ex 3:3-5, Deut 4:1-2 & 6:1-7; 8:3, 2Sam 22:31, 1Kg 17:1-2, 2Chron 34:20-21, Neh 8:1-3 & 8, Job 22:21-22; 23:11-12, Ps 19:7-10; 78:1-4; 119:8-18; 41-45; 119:101-105; 119:130,& 160-165, Prov 4:20-22, 28:9; 30;5-6; Isa 1:1-4;& 10-11; 55:10-11; 66:1-2 & 5, Jer 15:16; 20:8-9, Amos 8:1-6 & 11-12, Mat 7:24-27; 8:8 & 16; 11:25; 22:29; 26:54, Lk 7:6-7; 24:25-27 & 44-45, Jn 5:39-40; 7:16-17; 15:3; 16:13; 17:14-17, Acts 17:1-2 & 11-12, Rom 1:1-2; 12:1-2; 15:3-4; 16:25-26, 1Cor 2:14, 2Cor 3:18; 4:2, Eph 1:13;

5:25-26; 6:17, Col 1:24-25; 2:2-3; 3:16, 1Thess 2:13, 1Tim 4:13, 2Tim 2:8-9 & 15, Jas 1:21-22; 1Pet 1:23-25; 2Pet 1:19-21; 3:16, 1Jn 2:4-5; Rev 22:18-19

D2

GOD'S PROVISION

- THE CHURCH -

Biblical Definitions

The Church – Its Nature and Effect

The whole concept of 'church' is frequently misunderstood – it is thought of as a 'building' and as a place people go, to conduct weddings and funerals etc. In fact, the word' Church' is a collective term referring to the community of all true Christian believers, and is nothing to do with a building. This community has existed since the time of Christ to the present day.

The 'Church', the group of Christians, should be characterised by love that is shown in helpful and caring words where biblical truth is expressed with a clear, bold and humble attitude and matched with practical help.

The Church family meets regularly in different locations for worship and fellowship. This takes a number of different but reverent forms to accommodate the varying and different approaches of people from differing backgrounds.

There is, however, much misunderstanding and ignorance of the true nature of the church in the general population of many countries causing some to consider it irrelevant to their needs, too challenging to their lifestyle or being dismissed by others due to an unhelpful experience of church. All these situations cause sadness with Christians because the church has been founded by the Lord Himself to meet the needs of all people, and to address the above lack of knowledge and hurt Christians are commissioned to go into all the world to present the good news about the Lord Jesus Christ and make disciples. In fact most churches have some form of outreach activity to take the message of love faith, and hope to non-Christians.

It is most necessary to understand that the Church is an organism of God, not an organisation of man. Through it, God acts supernaturally and empowers those in it. If it becomes just an organisation of man it is no longer the real Church

The Church is local and universal

In the New Testament the word *church* may be applied to a group of believers at any level, ranging from a very small group meeting in a private home all the way to the group of all true believers in the universal church, A "*house* church" is called a "church" in Romans 16:5 ("greet also the church in their house") and 1 Corinthians 16:19 ("Aquila and Prisca, together with *the church in their house* send you hearty greetings in the Lord"). The church in an entire *city* is also called "a church" (1Cor 1:2; 2Cor 1:1; 1Thess 1:1).

The church in a *region*_is referred to as a "church" in Acts 9:31: "So *the church throughout all Judea and Galilee and Samaria* had peace and was built up." Finally, the church throughout the entire world can be referred to as "the church." Paul says, "Christ loved *the church* and gave himself up for her" (Eph 5:25).

The above statements are from the book "Bible Doctrine" by Wayne Grudem.

Saints

All true believers in the New Testament are referred to as 'saints'(Rom 1:7). It refers to the 'saints' or 'holy people' in 2Thess 1:10 as 'those who have believed' i.e. the whole number of the redeemed - from the book: "Expository Dictionary of Bible Words" by W.E. Vine.

They are called to a life of holiness (separation to God) as it says in 1Pet 1:15-16 "Be holy, because I am holy".

The Church Body and the Giftings Given to it

In Rom 12:4-8 it says that those who are 'in Christ' are members of one body and have different functions that relate to various gifts, and in the book "Bible Doctrine" by Wayne Grudem, he classifies the gifts into two groups, as Common Gifts and Special gifts in the following way:

Common gifts are listed in the above Scripture as:

prophesying - "telling something that God has spontaneously brought to mind" on an occasional basis,

serving - being of service to those around us and the church,

teaching - to teach with gentleness (2Tim 2:24-25), and humility,

encouraging - encourage one another with words and actions of love,

contributing - to the needs of others around us and in the church,

leadership - one who leads others by assisting the main church leadership and seeking at all times to emulate their characters by showing humility and a shepherds' heart (1Pet 5:1-11), and being dependant on God for wisdom, (see Section E5 for further details),

showing mercy - out of a heart of one who themselves' has received mercy, being forgiving and prepared to offer others a fresh start.

Also: In the Scripture 1Cor 12:4-13, it refers to a variety of spiritual gifts given to the Body of Believers as determined by God's Holy Spirit, for the common good. In this Scripture it refers to the spiritual gifts of: *the message of wisdom; the message of knowledge; healing; miraculous powers; prophecy; the ability to distinguish between spirits; speaking in different kinds of tongues;* and *interpretation of tongues.*

It follows, therefore, that each true believer needs to ascertain the gifting they have been given, and use them for God's glory.

Special gifts given in Eph 4:11-13 are listed as: apostles, prophets, evangelists, pastors and teachers. These gifts were given with a special calling (to Paul Rom 1:1, to Timothy 2Tim 1) to "prepare God's people for works of service, so that the body of Christ may be built up until we all reach unity in the faith and in the knowledge of the Son of God - - - - - -" Eph 4:12-13.

Apostle

L.O. Richards in his book "Expository Dictionary of Bible Words" defines 'apostle' as;

"An apostle is an envoy, sent on a mission to speak for the one sending him and having the sender's own authority." -.

Jesus chose twelve apostles to be with him in his earthly ministry. These were called to be followers of Jesus, up to and beyond his resurrection. After his resurrection they focused particularly on prayer and teaching.

Scriptures such as Acts 14:14 and 1Cor 12:28 indicate that others were also referred to as apostles, but the use of this term to-day is a matter of some debate. It is also clear that some of the apostles spoke and wrote God's very words and they became included in the scriptures, and are in fact a large proportion of the New Testament.

Prophet and Prophecy

Wayne Grudem in his book "Bible Doctrine" defines prophecy as "telling something that God has spontaneously brought to mind". He also states that "The New Testament counterparts of Old Testament prophets are New Testament apostles," - for which he has much scriptural support.

Concerning Old Testament prophets he again states, "they were able to speak and write words that had absolute divine authority. They could say, "Thus says the Lord," and the words that followed were the very words of God."

He further states, "In the New Testament there were also people who spoke and wrote God's very words and had them recorded in scripture, but we may be surprised to find that Jesus no longer calls them "prophets" but uses a new term "apostles.""

The gift of prophecy is given to many Christians and Peter said this would happen - see Acts 2:16-18.

Further statements by Wayne Grudem: "The gift of prophecy is widely distributed to God's people, but the authority of prophecy is a lesser authority, no longer the authority of God's very words."

"It does not threaten or compete with Scripture but is subject to Scripture, as well as the mature judgement of the congregation."

"In 1Thessalonians 5:19-21, Paul tells the Thessalonians, "Do not despise prophesying, but *test everything;* hold fast what is good." Similarly in 1Corinthians 14:29-38, Paul says "Let two or three prophets speak, and *let the others weigh what is said"*, he suggests that they should listen carefully and sift the good from the bad." Or this could be considered as meaning, sifting the words that have come from God from those that have come human thought.

<u>Evangelist</u>
"An evangelist is a messenger of good news, one who proclaims the glad tidings of the Gospel" - W.E.Vine.

Those who receive the special gifting of an evangelist will be enabled to communicate the Gospel in an effective way to others.

In Matthew 28:19 the disciples were told by Jesus to "make disciples of all nations," and this means that He wants us to be sensitive and obedient to His voice so that He can draw people to Himself. Also in Acts 1:8 it says "you will be my witnesses", so we are each called through our lifestyle, attitude and words to be His witnesses of who the Lord is and what He has done for us personally.

To provide an opportunity to 'proclaim' the Gospel often means that first of all genuine love and practical care should be shown to the people we are trying to reach. This may entail considerable cost of time and money before we can share with them the love of God.

<u>Pastor</u>
A pastor is like a shepherd who tends his flock and leads them to pasture to feed. So a pastor keeps watch over those in his charge and sees that they are cared for, discipled and fed on the Word of God, - see Acts 20:28-31, and Hebrews 12:5-6.

In John 21:15-17 Jesus says to Peter "Feed my lambs; take care of my sheep; and feed my sheep. The lambs and sheep in this passage are commonly considered to refer to children and adults respectively.

In Ephesians 4:12-13 it says concerning pastors and teachers that they are "to prepare God's people for works of service, so that the body of Christ may be built up until we all reach unity in the faith and in the knowledge of the Son of God and become mature, attaining to the whole measure of the fullness of Christ."

Teacher

A teacher, in this context, is one who teaches Biblical Truth to the Church.

The Lord Jesus Christ Himself was the supreme teacher, and this is supported by numerous Scriptures where His unique ability to convey and illustrate truth is further substantiated by miraculous demonstrations.

In John 3:2 a Pharisee named Nicodemus said to Jesus "Rabbi, we know you are a teacher who has come from God." Again in Mark 1:22 it says "The people were amazed at His teaching, because He taught them as one who had authority, not as the teachers of the law."

There is a warning given in Matthew 5:19-20 that teachers who do not obey the teaching they are giving will not enter the kingdom of heaven.

It follows, therefore, from these and other Scripture references that the character of a person who teaches Biblical truth should be one who: has integrity; follows Biblical teaching in their lifestyle; graciously teaches Scripture using the Word of God as the only Word of divine authority; endeavours to follow the way Jesus taught and lived.

Church Leadership

In the early church two types of leadership role were recognised and appointed, namely: elders and deacons. These people were chosen from the local congregation of believers.

Note:

For a fuller account of Church Leadership please see Section E5 under the heading 'Biblical Definitions'.

Elders

In Acts 14:23 we see that "Paul and Barnabas appointed elders for them in each church and, with prayer and fasting, committed them to the Lord in whom they had put their trust."

L.O. Richards states, "The word 'elder' probably suggests age, and certainly indicates spiritual maturity."

In 1Timothy 3:1-7 and Titus 1:5-9 we are given a clear indication of the quality of person and lifestyle expected for those to be appointed as elders. These Scriptures clearly state the sex of the elder to be male, when it says "the *husband* of one wife" and "*He* must manage *his* own family well". Also, these were to be people who had 'a good reputation with outsiders'.

The function of elders is not spelled out in detail, but in 1Timothy 5:17 it says "The elders who direct the affairs of the church well are worthy of double honour, especially those whose work is preaching and teaching."

<u>Deacons</u>

In 1Timothy 3:8-13 it refers to people who can be appointed as deacons, and it concentrates on the quality of the person and their lifestyle similar in fact to those required for elders. In this passage of Scripture it also states that "A deacon must be the husband of but one wife and must manage his children and his household well." So again, it indicates that a deacon should be male.

Another passage of Scripture that seems to refer to deacons, again as male, is Acts 6:1-6, and this gives some indication of their role, and again, Acts 6:8 and Acts 7 shows an increase in the width of that role.

The maturity process of the Christian is not automatic, but can be likened in some ways to the growth of plants in the sense that they need nourishment and the right environmental conditions. However, with the growth of the Christian the process is made up of two interlinked parts; the natural part and the supernatural part.

The natural part is our responsibility and the supernatural part is God's, with a corresponding interaction between them.

These aspects of growth are well stated by L.O. Richards in his book "Expository Dictionary of Bible Words." where he says: "But Christian growth is not automatic. The NT makes it clear that we need to feed on the Word of God (1Pet 2:2; Heb 5:11-14). We need to root ourselves deeply in the shared life of the believing community (Eph 3:17-19; 4:13-16). We are also called on to make personal choices that will facilitate our growth (Heb 5:14; cf. 2Cor 9:6-11). God is deeply involved in the process of our growth, and He has ordained its direction. Moreover, He has given us the privilege of co-operating with Him as he works within us."

<u>The Numerical Growth of the Church</u>

Much has been written on this subject, but given here are just a few salient points to consider.

In Acts 6 we are told that the number of the disciples was increasing and this was at a time when they had particularly given their attention to prayer, and to the ministry of the Word of God (the Bible). Then we are told that the Word spread, and this was closely followed by opposition. Similarly in Acts 12 it says that "the word of God continued to increase and spread," and in the story told here we see there was persecution followed by earnest prayer and a miracle. Again in Acts 19 it says "In this way the word of the Lord spread widely and grew in power," and this took place in the midst of opposition, miracles and prayer.

In these, and other stories of the early church, we see something of a pattern emerging, having the common factors of preaching the Word of God to unbelievers, and this is in some way mixed with opposition, persecution, miracles and prayer.

We may well ask the question, therefore, "who has the responsibility for the growth of the Church?" and the answer seems to be in two parts. We do our part of faithfully and 'fully' preaching the Word of God to unbelievers (see Rom 10:14-15, & 15:18-19), coupled with listening and co-operating with God in earnest prayer, then God in His own time and way will do His part by building the Church and performing miracles, which may occur with opposition and persecution - see Acts 11:19-21; 13:46-52.

In the final analysis it is God who gives the increase – see Acts 2:47; 11:21; 1Cor 3:6-7.

<u>Note:</u>

The key Scriptures referred to under 'Biblical Definitions' are given in the D2 Texts.

GOD'S PROVISION

- THE CHURCH -

Notes and Quotations

Those who are disciples of the Lord Jesus Christ i.e. the Church, are meant to represent the living organism on earth of our Lord and Saviour Jesus Christ.

All true Christians do in fact belong to one universal Church, however, there are many different types of Church groupings with a vast number of names, and having a variety of Church meeting places, all of which may well cause some confusion to outsiders. Many of these types of Church groupings are sound, and their differences have come about due to an emphasis on one particular aspect of Scripture, lifestyle or tradition.

A basic test for any Christian group is to ascertain whether they proclaim the Good News of personal salvation through repentance and faith in the Lord Jesus Christ as the only and all sufficient Saviour who died on the cross to pay the penalty for every person's sin. It follows, therefore, that we cannot earn our salvation through doing good works, - the good works should be seen after the person has become a Christian.

It should be noted that the distinctive feature of the Early Church, as shown in the Book of Acts, was much evidence of the supernatural.

The Responsibilities and Tasks of the Church

An outline of the responsibilities and tasks of every person in the Church is listed below:

To worship God - Ps 95:6, Jn 4:23-24
To give God sacrificial praise - Ps 34:1, Heb 13:15-16

To read and obey His Word the Bible - Ps 119:105, 2Tim 2:15
To seek His Will for our lives - Rom 12:1-2, Eph 1:9-12
To pray personal prayers, and pray for others - Phil 1:9, Col 1:9
To pray in the Holy Spirit - Eph 6:18, Jude 20
To pray for healing and confess your sins to one another - Jas 5:14-16, 1Jn 1:9
To encourage one another - 1Thess 5:11, Heb 10:24-25
To give sacrificially to God of ourselves, our substance and talents - Rom 12:1-2, 2Cor 9:7
To love God - Jn 14:23, 1Jn 5:1-2
To serve God in the way He shows us - Rom 12:11, 1Tim 6:2
To show God's grace in our lives - 2Tim 2:1, 2Pet 3:18
To live and conduct our lives in an attitude of humility - Mat 23:12, 1Pet 5:5-6
To live in the power and boldness of the Holy Spirit - Acts 4:29-31, Rom 15:18-19
To be His witnesses - Acts 1:8, Heb 12:1-2
To act as salt and light in the world - Mat 5:13, Col 4:6
To be self-controlled, alert and wary of the devil's schemes - Eph 6:11-18, 1Pet 5:8
To give love and care to those around us Rom 12:10 & 13, Rom 13:10
To get beside people - Rom 12:15-16, Gal 6:1-2
To live at peace with others, as far as it depends on you Rom 12:18, Heb 12:14
To answer with grace and patience those who question our Faith -Lk 12:11-12,
1Pet 3:15-16
To overcome evil with good - Mat 5:11-16, Rom 12:21
To seek to glorify God in all that we do - Rom 2:6-8, Phil 4:8-9
To offer fellowship to others Christians - Acts 2:42, Gal 2:9

<u>An outline of special responsibilities and tasks given to some is listed below:</u>

To teach the Scriptures to believers - Rom 12:7, 2Tim 3:15-17
To preach the Word of God - Rom 10:14-15, 1Tim 2:7
To evangelise the world - Mat 28:19, Acts 1:8
To make disciples of all peoples - Mat 28:18-20, Lk 14:26-27
To lead other Christians - Rom 12:8, Heb 13:17

To discipline believers - Col 3:16, 1Thess 5:12-13
To baptise believers - Mat 28:19, 1Cor 1:17
To heal - 1Cor 12:9, Jas 5:14-16
To prophesy - Rom 12:6, 1Cor 14:1 & 39-40
To speak and interpret tongues - 1Cor 12:10, 1Cor14:6-12

Church Leadership

In Eph 4:11-13 it gives the titles of Church leaders whose ministry was to build up Christ's Body, namely, apostles, prophets, evangelists, pastors, and teachers. Regarding this area of church leaders, Selwyn Hughes in his "Every Day with Jesus" Notes makes the following comment: "Some believe that the ministry of apostles and prophets ceased a few decades after Pentecost. That is not my view. The first apostles were men who had seen the risen Lord and who had been commissioned by Him to preach the gospel, but the ministry of apostles and prophets has continued throughout the entire life of the Church.

An apostle is a person who goes ahead to pioneer and plant. A prophet brings the word of God and applies it to specific situations. An evangelist enlarges the Church both by presenting the gospel and by inspiring others to reach out to their non-Christian friends. A pastor shepherds and cares for the flock and a teacher instructs them. Christ has given the Church five "ministry gifts", as they are called, to equip believers for service and to help them become mature in the faith."

Note:
For a fuller account of Church Leadership please see Section E5 under the heading 'Biblical Definitions'.

Church Growth

There has been much heart searching over many years by sincere godly people wanting to see people saved – coming to a personal knowledge of Jesus Christ as Lord and Saviour, and to this end many schemes and strategies have been devised. Sadly, many of these efforts have produced less than encouraging results. However, one approach that stands out with God's blessing is biblical and simple, but costly in time, discipline and determination and this is demonstrated on the 'Transformation' video tapes. The tapes show how a few Christians, sold out to God, come together firstly to identify the particular 'forces' of the Evil One that are at work in their area and then pray against those 'forces' until there is a breakthrough. See Eph 6:10-13. To get to this point they pray and fast, and wait on God. Then, as attitudes change in openness they come into contact with these people, often one by one and have the joy of pointing them to Jesus Christ, and they willingly respond to Him, - the One who can meet every need.

The Christians continue to pray, and also follow up the new converts to teach and disciple them.

As God is sovereign we must remember that He 'added to their number', see Acts 2:47; 11:21; 1Cor 3:6-7.

The words, actions and lifestyle of the Lord Jesus Christ brought reaction/response – hostility or blessing, and using Him as the model, our words, actions and lifestyle should also produce a similar reaction/response.

With reference to the Scripture Neh 1:1-9 Terry Virgo has made the following observation:

"Until we have wept over the ruins we will never build the wall."

GOD'S PROVISION

- THE CHURCH -

Biblical Texts & Text References

The Church - Its Nature and Effect

13 Therefore, prepare your minds for action; be self-controlled; set your hope fully on the grace to be given you when Jesus Christ is revealed.
14 As obedient children, do not conform to the evil desires you had when you lived in ignorance.
15 But just as he who called you is holy, so be holy in all you do;
16 for it is written: "Be holy, because I am holy."

1Pet 1:13-16

Additional Scripture references

Isa 66:1-2, Jn 13:34-35; 17:20-21, Acts 2:42-43; 4:32-33; 7:47-50; 8:1-4; 12:5, Rom 1:7, 16;5; 1Cor 1:2; 6:19-20; 10:31-33, 2Cor 1:1; 8:1-5, Eph 1:22-23; 3:20-21; 4:1-3; 5:24-29, Col 3:1-4; 3:12-17, 1Thess 1:1-3; 2Thess 1:3-10; 2:13-15, 1Pet 2:9-10, 2Pet 1:3-9

The Church Body & the Giftings Given to it

In Acts 2:16-18 the N.T. writer records the words of the O.T. prophet Joel saying how God's Spirit would be poured out with various gifts in the future as referred to in Acts 1:8 below.

There are two principle lists of these Holy Spirit Gifts, one in Rom 12:4-8 and the other in 1Cor 12:4-11. These Gifts are given for the common good.

The Gifts are given by God, and those mentioned in Rom 12:4-8 are:

prophecy, serving, teaching, encouraging, contributing, leadership, and showing mercy.

In 1Cor 12:4-11 the Gifts mentioned are: wisdom, the message of knowledge, faith, healing, miraculous powers, distinguishing between spirits, to another speaking in different kinds of tongues, and to still another the interpretation of tongues.

8 But you will receive power when the Holy Spirit comes on you; and you will be my witnesses in Jerusalem, and in all Judea and Samaria, and to the ends of the earth."

Acts 1:8

The two scriptures given below explain the use and purpose of the gifts.

27 Now you are the body of Christ, and each one of you is a part of it.
28 And in the church God has appointed first of all apostles, second prophets, third teachers, then workers of miracles, also those having gifts of healing, those able to help others, those with gifts of administration, and those speaking in different kinds of tongues.
29 Are all apostles? Are all prophets? Are all teachers? Do all work miracles?
30 Do all have gifts of healing? Do all speak in tongues? Do all interpret?
31 But eagerly desire the greater gifts. And now I will show you the most excellent way.

1Cor 12:27-31

In Eph 4:11-13 it states that the purpose of apostles, prophets, evangelists, pastors and teachers is to prepare God's people for works of service, so that the body of Christ may be built up

Additional Scripture references
Mat 5:19-20, 28:18-19; Mk 1:22, Jn 3:2; 21:15-17, Acts 5:12-15; 5:38-6:1; 6:1-7; 20:27-31; 28:19, Rom 1:1; 15:18-20, 1Cor 12:1-14; 14:4-5; 14:23-33, Eph 5:23-26, Col 1:17-18; 3:12-17, 1Thess 5:11-24, 1Tim 5:17-18, 2Tim 2:24-25; Heb 12:5-6

Church Leadership

23 Paul and Barnabas appointed elders for them in each church and, with prayer and fasting, committed them to the Lord, in whom they had put their trust.

Acts 14:23

The qualities required for those who would be leaders are given in 1Tim 3:1-7 and can be summarised as someone who is: above reproach, the husband of but one wife, temperate, self-controlled, respectable, hospitable, able to teach, not given to drunkenness, not violent but gentle, not quarrelsome, not a lover of money. Someone who can manage his own family well and see that his children obey him with proper respect. He must not be a recent convert and must also have a good reputation with outsiders

Deacons are required to have similar moral and spiritual qualities – See 1Tim 3:8-13

Additional Scripture references

Acts 6:1-8; 14:14, Rom 16:1-2, Eph 4:11-13, Tit 1:5-9, 1Pet 5:1-11

The Growth and Maturity of the Christian

In Eph 4:13-16 it describes the characteristics that are looked for growth and maturity of the Christian as unity in the faith, and knowledge of the Son of God. These qualities will prevent them from being unsettled and unstable through hearing teaching that is unsound. Instead, speaking the truth in love, they will grow up more into the likeness of Christ.

Additional Scripture references

2Cor 9:6-11; Eph 3:16-20; Heb 5:13-14; 1Pet 2:1-3

The Numerical Growth of the Church

In the early days the church quickly – see Acts 2:46-47

6 I planted the seed, Apollos watered it, but God made it grow.
7 So neither he who plants nor he who waters is anything, but only God, who makes things grow.

1Cor 3:6-7

Additional Scripture references

Acts 11:19-21; 13:46-52, Rom 10:12-15; 15:18-20; Eph 6:10-13

D3

GOD'S PROVISION

- SALVATION --BELIEF, FORGIVENESS, HOPE, JOY, AND PEACE -

Biblical Definitions

Salvation - and its Benefits

A deep down desire in the heart of all people, surely, is to find peace and happiness in a turbulent uncertain world, and want to be assured that they can find the path to forgiveness for things they have done wrong against others, and God, if there is a God. They are also looking for acceptance and satisfying purpose in this life, and at the end, assurance that they will not be punished for their misdeeds in the afterlife, if there is an afterlife.

Well, all these quests are met in the best possible way when a person comes into the position of knowing God's salvation as explained underneath.

Let us begin by defining the word 'salvation', and the meaning given in the Oxford dictionary is: "deliverance from sin and its consequences and admission to heaven, brought about by Christ".

This describes a very satisfactory and secure state for the person who claims 'being saved', and has entered into the benefits that spring from it. The benefits that come from salvation are many, but the basic ones being addressed here are: belief, forgiveness, hope, joy and peace. Briefly, it means that a 'saved' person has resolved their questions of belief and forgiveness, and has discovered the source of true hope, joy and peace.

So, it can be said that such a person has:

established with proof, where their belief or trust is founded, - in the Lord Jesus Christ, the One who has made salvation possible;

found the relief of knowing that they are a forgiven sinner;

and is beginning to enjoy a hope, joy and peace that is not dependant on earthly wealth, good health or pleasant circumstances.

Salvation covers many beneficial aspects of our well-being as outlined above, and these are further explained below.

Many search for such benefits in every place but the right place, and that is, through knowing a personal salvation that comes from the God of the Bible.

The very offer of eternal salvation shows us our need to be saved and only God has the power and authority to save us - see Acts 4:12. This Scripture shows us that God alone, through the Lord Jesus Christ, is the only one who can give eternal salvation to a person.

The Bible shows us that we are in great need to be 'SAVED FROM' the consequences of just remaining in our natural and inherited state of sin – (Please see the passage below).

<u>Note:</u> The process of personal salvation is further described in Sections E2 and E4.

<u>Sin and Salvation</u>

When people fail to keep God's laws, ignore them, or just want to please themselves how they live, then they are showing a rebellious attitude towards God, their creator. This attitude is referred to as 'sin' in the Bible. Sin is defined as lawlessness in the Bible (1Jn 3:4), and refers to the failure of people to keep God's moral laws. The Scriptures further reveal that this failure to keep God's laws and prefer to live their lives to please themselves is due to an inborn weakness in all people, so all are guilty. Furthermore, God has always demanded a blood sacrifice to pay the penalty for the person's guilt.

In the times before Christ came the Hebrew people were required to sacrifice an unblemished lamb to cover their personal sin, but the good news is, that when the Lord Jesus Christ came He paid the ultimate blood sacrifice by dying on the cross, and He was the only One who was able to pay the penalty for sin for all mankind because He alone was sinless.

It follows from the above statement that for a person to know God's salvation there must be recognition and confession of their sin to God, coupled with a belief in and submission to God – this process of coming to know God's salvation is further explained under the heading of 'Belief', given below, and in Sections E2 and E4 of the book.

Lastly, the word 'sin' should not be confused with 'sins', which refers to acts, attitudes and thoughts that are abhorrent to God and are the result of a person's 'sin'.

Continuing the theme of salvation it can be said that coming into the experience of being 'SAVED FROM' will lead us into the situation of being 'SAVED TO'. Saved to live for God by fulfilling His will for our lives' (see Section E1), and to enable us to live this new life with new priorities He has made all sufficient provision, as given in the D Section of the book, but here we are only considering His provision of forgiveness, hope, joy and peace. For our response to God's offer of salvation see Section E2, and the passage headed 'Religion or Living Faith'.

Given below is an extract taken from the book "Expository Dictionary of Bible Words" by L.O. Richards.

"The NT concept. The core concept established in the OT is carried over into the NT. In fact, the Greek verb *sozo* ("to save") also implies rescue from some life-threatening danger.

In the NT, it is God or Jesus who acts to deliver believers from dangers that threaten not only their physical life but also their prospect of eternal life."

The writer also goes on to refer to three aspects of salvation that Jesus has won for believers, relating to the past, present and future. The past aspect is historical in that Jesus died for us and thus accomplished our salvation, - see 2Tim 1:9 & Tit 3:5. Secondly, in the present, it is also true that Jesus is saving us. We are being saved through Jesus' life, - see Rom 5:10 & Rom

6. Finally, it is true that we will be saved, and the certainty of this future is beautifully expressed in Rom 8:18-39, 1Cor 15:12-58 & 1Pet 1:8-9.

Belief

To receive salvation it is essential that the person must believe, have complete faith in, what the Bible says concerning a desperate need of forgiveness for their sin, also they must fully believe in the Lord Jesus Christ as God's Son and accept that through His death to pay the penalty for their sin He is the only one who can forgive and grant eternal salvation - see Jn 3:16-18, Acts 16:29-34 & Rom 3:21-24. When a person has received God's salvation a new spiritual life has begun, and character changes begin to take place. Their priorities and aims in life begin to change. All these changes provide proof that the process of salvation has started and also the benefits of salvation begin to be realised like; forgiveness, hope, joy, peace and purpose etc.

Forgiveness

As L.O. Richards in his book: "Expository Dictionary of Bible Words" states; "The NT relates forgiveness to Jesus, specifically to his sacrificial death. The basis on which God can forgive sin and remain righteous has been provided by Jesus' sacrifice of Himself as atonement, in that ultimate sacrifice to which OT offerings merely pointed. As Hebrews puts it, "By one sacrifice he has made perfect forever those who are being made holy" (10:14)."

John Gill in his book: "A Body of Doctrinal Divinity" has much to say about this subject, and some of the factors concerning forgiveness that we can receive from God are listed below:

In the OT David refers to forgiveness he had received in Ps 103:3, and Daniel reminded God that He was a merciful and forgiving God in Dan 9:9.

In Ps 32:1 David refers to this subject again when he says: "Blessed is he whose transgressions are forgiven, whose sins are covered." 'Forgiven' meaning "lifted up," taken off from him, and carried away. And 'covered' relates to the fact that our sin is impure and needs to be covered from the all seeing eyes of God, and this is now effectively done through the blood of Christ.

In the NT the disciples of Jesus were commissioned to preach forgiveness in His name - Lk 24:47.

A full and free pardon of sin is a blessing provided and promised in the covenant of grace - Heb 8:10-12.

In Col 2:13-15 it likens our sins to debts which God has cancelled out for the person who comes to Him in repentance and faith, because they are totally unable to pay.

It is also good to know that our sins are pardoned with respect to quality and quantity, and for our part we are required to confess our sins, renouncing and regretting our former rebellion against God through going our own way - 1Jn 1:8-10.

Pardon of sin cannot be obtained by works of any kind because it is only received by grace, the unmerited favour, of God - Eph 2:8-10.

Hope

W.E. Vine defines 'Hope' in the N.T. as a "favourable and confident expectation. It has to do with the unseen and the future, Rom 8:24-25. Hope describes (a) the happy anticipation of good (the most frequent significance), e.g. Tit 1:2; 1Pet 1:21; (b) the ground upon which hope is based, Acts 16:19; Col 1:27, "Christ in you the hope of glory;" (c) the object upon which the hope is fixed, e.g. 1Tim 1:1."

Each true believer has the sure hope of resurrection - see Acts 23:6; 24:14-15; 1Thess 4:13-14. Also in Rom 5:1-5 we see that 'hope' has links with many other characteristics.

The biblical word 'Hope' in the context it is used has no element of uncertainty in it, as used typically in Rom 8:24-25.

Joy

An extract from The Online Bible Foundations' Biblical definition concerning Spiritual Joy is that "Joy is a fruit of the Spirit, which follows love; "The fruit of the Spirit is love, joy . . . .", Gal 5:22 it attends faith and hope; and as these graces are in exercise, and increase, so does spiritual joy; hence we read of "the joy of faith", and "the rejoicing of hope", Phil

1:25 Heb 3:6 it enters very much into the Christian's character and experience, and is peculiar (special) to saints and believers in Christ."

The definition continues with the following:

That the object of joy is God Himself - Ps 43:4, Isa 61:10, Hab 3:17-18.

Also we find joy in the attributes of God and receive benefit and advantage not only from his power, wisdom, truth, faithfulness, goodness, grace and mercy, but even in his justice and holiness - Ps 97:12, Isa 9:7.

In addition, the everlasting love of God is a matter of joy to believers - Ps 30:4-5, Ps 103:17, Jer 31:3. True believers are also told it is a matter of joy, that, "their names are written in heaven" - Lk 10:20.

Peace

John Gill states: "Next to Love and Joy, in order, stands Peace - Gal 5:22. "Love" and "peace", are sometimes mentioned together, 2Tim 2:22 and where the one is there is the other; especially if joy is in company with love, peace must be an attendant."

He also defines this peace not as an external peace; which may be enjoyed when people are free from wars, persecution, troubles and can be experiencing prosperity and happiness. But it is an internal, spiritual peace of soul, which is to be inquired into; which is an ease of mind from distress through sin and a sense of wrath.

This peace is "from God our Father and from the Lord Jesus Christ" - 1Cor 1:3, Eph 1:2, Phil 1:2, Col 1:2,---and many other references.

All people need peace with God, and this is made available to all true believers through Jesus Christ - Rom 5:1 states; "we have peace with God through our Lord Jesus Christ."

GOD'S PROVISION

- SALVATION --BELIEF, FORGIVENESS, HOPE, JOY, PEACE -

Notes and Quotations

Salvation

Selwyn Hughes in his "Every Day with Jesus" Notes, has said "Salvation is the offer of divine forgiveness of our sin and the gift of eternal life; conversion is the way we enter into that experience and receive the gift. The word "conversion" means to turn about or change one's direction. Though other religions talk about spiritual conversion, the experience they speak of bears no relation whatsoever to the thought in the mind of Jesus when he said: "Except ye be converted.....ye shall not enter into the kingdom of heaven" (Mat 18:3, AV)."

Selwyn Hughes goes on to say: "Conversion can be explained like this: it is the change, gradual or sudden, by which one passes from the kingdom of self to the kingdom of God. And if there is no change there is no conversion."

The Bible states very clearly that people cannot be saved *by* good works, but are saved *for* good works, see Eph 2:8-10, Jas 2:14-17.

Conversion: Someone has stated that conversion affects us in three stages:

1 - The emotions,
2 - The intellect,
3 - The will (a full commitment).

The process 1 to 3 may be a slow or fast progression to reach a commitment, but having arrived at this point salvation is immediate - Mat 13:23, Acts 8:26-39, Acts 16:27-33.

In Jn 3:3 Jesus declared "I tell you the truth, unless a man is born again, he cannot see the kingdom of God."

Someone has referred to the character of the new birth in the following way:

New Birth is not - Reformation of the outward man
- Education of the natural man
- Purification of the old man
But it is - *Creation* of the new man.

God offers people 'Complete' salvation, requiring nothing to be 'added' by us, because He is a 'Perfect' saviour - Heb 7:23-28.

Selwyn Hughes in his "Every Day with Jesus" Notes, when referring to Col 1:12-14 reminds the Colossians (and us) that "they had been 'rescued' .... from the dominion of darkness and brought ... into the kingdom of the Son he loves." We must never forget that salvation is a rescue mission -- a deliverance. We don't climb out of the darkness; we are delivered from it."

Selwyn Hughes also provides the following statement made by someone (unknown) who has a deep insight into human nature: "Men and women need two things .... light on the mystery of life and power for the mastery of life."

He comments: "In Jesus these two needs are met. He gives light on the mystery of life through the things He said, and He gives power for the mastery of life by saving us from our sins and from sinning."

Christianity is not a pain killer – our wounds and hurts must be brought into His light to be cleansed and healed. The connection between mental stress, emotional illness, demonic influence and sinful disobedience can be complex and needs the wise discernment of God's Holy Spirit. King Saul had a mixture of the above problems (1Sam 13-18). Author unknown.

See also Isa 53:4-5 which was fulfilled in Mat 8:16-17.

There are many passages of Scripture that refer to the way a person can be eternally saved and the following texts outline the basic conditions that apply:

You must call on the name of the Lord Jesus Christ – Acts 2:21.

You must repent (turn from the basic rebellion you have against God's rule in your life) and so receive His forgiveness – Acts 2:38.

Acknowledge that there is no other Name, or way, through which you can be saved – Acts 4:12.

Believe, and rely utterly, on the Lord Jesus Christ for your salvation – Acts 16:30-31.

Thank Him for dying to procure your salvation – Jn 3:16-18; Rom 5:8; 1Thess 5:10.

When we trust only in Jesus Christ for our salvation, then we are seen as being "in Christ", for it says in (Rom 8:1) "there is now no condemnation for those who are in Christ Jesus," and as Bob Gass points out in his "The Word for Today" Notes: "you are made righteous before God." And he refers to (Rom 5:19) and explains: "That the word "made" means "*a permanent condition of being.*""

Forgiveness

Philip Yancey in his book "What's so Amazing about Grace?" states: "Forgiveness is an act of faith. By forgiving another, I am trusting that God is a better justice-maker than I am. By forgiving, I release my own right to get even and leave all issues of fairness for God to work out. I leave in God's hands the scales that must balance justice and mercy."

Bob Gass in his "The Word for Today" Notes states: "If you take 'the blood' out of your church, 'the body' becomes a corpse. If you take it out of your Bible, it's reduced to a book of good advice – not good news. If you take it out of your preaching, you have no power to forgive sin and remove guilt. Listen: "without the shedding of blood there is no forgiveness" (Heb 9:22)."

Hope

"The word *hope* in scripture means a sure and certain expectation with no shadow of doubt, no trace of dubiety. 'Christ in you the hope of glory' - Col 1:26-27." By Selwyn Hughes.

"The concept of hope was something the ancients repudiated. They regarded it as dubious and uncertain. But Christian hope is as certain (if not more certain) as tomorrow's dawn.

Note too that hope is not a consequence of faith and love but its origin. Faith and love *spring* from hope. When we hold before us the sure and certain hope of our accommodation in heaven then out of that hope spring faith and love. They don't just saunter into our lives -- they *spring!"*

By Selwyn Hughes from his "Every Day with Jesus" Notes.

Joy

In the "The Word for Today" Notes by Bob Gass there is a quotation by Sherman Owens where he states: "Happiness is of the mind, but joy is of the spirit. Happiness has to do with your circumstances, but joy is to do with your outlook.

10 Nehemiah said, "Go and enjoy choice food and sweet drinks, and send some to those who have nothing prepared. This day is sacred to our Lord. Do not grieve, for the joy of the LORD is your strength."

Neh 8:10

"Joy is a deep sense of exhilaration and confidence in God even in times of suffering."

Author unknown

Christians are exalted in Phil 4:4 to: "Rejoice in the Lord always." – all the time and in all circumstances, and in Neh 8:10 it states: "Do not grieve, for the joy of the LORD is your strength."

Peace

In the OT this word is *shalom* (Heb), and in the NT is *eirene* (Gk). Someone has stated that this word does not mean 'absence of strife' or 'tranquillity of mind' but rather wholeness, health and completeness.

This peace is shown by a calmness of spirit resting on God's character and promises, through tough and smooth times. It can be realised only by God's grace as a gift, Ps 29:11, Jn 14:27, Gal 5:22, 2Thess 3:16. It involves right relationships with God and man. Peace is through Jesus Christ - Acts 10:36.

God works with us to bring about His 'shalom' - the harmony and wholeness of a person with God.

Another person has defined peace as the ability to trust in the wisdom, sovereignty and protective care of God in all circumstances.

Selwyn Hughes in his "Every Day with Jesus" Notes states with reference to Phil 4:1-13 and especially verse 7 below:

7 And the peace of God, which transcends all understanding, will guard your hearts and your minds in Christ Jesus.

"You cannot have peace of mind until you have something deeper than peace of mind. When you have peace at the depths of your spirit then peace of mind is an outcome of that deeper peace. In other words, you cannot experience the peace *of* God until you have experienced peace *with* God."

GOD'S PROVISION

- SALVATION --BELIEF, FORGIVENESS, HOPE, JOY, PEACE -

Biblical Texts & Text References

Salvation

In Acts 4:12 it states that salvation is only found through Christ. There is no other way to be eternally saved.

16 "For God so loved the world that he gave his one and only Son, that whoever believes in him shall not perish but have eternal life.

Jn 3:16

35 The Father loves the Son and has placed everything in his hands.
36 Whoever believes in the Son has eternal life, but whoever rejects the Son will not see life, for God's wrath remains on him."

Jn 3:35-36

Additional Scripture references

Deut 4:34-35, Ps 23:1-6; 40:1-4; 103:2-5; 111:9-10; 147:10-11, Isa 1:18-20, Ezek 18:23; 33:11, Mat 4:4; 13:23; 19:24-26, Mk 8:34-38, Jn 1:10-12; 5:24; 8:23-24; 10:9-11; 12:44-46; 14:6-7; 20:27-31, Acts 2:36-38; 4:12; 16:29-33, Rom 3:20-24; 5;10-11 & 19; 10:8-11, 1Cor 1:17-21; 15:1-2, 2Cor 5:17-19; 6:1-2; 8:9, Gal 3:10-14, Eph 1:7-8; 2:4-10, Col 1:12-14, 2Thess 2:9-10, 1Tim 2:3-6, 2Tim 1:8-9, Tit 3:3-7, Heb 2:1-3; 7:25; Jas 2:14-17, 1Pet 1:8-9; 2:24-25; 3:18, 1Jn 4:14-15

Belief

Jesus is speaking:

23 But he continued, "You are from below; I am from above. You are of this world; I am not of this world.
24 I told you that you would die in your sins; if you do not believe that I am *the one I claim to be,* you will indeed die in your sins."

Jn 8:23-24

In Rom 3:21-24 it says that whilst we have all sinned we can be accepted by God as being righteous through having faith in Jesus Christ and so are redeemed.

Additional Scripture references

Mk 1:14-15, Jn 3:16-18; 12:44-46; 14:10-11, Acts 16:30-33; Rom 4:2-3; 4:23-25, 1Cor 1:19-21, Gal 3:6-8, 1Thess 4:14-16, 1Pet 1:21-23; 2:6-8

Forgiveness

If people confess their sins to the Lord he is faithful and just and will forgive us our sins and purify us from all unrighteousness. See 1Jn 1:8-10

46 He told them, "This is what is written: The Christ will suffer and rise from the dead on the third day,
47 and repentance and forgiveness of sins will be preached in his name to all nations, beginning at Jerusalem.

Lk 24:46-47

Additional Scripture references

Ps 103:2-4; Lk 15:16-24, Acts 10:42-43; 13:37-39, Rom 2:4-5; Eph 2:8-10, Col 1:12-14, 2:13-15; Heb 8:10-12; 9:13-14 & 22; 10:16-18, 1Jn 4:9-10

Hope

22 Not only so, but we ourselves, who have the firstfruits of the Spirit, groan inwardly as we wait eagerly for our adoption as sons, the redemption of our bodies.
24 For in this hope we were saved. But hope that is seen is no hope at all. Who hopes for what he already has?
25 But if we hope for what we do not yet have, we wait for it patiently.

Rom 8:23-25

Additional Scripture references

Ps 27:13-14; 73:24-26, Lam 3:21-25, Prov 13:14; 14:27, Jer 29:10-11, Acts 23:6; 24:14-15, Rom 5:1-5; 15:4 & 13, 2Cor 4:16-18, Gal 5:5-6, Eph 1:18-19, Col 1:22-23; 1:25-27, 1Thess 4:13-14; 1Tim 1:1; Heb 7:23-26; 10:23, 1Pet 1:3-5; 1:21; 3:14-15, 1Jn 3:1-3

Joy

20 However, do not rejoice that the spirits submit to you, but rejoice that your names are written in heaven."

21 At that time Jesus, full of joy through the Holy Spirit, said, "I praise you, Father, Lord of heaven and earth, because you have hidden these things from the wise and learned, and revealed them to little children. Yes, Father, for this was your good pleasure.

Lk 10:20-21

Additional Scripture references

Ps 30:4-5; 33:1-3; 43:3-4; 97:11-12; 118:22-24, Isa 9:7, 61 10-11; Hab 3:17-18, Lk 15:8-10, Jn 15:10-11; 17:13; Gal 5:22-23; Phil 1:25-26

Peace

1 Therefore, since we have been justified through faith, we have peace with God through our Lord Jesus Christ,

2 through whom we have gained access by faith into this grace in which we now stand. And we rejoice in the hope of the glory of God.

Rom 5:1-2

Additional Scripture references

Ps 29:10-11; 119:165, Isa 9:6; 26:3-4; 32:16-17; 48:17-18; 52:7; 57:18-21, Lk 1:76-79; 2:13-14, Jn 14:27; 16:32-33, Acts 10:34-36; Rom 14:16-18, 1Cor 1:3, Gal 5:22-23; Eph 1:2; 2:13-17, Phil 4:6-7, Col 3:13-15, 2Thess 3:16, 2 Tim 2:22, Heb 13:20-21

D4

GOD'S PROVISION

- TEACHING and GUIDANCE -

Biblical Definitions

The Importance of Teaching and Guidance

As an introduction to this subject matter it is worth considering the words and application of what we hear with the following statement in mind, that:

Knowledge is what we know, and
Wisdom is the right application of what we know.

If anyone is going to learn about any subject, they must be prepared to admit, if only to themselves, that they are lacking in knowledge in that subject and have a desire to know about it. Hence, having the right attitude is most important, and someone has addressed this attitude by the following statements:

"If you are not teachable you're not reachable"
and "learning requires submission"

Please see the Scriptures below, and also Prov 19:20.

15 The way of a fool seems right to him, but a wise man listens to advice.
Prov 12:15

18 He who ignores discipline comes to poverty and shame, but whoever heeds correction is honoured.
Prov 13:18

Some people want to learn whilst others are happy to live in a less structured, more relaxed fashion, and perhaps are less academic and more practical in their outlook on life. But whatever outlook, ability and background a person has in life, it is important to realise that there are a minimum number of things they should know about life, and consider.

The essential things everyone should know about concern the guidelines that determine the direction their lives take, and the destiny they could lead to.

These guidelines may be followed almost unknowingly from our families and those around us, or can be adopted willingly, or not so willingly, from family members or others. The guidelines are usually in the form of a lifestyle that evolves through circumstances and ambitions, or a lifestyle that results from following a Faith. Whatever type of lifestyle is adopted, will have a bearing on the person's character and their destiny.

Hence, it is very important that a person receives the type of 'teaching' and 'guidance' that leads to a fulfilled life, having an assured hope and prospect that leads to eternal life with God. All this, and much more is offered through the Christian teaching and guidance given in this Section.

Teaching - Also see Section E4

In Acts 1:1 the writer refers to "all that Jesus began to do and to teach until the day he was taken up to heaven, after giving instructions through the Holy Spirit to the apostles he had chosen." From this Scripture it is interesting to note that the *DO* comes before the *TEACH,*

and this was true of so much of Jesus' lifestyle that his actions preceded so much of his teaching and were also an integral part of it. For example, soon after Jesus had called his disciples he started his ministry with action by going to a wedding and changing their water into wine - Jn 2:1-11, and v11 gives the purpose for this action: "He thus revealed his glory, and his disciples put their faith in him."

In many Scriptures we see the coupling of actions and teaching, as in Mat 4:23 we read that he was "teaching in their synagogues, preaching the good news of the kingdom, *and* healing every disease and sickness among the people." He then proceeds to give 'The Sermon on the Mount' Mat 5-7. Another instance of this combined approach is given in Lk 5:17-26.

In Mk 11:15-17 we see Jesus driving out those who were buying and selling in the temple, closely followed by teaching.

The action of Jesus in prayer caused the disciples to say, "Lord teach us to pray," and he then gave them 'The Lord's Prayer' - Lk 11:1-4.

A unique feature of Jesus' teaching, which is mentioned in a number of Scriptures, is that: "He taught as one who had authority" - Mat 7:29, Mk 1:22, Lk 4:22, Jn 2:18-22, Jn 10:17-18. He used this authority when He warned people against teaching for doctrine the rules of men - Mat 15:9, Mk 7:7.

It is apparent through His ministry that Jesus taught with compassion, and showed that He cared about people, and that His strongest words of rebuke were mostly reserved for religious leaders because of their pride, self-righteousness and hypocrisy.

Methods of Teaching used by Jesus – See also Section E4

He taught through his actions and lifestyle, and also through direct speech and parables. The direct or straight teaching was given to his disciples and this was well illustrated with common objects and life situations, see Mat 5-7. He also related his teaching to the common sayings and thinking of the day with words such as "You have heard that it was said, 'Do not commit adultery,' but I tell you --------"

See Mat 5:27-28

Parables

The Universal Bible Dictionary edited by A.R. Buckland states: "A parable is a narrative, imagined or true, told for the purpose of imparting a truth. It differs from the proverb in that the picture presented is not so concentrated, but contains more detail, and so requires less mental effort to its understanding."

Jesus taught the people by using parables, and when the disciples asked him why he did this, he replied, "The knowledge of the secrets of the kingdom of heaven has been given to you, but not to them." - Mat 13:10-11. In a number of passages of Scripture Jesus states that he speaks to the people in parables, but he will explain them to the disciples, see Mat 13:16-18, Mk 3:23, Mk 4:10-13, Mk 4:33-34, Lk 8:9-11.

In Hosea 12:10 God says, "I spoke to the prophets, gave them many visions and told parables through them." - 2Sam 12:1-7, Isa 5:1-7.

There are many parables told in the Gospels, but most are found in the Books of Matthew and Luke, well known ones being:

The Sower - Mat 13:3-23, Mk 4:3-20, Lk 8:4-15.
The Unforgiving Servant - Mat 18:23-35.
The Good Samaritan - Lk 10:25-37.
The Prodigal Son - Lk 15:11-32.
The Vine - Jn 15:1-8.

Jamie Buckingham in his book "Parables" refers to parables as "stories with spiritual meaning." He relates how Jesus "used earthly things to convey spiritual truth." While speaking Jesus would no doubt point to a shepherd, or to a person planting seeds. Jesus used stories from real-life situations, many of them tough situations.

He further states concerning parables that "They were designed not only to be remembered, but to stimulate His listeners to think. Many of His stories closed with a question rather than an answer."

Guidance

The concept of God guiding and leading his people is a very important issue in the lives of believers and the Bible provides us with many stories and statements of the ways that God guides, both in the O.T. and the N.T. From these stories and statements many scriptural truths and principles can be extracted.

Guidance and leading from God is received in a number of ways including:

(1) Through prayerfully knocking 'on doors'.
(2) Through miracles, and words of knowledge.
(3) Through prayer and waiting on God.
(4) Through reading the Bible, and being convinced that God, by

His Holy Spirit, has spoken to you by highlighting a passage of Scripture for you to accept and act on.

Guidance Through Miracles

Many miraculous interventions by God have occurred in the past as recorded in the O.T. and the N.T. and still occur in the present day. A few examples from the Bible are listed below:

The Flood-see-Gen 6-8, Mat 24:37-39.
Moses spoken to through the burning bush -see--Ex 3
The deliverance of the Hebrews from slavery in Egypt - through plagues, -see--Ex 6-12.
God tells Elijah there will be no rain until He says so, and feeds Elijah by ravens ---see 1Kg 17-18.
The healing of Hezekiah -see--2Kg 20:1-11
The handwriting on the wall in Belshazzar's palace --see-Dan 5
The swallowing of Jonah by a fish --see-Jon 1:17-2:10
The many miracles recorded in the O.T. by Joseph, Moses, Joshua, Samson, Elijah, Elisha, Daniel, etc.
The birth of a son to Elizabeth who was barren --see-Lk 1:5-16, 57
The Virgin birth of Jesus Christ --see-Lk 1:26-38
The star that guided the wise men to the infant Jesus --see-Mat 2:1-12
The transfiguration of Jesus --see-Lk 9:28-36
The numerous miracles performed by Jesus and recorded in the four Gospels.
The lame man for thirty eight years healed by Jesus -see-Jn 5:5-9
The paralysed man healed and the teachers of the law had their thoughts read by Jesus--see-Mk 2:3-12
The Resurrection of Jesus --see-Lk 24, Jn 20
The Ascension of Jesus --see-Lk 24:50-52, Acts 1:4-11
The Holy Spirit comes at Pentecost --see-Acts 2:1-4
The judgement of Ananias and Sapphira -see Acts 5:1-11
The blinding of Saul --see-Acts 9:3-9
The freeing of Paul and Silus from prison --see-Acts 16:19-40
The healing miracles performed by Peter and Paul recorded in Acts.
The cripple from birth healed through Peter -see-Acts 3:1-8
The vision given to Peter causes him to go to the Gentiles -see-Acts 10:9-35

GOD'S PROVISION

- TEACHING and GUIDANCE -

Notes and Quotations

Teaching and Guidance

There are many Scriptures that relate to God teaching and guiding his people, and a few of these are given below with notes.

In Psalm 23 below one can see how David was secure in the Lord's leading, and notice the personal references: I shall; he leads me; he restores my; he guides me; you are with me; I will dwell, etc.

1 *A psalm of David.* The LORD is my shepherd, I shall not be in want.
2 He makes me lie down in green pastures, he leads me beside quiet waters,
3 he restores my soul. He guides me in paths of righteousness for his name's sake.
4 Even though I walk through the valley of the shadow of death, I will fear no evil, for you are with me; your rod and your staff, they comfort me.
5 You prepare a table before me in the presence of my enemies. You anoint my head with oil; my cup overflows.
6 Surely goodness and love will follow me all the days of my life, and I will dwell in the house of the LORD for ever.

In the Mark 7:6-8 Jesus gave a clear warning for people not to teach for doctrine the rules or traditions of men.

The person of the Holy Spirit has a key role in guiding God's people. Being led by God's Holy Spirit implies commitment and obedience, and given below are Scriptures which show things revealed and people led by Him:

In Mat 4:1 Jesus was led by the Spirit into the desert.

In Lk 2:25-26 it speaks about a devout man named Simeon who had it revealed to him by the Holy Spirit that he would not die before he had seen the Lord's Christ.

It is helpful to note the conditions under which a 'voice' of guidance was given in the Scripture stated below:

2 While they were worshipping the Lord and fasting, the Holy Spirit said, "Set apart for me Barnabas and Saul for the work to which I have called them."
3 So after they had fasted and prayed, they placed their hands on them and sent them off.
4 The two of them, sent on their way by the Holy Spirit, went down to Seleucia

Acts 13:2-4

In 2Pet 1:21 it states that:" prophecy never had its origin in the will of man, but men spoke from God as they were carried along by the Holy Spirit."

Teaching

What we are privileged to teach is 'The Truth' - absolute Truth, and in Jn 8:31-32 it says "The Truth will make you free," free From - the dominion and power of sin (Rom 6:17-18), error, deceit and condemnation (Rom 8), and free To - live for God (Eph 2:1-5).

'If you are not TEACHABLE, you're not REACHABLE.' Someone has said, because learning requires submission. See Prov 12:15 & 19:20

Guidance

We know that God is sovereign and can do what he likes, when he likes, but he still asks Christians to exercise faith, follow the lead of his Holy Spirit and thus provide Him with further opportunities to show Himself as the only God of mercy, love, grace and power. If faith is not exercised and the Holy Spirit is not listened to or obeyed, then all that people outside the Faith see is ceremonies, words and actions that are not empowered by God, and therefore, will achieve little or nothing that He intended.

Bob Gass in his 'The Word for Today' Notes has said regarding guidance and leading of the Holy Spirit: "If you can get 'there' without God - He didn't lead you."

On another occasion he told the following story: "A captain of the Queen Mary has said "It takes about one mile to stop the ship. - A good captain thinks at least a mile ahead." - Our Lord Jesus Christ has thought eternity ahead for us.

On a further occasion he set out some guidelines for hearing 'His voice': "

1. *Have a regular prayer time.* Jesus said, "My sheep listen to my voice . . . . and they follow Me" (Jn 10:27). Spend time with the Shepherd and you'll get to know His voice.

2. *Be careful what you hear.* Get rid of the 'filters' of doubt and unbelief that you listen through. Create a faith-filled atmosphere that's conducive to hearing from God.

3. *Want His will more than your own.* That means crucifying your carnal desires day by day.

4. *Know that God leads step-by-step, not mile-by-mile.* He won't show you the entire plan, just the next phase.

5. *Develop an attitude of gratitude.* Grumblers die in the wilderness; only the thankful enter and enjoy God's blessings.

6. *Don't move until you have a sense of peace.* Listen, "Let the peace of God rule in your hearts . . . (Col 3:15). Allow God's peace to rule what's <u>in</u> – and what's <u>out.</u> Today you can be led by God's Spirit."

Selwyn Hughes on the subject of guidance has said: "Let our actions be guided by first considering, 'what would Jesus do' (WWJD) in these circumstances.

Alex Buchanan has said with reference to Ex 13:21-22, "Move on with the Cloud. For us the 'Cloud' is His presence. When He moves, we move - God is not static." Also, "When we walk with God we will never be bored or redundant." - Mk 8:34-38.

George Muller said: "God not only orders our steps; He orders our stops." Steps - Mk 6:7-13. Stops - Mk 6:30-32.

The Scripture referred to here concerns Joseph who had been sold as a slave into Egypt by his brothers and later slandered by his employer's wife, and for this he was put in a dungeon for a few years. But in all this time God was with him and he was then raised to high office, and a famine brought his brothers to Egypt and he does not treat them with vengeance but says: "You intended to harm me, but God intended it for good ......"

20 You intended to harm me, but God intended it for good to accomplish what is now being done, the saving of many lives.

Gen 50:20

It is not uncommon for things to happen in our lives which we wish had not occurred and we didn't understand, yet later realise were for our good and our maturity as Christians. When these things occur we must learn to be patient and trust God.

In the jungle the guide says: "There is no path, I am the path, follow me." – See the Scriptures below, and note the promises God (the Guide for life), makes to His followers:

13 I will lead the blind by ways they have not known, along unfamiliar paths I will guide them; I will turn the darkness into light before them and make the rough places smooth. These are the things I will do; I will not forsake them.

Isa 42:16

Jesus said ;" The watchman opens the gate for him, and the sheep listen to his voice. He calls his own sheep by name and leads them out". See Jn 10:3-4

In Jn 14:6 Jesus says:" I am the way and the truth and the life. No-one comes to the Father except through me." This statement makes the claim that he is, the Way to God, the Truth about God and the Life of God.

The following extract has been taken from 'The Word for Today' Notes by Bob Gass regarding guidance:

"God guides us by closing one door then opening another. Abraham didn't know where he was going, but he knew he couldn't stay where he was; and that's enough to create movement in the right direction. Knowing you can't stay where you are is often the starting point of God's guidance. - - - - - - - When a season is over, you sense it's time to move!"

He also refers to the guidance that was given to Paul (Acts 16:7-10) in terms of where he was not to go, and then, where he should go. Noting that he didn't ask why, but just obeyed.

Paul in the Bible speaking about the time when he was shipwrecked (Acts 27:9-44) is referred to by Bob Gass in his 'The Word for Today' Notes when he says: "The idea that circumstances will always line up favourably with God's guidance is not scriptural. Sometimes God leads you through the wilderness. And He'll never lead you anywhere that doesn't require His provision and protection. If you can get there without God He didn't send you. So if you want to avoid shipwreck ask God to show you the right way, which is His way!"

Vision

Helen Keller, the first deaf blind person to earn a Bachelor of Arts degree said many notable things during her life, and concerning vision stated: "One thing worse than being blind is having sight but no vision".

Christians need to have spiritual insight/discernment – so what good thing do we feel passionate about? and what is our heart's desire? see 1Cor 9:16, Ps 20:4; 145:19, Rom 10:1.

When Christians have a vision or dream of achieving something for God they often want to see the resources in place before they make a start, but, if the vision is of God, then He usually wants them to move by faith and then the resources will be provided.

Guidance and Maturity

At times God allows his people to go through difficulties and pain, and this is not because he enjoys doing so, but because he wants them to attain more of the characteristics of Jesus.

Someone has made the following observations:

"It's not a sin to hurt - growing up in Christ will hurt. It hurts to mature in Christ. Flight from pain is flight from reality."

"Metal is heated so that it can be shaped - into His likeness."
See Heb 12:3-11

His revealed Will for us is that we conformed to His likeness - see Rom 8:29 - "For those God foreknew he also predestined to be conformed to the likeness of his Son, that he might be the firstborn among many brothers." Someone has interpreted this as: 'His determined ruthless love to change and shape us into His Likeness whatever it costs – through trials of faith, difficulties, disappointments, seeming failures, mistakes and encouragements because His perspective is eternal.

He is more concerned with who we *become* in God (e.g. with the godly character that is developed in us), than what we can *do* for Him. His mind is set on transforming us into His *likeness* - see Rom 8:14-17, 12:1-2, 2Cor 5:17. God often achieves this *likeness* with a sharp chisel and a mallet - see 2Cor 4:8-11.

His love will not allow Him to deviate from His intention. God loves us as we are, but loves us too much to leave us as we are.'

In Rom 12:6 it states: "We have different gifts, according to the grace given us. . . . . ." This statement shows us that we are given different gifts, but we must bear in mind that we all have different personalities and live in different circumstances and hence, should each endeavour to understand and fulfil God's will for the life He has given us.

Through problems and difficulties we have an opportunity of getting to know God better by learning to be more dependent on Him - See 2Cor 12:7-10.

In Deut 8:1-7 it states that God led the Israelites forty years in the wilderness to humble them. This was His purpose, so that they live pleasing to God and be a people that he could use more.

Bob Gass in his 'The Word for Today' Notes has stated that the way to the Promised Land is through the wilderness .

A place where He gets our attention;

- learn to be dependent on Him,
- stripped of self-sufficiency,
- humble ourselves,

and provides us with a positive satisfying aim in life, and provides the ability to fulfil it.

He is not punishing us - no, He is allowing some things in you to die so that other qualities can be born and grow and be fruitful. There is no other way to the Promised Land.

Part of God's provision to guide us is knowledge and wisdom: where 'knowledge' includes the knowledge of Him and His Word,
so *Knowledge* is what we know, and
Wisdom is the right application of what we know.

Someone has said concerning the Book of Proverbs that: "The purpose of the Book is to put godliness into working clothes, as it addresses our lifestyle in home, business and society.

Proverbs provide practical wisdom for all aspects of life, including for making decisions - Mat 7:24-27.

GOD'S PROVISION

- TEACHING and GUIDANCE -

Biblical Texts & Text References

Teaching

7 They worship me in vain; their teachings are but rules taught by men.'

Mk 7:7

The following Scripture is commonly referred to as 'The Lord's Prayer'.

1 One day Jesus was praying in a certain place. When he finished, one of his disciples said to him, "Lord, teach us to pray, just as John taught his disciples."
2 He said to them, "When you pray, say: "'Father, hallowed be your name, your kingdom come.
3 Give us each day our daily bread.
4 Forgive us our sins, for we also forgive everyone who sins against us. And lead us not into temptation.'"

Lk 11:1-4

Additional Scripture references

Deut 4:5, Isa 40:13-14; 50:4; 54:13, Mat 5-7 & 27-28; 7:28-29; 15:9, Mk 1:21-22; 10:1, 11:17; Lk 4:22; 5:17-26, Jn 2:1-11; 10:17-18; 18:19-20, Acts 1:1, 1Cor 2:12-13, Gal 1:11-12, 1Thess 4:7-9, 2Tim 2:1-2

Parables

10 The disciples came to him and asked, "Why do you speak to the people in parables?"
11 He replied, "The knowledge of the secrets of the kingdom of heaven has been given to you, but not to them.

16 But blessed are your eyes because they see, and your ears because they hear.
17 For I tell you the truth, many prophets and righteous men longed to see what you see but did not see it, and to hear what you hear but did not hear it.
18 "Listen then to what the parable of the sower means:

Mat 13:10-11 & 16-18

Now see Mk 4:10-13 & Jn 15:1-8

Additional Scripture references

2Sam 12:1-7, Isa 5:1-7, Hos 12:10, Mat 13:3-23; 18:23-35, Lk 8:9-11; 10:25-37; 15:11-32

Guidance

105 Your word is a lamp to my feet and a light for my path.

Ps 119:105

27 My sheep listen to my voice; I know them, and they follow me.

Jn 10:27

In Jn 14:5-6 one of the disciples said to Jesus:" Lord, we don't know where you are going, so how can we know the way?" Jesus answered, "I am the way and the truth and the life."

Additional Scripture references

Gen 24:26-27, Ex 13:17-18 & 21-22, Deut 8:1-3 ; 29:5-6; 31:6, 2Chron 31:20-21; 32:7-8, Ezra 8:21-23, Job 22:21-30, Ps 1:1-3 ; 23:1-6; 25:8-10; 27:10-14 ; 32:6-8; 73:23-24; 78:13-14; 107:6-8; 119:98-99, Prov 3:5-10; 14:12; 16:1-3; 19:1-3; 25:11-12, Isa 40:10-11; 42:16-17; 58:9-11, Amos 3:7, Mat 4:4; Mk 6:7-13; 6:30-32; 8:34-38, Jn 15:15; 16:13-15, Acts 8:26-27; 13:1-3, Rom 8:13-14; 2Cor 4:16-18; 12:7-10, Gal 5:17-18, 2Tim 2:22-25, Rev 7:16-17

Guidance through Miracles

Saul (who became Paul) as he travelled to Damascus to arrest Christians was surrounded by a bright light from heaven and fell to the ground and heard a voice say to him, "Saul, Saul, why do you persecute me?" and Saul asked "Who are you, Lord?" "I am Jesus, whom you are persecuting," he replied. "Now get up and go into the city, and you will be told what you must do." When Saul got up from the ground he was blind .and was led into Damascus. – See Acts 9:3-9

Additional Scripture references

Mat 24:37-39, Lk 9:28-36; Jn 9;5-9; Acts 2:1-4; 10:9-35; 16:16-34

Guidance and Maturity - See also Section E5

Jesus told this parable saying "everyone who hears these words of mine and puts them into practice is like a wise man who built his house on the rock. The rain came down, the streams rose, and the winds blew and beat against that house; yet it did not fall, because it had its foundation on the rock.

But everyone who hears these words of mine and does not put them into practice is like a foolish man who built his house on sand, but when the rain came down, the streams rose and the winds blew against that house it fell. – See Mat 7:24-27

1 Therefore, I urge you, brothers, in view of God's mercy, to offer your bodies as living sacrifices, holy and pleasing to God—this is your spiritual act of worship.
2 Do not conform any longer to the pattern of this world, but be transformed by the renewing of your mind. Then you will be able to test and approve what God's will is—his good, pleasing and perfect will.

Rom 12:1-2

Additional Scripture references

Ex 18:13-24, Deut 8:1-7, Rom 8:14-17 ; 2Cor 4:8-11; 5:17

D5

GOD'S PROVISION

- THE PERSON AND WORK OF THE HOLY SPIRIT -

Biblical Definitions

Introduction

To many people this whole topic of the Holy Spirit is difficult to understand, to others it is simply avoided or is a source of embarrassment, but in whatever way it is viewed, it certainly contains elements of mystery. However, so many aspects of Almighty God and the Godhead are mysterious, and would it be God if they could be plainly understood? No, it would not.

When one looks at the Trinity – the teaching concerning the three Persons that make up the Godhead i.e. God the Father, God the Son and God the Holy Spirit (see Section B2) – we note that it refers to 'The Person of the Holy Spirit'. This Person is revealed many times in the N.T. Scriptures, and His character and work are described below. From these Scriptures it will be seen that He makes very significant contributions of enlightenment, encouragement and empowerment to the Christian believer, so please read on.

The Person and Work of the Holy Spirit

The Holy Spirit is spoken of under various names and titles in the N.T. and in Jn 14:16 He is referred to in the Greek as *'parakletos'* and this is defined by W.E. Vine as someone who is: "called to one's side, i.e., to one's aid, and suggests the capability or adaptability for giving aid. It was used in a court of justice to denote a legal assistant, counsel for the defence, an advocate; then, generally, one who pleads another's cause, an intercessor, advocate, as in 1Jn 2:1, of the Lord Jesus. In the widest sense, it signifies a succourer, comforter. Christ was called this to His disciples, by the implication of His word "another (*allos,* another of the same sort, not *heteros,* different) Comforter," when speaking of the Holy Spirit."

The triune Godhead comprises The Father, The Son and The Holy Spirit - see Section B2, The Trinity.

In the following Scriptures we see aspects of the Holy Spirit's character and function:

He is Holy, a Counsellor, Teacher and Prompter - sent by The Father in the name of The Son. See the Scripture below:

Jesus is speaking here to His disciples:

"But the Counsellor, the Holy Spirit, whom the Father will send in my name, will teach you all things and will remind you of everything I have said to you."

Jn 14:26

He is the absolute Speaker of Truth and giver of Counsel - from God The Father - who will testify about Jesus. See Jn 15:26 where Jesus is speaking here to His disciples

He will convict (convince) people of guilt - concerning the true nature of sin, righteousness and judgment, because He knows all about us. On Jesus' return to the Father (when He Ascended) the Holy Spirit was sent in a general way into our domain.

Jesus speaking to His disciples says: That when he (the Holy Spirit) comes he will convict the world of guilt in regard to sin and righteousness and judgment: in regard to sin, because men do not believe in me; in regard to righteousness, because I am going to the Father, where you can see me no longer; and in regard to judgment, because the prince of this world now stands condemned. – Jn 16:7-11

He reveals the very Person of God to us.– See the Scripture 1Cor 2:10-11 which states that/;" God has revealed it to us by his Spirit. The Spirit searches all things, even the deep things of God, for who among men knows the thoughts of a man except the man's spirit within him? In the same way no-one knows the thoughts of God except the Spirit of God". It also says that we (the believers) have not received the spirit of the world but the Spirit who is from God, that we may understand what God has freely given us.

<u>He reveals God's thoughts to us</u>- See the Scriptures Jn 14:16-17 below and Jn 14:26 above.

"And I will ask the Father, and he will give you another Counsellor to be with you for ever— the Spirit of truth. The world cannot accept him, because it neither sees him nor knows him. But you know him, for he lives with you and will be in you."

<u>He is powerful</u> – See the Scriptures below:
"I will not venture to speak of anything except what Christ has accomplished through me in leading the Gentiles to obey God by what I have said and done—by the power of signs and miracles, through the power of the Spirit. So from Jerusalem all the way round to Illyricum, I have fully proclaimed the gospel of Christ."

Rom 15:18-19

In 1Cor 2:4-5 the apostle Paul said his message and preaching were not with wise and persuasive words, but with a demonstration of the Spirit's power.

<u>He should not be grieved</u> – See the Scripture Eph 4:29-32 and the one given below.

19 Do not put out the Spirit's fire;
20 do not treat prophecies with contempt.

1Thess 5:19-20

Information regarding the gifts of the Holy Spirit have been taken from the book: "Willmington's Book of Bible Lists" by H.L.Willmington, and are shown below:

<u>Facts about and Giftings of the Holy Spirit</u>

1	He is omnipresent	Ps 139:7
2	He is omniscient	1Cor 2:10-11
3	He is omnipotent	Gen 1:2
4	He is eternal	Heb 9:14

5	He is called God	Acts 5:3-4
6	He is equal with the Father and with the Son	Mat 28:19-20
7	He has a mind	Rom 8:27
8	He searches out the human mind	1Cor 2:10
9	He has a will	1Cor 12:11
10	He forbids	Acts 16:6-7
11	He leads	Acts 16:10
12	He speaks	Acts 8:29
13	He loves	Rom 15:30
14	He grieves	Eph 4:30
15	He prays	Rom 8:26

<u>Gifts of the Holy Spirit</u>

1	Apostleship	Eph 4:11, 1Cor 12:28
2	Prophecy	Rom 12:6, 1Cor 12:10
3	Miracles	1Cor 12:28
4	Healing	1Cor 12:9, 28, 30
5	Tongues	1Cor 12:10
6	Interpretation of tongues	1Cor 12:10
7	Knowledge	1Cor 12:8
8	Wisdom	1Cor 12:8
9	Discerning of spirits	1Cor 12:10
10	Giving	Rom 12:8
11	Ministering (service, administration).	Rom 12:7, 1Cor 12:28
12	Exhortation	Rom 12:8, see also Prov 25:11
13	Showing of mercy	Rom 12:8
14	Ruling (leadership).	Rom 12:8
15	Faith	Rom 12:3
16	Teaching	Rom 12:7
17	Evangelism	2Tim 4:5, Acts 8:26-40, Acts 21:8
18	Pastoring-teaching	1Pet 5:1-4

Wayne Grudem in his book “Bible Doctrine” states: “Spiritual gifts are given to equip the church to carry out its ministry until Christ returns. Paul tells the Corinthians, “You are not lacking in any spiritual gift, as you wait for the revealing of our Lord Jesus Christ” (1Cor 1:7). Here he connects the possession of spiritual gifts and their situation in the history of redemption (waiting for Christ’s return), suggesting that gifts are given to the church for the period between Christ’s ascension and his return.”

O.T. and N.T. Prophecy

It is important to note the difference between O.T. and N.T. prophecy. Prophets in the O.T. carried the responsibility of giving to the people the very words of God and they were to be recorded as part of Scripture – later to become included in the Bible. It was, therefore, a very serious matter if a prophet was unfaithful and failed to give all the words, or changed the words they were given, and they suffered death by stoning. Their words were also recorded in Scripture as a warning to others.

Prophecy in the N.T. to the present day is quite different, as the biblical Scriptures were completed in the first few years of the N.T. times, so that when people receive 'prophetic words' from God they are not to be recorded in Scripture. Also it must be remembered that these 'words' now come through imperfect human channels and can be subject to partial impartation or interpretation, and hence it says in 1Cor 14:29-32 that these 'words' should be 'weighed' by others. It also states that these 'words' are for instruction and encouragement.

It follows, therefore, that those who give 'prophetic words' should be in close fellowship with God and dependant on the Holy Spirit and not their own wisdom or knowledge.

In addition it should be remembered that in 1Cor 14:1-3 Christians are encouraged to prophecy.

Additional facts concerning the Holy Spirit

He must live in us if we belong to Christ.	Rom 8:9
He should be called to aid our prayers.	Eph 6:18, Rom 8:26
He should be the one we live by.	Gal 5:16
He should be the one who leads us.	Gal 5:18
He is the one to produce the fruit of the Spirit in us.	Gal 5:22-23
He can be resisted.	Acts 7:51
His zeal, like fire, can be put out.	1Thess 5:19

The Fruit of the Holy Spirit

In Jn 15:4-8 it states:

4 Remain in me, and I will remain in you. No branch can bear fruit by itself; it must remain in the vine. Neither can you bear fruit unless you remain in me.

5 "I am the vine; you are the branches. If a man remains in me and I in him, he will bear much fruit; apart from me you can do nothing.
6 If anyone does not remain in me, he is like a branch that is thrown away and withers; such branches are picked up, thrown into the fire and burned.
7 If you remain in me and my words remain in you, ask whatever you wish, and it will be given you.
8 This is to my Father's glory, that you bear much fruit, showing yourselves to be my disciples.

This Scripture reveals the conditions for a believer to bear fruit, namely, by remaining in fellowship with God, and by absorbing and living by His Word (both read and received). This will result in glorifying God and bearing godly character in the believer, thus providing evidence that the person is a disciple of Jesus.

The Scripture also links the 'fruit' to the natural growing process, and it will grow when it is fed and watered (time spent in His presence, receiving His Word and enjoying His fellowship), and in due time the 'fruit of the Spirit' will be seen. The 'fruit' will thus flourish in the right environment and this will be subject to the 'natural elements' of disappointments. joys, difficulties, encouragements, loss and many changes.

For the character 'fruit' of the Spirit see Gal 5:22-26 given below:

22 But the fruit of the Spirit is love, joy, peace, patience, kindness, goodness, faithfulness,
23 gentleness and self-control. Against such things there is no law.
24 Those who belong to Christ Jesus have crucified the sinful nature with its passions and desires.
25 Since we live by the Spirit, let us keep in step with the Spirit.
26 Let us not become conceited, provoking and envying each other.

The Work of the Holy Spirit

The following aspects of the work of the Holy Spirit have been extracted from notes written by David Allen Reed and supplied on The Online Bible software.

The Father and the Son work by, and through, the Holy Spirit.

<u>His special individual work</u>

1) To convict of sin
   Jn 16:8 Acts 2:37

2) To regenerate
   Jn 3:3 -5 6:63 Tit 3:5 -7

3) To witness concerning Jesus
   Heb 10:15 1Jo 5:7

4) He is the author of assurance to us
   Rom 8:14-16 1Jn 4:13

5) He is the inspirer of the scriptures and our personal teacher
   Jn 14:26 16:13 1Cor 2:9-13 12:3 -8 1Thess 1:5 2Ti 3:16
   Heb 3:7 2Pet 1:21

6) He dwells in the disciples of Jesus
   1Cor 2:9-16 6:17 12:13 Ga 3:5 4:6 5:25
   Eph 2:22 3:16 5:18 1Pet 1:11 1Jn 3:24

7) He sheds abroad the love of God in our hearts
   Rom 5:5

8) He gives hope, joy, peace, liberty
   Ga 5:22 2Cor 3:17

9) He is the Comforter
   Jn 14:16,26 15:26 16:7 Acts 9:31 Rom 15:13

10) He sanctifies
    Rom 8:6-11 1Cor 6:11 Gal 5:22-26 2Thess 2:13

<u>The Holy Spirit for Service</u>

1) The gift
   Jn 14:17 1Cor 3:16 6:19,20 Lk 4:17-21 Jn 3:34
   Acts 10:38 Isa 44:3 Acts 1:5,8 2:4,38,39 4:31 6:3 9:17

2) How given
   Lk 11:13 24:49 Jn 20:22 Acts 1:4 2:38 5:32 8:17 19:6 1Jn 5:14,15

3) As to the renewal of the gift
   Acts 4:31 10:44 11:15 13:52

<u>In Section D5 Texts there are additional headings as listed below:</u>

- The Holy Spirit in the Believer.
- Filling with the Spirit.
- The effect on Believers of 'Filling' or 'Fillings' of the Holy Spirit.
- Warnings regarding the Holy Spirit.

<u>Features of the Believers Relationship with the Holy Spirit.</u>

(1) Receiving the Holy Spirit
(2) Being filled with the Holy Spirit
(3) Receiving God's love through the Spirit
(4) Walking in the Spirit
(5) Being led by the Spirit
(6) Bearing fruit by the Spirit
(7) Living by the Spirit
(8) Sowing to the Spirit
(9) Setting one's mind on the things of the Spirit
(10) Praying in the Spirit
(11) Receiving the Gifts of the Spirit

GOD'S PROVISION

- THE PERSON AND WORK OF THE HOLY SPIRIT -

Notes and Quotations

The Holy Spirit in the Believer

L.O. Richards in his book "Expository Dictionary of Bible Words" has much to say on this subject, and given below are a few extracts on this topic. These hopefully will act as a spur to further study of this important subject. The extracts are placed under the following two headings:

Filling with the Spirit

The O.T. speaks of the spirit of God coming upon various O.T. leaders (Judg 6:34; 11:29; 14:19); these leaders subsequently performed special tasks. Then the N.T. unveils one of the great wonders of our present age: every believer is given the gift of the Holy Spirit. Each of us can be filled with the Spirit, and by the Spirit we are qualified and equipped both for any service to which we are called and for living a victorious Christian life.

Acts 6 gives us a hint of how filling affects character. The men chosen as Spirit-filled men were known for their wisdom (6:3) and their faith (6:5). Paul in Galatians focuses our attention on how the Spirit shapes character. Sinful nature shows itself in immorality, interpersonal discord, jealousy, anger, selfish ambition, and lack of self-control. But someone filled with the Spirit - led and enabled by him - demonstrates love, joy, peace, patience, kindness, goodness, faithfulness, gentleness, and self-control (5:19-23).

The Holy Spirit in the believer's life

As we trace the N.T's teaching on the work of the Holy Spirit in the believer's life, we begin to see why Jesus spoke as he did. We see this both in the named works of the Spirit and in the works ascribed to him in description.

Later he states: "Several specific works of the Holy Spirit linked with the believer's experience are identified. We are told that the Spirit baptises, fills, seals, and indwells Christians. We are also told that the Holy Spirit gives "gifts" to believers."

Also: "Perhaps the most significant in these specified works of the Spirit is the repeated emphasis on the fact that the Holy Spirit maintains a unique relationship with all believers.

Gifts are given "to each one" (1Cor 12:7), for "we were all baptised by one Spirit into one body" (v 13). In Romans, Paul goes so far as to say that "if anyone does not have the Spirit of Christ, he does not belong to Christ" (Rom 8:9). The specific interplay between the Holy Spirit and the believer in these and other areas (as in the need for repeated "fillings") must be explored case by case. But the basic assurance that the Holy Spirit has established a permanent relationship with each Christian is foundational to understanding the Spirit's ministry in our lives."

In the above notes it refers to repeated "fillings" of the Holy Spirit, and it was thought the best explanation of this would be to let the Scriptures speak for themselves. Hence, from the list of references given below one can get some indication of the frequency and repeated nature of this "filling" and the purpose behind it.

Lk 4:1-14 - Jesus was led into the desert, tempted by the devil. Defeated Satan.
Acts 2:1-4 - Initial filling of all disciples - they witnessed in other tongues (languages).
Acts 2:15-21 - O.T. Prophecy fulfilled - people to prophesy, have visions, dreams, etc.
Acts 4:8 - Peter given boldness to witness.
Acts 4:31 - Peter, John and a group of Christians - spoke the word of God boldly.
Acts 6:3-6 - Stephen and others commissioned for service, and hands laid on them.

Acts 6:8 - Stephen did great wonders and miraculous signs among the people.
Acts 7:54-60 - Stephen stoned to death - and prayed for those stoning him.
Acts 8:29 - Philip spoken to directly by the Holy Spirit.
Acts 9:17-22 -Saul (Paul) given his sight back, commissioned for service-hands laid on him.
Acts 10:38 - Jesus anointed - he did good, healed and overcame demonic powers.
Acts 10:44-48 - Peter spoke - Gentiles received Holy Spirit, spoke in tongues, praised God.
Acts 11:23-26 - Barnabas spoke, people believed. Christians taught and encouraged.
Acts 11:27-28 - Agabus predicted a severe famine.
Acts 13:9-12 - Paul discerns evil and pronounces judgment against a sorcerer.
Acts 13:48-52 -Paul and Barnabus spoke boldly, were expelled, yet rejoiced. Many believed.
Acts 16:6-10 - Paul and others redirected from one area, and towards Greece by a vision.
Eph 5:18 - We are charged to be filled with the Spirit, it is not an option.
Eph 4:30-32 - We are warned not to grieve the Holy Spirit.
1Thess 5:19-21 - We are warned not to put out the Spirit's fire - subdue His voice.

It would appear from the above list that the overarching purpose of "being filled with God's Holy Spirit" is to bring glory to God, and this enables bold witness, service, testing, gifts of the Spirit to be used, miracles, healings, prophetic words, tongues, spiritual discernment, etc. To this end God is glorified as all these means are used to bear spiritual fruits for the conversion of unbelievers and also maturity and encouragement to Christians. This may, however, come about through God using and allowing channels of hardship and suffering for Christians, accompanied by joy.

Jesus is the Model of the Spirit-Filled person –see Jn 3:34

A question to ask ourselves - We may have God's Holy Spirit, but how much does He have of us?

The following statement, concerning Christians, is very challenging:

"The fullness of the Holy Spirit is in proportion to the degree of our surrender", taken from the book "Bursting the Wine Skins" by Michael Cassidy.

In the reference notes of the Open Bible - New King James Version it states against Eph 3:30 "do not grieve the Holy Spirit of God" is explained as: "Do not push the Spirit away, ignore Him, or cause Him to grieve by rejecting His counsel."

Also the note for Eph 5:18 "Be filled with the Spirit" reads: "is a command to be obeyed, not an option for the Christian. *Be filled* is a present tense meaning "go on being filled with the Spirit." It is also plural; all believers are to be filled.

The image is of a container so full that there is no room for anything else. The Spirit-filled Christian is so given over to the Spirit's leadership that other, conflicting influences have no place."

Someone has said: "The Holy Spirit does not operate automatically in a believer, but waits to be depended on" - Rom 8:1-6.

Dr R.T. Kendall in his book "The Word and the Spirit" states: "My thesis then is that the Holy Spirit wants to be himself and reach those I address unhindered, ungrieved, unquenched and undisguised" – see Eph 4:30-32, Gal 3:2-5.

The Holy Spirit is certainly resident in the life of the Christian, but the question is: Is He President? Prayer: "Lord help me to <u>*work out*</u> with your Holy Spirit what you have <u>*worked in.*"</u> - Phil 2:12-13.

A number of people have quoted that one aspect of the Holy Spirit's work is to: "Comfort the afflicted and afflict the comfortable."

<u>The Believers Relationship with the Holy Spirit</u>

At the time of Christ's ascension the Early Church was born and the commencement was signalled by the giving of the Holy Spirit as promised (Lk 24:48-49), and this was fulfilled in Acts 1:8 when the Lord said: "you will receive power when the Holy Spirit comes on you." A typical example of the effect this had on Peter is given in Acts 3 where a cripple at the gate Beautiful was healed through Peter, and his answer to those who question him is: "Why do you stare at us as if by our own power or godliness we had made this man walk"?

In view of this and many other Scriptures it is revealed that firstly the Christian's utter weakness and impotence to achieve God's objectives by natural means, and secondly, they should have an attitude of utter dependence on God's Holy Spirit to fulfil His will and purposes through them. This means that the Christian lives and works as though it all depended on themselves, yet at the same time, is completely dependent on God. (I believe a similar statement has been made by someone else).

The above statements are supported by many Scriptures, and a sample of these are given below:

Regarding the casting out of demons, Jesus tells his disciples that they need to have faith and: "Nothing will be impossible to you." - Mat 17:14-21.

Jesus' answer to the rich young ruler's question regarding how he could obtain eternal life, brought a response from his disciples: "Who then can be saved?" and Jesus said:

"With man this is impossible, but with God all things are possible." - Mat 19:16-30.

Regarding the casting out of an evil (deaf and dumb) spirit, Jesus says to his disciples: "This kind can come out only by prayer." - Mk 9:20-29 (some manuscripts state "prayer and fasting"). See also Mat 6:16-18.

Concerning the virgin birth of Jesus, an angel says to Mary: "For nothing is impossible with God." - Lk 1:26-38.

Concerning being born of the Spirit, Jesus tells the Pharisee Nicodemus: "that everyone who believes in him (Jesus) may have eternal life." - Jn 3:1-18.

Jesus speaking to his disciples about bearing spiritual fruit in their lives says: "If a man remains in me (Jesus) and I in him, he will bear much fruit; apart from me you can do nothing." - Jn 15:1-8.

The Lord said to Paul: "My power is made perfect in weakness" - 2Cor 12:9.

Paul writing to the Ephesians and referring to the Holy Spirit says: "his incomparably great power for us who believe" - Eph 1:19-20.

Concerning faith, the writer of the Book of Hebrews states: "And without faith it is impossible to please God, because anyone who comes to him must believe that he exists and that he rewards those who earnestly seek him." - Heb 11:6.

In an endeavour to summarise the above statements, a set of essential conditions are set out below by which God works through believers by his Holy Spirit to enable them to fulfil His spiritual objectives, which are miraculous in essence and /or timing:

Having the faith to believe God,
Having the godliness of life to be available to God,
Having the humility to be God dependent,
Having the prayerfulness to commit everything to God,
Having the spiritual perception to understand God's Will,
Having the wisdom to await God's timing,
Having the fullness of his Holy Spirit, and so be prepared for God's use,
<u>Then,</u> having the boldness to act.

However, it would seem that sometimes God acts out of grace, when these conditions are not in place.

Biblical commentators have stated regarding the following Scripture:

"This is the word of the LORD to Zerubbabel: 'Not by might nor by power, but by my Spirit,' says the LORD Almighty. Zech 4:6

'might' - can relate to the force of men (army), wealth or other resources.

'power' - can be good or bad power, relating to chameleon - subtle disguise, cunning or cleverness.

Thus, God's Divine Power provided by his Holy Spirit is the only means by which the believer can accomplish the purposes of God.

In "The Word for Today" Notes by Bob Gass, he states regarding 'being filled with the Holy Spirit': "The Holy Spirit fills the places vacated by our personal priorities. The more personal priorities that are surrendered up to God means that there is more time and energy available for the Holy Spirit to occupy and use. (Acts 2:4, 4:8, 4:29-31).

These priorities can even be 'our' Christian priorities - not God's."

As all believers have received the Holy Spirit (Acts 1:8, 2:4, 2:38-39, 19:1-7, Gal 3:2-5), they are encouraged by the Scriptures to continuously improve their relationship with Him by:

Being filled with the Spirit	Acts 2:1-4, Eph 5:18-20
Receiving God's love through the Spirit	Rom 5:5
Walking in the Spirit	Rom 8:4, Gal 5:16
Being led by the Spirit	Jn 16:13-14, Rom 8:14, Gal 5:18
Bearing fruit by the Spirit	Jn 15 1-8, Gal 5:22-24
Living by the Spirit	Rom 6:4, 8:4, 2Cor 3:4-6, Gal 5:25
Sowing to the Spirit	Gal 6:8
Setting their minds on the things of the Spirit	Rom 8:5-6
Praying in the Spirit	Eph 6:18, Jude 20
Receiving the gifts of the Spirit	Rom 12, 1Cor 12

The Gifts of the Holy Spirit

The main Scriptures that mention these gifts are found in Rom 12 and 1Cor 12-14.

In any study of this subject it is recommended that a foundational starting point should be 1Cor 12:7 & 18, where it states that gifts of the Spirit are "given for the common good", and with reference to parts of the body says, He has given them "just as he wanted them to be."

Also, take into account Rom 12:10-11 where it says: "Be devoted to one another in brotherly love, Honour one another above yourselves. Never be lacking in zeal, but keep your spiritual fervour, serving the Lord."

Use of the Gifts of the Spirit

Given below are some Biblical references that illustrate typical examples of the use of the gifts of the Spirit.

Acts 2:1-4, 3:1-10, 4:29-31, 6:8, 8:4-8, 9:10-17, 10:1-8, 10:9-20, 11:27-28, 13:9-11, 14:1-3, 14:8-11, 16:6-10, 19:1-7, 21:8-12.

A note of caution: Those who exercise the Gifts of the Spirit should ensure that they do so with humility, love, and in dependence on God, as evidence of the Fruit of the Spirit. The reason for this is that any incompatibility between the use of the Gifts and the absence of the Fruit of the Spirit (Gal 5:22-26) can bring God's work into disrepute, - see 1Pet 4:10 below:

"Each one should use whatever gift he has received to serve others, faithfully administering God's grace in its various forms."

Tests to be applied to spiritual gifts

David Watson in his book "Discipleship" states: "What are the tests for prophecy, or for any other spiritual gift, especially that which purports to bring the word of God? These should be some of the questions to ask:

(a) Does it glorify Christ? (Jn 16:14; 1Cor 12:1-4).
(b) Does it edify the body of Christ? 1Cor 14
(c) Is it in accordance with the written word of God in the scriptures? (2Pet 3:16).
(d) Is the word given in the spirit of love?
(e) Is Jesus Lord of the speaker's life? Mat 7:15-20.
(f) Does the speaker submit to the leaders of the church? Acts 20:19-31.
(g) Does the speaker allow others to judge or weigh what he has said? 1Cor 14:29.
(h) Is the speaker in control of himself when speaking? 1Cor 12:2, & 14:32.
(i) Is the prophecy fulfilled, if it speaks about some future event? Most prophecy is forth-telling, not foretelling.

The Fruit of the Holy Spirit

The Scripture Jn 15:4-8 that details the Fruit of the Holy Spirit is given in the Biblical Definitions in this Section.

This Scripture reveals the conditions for a believer to bear fruit, namely, by remaining in fellowship with God, and by absorbing and living by His Word (both read and received). This will result in glorifying God and bearing godly character in the believer, thus providing evidence that the person is a disciple of Jesus.

The Scripture also links the 'fruit' to the natural growing process, and it will grow when it is fed and watered (time spent in His presence, receiving His Word and enjoying His fellowship), and in due time the 'fruit of the Spirit' will be seen. The 'fruit' should thus flourish and be seen in the 'natural seasons' of disappointments. joys, difficulties, encouragements, loss and many changes.

For the character 'fruit' of the Spirit see Gal 5:22-26.

With reference to the 'fruit' of the Spirit in Gal 5:22-26 someone has provided the following definitions:

Love – the unselfish affection that promotes the well-being of others.
Joy – the ability to rejoice in God when life is tough.
Peace – the ability to trust in the wisdom, sovereignty and protective care of God in all circumstances.
Patience – the determination to keep going even when you are not enjoying what God is asking you to do.
Gentleness – the refusal to inflict pain on others.
Goodness – the freedom to reject all that is not of God.
Self-control – the ability to discipline one's rebel emotions.

GOD'S PROVISION

- THE PERSON AND WORK OF THE HOLY SPIRIT -

Biblical Texts & Text References

The Person and Work of the Holy Spirit

When God created the heavens and the earth the Spirit of God was hovering over the waters. – See Gen 1:1-2
He speaks the words of God. – See Jn 3:34
He spoke to Philip. – See Acts 8:29

26 In the same way, the Spirit helps us in our weakness. We do not know what we ought to pray for, but the Spirit himself intercedes for us with groans that words cannot express.
27 And he who searches our hearts knows the mind of the Spirit, because the Spirit intercedes for the saints in accordance with God's will.

Rom 8:26-27

See also 1Cor 12:11

Additional Scripture references

Ps 139:7, Mat 28:19-20, Jn 14:16-17; 16:7-11, Acts 5:3-4; 16:6-7; 16:10, Rom 1:11-12; 15:30, 1Cor 2:10-11, Eph 4:30, Heb 9:14, 1Jn 4:12-13

The Person of the Holy Spirit in the Believer

Speaking about the believers in Lk 11:13 it says the Holy Spirit will be given to those who ask him, - See Lk 11:13

9 You, however, are controlled not by the sinful nature but by the Spirit, if the Spirit of God lives in you. And if anyone does not have the Spirit of Christ, he does not belong to Christ.

Rom 8:9

In Rom 8:15-16 it states that:" The Spirit himself testifies with our spirit that we are God's children.

See also Gal 5:22-23

Additional Scripture references

Mat 3:11, Rom 8:1-6, 1Cor 12:7 & 13, Gal 3:2-5, Eph 4:30-32, 2Tim 1:13-14, Heb 2:3-4, 1Jn 3:23-24; 4:12-13, Jude 18-19

Filling with the Spirit

3 Brothers, choose seven men from among you who are known to be full of the Spirit and wisdom. We will turn this responsibility over to them

4 and will give our attention to prayer and the ministry of the word."

5 This proposal pleased the whole group. They chose Stephen, a man full of faith and of the Holy Spirit; also Philip, Procorus, Nicanor, Timon, Parmenas, and Nicolas from Antioch, a convert to Judaism.

6 They presented these men to the apostles, who prayed and laid their hands on them.

Acts 6:3-6

Additional Scripture references

Jud 6:34; 14:19, Isa 61:1-3, Lk 4:18, Acts 10:38, Gal 5:19-26

The Effect on Believers of 'Filling' or 'Fillings' of the Holy Spirit

Jesus was full of the Holy Spirit

1 Jesus, full of the Holy Spirit, returned from the Jordan and was led by the Spirit in the desert,

2 where for forty days he was tempted by the devil. He ate nothing during those days, and at the end of them he was hungry.

13 When the devil had finished all this tempting, he left him until an opportune time.

14 Jesus returned to Galilee in the power of the Spirit, and news about him spread through the whole countryside.

Lk 4:1-2-&-13-14

Believers were all filled with the Holy Spirit

On the day of Pentecost the disciples were: "All of them filled with the Holy Spirit and began to speak in other tongues as the Spirit enabled them". See Acts 2:1-4

15 These men are not drunk, as you suppose. It's only nine in the morning!
16 No, this is what was spoken by the prophet Joel:
17 "'In the last days, God says, I will pour out my Spirit on all people. Your sons and daughters will prophesy, your young men will see visions, your old men will dream dreams.
18 Even on my servants, both men and women, I will pour out my Spirit in those days, and they will prophesy

Acts 2:15-18

Peter filled with the Holy Spirit

In Acts 4:8-10 it states that Peter was filled with the Holy Spirit

Believers filled with the Holy Spirit and spoke boldly for God

In Acts 4:29-31 the believers prayed asking to be enabled to speak God's word with great boldness, and to perform miraculous signs and wonders through the name of Jesus, and it was answered by them being filled with the holy Spirit.

Stephen full of the Holy Spirit did great wonders and miracles

The Apostles were asked (in Acts 6:3-6) to choose seven men who were known to be full of the Spirit and wisdom to serve out the daily distribution of food, and one of those was Stephen.

8 Now Stephen, a man full of God's grace and power, did great wonders and miraculous signs among the people.

Acts 6:8

The Holy Spirit spoke to Philip

26 Now an angel of the Lord said to Philip, "Go south to the road--the desert road--that goes down from Jerusalem to Gaza."
29 The Spirit told Philip, "Go to that chariot and stay near it."

Acts 8:26 & 29

<u>The Holy Spirit was poured out on the Gentiles and they spoke in tongues and praised God</u>

This event came about when Peter obeyed a vision that he had received from God.- See Acts 10:44-48

<u>Barnabas, full of the Holy Spirit, was used by God for the conversion of others</u>

24 <u>He was a good man, full of the Holy Spirit and faith,</u> and a great number of people were brought to the Lord.

Acts 11:24

<u>Paul filled with the Holy Spirit was given a word of knowledge</u>

When Paul travelled to Cyprus the proconsul Sergius Paulus asked to meet him, but this was opposed by an attendant called Elymus who was a sorcerer. <u>Then Paul, filled with the Holy Spirit</u> told him he was full of all kinds of deceit, that the hand of the Lord was against him and he was going to be blind for a period of time. See Acts 13:6-12.

<u>All Believers are urged to be filled with the Holy Spirit</u>

In Eph 5:18 it asks believers to be filled with the Spirit.

<u>Additional Scripture references</u>

Acts 4:29-31; 6:8-13; 7:54-60; 8:26-29; 9:17-22; 10:37-38; 11:22-24; 11:27-28; 13:48-52; 16:6-10

<u>Warnings Regarding the Holy Spirit</u>

30 And do not grieve the Holy Spirit of God, with whom you were sealed for the day of redemption.

31 Get rid of all bitterness, rage and anger, brawling and slander, along with every form of malice.

32 Be kind and compassionate to one another, forgiving each other, just as in Christ God forgave you.

Eph 4:30-32

<u>Additional Scripture references</u>

Mk 3:28-29, 1Thess 5:18-22; Heb 3:7-8

Features of the Believers Relationship with the Holy Spirit

(1) Receiving the Holy Spirit

When people receive the Holy Spirit they will:

i) Get power to be witnesses for the Lord. See Acts 1:8
ii) Speak in tongues when enabled by the Spirit. See Acts 2:4

38 Peter replied, "Repent and be baptised, every one of you, in the name of Jesus Christ for the forgiveness of your sins. And you will receive the gift of the Holy Spirit.
39 The promise is for you and your children and for all who are far off--for all whom the Lord our God will call."

Acts 2:38-39

(2) Being filled with the Holy Spirit

See Acts 2:4 and Eph 5:17-18

(3) Receiving God's love through the Spirit

5 And hope does not disappoint us, because God has poured out his love into our hearts by the Holy Spirit, whom he has given us.

Rom 5:5

(4) Walking in the Spirit

See Gal 5:16 and Gal 5:16

(5) Being led by the Spirit

13 But when he, the Spirit of truth, comes, he will guide you into all truth. He will not speak on his own; he will speak only what he hears, and he will tell you what is yet to come.
14 He will bring glory to me by taking from what is mine and making it known to you.

Jn 16:13-14

See also Rom 8:13-14

(6) Bearing fruit by the Spirit

In Gal 5:22-23 it refers to the fruit of the Spirit as love, joy, peace, patience, kindness, goodness, faithfulness, gentleness and self-control.

See also Jn 15:4-6

(7) Living by the Spirit

Those who have received The Holy Spirit are enabled to live by the Spirit. See Rom 8:3-4

See4 also Gal 5:25-26

(8) Sowing to the Spirit

In Gal 6:7-9 it says that God is not mocked. A man reaps what he sows, so that if we sow to our sinful nature we will reap destruction, but if we sow to please the Spirit we will reap eternal life.

(9) Setting one's mind on the things of the Spirit

Those who live in accordance with the Spirit have their minds set on what the Spirit desires. See Rom 8:5-6

(10) Praying in the Spirit

Believers are asked to pray in the Spirit on all occasions with all kinds of prayers and requests. See Eph 6:17-18 and Jude 20

(11) Receiving the gifts of the Spirit

See Rom 12:4-8 & 1Cor 12:7-11 & 31

Additional Scripture references

(1) Mat 6:16-18, Jn 3:1-7, Acts 19:1-7, 2Cor 12:9, Gal 3:2-5, Eph 1:19-20. (2) Acts 2:1-4. (5) Mat 10:16-20, Jn 10:27. Gal 5 :17-18. (6) Jn 15:1-8. (7) 2Cor 3:4-6. (11) 1Cor 12:1-31.

D6

GOD'S PROVISION

-FELLOWSHIP. SUPPORT IN TRIALS -

Biblical Definitions

Fellowship

There are those who prefer their own company for most of the time, but the vast majority of people prefer to share their lives with others in companionship, friendship and love. They want to communicate and be part of a group.

The sad situation for many is that for various reasons they suffer loneliness, but for these, and those who have found a level of friendship the Christian Faith can meet this need of friendship at a deeper level. The friendship that can come through Christians is special because it is a true sharing and bonding of hearts that comes through a common relationship that they have with the Lord Jesus Christ, and this is referred to as Christian Fellowship.

Let us now consider statements on this topic from renowned Christian writers below.

This term 'fellowship' is referred to by W.E.Vine in his book, "Expository Dictionary of Bible Words" as: "sharing in common, communion." See 1Cor 10:16 AV, RSV and NIV below:

16 Is not the cup of thanksgiving for which we give thanks a participation in the blood of Christ? And is not the bread that we break a participation in the body of Christ?

1Cor 10:16

L.O. Richards states: "Fellowship is a particularly significant concept in the N.T. There it expresses shared participation in Christ and the bond that Christ creates between believers." See Acts 2:42-47, Rom 15:26, 1Cor 1:9, 10:16, 2Cor 6:14, 8:4, 9:13, 13:14, Gal 2:9, Eph 3:9, Phil 1:5, 2:1, 3:10, Heb 13:16, 1Jn 1:3-6

The Scriptures below show how this word is used in the context of Christian living.

This 'Fellowship' is part of, and interconnected with, many aspects of Christian living such as:

The Friendship of God - Ex 33:11, Num 12:7-8, Deut 34:10, 2Chron 20:7, Jas 2:23.
The Friendship of Christ - Jn 11:5, 35-36, 13:23, 15:15.
Walking with God - Gen 5:22-24, 6:9, 2Kg 23:3, Mic 4:5, Rev 3:4.
Nearness to God - Ps 16:8, 34:18, 145:18, Jer 23:23-24, Acts 17:27.
Nearness to God in prayer and submission - Ps 73:28, Heb 7:18-19, 10:22, Jas 4:7-8.
Remaining in Christ - Jn 15:1-10, 1Jn 2:6, 28, 3:6, 2Jn 1:9.

Knowing the Divine Presence - a comfort to the saints (believers):

(a) In the pilgrimage of life - Gen 28:15, 31:3, Ex 3:11-12, 29:45-46.
(b) Affords Rest - Ex 33:14, Lev 26:11-12, Heb 4:10.
(c) Gives courage in life's battles - Deut 20:1, Josh 1:6-9, Mat 14:26-27.
(d) Provides comfort in trials - Isa 43:1-2, Zech 2:10-11.
(e) Assured to the smallest company of believers - Mat 18:20.
(f) Continually to the End - Mat 28:19-20.

The friendship and support of other Christians - as outlined below:
Love one another - Jn 13:34-35
Depend on one another - Rom 12:4-5
Honour one another above yourselves - Rom 12:10
Accept one another just as Christ accepted you - Rom 15:7
Care for one another - 1Cor 12:25-26
Serve one another in love - Gal 5:13
Submit to one another - Eph 5:21
Encourage one another - 1Thess 4:18

Confess your faults to one another - Jas 5:16
Pray for one another - Jas 5:16
Offer hospitality to one another - 1Pet 4:9

Support in Trials

Difficulties come to all people, those of every Faith or no Faith, and subject them to a time of testing, These tests or trials can occur through their own actions, through the actions of others, or the reason may be unknown. However they come they cause a range of responses from anger or revenge to bewilderment or resigned acceptance.

In such situations it is good to get support and understanding from those who have had similar experiences. It follows, that when people become Christians they will not only experience blessings, but also difficulties. The difficulties are inevitable, and often arise as a result of the person's lifestyle being different from those around them. As the person grows in their Christian life their priorities change and they begin to want to live to please God and whatever that entails to fulfil God's will for their lives'. These higher moral and caring standards act as a challenge to others, and can thus lead to testing of character, trials and suffering.

Given below are a number of aspects relating to this topic:

The believer subjected to testing

Every believer will experience testing of their character, discernment, judgment and actions, thus proving them and encouraging them to compare themselves to the Lord Jesus Christ and be ever more depended on Him. See the following Scriptures:

Jud 3:1-4, 1Chron 29:17, 2Chron 32:31, Job 7:17-18, Ps 17:3, 26:2, 139:23, Jer 6:27, 9:7, Lam 3:40, Dan 1:12, Lk 8:13, Rom 12:1-2, 1Cor 3:12-13, 2Cor 2:9, 8:8, 13:5-7, Gal 6:4-5, 1Thess 5:21, Heb 3:7-8, 12:10-12, Jas 1:3, 1:12, 1Jn 4:1, Rev 2:10.

The believer subjected to trials

The severity of trials experienced by believers will vary from a testing of patience to being condemned to death. See the following Scriptures: Ps 37:32-33, Mk 13:11, Lk 22:38, Acts 12:4-6, 16:37, 23:6, 2Cor 8:2, 1Thess 3:2-3, 2Thess 1:4, Jas 1:2, 1:12, 1Pet 1:6, 4:12, 2Pet 2:9, Rev 3:10.

Suffering for Christ and the Gospel

In seeking to proclaim and maintain the truths concerning the Lord Jesus Christ, and the whole truth concerning the Gospel message there is often opposition from both the world and from some sections of the established Christian community. This should not be considered surprising as Christ told us to expect such treatment. See the following Scriptures: Jn 15:18-21, Acts 5:41, 9:16, Rom 8:17, 36, 2Cor 1:7, 11:23, Phil 1:27-30, Phil 3:10, 2Tim 2:12, Heb 11:25, Jas 1:2-3, 5:10, 1Pet 2:20-21, 3:14, 4:16, 5:10.

Support for the weak and those who suffer

Throughout the Bible we see that God supports the weak and shows compassion to those who suffer, and so calls on His followers to do the same. See the following Scriptures:

Ex 19:4, Deut 1:30-31, 33:27, Ps 18:35, 37:16-17, 41:12, 68:19, 91:12, Isa 41:10, 46:4, 63:9, Mat 11:28, Acts 5:41, 1Cor 9:22, Gal 6:2, Phil 1:29, 2Tim 1:7-8, 1Pet 3:17, 4:16.

Believers are called to persevere

They are frequently encouraged in the Bible to continue in the Faith and persevere in spite of difficulties; they are called on to show courage in adversity or pain, and are further called on to show determination, endurance and firmness with a gracious attitude, being patient towards all people and revealing a generous spirit.

"Be on your guard; stand firm in the faith; be men of courage; be strong. Do everything in love." 1Cor 16:13-14.

"For God did not give us a spirit of timidity, but a spirit of power, of love and of self-discipline." 2Tim 1:7.

See also the following Scriptures: Rom 11:22, Col 1:21-23, 2:6-7, 2Thess 1:4, 1Tim 4:16, 2Tim 3:14, Heb 12:1-3, Jas 1:2-4, 5:11, Rev 2:3.

GOD'S PROVISION

-FELLOWSHIP. SUPPORT IN TRIALS -

Notes and Quotations

Fellowship

Fellowship is connected to maturity - quoted from 'Every Day With Jesus' Notes by Selwyn Hughes.

"The central thing in maturity, said Dr E Stanley Jones, is fellowship. Those who cannot have fellowship with others are ingrown and hence immature persons. Spiritual maturity is when we can relate correctly to God, to others and to ourselves."

See Mal 3:16-18, Acts 2:42-47, 1Cor 3:1-9, Eph 4:13-15, Heb 5:11 - 6:3.

Testing

We are encouraged to 'give thanks in all circumstances' - however difficult that may be, see the following Scriptures: Acts 10:44-47, 1Cor 2:12-16, 2Cor 5:5.

Someone has said: "A Christian is like a tea bag - not much use till it has been through some hot water."

Goerthe said: "Difficulties prove men, as we grapple we grow."

Christians are meant to be STRONG IN THE LORD - Jesus said in Jn 15:5 "I am the vine; you are the branches. If a man remains in me and I in him, he will bear much fruit; apart from me you can do nothing." This Scripture clearly states that while we remain in a close relationship with Him then our words and actions will bring glory to Him, and achieve His ends. Whilst those things accomplished by us that do not depend on Him in any way will not achieve anything spiritually.

<u>Bob Gass in his "The Word for Today" Notes refers to Ps 26:2 and states:</u>
<u>The Wilderness Test</u>
This test comes when we feel spiritually dry and our joy level is low. It reveals our ability to adapt to adversity and change, and as a result enter a new level of growth. It proves we're able to perform even when life isn't fun. 'He led you through the vast and dreadful desert....to test you so that in the end it might go well with you'(Deuteronomy 8:15-16 NIV). The wilderness test is where we submit to short-term pain, confident that in the end it'll produce long-term gain.

<u>Trials</u>

Trials and difficulties are often described as "Wilderness experiences", and Selwyn Hughes in his "Every Day with Jesus" Notes makes reference to Ps 56:1-13 and states: "The true wilderness experience is a period of deep and prolonged testing which God either arranges or allows. Observers of this strange phenomenon down through the ages are almost unanimously agreed that the true wilderness experience can be divided into seven types: (1) humiliation, (2) suffering, (3) bereavement, (4) estrangement, (5) doubt, (6) failure, (7) dereliction. Some of God's people have met them all, but not all of them had all to meet."

Jesus told us to expect trials and troubles when we follow Him, it is part of the journey of faith. See Jn 16:33

"Wisdom is knowing enough about God's ways and character to be able to bear life's trials."

Author unknown.

"Wisdom is the ability to interpret things through God's eyes. (Ps 119:130).

Bob Gass

Let us remember that 'Passion feeds perseverance'

Author unknown

A quotation from "The Word for Today" Notes by Bob Gass, with reference to 2Sam 10:12.

"Today as you face your difficulties keep these seven things clearly in mind:

(1) never give up when you know you are right;
(2) believe that all things work together for good, if you just persevere;
(3) do not let the odds discourage you, God is bigger than all of them;
(4) never let anyone intimidate you or deter you from your goals;
(5) fight and overcome every limitation;
(6) remember, every winner has dealt with defeat and adversity;
(7) keep trying, confident that in God's strength you will surely succeed."

Trials and Help

It is comforting to note that in Isa 43:2-5 it states that: "*when* you pass through the waters"(of difficulty) that God is with us and that His people are "precious and honoured" in His sight. We need to be reassured of this because we are forewarned that it is not *IF* difficulties come, but *WHEN*. The same thought is expressed in Jer 17:7-8.

Butterfly/Chrysalis Struggle

It has been found that if a butterfly, struggling to get out of its chrysalis, was helped by someone to escape then it would result in the butterfly being unable to fly because in the effort and struggle to emerge it develops the strength to fly. So the helper, with the best of intensions, sadly caused it to have an early death.

What we can learn from this is that people should be left to struggle through the process and difficulties that repentance brings, but let them know that you care and are praying for them. This approach applies to many of the difficulties we experience as Christians, and working through these unwelcome situations will enable our faith to grow. It follows, therefore, that others should not interfere but support them in prayer and so allow them to mature.

Extract from the book "In All Their Affliction" by Murdoch Campbell.

"Let us remember that although the grace of God is always sufficient and ever available it is not given in advance, "As thy days, so shall thy strength be." Dr Payson once said: "Anticipated sorrows are harder to bear than real ones, because Christ does not support us under them." Whatever the future may bring God will adapt His strength to every situation. With the need - and only then - comes His grace. This promise is in the present tense. This grace was not given to Paul in the third heaven - a few hours before the trial came. It was given in answer to prayer when Satan had arrived at his door."

In Heb 4:16 it says:

"Let us then approach the throne of grace with confidence, so that we may receive mercy and find grace to help us in our time of need." And a comment has been made on this *"grace to help us"* recorded in the "The Word for Today" Notes by Bob Gass, where he states: "What is this "grace" that we get when we pray? Gerald Brooks says, "Grace is the strength to stand and take it; the will to hold on to a job that stinks, a marriage that gets difficult or a promise I could break. It's the power to let go of what others are holding on to – my achievements, my social class, my possessions, my power. It's the strength to grasp what lasts – and the will to let go of what vanishes. None of that is possible on our own; it's *simply* a gift from God and we get it through prayer." In other words, grace will not give you the easy way <u>out</u>, but it will show you the right way <u>through</u> – and you'll be stronger on the other side of it!"

<u>Adversity – Opportunities for Advancement</u>

Bob Gass in his "The Word for Today" Notes quotes the following statement by Bob Yandian: "All adversity is just opportunity – if you understand seven things."

Adversity is an opportunity:

(1) For advancement. Once you stop trying to escape the problem and accept the challenge, you begin to advance.
(2) For victory. Without a battle, there can be no victory. Listen, "But thanks be to God, who always leads us in triumphal procession

in Christ and through us spreads everywhere the fragrance of the knowledge of him." (2Cor 2:14).

(3) For growth. Maturity comes through struggle. We hate to see our children struggling, but it's the *only* way they can grow.

(4) To glorify God. God's glorified when you rise up in faith and deal with adversity. Listen, "[Abraham] staggered not at the promise of God through unbelief; but was strong in faith, giving glory to God" (Rom 4:20).

(5) To develop endurance. Sometimes we wish there was an easier way, but Paul says, "problems . . . . are good for us – they help us learn to endure" (Rom 5:3).

(6) To develop character. Sometimes we think God is anxious for us to come out of a trial, when in reality He's more interested in developing our character through it.

(7) For blessing. God can turn every crushing into a blessing, every battle into a victory – *if you let him* (Rom 8:28).

The following is an extract from "The Word for Today" Notes by Bob Gass where he refers to the <u>benefits</u> of going through hard times:

(1) "so that we can comfort those in any trouble with the comfort we ourselves have received from God. (2Cor 1:4). He then quotes from Mike Murdock who says: "Only the broken become the masters at mending." "He's right! Built into any problem that forces you to grow or find a solution is the medicine that can make others whole. When you can say, "I've been there," people listen. Experience is one of your greatest assets – and God never wastes it.

(2) "....that we might not rely on ourselves....."(2Cor 1:9). Anything that causes you to turn to God and lean harder on Him is a blessing!"

Paul speaking to the Christians at Philippi (Phil 1:12-14) reflects on the tough times he has been through and the results that he sees has come from them, namely: the gospel had been advanced; his chains have provided the opportunity for witnessing to the palace guards; and Christians 'have been encouraged to speak the word of God more courageously and fearlessly'.

Suffering and Sacrifice

We see David's attitude towards sacrifice to the Lord and how it is linked to paying a cost of suffering in some way, financially, physically, emotionally, etc; when he says, "I will not sacrifice to the Lord my God burnt offerings that cost me nothing." 2Sam 24:24.

This theme is borne out also by the following Scriptures: 2Sam 23:16, 1Chron 21:24, Ps 40:6, 51:16-17, 116:17, Hos 6:6, 8:13, Amos 4:5, Mat 9:13, Rom 12:1, Eph 5:2, Heb 9:26, 10:5, 8, 12, 26, 13:15-16.

Selwyn Hughes states in his 'Every Day With Jesus' Notes: "If our faith costs nothing it will contribute nothing."

Suffering and Glory

Suffering is also linked with the Glory of God as shown in Jn 11:38-40 where Lazarus is raised from the dead and comes out of the tomb. This theme is found in many Scriptures including; Jn 17, Phil 3:10-11.

GOD'S PROVISION

-FELLOWSHIP. SUPPORT IN TRIALS -

Biblical Texts & Text References

Fellowship

1 If you have any encouragement from being united with Christ, if any comfort from his love, if any fellowship with the Spirit, if any tenderness and compassion,

2 then make my joy complete by being like-minded, having the same love, being one in spirit and purpose.

Phil 2:1-2

Additional Scripture references

Acts 2:42-47, Rom 15:26, 1Cor 1:9-10; 10:16, 2Cor 6:14, Gal 2:9-10, Phil 1:4-5; 3:10, Heb 13:16; 1Jn 1:3-6

The Friendship of God

"Abraham believed God, and it was credited to him as righteousness," and he was called God's friend. See Jas 2:23

Additional Scripture references

Ex 33:11; 2Chron 20:7, Num 12:7-8; Deut 34:10

The Friendship of Christ

35 Jesus wept.

36 Then the Jews said, "See how he loved him!"

Jn 11:35-36

Jesus referred to his followers as friends if they did what he asked them, and not servants because a servant does not know his master's business See Jn 15:14-15

Additional Scripture references

Jn 11:5; 13:23

Nearness to God

It says in Ps 34:18 that the Lord is close to the broken-hearted

Additional Scripture references

Ps 16:8; 145:18; Jer 23:23-24, Acts 17:26-27

Nearness to God in Prayer and Submission

22 let us draw near to God with a sincere heart in full assurance of faith, having our hearts sprinkled to cleanse us from a guilty conscience and having our bodies washed with pure water.

Heb 10:22

Additional Scripture references

Ps 73:28, Heb 7:18-19; Jas 4:7-8

Remaining in Christ

In Jn 8:31-32, Jesus said, "If you hold to my teaching, you are really my disciples,"

Additional Scripture references

Jn 15:1-10, 1Cor 15:1-2; 1Jn 3:6, 2:6 & 28; 2Jn 1:9

Knowing the Divine Presence is Assured to the Smallest Company of Believers

See Mat 18:20

Knowing the Divine Presence Continually to the End

See Mat 28:19-20

The Friendship and Support of Other Christians is Shown as they:

Love One Another;

See Jn 13:34-35

Depend on One Another;

See Rom 12:4-5

<u>Honour One Another Above Yourselves;</u>
See Rom 12:10

<u>Accept One Another Just as Christ Accepted You;</u>
See Rom 15:7

<u>Care for One Another;</u>
See 1Cor 12:25-26

<u>Serve One Another in Love;</u>
13 You, my brothers, were called to be free. But do not use your freedom to indulge the sinful nature; rather, serve one another in love.

Gal 5:13

<u>Submit to One Another;</u>
See Eph 5:21

<u>Encourage One Another;</u>
See 1Thess 4:18

<u>Confess Their Faults to One Another;</u>
See Jas 5:16

<u>Pray for One Another;</u>
See Jas 5:16

<u>Offer Hospitality to One Another;</u>
See 1Pet 4:9

<u>Support in Trials:</u>

<u>The Believer Subjected to Testing;</u>
13 No temptation has seized you except what is common to man. And God is faithful; he will not let you be tempted beyond what you can bear. But when you are tempted, he will also provide a way out so that you can stand up under it.

1Cor 10:13

<u>Additional Scripture references</u>
Job 7:17-18, Ps 17:3, Isa 43:2, Jer 17:7-8, 1Cor 3:12-13, Gal 6:4-5; Heb 3:7-8

The Believer Subjected to Trials;

11 Whenever you are arrested and brought to trial, do not worry beforehand about what to say. Just say whatever is given you at the time, for it is not you speaking, but the Holy Spirit.

Mk 13:11

Additional Scripture references

Ps 37:32-33, Acts 12:4-6, 2Cor 8:2, 1Thess 3:2-3; Jas 1:12, 1Pet 1:6; 4:12-16

Suffering for Christ and the Gospel

Jesus reminded his disciples:" If they persecuted me, they will persecute you also. If they obeyed my teaching, they will obey yours also". See Jn 15:20-21

14 Now if we are children, then we are heirs--heirs of God and co-heirs with Christ, if indeed we share in his sufferings in order that we may also share in his glory.

Rom 8:17

Additional Scripture references

Acts 5:41, 2Cor:1:7, Phil 3:10, 2Tim 2:8-13, 1Pet 3:14-17

Support for the Weak and those who Suffer

28 "Come to me, all you who are weary and burdened, and I will give you rest.

Mat 11:28

Additional Scripture references

Deut 1:30-31, Ps 37:16-17, Isa 41:10; 1Cor 9:22; 2Tim 1:7-8

Believers are Called to Persevere

16 Watch your life and doctrine closely. Persevere in them, because if you do, you will save both yourself and your hearers.

1Tim 4:16

Additional Scripture references

Ps 46:1-10, Rom 11:22, 1Cor 15:55-58, Col 1:21-23; 2Thess 1:4; 2Tim 3:14; Jas 5:11

D7

GOD'S PROVISION

-HOLY COMMUNION-

Biblical Definitions

There is only one act of remembrance Christians are called upon to observe and only one specially worded prayer they are asked to pray. The act of remembrance being referred to as Holy Communion, and the prayer is commonly called the Lord's Prayer (Mat 6:9-15).

This act of remembrance is incorporated into a Church service or is a separate Holy Communion service.

The Holy Communion service is also referred to as:
The Lord's Supper - 1Cor 11:20,
The Breaking of Bread service - Acts 2:42 & 46.

This service is derived from a simple meal that Jesus Christ had with His disciples shortly before He was crucified. It was during this meal that this special act of remembrance was requested by the Lord Jesus Christ as described in the following Scripture:

26 While they were eating, Jesus took bread, gave thanks and broke it, and gave it to his disciples, saying, "Take and eat; this is my body."
27 Then he took the cup, gave thanks and offered it to them, saying, "Drink from it, all of you.
28 This is my blood of the covenant, which is poured out for many for the forgiveness of sins.
29 I tell you, I will not drink of this fruit of the vine from now on until that day when I drink it anew with you in my Father's kingdom."

Mat 26:26-29

The above words were later taken by the Apostle Paul when he wrote to the Corinthian Church asking them to remember the Lord Jesus Christ in this way and reminding them of their significance when he said, "For whenever you eat this bread and drink this cup, you proclaim the Lord's death until he comes." (1Cor 11:26).

In some branches of the Christian Church, however, this essentially simple but deeply significant service has been overlaid with much ritual and ceremony that can obscure it's true meaning and application to people's lives, so the essential teaching that should come from this type of service is set out below.

The meaning of the Lord's Supper is rich, in that symbols used have great significance for Christians, as outlined below:

The broken bread symbolizes Christ's body being given for us when He died on the cross (Jn 19:31-36), and the poured out cup symbolizes the pouring out of Christ's blood for us, and through this act has obtained forgiveness for our sins.

When participating in the Lord's Supper, and following Christ's invitation to "take and eat -----"(Mat 26:26), we are taking the benefits of Christ's death to ourselves.

Jesus had spoken previously in a symbolic way about His death and what it meant when He referred to Himself as the 'bread of life' - 'which I will give for the life of the world' (Jn 6:48-51), and He continues in this symbolic manner by saying: "unless you eat the flesh of the Son of Man and drink his blood, you have no life in you." (Jn 6:52-54). This illustrates again the benefits we, as Christians, receive from His redemptive work on the cross.

The Scriptures show that participation in the Lord's Supper is an open and continual invitation to Christians when they come together, and in Lk 22:17-20 Jesus says: "do this in remembrance of me." An indication, accepted by some, that this was a weekly event can be taken from Acts 20:7 where it says: "On the first day of the week we came together to break bread."

When Christians meet together for this event they come at the Lord's invitation and on each occasion are reminded of Christ's redeeming love, that they are included in His family, and that the act of meeting together in this way is a sign of unity with one another and with Him. The Scripture given below supports this aspect of unity:

16 Is not the cup of thanksgiving for which we give thanks a participation in the blood of Christ? And is not the bread that we break a participation in the body of Christ?
17 Because there is one loaf, we, who are many, are one body, for we all partake of the one loaf.

1Cor 10:16-17

In the passage 1Cor 11:23-29, Paul sets out the conditions that should pertain when Christians meet to celebrate the Lord's Supper, and asks them to break bread to remind them of the Lord's body broken for them, and to take wine in remembrance of the Lord's blood poured out for them. When they do this they proclaim the Lord's death until he comes.

Also everyone taking part should examine themselves before they eat of the bread and drinks of the cup.

In the above Scripture he warns people in v27 against eating or drinking 'in an unworthy manner,' and this is further emphasised and explained in v28-29, where each person is reminded to examine themselves in respect of discerning the true nature of the church, that it is His Church, and they are part of one united body. In which case if any person is not in a forgiven and restored relationship with God and others, then this should be put right first before they come to this service. If these things are not put right then, this person, and perhaps others, will not receive the benefit that can be expected from this special time of meeting with God.

GOD'S PROVISION

-HOLY COMMUNION-

Notes and Quotations

Wayne Grudem in his book, "Bible Doctrine" referring to 'The Meaning of the Lord's Supper' states: "The meaning of the Lord's Supper is complex, rich, and full. Several things are symbolized and affirmed in the Lord's Supper."

In the above book he gives many insights and explanations into this subject, and outlined below are a few brief extracts from this material:

Referring to Christ's death he states: "participating in the Lord's Supper is also a kind of proclamation," 'For as often as you eat this bread and drink the cup, *you proclaim the Lord's death* until he comes' (1Cor 11:26).

He also makes the following points:

"As we individually reach out and take the cup for ourselves, each one of us is by that action proclaiming, *I am taking the benefits of Christ's death to myself.*"

"Just as ordinary food nourishes our physical bodies, so the bread and wine of the Lord's Supper give nourishment to us," - He refers here to spiritual nourishment and refreshment.

"When Christians participate in the Lord's Supper together, they also give a clear sign of their unity with one another. In fact, Paul says, '*Because there is one bread, we who are many are one body, for we all partake of the one bread'* (1Cor 10:17)."

Randy Petersen in his book "The Christian Book of Lists" quotes seven reasons for coming to the Lord's Supper:

1. It is an act of obedience (Mat 26:26-27; 1Cor 11:24-25).
2. It is an act of remembrance (Lk 22:19; 1Cor 11:24-25).
3. It is a testimony to his death (1Cor 5:7; 11:26).
4. It is a confession that salvation is through his blood (Mat 26:28; Rev 1:5).
5. It is an act of fellowship (1Cor 10:16-17).
6. It is an act of praise and thanksgiving (Lk 22:19; 1Cor 10:16; 11:26).
7. It proclaims his second coming (1Cor 11:26).

GOD'S PROVISION

-HOLY COMMUNION-

Biblical Texts & Text References

Jesus Christ is speaking:

17 After taking the cup, he gave thanks and said, "Take this and divide it among you.
18 For I tell you I will not drink again of the fruit of the vine until the kingdom of God comes."
19 And he took bread, gave thanks and broke it, and gave it to them, saying, "This is my body given for you; do this in remembrance of me."
20 In the same way, after the supper he took the cup, saying, "This cup is the new covenant in my blood, which is poured out for you.

Lk 22:17-20

It states in Heb 9:27-28 that: "man is destined to die once, and after that to face judgment", and that Christ was sacrificed once to take away the sins of many people.

Additional Scripture references

Jn 6:47-59, Acts 2:42 & 46; 1Cor 5:7, Heb 10:3-10; Rev 1:3-6

D8

GOD'S PROVISION

-RENEWAL, RESTORATION, WHOLENESS, REVIVAL-

Biblical Definitions

Renew

It is a general principle in life that people age and deteriorate health wise, and this principle can apply to people spiritually. When a person becomes a Christian, as explained in Part 1 of the book and also in Section E4, they begin a relationship with God and in time this should strengthen, but from the outset it will be attacked in various ways. Attacks can be in the form of doubts, negative and discouraging comments and experiences, so there will always be a need for spiritual renewal. All these factors seem to indicate that a spiritual leakage principle can be at work, so Christians need to develop a way of life that is continually dependant on God for His resources to renew them spiritually. This same principle relates to us in the physical realm in that we cannot rely on the food that we ate yesterday or last week to keep us nourished and in good health, it is an ongoing daily process.

With these thoughts in mind let us look further into this subject by reading the following notes by W.E. Vine.

RENEW, RENEWING - VERB

W.E.Vine in his book:(Expository Dictionary of Bible Words) refers to 2Cor 4:16 where the Scripture says: "Though our outer nature is wasting away, our inner nature is being renewed every day." He refers here to the renewal of spiritual power, and in Col 3:10 it states: "and have put on the new nature, which is being renewed in knowledge after the image of its creator." Here again he refers to "the new man" (in contrast to the old unregenerate nature), which "is being renewed in knowledge," i.e. the true knowledge in Christ, as opposed to heretical teachings.

RENEWAL - NOUN

W.E.Vine refers to Rom 12:2 "Do not be conformed to this world but be transformed by the renewal of your mind, that you may prove what is the will of God, what is good acceptable and perfect." He describes "the renewal of your mind" as "the adjustment of the moral and spiritual vision and thinking to the mind of God, which is designed to have a transforming effect upon the life." With reference to Tit 3:5 where the Scripture refers to, "renewal in the Holy Spirit" he further states that this:"is not a fresh bestowment of the Spirit, but a revival of His power, developing the Christian life; this passage stresses the continual operation of the indwelling Spirit of God; the Romans passage stresses the willing response on the part of the believer.

Restore

Due to human weakness Christians can fail God for various reasons, such as, giving in to temptation or selfishness, or being guilty of cowardice etc. When the person becomes aware of their failure they can feel depressed or dispirited, and can wonder if they should carry on?, or could they have their relationship restored with God? In these quite common circumstances, however, there is good news – God is waiting to forgive and restore the relationship when that sin is confessed as stated in the Scripture 1Jn 1:8-9.

There are further comments from W.E. Vine in his book: (Expository Dictionary of Bible Words), that provide more Scriptures to back up and expand on this theme as outlined below.

W.E.Vine refers here to three words:

1. to give back - translated "I restore" in Lk 19:8.
2a. to restore to a former condition of health in - Mat 12:13; Mk 3:5; 8:25; Lk 6:10.
2b. of the Divine restoration of Israel and conditions affected by it, including the renewal of the Covenant broken by them, Mat 17:11; Mk 9:12; Acts 1:6.
2c. of giving or bringing a person back, Heb 13:19.
3. to mend, to furnish completely, is translated "restore" in Gal 6:1.

Wholeness

It is a fact that people may suffer from a wide variety of illnesses and medical conditions throughout their lives, and that when they occur healing is required. There are many occurrences, however, where people deny that they have a health problem, and this is frequently true for things spiritual, where people think they are alright with God and have no need of 'healing'. Whilst a person remains in denial not very much can be done, so they must be persuaded to face the problem of spiritual pride, or whatever the problem is, so that their relationship with can be restored.

It is always good to know that help is available for the asking from God, and we shall see from the following statements concerning the word 'wholeness' that God's ultimate desire for us is to be 'whole' or 'complete'. Let us remember the words of Jesus Christ when He said to the sick: "what do you want me to do for you?". With these thoughts in mind let us look further at the word 'wholeness'.

According to the Biblical scholars there are a number of words which are used in the N.T. for "whole" many refer to "all; a lot; entire; complete, etc. but one word of particular interest is the word that is used especially in the Gospels for making sick folk "whole"- Mat 12:13 N.I.V. "Then he (Jesus) said to the man, "Stretch out your hand." So he stretched it out and it was completely restored, just as sound as the other."

In the R.S.V. it reads: "Then he (Jesus) said to the man, "Stretch out your hand." And the man stretched it out, and it was restored, whole like the other."

There are many references in Scripture to Jesus making people "whole" completely healed whatever the condition, and as He is THE CREATOR GOD nothing is too difficult for Him.

Revival

There is a general tendency among people to want to be comfortable and to resist change. So, therefore, there is always a need to be spiritually re-ignited, fired up, to strive to know more of the power and character of God in their lives. This though, is not comfortable talk it is unknown territory, so there is often a response: "I'm alright where I am, thank you", or perhaps: "I'm more spiritually minded than Mr X or Mrs Y". So as in life we are usually subjected to the principle of physical deterioration with age, so this principle can apply to us spiritually, leaving us in a place, therefore, needing to be spiritually refreshed, and indeed revived. Please now read what other contributors have to say on this topic.

"There have been three great *Protestant* Revivals - the Reformation, the Puritan, and the Evangelical, this last starting about the middle of the eighteenth century, all whose first apostles were ministers of the Church of England, but by means of which all the Reformed Churches everywhere were visited from on high by a marvellous time of refreshing. Nor was its influence limited to those Churches then; whilst to-day, perhaps, throughout the world that influence is stronger and more widely felt than ever before." - from "The Protestant Dictionary" Published by The Harrison Trust - London.

Winkie Pratney in his book "Revival" states at the front of the book: "This book focuses especially on two subjects: young people and revivals. About the only thing more written on and less understood than the subject of "Youth" is the subject of "Revival." I hope this will not add to the confusion. I am, nevertheless, persuaded that revival - true, heaven-born, God-authorised revival - is the critical need of the hour and the hope of this country's young. We had better understand something about this thing called revival and know how to call on God concerning it if the bright western youth of the 1980's are going to spiritually survive and triumph in the world of the 1990's."

He begins his definition of Revival by referring to Webster's dictionary meaning of the word *revive* as a:

1. "Return, recall or recovery to *life from death* or *apparent death*; as the revival of a drowned person." Revival brings something back to life that is either now dead or seemingly dead. Revival is not for something that has never lived at all.

2. "Return or recall to *activity* from a state of languor; as the revival of spirits." Revival brings a holy shock to apathy and carelessness. Isaiah, calling for God to show His manifest power, says: "Oh that Thou wouldest rend the heavens, that Thou wouldest come down, that mountains might flow down at Thy presence.......to

make Thy name known to Thine adversaries, that the nations may tremble at Thy presence! When Thou didst terrible things which we looked not for, Thou camest down." Isa 64:1-3.

3. "Recall, return or recovery from a state of *neglect, oblivion, obscurity,* or *depression*; as the revival of letters or learning." Revival restores truth and recalls to obedience that which has been forgotten. Invariably, as either its cause or result, it is associated with reformation of doctrine and preaching.

4. "Renewed and more active attention to religion: an awakening of men to their *spiritual concerns."* Revival accomplishes what our best spiritual efforts cannot. - - - - - - - .

In the book he gives a wide coverage of the whole subject of revival, including its history, effects, characteristics and the principal people involved in it.

GOD'S PROVISION

-RENEWAL, RESTORATION, WHOLENESS, REVIVAL-

Notes and Quotations

Renewal / Revival

"Revival is always related to holiness. True revival is a revival of holiness."

"Holiness is not just a doctrine to be taught, it is a way of life - it is the LIFE of Jesus."

A quotation by Duncan Campbell.

A few quotations are given below from the very challenging book "Why Revival Tarries" by Leonard Ravenhill. In this book he explains why he considers revival tarries and gives the following statement headings:

"It tarries because evangelism is so highly commercialised"
"It tarries because of cheapening the Gospel"
"It tarries because of carelessness"
"It tarries because of fear"
"It tarries because we lack urgency in prayer"
"It tarries because we steal the glory that belongs to God"

He further quotes: "Two hundred years ago, Charles Wesley sang,
"O that in me the sacred fire
Might now begin to glow,
Burn up the dross of base desire,
And make the mountains flow!"

Dr Hatch cried,
"Breathe on me, Breath of God,
Till I am wholly Thine,
Until this earthly part of me
Glows with Thy fire divine."

"Holy Ghost fire destroys, purifies, warms, attracts, and empowers."

Selwyn Hughes in his "Every Day with Jesus" Notes reminds us of words used by Evan Roberts when he stated 'The Four Great Tenets'.

Evan Roberts, a man greatly used by God in the 1904 Welsh revival claimed that there were four essential conditions which needed to be fulfilled before revival could come:

1. All sin must be confessed to God.
2. There must be no cloud between the believer and God and the believer and everyone else.
3. The Holy Spirit must not only be invited but *obeyed.*
4. There must be continued public confession of Christ as Saviour and Lord.

"*Will you not revive us again, that your people may rejoice in you*".

Ps 85:6

Someone has said: "A form of Renewal is Revival."
Someone has said: "There is no revival without repentance."
Somebody has provided the following:

"<u>Recipe for Revival</u>
If all the Sleeping folks would Wake Up,
And all the Lukewarm would Fire Up,
And all the Disgruntled would Sweeten Up,
And all the Discouraged would Cheer Up,
And all the Depressed would Look Up,
And all the Estranged would Make Up,
And all the Gossipers would Shut Up,
Then there might come a revival."

Consider the words of Jesus in Mat 18:19,

"Again, I tell you that if two of you on earth agree about anything you ask for, it will be done for you by my Father in heaven."

There seems to be a balance between the sovereignty of God and the responsibility of man, where revival is transported to earth on the wings of fervent, believing, intercessory prayer. John Wesley said: "God does nothing redemptively in the world, except through prayer," and "He touches the hearts of certain people to pray."

See Lk 1:10-13, Acts 1:14-15, 4:24-31, 12:12-17.

Roy Hession in his book "The Calvary Road – Be Filled Now" states: "Revival is just the life of the Lord Jesus poured into human hearts. Jesus is always victorious. In heaven they are always praising Him all the time for His victory. Whatever may be our experience of failure and barrenness, He is never defeated. His power is boundless. We, on our part, have only to get into a right relationship with Him, and we shall see His power being demonstrated in our hearts and lives and service, and His victorious life will fill us and overflow through us to others. That is revival in its essence." He then goes on to say that to come into this right relationship our will must be broken to His will, and that is painful.

2 O LORD, I have heard thy speech, *and* was afraid: O LORD, revive thy work in the midst of the years, in the midst of the years make known; in wrath remember mercy. Hab 3:2 AV.

Bob Gass in his "The Word for Today" Notes states with reference to Hab 3:2 AV above:

"We all need to pray, "O Lord, revive *Thy* work," but we also need to remember that He'll revive only *His* work; He'll let *yours* die!"

<u>Restoration</u>

God's heart is always to restore, rebuild, and straighten out people's lives that have strayed away from Him, and wish to return. Some of these thoughts are reflected in the Scriptures below.

We see in the Scripture below something of God's attitude and resulting action towards people who sin:

3 So I went down to the potter's house, and I saw him working at the wheel.

4 But the pot he was shaping from the clay was marred in his hands; so the potter formed it into another pot, shaping it as seemed best to him.

Jer 18:3-4 (N.I.V.)

3 So I went down to the potter's house, and there he was working at his wheel.

4 And the vessel he was making of clay was spoiled in the potter's hand, and he reworked it into another vessel, as it seemed good to the potter to do.

Jer 18:3-4 (R.S.V.)

We see here that when we sin and become 'marred' or 'spoiled' clay, God does not discard or throw the clay away, but He reworks it. This is like us when we turn back to God in faith and repentance, He works on us again to reshape us as He desires.

In Isa 40: 28-31 we see something of God as one who gives encouragement and hope, and one whose heart is to see lives rebuilt, giving strength to the weary and power to the weak.

Here God is calling for people's lives to be built anew with his help.

In the Scripture Joel 2:12-13, 24-26 we see God's conditional promise of restoration to those who come back to Him in repentance.

In Joel 2:25 (RSV) given below, is seen God's heart to restore those who have turned away from him.

25 "I will restore to you the years which the swarming locust has eaten,"

Jesus loves to take the *lost,* the *last,* the *least* and the *lowest* and make something beautiful of them. See Jn 4:13-26

Regarding revival and miraculous happenings the author holds the view, no doubt common to many who want to see the maximum involvement of God in these matters, with the minimum involvement of man.

Wholeness

W.E. Vine states when referring to "The God of peace" (Rom 15:33, 16:20, Phil 4:9, 1Thess 5:23, ---------), "that the corresponding Hebrew word *'shalom'* primarily signifies wholeness." And included in his exposition of *'shalom/wholeness'* he relates its meaning to such words as: "full", "finished", "made perfect", "entire", "salvation". He gives further explanation of what it means to be "whole" with reference to the Gospels (Mat 12:13, Mk 3:5, Lk 6:10, Jn 5:4-14) where he also includes the words to be "sound" and "healthy."

Something of the desire of God's heart can be seen in Isa 57:15-19,
His desire - v15 - to revive,
- v18 - to heal, guide and comfort,
- v19 - to give peace.

Someone has said that "wholeness" means: "having every part of our lives exactly as God wants."

Wholeness - Spiritual Maturity

Someone has said 'spiritual maturity' can be measured by where we put our trust. Is it in God, or people, or things (science, education, possessions, traditions, etc.), or self?

God wants us to be dependant on Him for direction in life and not ourselves, and this requires the revelation of and submission to His Will. This means that we will use the energy and abilities we have been given to ultimately fulfil His purposes. For most people this will not mean being in full-time Christian work, but will entail listening for and obeying His voice.

For the majority of people spiritual maturity is a slow process, because our submission to His Will is partial and slow. We need to be *weak* in our own strength and *strong* in His, see Jud 6:15-16, 2Cor 12:9-10 (where God says: "my power is made perfect in weakness," ----- and Paul confirms that by saying: "For when I am weak, then I am strong."

Dr R.T.Kendall has said: "Spiritual maturity can be measured by the time gap between when we sin and when we repent - is it years, months, weeks, days, hours, minutes, seconds, or is it immediate."

GOD'S PROVISION

-RENEWAL, RESTORATION, WHOLENESS, REVIVAL-

Biblical Texts & Text References

Renewal / Revival

In Rom 12:1-2 believers are urged to offer their bodies as a living sacrifices, holy and pleasing to God, and not to conform to the pattern of this world, but be transformed by the renewing of your mind.

3 At one time we too were foolish, disobedient, deceived and enslaved by all kinds of passions and pleasures. We lived in malice and envy, being hated and hating one another.
4 But when the kindness and love of God our Saviour appeared,
5 he saved us, not because of righteous things we had done, but because of his mercy. He saved us through the washing of rebirth and renewal by the Holy Spirit,
6 whom he poured out on us generously through Jesus Christ our Saviour,
7 so that, having been justified by his grace, we might become heirs having the hope of eternal life.

Tit 3:3-7

Note: W.E. Vine refers to verse 5 and the Greek word for 'renewal' and states: "'the renewing of the Holy Spirit' is not a fresh bestowment of the Spirit, but a revival of His power, developing the Christian life; this passage stresses the continual operation of the indwelling Spirit of God."

Additional Scripture references

Ps 86:6-7; 103:1-5; Isa 32:12-18; 40:28-31; 57:14-15; 64:1-3, Jer 31:23-25, Hos 14:4-7, Hab 3:1-2, Zeph 3:17-18, Mat 18:19-20, Lk 1:10-13, Acts 1:14-15; 2:1-4; 4:24-31; 12:12-17, 2Cor 4:16-18, Eph 4:22-24; Col 3:9-12

Restoration

When David committed adultery with Bathsheba he earnestly sought God's forgiveness and restoration of his relationship with him, and also wanted to receive the renewal of God's spirit within him, and avoid being cast from his presence. See Ps 51:10-12

17 Therefore, if anyone is in Christ, he is a new creation; the old has gone, the new has come!
18 All this is from God, who reconciled us to himself through Christ and gave us the ministry of reconciliation:

2Cor 5:17-18

In 1Jn 1:8-9 the reader is reminded that nobody is without sin, but if people confess their sins God is faithful and will forgive and purify them.

Additional Scripture references

1Sam 2:8, Ps 80:3-7; 147:1-3, Isa 40:3-5 & 25-31, 44:3; 61:1-3; Jer 15:19-20; 17:14; 31:25-26, Joel 2:12-13 & 24-26, Mat 12;13; 17:11, Mk 3:5; 9:12, Lk 17:15-19; 19:8, Acts 1:6-7, Rom 7:4; 15:31-33, Gal 6:1, Eph 2:6-9, Col 1:19-23

Wholeness

33 There he found a man named Aeneas, a paralytic who had been bedridden for eight years.
34 "Aeneas," Peter said to him, "Jesus Christ heals you. Get up and tidy up your mat." Immediately Aeneas got up.
35 All those who lived in Lydda and Sharon saw him and turned to the Lord.

Acts 9:33-35

Additional Scripture references

Jud 6:15-16, Isa 57:15-19, Mat 9:21-22; 12:12-13, Mk 3:4-5; Lk 5:17-25; 6:10; 7:7-10, Rom 15:33; 16:20, 2Cor 12:9-10; Phil 4:9, Col 3:15, 1Thess 5:23; Heb 7:23-26

E1

OUR RESPONSE TO GOD - DISCIPLESHIP

- FULFILLING HIS WILL -

Biblical Definitions

Fulfilling God's Will

It is to be remembered that even The Lord Jesus Christ, God's Son, did not come on earth to do His Will, but that of His Father, and in Jn 5:30 Jesus says:"I seek not to please myself but him who sent me", and this is the same commitment that God asks of those who become Christians.

So to understand how this commitment can be made people must know that the process of becoming a Christian entails submitting our will to the will of God. It follows, therefore, that nobody can begin to fulfil God's will until they become a Christian, so given below is an outline of the essential steps for becoming a Christian, and so coming into Christ's family.

Becoming a Christian

Some people think that if they were born into a Christian family or country, or that if they live as good a life as they can and did many good deeds, - they could consider that makes them a Christian. Unfortunately none of these is the way. This thinking could be likened to the analogy of saying, that if they were born in a garage that would make them a car. As far as doing good deeds are concerned, it is like people saying they can become a Christian by building a credit with God through doing good deeds, - this also is not the way to become a Christian. In fact, the good deeds are expected *after* they become a Christian.

The way to become a Christian is quite simple to understand, but it does require that the person is open and honest and sees the true need that they have. To discover the truth in this very important matter please read on.

The first thing to understand is that a person cannot be born a Christian, and someone is not found to be acceptable or unacceptable based on whether their parents or family were Christians or not. The fact is, that each person must always have a direct meeting with God – initially through recognition of the deity of the Lord Jesus Christ as God, coupled with confession and repentance, as explained below.

The person must realize that they have a need to come to God and seek forgiveness, and that they are coming to God, the only God, who loves them and has proved His love by the Lord Jesus Christ dying for them. He did this to pay the price required to deliver every person from the penalty they would have to pay for the sin they had committed. The sin being the basic rebellion against the rule of God that everyone has in their makeup, e.g. -I'll live my own life, good or bad, in my own way, - I'll do it my way, - I'll paddle my own canoe. This attitude of mind, which wants to live independent of God and a relationship with Him, is one that unfortunately, we are born with.

To come then into a right relationship with God is the most important thing in peoples lives., as they will then find acceptance, forgiveness, a fresh start, unconditional love, power for living, and the certainty of an eternal place in heaven, - to name but a few of the things they will receive.

Like anything that is worthwhile, there is always 'price' to pay, and the Christian life does not promise to be easy, but it does promise to be fulfilling and eternally worthwhile.

Essential Steps to Becoming a Christian

These steps are fully explained in Section E4, but they can be outlined in the following way.

The process of becoming a Christian must contain the elements of belief, repentance, confession and commitment

Every person must confess to God by admitting that they have left Him out of their lives, and have ignored His rightful claims on them, because this is the main, the cardinal sin, that everybody is guilty of, and is the sin from which all other sins originate.

This confession must be coupled with a truly repentant attitude (have a changed mind – and this should result in a changed lifestyle) and of asking Him to forgive them. Then proceed to thank Him for dying for them. See the Scriptures below:

In Acts 26:20 it states:" First to those in Damascus, then to those in Jerusalem and in all Judea, and to the Gentiles also, I preached that they should repent and turn to God and prove their repentance by their deeds."

In the above scripture there is a need to understand the term 'repentance', and the scripture below reveals a need to understand the meaning of 'sin'.

23 For the wages of sin is death, but the gift of God is eternal life in Christ Jesus our Lord.

Rom 6:23

For further information on this subject see Section E4.

<u>Warning to non believers</u>

To those who refuse or ignore all that God has done for them in love and so will not believe that Jesus Christ is God's Son, and will not accept His offer of forgiveness and new life, must seriously consider the consequences of that rejection of His action of love. As God has done all that is necessary to bring, to draw, to woo people, His creation, back to Himself and into His kingdom, it only remains to leave people in their present condemned state, which is not what He desires. It is as if a person is drowning and God has thrown them a life belt and they refuse to hold on to it, and so choose to drown.

The Scriptures Jn 3:18, & Rom 10:9-13 support the statement made here, and for more about this subject please read Section E4.

<u>*Let us now consider what it means as a Christian to be fulfilling the will of God.*</u>

The will of a person is like a ship's rudder, which is used to steer it in a certain direction. This is the effect of our will in that it determines our intentions to think or act in a certain way, to go in a deliberate direction in life. Stubbornness, causes a person to continue in a set direction, right or wrong, but as this can lead to many problems the person would be wise to check the likely consequences of their attitude *before* making important decisions affecting their lifestyle.

This is where everyone needs to look at the basis on which their life direction decisions have been made, and these decisions would normally relate to a life code of some type, e.g. a philosophy or religion.

The philosophy for living could range from just living to please yourself, to a way out mode of living. As far as adopting a lifestyle that is based on a religion, then there are plenty to choose from. However, on the authority of the Word of God, the Bible, people would be wise to consider the proven record of help and hope that the Christian Faith has given to people all round the world for more than two thousands years.

As the choice of lifestyle affects people in their present life and their eternal destiny, people are asked to read on to find out more about it.

There are many Scriptures that refer to this subject, and an outline of these is given below:

In the broad sense 'the Will of God' for our lives is fulfilling the 'Word of God'. God's Word (the Bible) has His authority as seen from a quote by Jesus Christ when he says, "It is written."

4 Jesus answered, "It is written: `Man does not live on bread alone, but on every word that comes from the mouth of God."

Mat 4:4 quoting from Deut 8:3

The 'Will of God' is also fulfilling the 'Word of God' when He speaks to a person individually from it, and they obey what they receive from the Bible. See part of the Lord's Prayer below:

9 "This, then, is how you should pray: "`Our Father in heaven, hallowed be your name,
10 your kingdom come, <u>your will be done on earth</u> as it is in heaven.

Mat 6:9-10

Another general point is that our aim in life is to please Him' - see 2Cor 5:9, & Col 1;10

Our responsibility is firstly one of obedience by putting aside our will and submitting ourselves to the will of God, then He begins transforming our character and renewing our minds, and this process is conforming us to live according to His will, as borne out by the Scripture Mat 7:21 in which it states that not everyone who says to Jesus 'Lord, Lord' will enter the kingdom of heaven, but only those who do the will of my Father.

The Scriptures below state that our underlying purpose (whatever our job or role) in life is to live for God and bear fruit to God, and this is where His love for us provides the driving force and the enabling motivation.

14 For Christ's love compels us, because we are convinced that one died for all, and therefore all died.
15 And he died for all, that those who live should no longer live for themselves but for him who died for them and was raised again.

2Cor 5:14-15

God wants the Christian to continually pursue the aim of having ever more of the character of Jesus. In the Scripture below we see (v7), Paul's determination and purpose. It is clear that his purpose did not finish at the grave, but went beyond it.

See 2Tim 4:7-8

God calls us, not just to *have* His Holy Spirit, which all true Christians have, but that His will is that we are *filled* with His Spirit, - see Section D5.

Jesus gave us a test for our aims and motives when He said in Mat 6:19-21 that we should not store up treasures on earth, but store up treasures in heaven where nothing can destroy them. The truth being that where your treasure is, there your heart will be also.

OUR RESPONSE TO GOD - DISCIPLESHIP

-FULFILLING HIS WILL-

Notes and Quotations

The Will of God

Archbishop William Temple said: "Every revelation of God is a demand, and the way to knowledge of God is obedience."

Selwyn Hughes commenting on this statement in his "Every Day with Jesus" Notes says: "Our relationship with God rises and falls at the point of obedience. When we stop obeying, God stops revealing. And always remember - whenever God's finger points the way to anything His hand always provides the power. It is ours to be willing; it is His to be supporting."

C.H. Spurgeon said: "A Man's chief end is to glorify God (1Cor 10:31) and to enjoy Him for ever." (Ps 73:25-26).

Christian discipleship involves every part of our personalities.
Our minds are to be renewed (Rom 12:2),
our emotions purified (Eph 4:26),
our conscience kept clear (Acts 24:16),
and our wills surrendered to God's will.
From "Every Day with Jesus" Notes by Selwyn Hughes.

"You were born for a purpose. Your greatest challenge is to discover it and live in the centre of it. In spite of his failures, the Bible says, "David had served God's purpose in his own generation ..... (Acts 13:36). There is no greater testimony than that!"

"Before you find life's purpose, you often go through a series of adversities that cause you to let go of the temporal and grasp the eternal! For Paul that meant the loss of everything ! (Phil 3:8)."

The notes shown above are extracts from 'The Word for Today' Notes by Bob Gass, and in another Note he refers to Ps 119:37 under the heading "Hold on to your vision". The verse states:

37 Turn my eyes away from worthless things; preserve my life [my vision] according to your word. He states: "Having a vision for your life will save you from three deadly foes: indecision; indifference; and impatience." He says the one thing you must have is 'vision', and states why: "Vision is the ability to . . . sense God's presence . . . . harness His power . . . and focus on His plan for your life – in spite of the obstacles.

Vision also means refusing to give in . . . to temptation . . .or to doubt . . . or to become jaded.

It means being determined to 'hang tough' when the going gets tough."

In another 'Note' Bob Gass says:"God created your uniqueness, so He certainly doesn't want to destroy it. Christ- likeness is about transforming your character, not your personality." see Rom 12:1-2, 2Cor 3:18, Eph 4:23-24

Knowing and fulfilling the Will of God is:

Rightly responding to the revealed Word of God - (Ps 40:8, 143:10), however that revelation comes: e.g. reading, hearing, or 'seeing' the revealed truth of the Word

- (Mat 6:10, 7:21, Mk 3:35, Jn 5:30).
- Jesus said: "I know my sheep and my sheep know me." (Jn 10:14).
- He also said: "My sheep listen to my voice, I know them, and they follow me." (Jn 10:27).
- What God initiates, He backs up with the resources of heaven. (Phil 4:19).

In life God's will is often only revealed a little at a time - Ps 119:105, but

His all-encompassing purpose for the lives of believers is 'to declare the praises of God' – 1Pet 2:9-10.

George Macdonald has said: "I find doing the will of God leaves me no time for disputing about his plans." A quote from "The Christian Book of Lists" by Randy Petersen.

<u>Checking our motivation</u>

Our true motivation, priorities, and heart desires are revealed through the words of Jesus when He said "out of the overflow of the heart the mouth speaks." (Mat 12:34).

<u>Leading and the Will of God</u>

Are you trying to find the will of God? If so, then you need to understand that God speaks to us in the following ways:

1. Through proven leadership - Heb 13:17.
2. Through your gifts - Prov 18:16.
3. Through your thoughts - 1Cor 2:16.
4. Through open doors - 1Cor 16:9.
5. Through 'sanctified desires' - Ps 37:4.
6. Through a word of confirmation - Isa 30:21. Please note, this word usually comes <u>after</u> you move. It is a word <u>*behind*</u> you, confirming that you're on the right track.
7. Through 'the peace test' - Col 3:15.
8. Through 'shaking up your comfort zone' - Deut 32:11-12. Eagles learn to fly by being <u>pushed</u> out of the nest and over the cliff's edge.

The note shown above is an extract from 'The Word for Today' Notes by Bob Gass.

Fred Smith, the author of 'Learning to Lead' once sent all his friends a letter with these three questions:

1. Am I enjoying what I'm doing?
2. Am I happy with where I'm going?
3. Am I satisfied with what I'm becoming?

See Prov 3:6 and Jer 29:11.

The note shown above is an extract from 'The Word for Today' Notes by Bob Gass.

These questions provide us all with an opportunity to review the direction of our lives.

In another extract from "The Word for Today" Notes by Bob Gass, he states: "The problem that infuriates you the most is often the one you've been called to solve. Situations that unlock your compassion are the very places you'll often find your greatest fulfilment. God doesn't waste experience. He can take your past and make it serve the future. He can turn your misery into a ministry and enable you to reach people you couldn't understand before, much less minister to."

He also states: "It was the trials of Job that made him a legend. It was the lion's den that made Daniel a governor. It was imprisonment that gave Paul an opportunity to write the Epistles."

In yet another extract from "The Word for Today" Notes by Bob Gass, he states: "Jesus said we'd have problems (John 16:33). Nobody gets a free pass. Solve one problem and another's waiting to take its place. They're not all big, but they're all ***necessary*** to your spiritual growth! How do you measure the strength of anything? By testing it! Listen: '....don't be....shocked that you are going through testing .... It will prepare you....'(1Peter 4:12-13 CEV). In this note he further states: "God could have kept Joseph out of jail, Daniel out of the lions' den, Jeremiah out of the slimy pit and Paul from being shipwrecked, but He didn't. And the result? Every one of them was drawn closer to God. – and impacted their world!"

In a further extract from "The Word for Today" Notes by Bob Gass, he states: "If the desire for something persists, that's a good indication that God's leading you. (Phil 2:13)." Consider this statement with other considerations, e.g. that this direction (plan) is to bring glory to God; that during this time His face is continually being sought in prayer; and that the person is listening for God's Holy Spirit and is prepared to obey His voice.

In the three verses of the poem "If" by Rudyard Kipling given below, we see some human qualities and attitudes which should be seen in the Christian as they respond to God's will.

If you can keep your head when all about you
Are losing theirs and blaming it on you,
If you can trust yourself when all men doubt you,
But make allowance for their doubting too;
If you can wait and not be tired by waiting,
Or being lied about, don't deal in lies;
Or being hated, don't give way to hating,
And yet don't look too good, nor talk too wise:
If you can dream - and not make dreams your master;
If you can think - and not make thoughts your aim;
If you can meet with Triumph and Disaster
And treat those two impostors just the same;
If you can bear to hear the truth you've spoken
Twisted by knaves to make a trap for fools,
Or watch the things you gave your life to, broken,
And stoop and build 'em up with worn-out tools:
If you can talk with crowds and keep your virtue,
Or walk with Kings - nor lose the common touch,
If neither foes nor loving friends can hurt you,
If all men count with you, but none too much;
If you can fill the unforgiving minute
With sixty seconds' worth of distance run,
And - which is more - you'll be a Man, my son!

Resources for the Will of God

God has all the resources we need to fulfil His will in terms of knowledge, spiritual wisdom and understanding, power, endurance, patience and joy, see Col 1:9-13.

By contrast to depending on Him and working out His will, Bob Gass in his: "The Word for Today" Notes relates to a writer who says:

"I was hungry and you formed a club to discuss it.
I was in prison and you stayed in church to pray for me.
I was naked and you debated the morality of my appearance.
I was sick and you thanked God for your health.

I was homeless and you told me about heaven's streets of gold. You seem so holy and so close to God, but I'm still hungry, lonely, cold and in pain. Does it matter?" - Mat 25:31-46.

<u>Power to live the Christian life.</u>
There are many Scriptures that show God has not intended the Christian convert, or the mature Christian, to attempt to live the Christian life without receiving His power to do so. God has made this provision because He knows that the power we need to make this life possible only comes through the Person of His Holy Spirit, as the Scripture below shows:

"But you will receive power when the Holy Spirit comes on you; and you will be my witnesses in Jerusalem, and in all Judea and Samaria, and to the ends of the earth." Acts 1:8

Other Scriptures which relate to this theme can be found in Rom 15:17-19; 2Cor 12:9-10; Col 1:10-11, and for further study please refer to Section D5.

Someone has made the following comment with reference to Acts 1:8 above:

"*Power* is the ability to complete a task given by God, and
authority is the right to use the *power* of God."

<u>Service in the Will of God</u>
<u>"The power of a goal.</u> (Phil 3:14)

What are your goals to-day?
Are they clear enough to write down?
Short enough to fit into a paragraph?
Strong enough to help you persevere?
Valuable enough to make you pay the price?
If they are, you'll see them fulfilled!"

The note shown above is an extract from 'The Word for Today' Notes by Bob Gass.

One could also ask, "What are the goals for your church?"

Comments from an unknown source:
"Be purpose driven - don't drift, only conforming to other people's wishes. Understand God's call on your life - be prepared to walk alone (e.g. Elijah v 850 prophets, David v Goliath - David was alone when he went out, but acclaimed when he came back).

We are called according to His purpose - Rom 8:28.

Purpose driven people 'never arrive'. They know that *'satisfaction'* is the enemy of 'success'."

All 'work' - whilst it may be a temporary means to an end, - honest, honourable, worthy occupation, - supporting the needs of family and others, - whether Christian or secular employment, can have an eternal effect on the lives of others. So let us reflect on the fact that God wants us to *'BE'* the people He wants us to *'BE'* in character, and THEN, to *'DO'* the things He has given, guided, and gifted us to *'DO'*. Let us always remember that "your labour in the Lord is not in vain." as stated in the following Scripture:

58 Therefore, my dear brothers, stand firm. Let nothing move you. Always give yourselves fully to the work of the Lord, because you know that your labour in the Lord is not in vain.

1Cor 15:58

God uses failures
In his "The Word for Today" Notes by Bob Gass he asks people to: "Look at Moses: an interrupted childhood, a foster family, a violent temper, a stammering tongue and a criminal record. What a résumé. He could have given up before he even started! Yet God used him to lead the greatest migration of people in the history of the world. And Peter: sinks trying to walk on water, and denies his Lord, yet he becomes head of the New Testament Church.

Failing does not make you a failure, quitting does. Get up and try again. Next time, with God's help, you'll make it."

A Blockage to Fulfilling His Will

"Are you harbouring a grudge? Dare to surrender it now. Grace may flow like a river but a grudge will dam the stream."

Quote from the "Every Day with Jesus" Notes by Selwyn Hughes.

Assessing Progress in Spirituality

D.L. Moody said you can assess your own spirituality by asking yourself: "What are our thoughts in the dark?"

Dr R.T.Kendall has said: "Spiritual maturity can be measured by the time gap between when we sin and when we repent - is it years, months, weeks, days, hours, minutes, seconds, or is it immediate."

Rudyard Kipling wrote: "If you don't get what you want, it's a sign that either you didn't want it seriously enough or that you tried to bargain over the price."

This leads us to ask ourselves: "How seriously do we want to fulfil God's purpose for our life?"

OUR RESPONSE TO GOD - DISCIPLESHIP

-FULFILLING HIS WILL-

Biblical Texts & Text References

God's Will - To Know Him and be Lead by Him

5 Trust in the LORD with all your heart and lean not on your own understanding;
6 in all your ways acknowledge him, and he will make your paths straight.

Prov 3:5-6

Jesus said in Jn 10: 27-28 that his sheep listen to his voice, he knows them and they follow him. Also he gives them eternal life, they will not perish and nobody can take them from him.

Additional Scripture references

Job 19:25, Ps 36:9-10; 40:8; 46:10; 73:25-26, Prov 18:16, Isa 30:21, Jer 24:7; 29:11, Mat 6:9-10; 9:12-13, Mk 3:35, Jn 5:30; 7:16-17; 10:3-4; 13:34-35, 1Cor 2:16; 10:31, 2Cor 4:16-18, Gal 4:8-9, Phil 2:13; 4:19, 1Tim 1:15-16, Tit 1:15-16, Heb 8:11; 13:17, 1Jn 4:7-8

God's Will and Purpose for Believers

Jesus said in Mat 6:20-21 that we should: "Store up for yourselves treasures in heaven, where moth and rust do not destroy, and where thieves do not break in and steal". He also stated the truth that 'your treasure is where your heart is'.

28 And we know that in all things God works for the good of those who love him, who have been called according to his purpose.

Rom 8:28

It is Christ's love that compels us, because we are convinced that Jesus died for all. Hence, we should no longer live for ourselves but for him who died for us. See 2Cor 5:14-15

Additional Scripture references

Gen 5:24, Deut 8:2-3; Job 42:1-2, Ps 37:23-24, Isa 58:9-11, Mat 4:4; 12:46-50, Jn 6:38-40; 10:7-11, Acts 13:36, Rom 7:4; 12:1-2, Gal 4:19-20, Eph 5:17-20, Phil 1:4-6; 2:12-13; 3:8-9 & 14, Col 1:9-10, 1Thess 4:1-8; 5:13-22, 2Tim 1:8-9; 3:16-17, Heb 10:35-36; 11:5, 1Pet 2:9-10; 2:12-15, 2Pet 1:5-8

The Will of God - Maturity

Scripture points out the need for, and the value of 'discipline'.

11 My son, do not despise the LORD's discipline and do not resent his rebuke,
12 because the LORD disciplines those he loves, as a father the son he delights in.

Prov 3:11-12

Additional Scripture references

Lk 8:14; 1Cor 2:6, Gal 4:18-19, Eph 2:10; 4:11-13, Phil 1:4-6; 3:14-15, Col 4:12, Heb 5:11-14; 10:35-36, Jas 1:2-4

E2

OUR RESPONSE TO GOD - DISCIPLESHIP

-CONFESSION AND REPENTANCE-

Biblical Definitions

Confession

The act of confession is often associated with criminals before a court of law, or Roman Catholics going to confess their misdeeds to a priest. In either case the person is expected to admit, or own up to, something that is deemed wrong according to the law of the land, the Church or some other religion. However, according to the Bible confession should be made directly to God, as stated by the Scriptures given below.

To make a confession is never easy because this brings the person into a place of self-humiliation and loss of pride. However, this is the 'price' that every person has to 'pay' if they are going to become a Christian. Yet, looking on the positive side, there is a wonderful release in the spirit and emotions of the person when they confess, and in the Scripture 1Jn 1:8-9 given below, there is an assuring promise given to all who are prepared to do this – the first time to become a Christian, and any subsequent time when they fail God in some way.

Note, particularly in verse nine where it says: "If we confess - - - - he - - - will forgive - -and purify (or cleanse) us" What a firm promise!

8 If we claim to be without sin, we deceive ourselves and the truth is not in us.
9 If we confess our sins, he is faithful and just and will forgive us our sins and purify us from all unrighteousness.

1Jn 1:8-9

Let us now continue and see what other contributors have to say about this topic and repentance.

In the Bible this particularly refers to the confession of a person's sin, that is, admitting that they are guilty of not keeping God's laws, ignoring them, and pleasing themselves how they live – it is this rebellious attitude towards God, their creator, that is referred to as 'sin' in the Bible. Also, it is this basic rebellious attitude from which all other sins such as, bad thoughts, attitudes and harmful actions towards others flow.

Also see E1 and E4.

<u>Repentance</u>

To repent involves making a decision that leads to a change of attitude and direction in life so that the person starts to go in the opposite direction. It's like the command being given on the parade ground to soldiers to 'about turn'.

True repentance should follow the confession of a person and should be seen in actions and attitudes and not just words.

It says in the Scripture Acts 26:20, that people," should repent and turn to God and prove their repentance by their deeds."

For example, people who at one time had no time for God in the direction of their lives, but were now prepared to follow the guidance of the Scriptures in their behaviour and relationships to others and their work ethic, and this was because they wanted to please God.

John Gill in his book "A Body of Practical Divinity" states a number of ways that the word 'repentance' is used:

(a) It is commonly expressed in the O.T. as a "turning" or "returning" and is signified by "a man's turning from his evil ways, and returning to the Lord; the term from which he turns is sin, the term to which he turns is the Lord, against whom he has sinned; and what most powerfully moves, encourages, and induces him to turn, is the pardoning grace and mercy of God through Christ, Isa 55:7 and so in the New Testament, repentance and turning are mentioned together, and the latter as explanative of the former; see Acts 3:19, 26:20."

Another word is used in Hos 11:8, 13:14 which also signifies comfort. This is "because such who sincerely repent of sin, and are truly humbled for it, should be comforted, lest, as the apostle says, they should be 'swallowed up with overmuch sorrow', 2Cor 2:7 and it is God's usual way to bring his people 'into the wilderness', into a distressed state, to lead them into a sense of sin, and humiliation for it, and then to speak comfortably to them, Heb 2:14 and the Spirit of God is first a reprover for sin, and a convincer of it, and then a comforter; - - - - - -"

(b) "Secondly, the Greek word more frequently used in the New Testament for repentance is metanoia, which signifies an "after understanding", or "after knowledge"; as when a man takes into serious consideration a fact after it is committed, and thinks otherwise of it, and wishes he had not done it, is sorry for it, and resolves, through the grace of God, to forsake such practices; this is a proof of a man's wisdom and understanding; now he begins to be wise, and to show himself an understanding man; even an heathen could say,"

"Repentance is the beginning of wisdom, and an avoiding of foolish works and words, and the first preparation to a life not to be repented of."

"It is a change of the mind for the better, and which produces change of action and conduct: this, as it is expressive of true repentance, flows from the understanding being enlightened by the Spirit of God, when the sinner beholds sin in another light than he did, even as exceeding sinful; and loaths it, and abhors it and himself for it. - - - - -"

(c) "Thirdly, The Latin's generally express repentance by "poenitentia", from "poena" punishment; hence our English word "penitence", and the popish "penance", which is a sort of corporal punishment for sin inflicted on the body by fastings, scourgings, pilgrimages, &c. but true penitence lies not in these things, but is rather an inward punishment of the mind, when a man is so displeased with himself for what he has done, and so severely reflects upon himself for it, that he takes as it were a kind of vengeance on himself within himself, which are the lashes of conscience; so the apostle observes of godly sorrow, "What indignation, yea what revenge" it wrought in you, as in the above quoted place; and this inward revenge is sometimes expressed by outward gestures, as by smiting upon the thigh, and upon the breast, Jer 31:19, Lk 18:13. - - - - - "

W.E. Vine refers to 'repentance' as signifying: "to change one's mind or purpose, always, in the N.T., involving a change for the better, an amendment, and always, except in Luke 17:3-4, of repentance from sin. - - - - - "

This is a brief extract taken from his book: "Expository Dictionary of Bible Words".

Also see E1 and E4.

OUR RESPONSE TO GOD - DISCIPLESHIP

-CONFESSION AND REPENTANCE-

Notes and Quotations

Confession

There is a need to:

(a) Confess our sin to God, (i.e. - where sin means having an attitude of rebellion against God's involvement in our lives). See E2 Biblical Definitions, and E4 The Human Condition.

Making this confession will include making confession to others of this step of faith and seeking to obtain the forgiveness from those whom we have hurt and offended.

(b) Find forgiveness from others and for ourselves. See the Scripture below:

Confession brings Healing - Someone has said: "Those who commit crime or war atrocities must accept it and confess the guilt to God and man, and mourn over it, then they can find forgiveness and healing and so get on with their lives.

Victims of crime and suffering must be prepared to talk through any attached shame, confess it and find the healing that the Lord can give." Read and consider Ps 107.

(c) Confess what we now believe concerning God. The essence of what Christians believe is summed up in the Nicene Creed as given below:

Nicene Creed

We believe in one God,

the Father almighty,
maker of heaven and earth,
of all that is,
seen and unseen.
We believe in the one Lord Jesus Christ,
the only Son of God,
eternally begotten of the Father,
God from God, Light from Light,
true God from true God,
begotten not made,
of one being with the Father.
Through Him all things were made.
For us men and for our salvation
He came down from heaven;
by the power of the Holy Spirit
He became incarnate of the Virgin Mary, and was made man.
For our sake He was crucified under Pontius Pilate;
He suffered death and was buried.
On the third day He rose again
in accordance with the Scriptures;
He ascended into heaven
and is seated at the right hand of the Father.
He will come again in glory
to judge the living and the dead,
and His kingdom will have no end.
We believe in the Holy Spirit,
the Lord, the giver of life,
who proceeds from the Father and the Son
With the Father and the Son he is worshipped and glorified
He has spoken through the Prophets.
We believe in one holy catholic and apostolic church.
We acknowledge one baptism for the forgiveness of sins.
We look for the resurrection of the dead,
and the life of the world to come. Amen.
(From Order for Holy Communion - Alternative Service Book 1980)

Council of Nicaea was held in 325AD. Nicaea is modern Iznik in Turkey.

Note: The word 'catholic' in this setting means universal.

Someone has said:

'Conviction without confession is dead and confession without conviction is just empty words'.

Confession must come out of conviction – see Rom 10:9-10

Repentance

Oswald Chambers speaking about sin and repentance in his book "My Utmost for His Highest" says: "When you get to the very core of SIN what you find is not just rebellion, but mistrust. Rebellion is there, he claims, but the root is mistrust. We are not sure God can be trusted to give what He says He will give - so we turn to other gods."

In Hos 8:14 we read at that time the Israelites put their trust in fortified cities instead of God.

In Psalm 51 we get a clear example of genuine repentance, as outlined below:

David asks for mercy, and for compassion to blot out his transgressions and cleansing from his sin (v1-3), - he makes no excuses, and realises he has to come to a point of being broken and so he says: "The sacrifices of God are a broken spirit; a broken and a contrite heart, O God, you will not despise." -see Ps 51:17.

Until we reach the end of ourselves, stop making excuses for our behaviour or situation, or both, and become completely honest, confess our utter need of God and totally depend on Him to meet that need, then nothing will change. See the difference that God makes in the following Scriptures: Ps 32:3-5; 34:2; 107:4-22, Acts 9:1-19, 16:25-34, 20:20-21, 26:19-28.

Randy Petersen in his book "The Christian Book of Lists" quotes from Martin Luther's theses that he posted on the door of the church in Wittenberg, sparking the Protestant Reformation.

Theses No 1 - When our Lord and Master Jesus Christ says repent, He means that the whole life of believers upon earth should be a constant and perpetual repentance.

Theses No 36 - Every Christian who truly repents of his sins, enjoys an entire remission both of the penalty and of the guilt, without any need of indulgences.

Somebody has said: "Remembrance is the shortest route to repentance", and opens the way to restoration - see Lk 15:17-20, Mk 14:72, Deut 30:1-10.

In 2Cor 7:9-11 we see a number of factors that are associated with repentance:

a) made sorry, (R.S.V. felt godly grief). b) earnestness. c) eagerness. d) indignation e) alarm. f) longing. g) concern, (R.S.V. zeal). h) readiness to see justice done, (R.S.V. punishment).

To those who repent comes joy through tears and gives joy to God's angels. See Lk 15:10.

God gives time for people to repent - see Rev 2:20-22.

"Until we have wept over the ruins we will never build the wall" a statement by Terry Virgo with reference to the Nehemiah in the Bible book of Nehemiah.

Someone has said: "Repentance is agreeing with God", see Isa 30:15-18.

Repentance is a process which we are always being called to, and by it we see ourselves as we really are, e.g. in need of making ourselves more like Jesus in all aspects of our character, thus requiring the ongoing surrender of self. During this process we also begin to see more and more of God as He really is: all-knowing, holy, majestic, all-powerful, gracious and waiting to forgive, cleanse and empower.

Repentance is a way of life that should prevent us from having an attitude, regarding our spirituality, that *says: 'I have arrived'.*

Someone has said: "Repentance is a change of mind, leading to a change of direction."

Bob Gass in his "The Word for Today" Notes states: "You can't fix what you won't face," - see Isa 55:6-7.

Confession and Repentance

There is hope for us if we confess with genuine sorrow that we have left God out of our lives, have just lived to please ourselves and ignored His claim on us, recognising that this lifestyle has spurned His love for us, because Jesus Christ died on the cross to save us from the penalty this type of lifestyle will bring.

Following this confession we must acknowledge the Lord Jesus Christ alone as God, recognise His rightful Kingship over our lives and submit our lives to His rule.

Let us be encouraged by two examples of people who recognised the error of their lifestyle and how they changed after repenting:

Zacchaeus (Lk 19:1-10) a wealthy, but cheating tax collector, owns up to his wrong doing by giving away half of his possessions to the poor and promises to pay back four times the amount to anyone he has cheated.

Paul a Jewish Pharisee and an ardent persecutor of Christians, when he met God on the road to Damascus (Acts 9:1-19) his life changed dramatically and he became the foremost apostle whom God used to take the Gospel to the Gentile world and to write much of the New Testament.

Note: The self-centred lives described above that contain no acknowledgement of God, to whom they are answerable, defines the condition of 'sin', which is not to be confused with 'sins', i.e. all forms of law breaking, and acts of inhumanity to man.

It is to be remembered that all 'sins' result from the basic human problem of 'sin'.

OUR RESPONSE TO GOD - DISCIPLESHIP

-CONFESSION AND REPENTANCE-

Biblical Texts & Text References

Confession

13 He who conceals his sins does not prosper, but whoever confesses and renounces them finds mercy.
14 Blessed is the man who always fears the LORD, but he who hardens his heart falls into trouble.

Prov 28:13-14

Jesus Christ speaking to the people said:

21 "Not everyone who says to me, 'Lord, Lord,' will enter the kingdom of heaven, but only he who does the will of my Father who is in heaven.
22 Many will say to me on that day, 'Lord, Lord, did we not prophesy in your name, and in your name drive out demons and perform many miracles?'
23 Then I will tell them plainly, 'I never knew you. Away from me, you evil doers!'

Mat 7:21-23

For a Scripture that explains about believing and confessing that "Jesus is Lord," will bring the person personal salvation, see Rom 10:9-11

Additional Scripture references

Ps 32:3-6; 38:16-18; 51:7-9; 73:24-28; 107:4-20, Mat 10:32-33, Lk 15:16-22, Jn 1:19-20, Acts 24:13-14, Rom 14:10-12; Phil 2:9-11, Heb 11:13, 1Jn 1:6-9; 4:14-15

Repentance

In Isa 55:6-7 people are cautioned to:" Seek the LORD while he may be found; call on him while he is near", and God will have mercy on those who turn to him.

9 The Lord is not slow in keeping his promise, as some understand slowness. He is patient with you, not wanting anyone to perish, but everyone to come to repentance.

2Pet 3:9

Additional Scripture references

Deut 30:1-3, 2Chron 7:13-14; Ps 32:3-5; 51:1-3; 51:10-13, Isa 1:18; 30:15-18, Jer 15:19; 31:19, Hos 11:8, Joel 2:12-13; Mat 4:17; 12:41, Lk 10:13-14; 16:27-31; 17:3-4; 18:13, Acts 2:37-38; 11:17-18; 20:20-21; 26:19-21, Rom 2:1-5; 2Cor 2:7; 7:8-10, 2Tim 2:24-26, Heb 2:1-3; 2:14

E3

OUR RESPONSE TO GOD - DISCIPLESHIP

-COMMITMENT TO TRUST AND LOVE-

Biblical Definitions

Introduction to 'Trust'

If a person can rely on someone else in a relationship it can be said that they have trust in them. This means that they have confidence to share their thoughts and lives with them.

So trust is a very important element in any human relationship, and lack of trust is a key cause of break-ups in friendships and marriages.

The trust factor is also the fundamental component that every person is asked to place in the Lord Jesus Christ for forgiveness, a new start, a new life and eternal salvation, etc.

Now let us see how this important element of 'trust' relates to the Christian Faith and the Bible.

Trust - In God

The verb, to trust, according to W.E. Vine in his book "Expository Dictionary of Bible Words" is to have confidence in. The word 'trust' is linked to 'believe in' and have 'faith in'. Again, he states 'to trust' signifies: "reliance upon, not mere credence."

Lawrence O. Richards in his "Expository Dictionary of Bible Words" relates the word 'trust' to Belief / Faith and states: "Few words are more central to the Christian message or more often used to describe Christian experience than "belief" and "faith." Yet these words are often corrupted by a misunderstanding of their biblical meaning. People today may use "faith "to indicate what is possible but uncertain. The Bible uses "faith" in ways that link it with what is assuredly and certainly true. Christians may sometimes speak of "believing," as if it were merely a subjective effort, as if our act of faith or strength of faith were the issue. But the Bible shifts our attention from subjective experience and centers it on the object of our faith - God himself.

It is exciting to look into the Scriptures and there rediscover the full meaning of faith and belief. There we grasp the great promise that faith holds out to all mankind: transformation through a personal relationship with God in Jesus Christ."

He further points out under the heading: 'The NT concept of faith' "One word group was used in classical Greek and in the common Greek of the NT era to express the idea of faith.

That word group encompassed a wide range of secular and religious ideas, but the underlying thrust is clear. *Pistis* ("faith," "belief") and related words deal with relationships established by trust and maintained by trustworthiness."

He further states: "In making a faith commitment, a person considers the evidence and accepts God's testimony about who Jesus is. The one who does not believe may be impressed with the evidence but will hold back from entrusting himself or herself to Jesus.

Yet it is only by believing, as a total commitment of oneself to the Lord, that life can be found. How vital, then, that we consider the testimony of Scripture, accept it, and believe on the one who speaks words of promise there."

He also states: "In Scripture a "believer" is not a person who holds a certain set of beliefs about God as if it were merely some theoretical conviction. A believer is a person who has responded to the gospel message by trusting Jesus and joining the company of others whose lives have found new focus in relationship with the Lord. A believer is a person who "has faith in Jesus" in the fullest, most biblical sense." These statements are just a fraction of the explanation Mr Lawrence O. Richards provides in his book.

Love - Towards God and Man

Over the years the word 'love' has been misused, abused, corrupted and misunderstood.

It has been used: when lust was intended; as a means to achieve selfish aims; to flatter or deceive; etc.

Children who grow up in a dysfunctional family, one where they are abused mentally or physically, or both, or where they are not wanted, where the parents split up, or where there are a number of partners, etc, will be deeply scarred and have a high probability of not understanding the true meaning of love.

Some parents interpret love to their children as giving them most or all of what they ask for; this means that neither parent nor child understands the true nature of love. A wise parent knows when to give and when to say no – for the child's own good and for their character development.

So if people want to understand the true meaning of love, then they need to consider the life and death of the Lord Jesus Christ. For example, the quality of His love entailed showing compassion and giving practical help to those in need, and in the end demonstrating that it was sacrificial, unconditional and selfless when He died on the cross for the sin of others.

W.E. Vine in his book "Expository Dictionary of Bible Words" states:

"Love had its perfect expression among men in the Lord Jesus Christ, 2Cor 5:14; Eph 2:4; 3:19; 5:2; Christian love is the fruit of His Spirit in the Christian, Gal 5:22.

The Lord Jesus Christ spent a significant amount of his time on earth meeting the spiritual and physical needs of people including healing many that were sick, and his motivation for doing this is clearly show in the Bible when it says: "When he saw the crowds, he had compassion on them, because they were harassed and helpless, - - - - -"Mat 9:36.

It is very important, therefore, that we follow in his footsteps through observing Scriptures like: Isa 58:6-12; Mat 25:31-46; Col 3:12-14.

Love: Towards God [illegible]

Over the years the word "love" has been misused, [illegible] corrupted and misunderstood.

It has been [illegible] to mean [illegible] a means to achieve [illegible] aims, to "make [illegible]" etc.

Children who grow up in a dysfunctional family, and where they are [illegible] or where they [illegible] where [illegible] there are [illegible] etc. [illegible] the [illegible] understanding the [illegible]

[illegible]

[illegible]

[illegible]

[illegible] Christianity is the [illegible]

[illegible] significant [illegible] on earth [illegible] spiritual and physical [illegible] including healing [illegible] and [illegible] Mt [illegible]

It is very important [illegible] through [illegible]

OUR RESPONSE TO GOD - DISCIPLESHIP

-COMMITMENT TO TRUST AND LOVE-

Notes and Quotations

Commitment

Bob Gass in his "The Word for Today" Notes quotes Jephthah when he says:"I have opened my mouth unto the Lord, and I cannot go back" (Jud 11:35 KJV). "That is commitment.

Each choice is a crossroad: one that will either confirm or compromise your commitment."

Trust - In God

C.H. Spurgeon said: "We trust as if it all depended on God, and we work as if it all depended on us." Ps 37:3-9, 46:1-3, Prov 3:5-8.

"Be still, and know that I am God; I will be exalted among the nations, I will be exalted in the earth."

The LORD Almighty is with us; the God of Jacob is our fortress.

Ps 46:10-11.

The question is: Do we have we a God we can be STILL WITH?

"Faith is usually about what <u>we</u> want, but Trust is about what <u>God</u> wants; that's a relationship." From "The Word For Today" Notes by Bob Gass.

What we believe in/trust in should affect the way we live.

Someone has said: "What do we do <u>when</u> trouble comes?"

a) Say it's unfair - people unjust.

b) Blame ourselves - feel guilty.
c) Lash out at those who caused the pain/trouble.
d) Withdraw into self pity.
e) Seek creative ways of getting back at those responsible.
f) Or turn our face to our Father in Heaven and trust that when He said: “in all things

God works for the good of those who love him” (Rom 8:28) He meant it.

God will use our trouble to make us more usable, - Jas 1:2-4.

Woe to the man or woman who has to learn principles when troubles come.

Commenting on how we do not like unanswered questions in our lives, Bob Gass in his “The Word for Today” Notes states: “But one of the tools God uses to crucify your carnal mind is unanswered questions. When we don’t know, we either: a. trust God, b. worry, or c. try to figure it out ourselves.

God doesn’t always give us answers to our questions, because He’s training us in trust.” See Prov 3:5.

Selwyn Hughes in his ‘Every Day with Jesus’ Notes states that there needs to be a balance between ‘Trusting’ and ‘Trying’, and in this connection he refers to 1Cor 15:10 where the apostle Paul says he worked harder than anyone, “yet not I, but the grace of God that was with me”. Selwyn Hughes points out, “He tried harder than anyone, yet his trust was not in his own strength, but in the strength given him by God. That’s the secret - working hard, but working in God’s strength and not our own.” See Neh 4:14-18, Ps 37:3-9, Prov 3:5-6, Phil 2:12-13.

Someone has defined ‘Worry’ as “accepting responsibility God never intended us to have,” From ‘Every Day with Jesus’ Notes by Selwyn Hughes.

An example of half-hearted commitment is seen in Rev 3:14-22. In this Scripture we see people that were ‘neither hot nor cold’ and God shows them their true condition and calls them to repent. If Christians, therefore, show half-hearted commitment, compromise, self-dependence and complacency when they relate to our relationship with God or our commitment to serve Him then they need to heed these words of Scripture. There is a cost in discipleship.

Trusting God is put to the test when our circumstances change so that we can learn to depend on Him more for our guidance and security and not ourselves. See Isa 43:18-19.

Love - Towards God and Man

Philip Yancey in his book "What's so amazing about Grace", refers to a British conference on comparative religions in which experts from around the world were debating what, if any, was Christianity's unique contribution among world religions. After much deliberation, C.S. Lewis came into the room and said "Oh, that's easy. It's grace."

"After some discussion, the conferees had to agree. The notion of God's love coming to us free of charge, no strings attached, seems to go against every instinct of humanity. The Buddhist eight-fold path, the Hindu doctrine of *karma*, the Jewish covenant, and the Muslim code of law -- each of these offers a way to earn approval. Only Christianity dares to make God's love unconditional."

Augustine said "My love is my weight". A measure of our true spirituality is the flow of God's love from our lives. See Rom 5:5 where it says "God has poured out his love into our hearts by the Holy Spirit, whom he has given us."

Bob Gass in his "The Word for Today" Notes states: "Love makes obedience a joy. Less obedience is simply less love. Often we replace grace with law, and love with rules. But we don't enjoy the rules because we don't exercise the love. Our new nature functions best when motivated by relationship, not rules. Rules without love lead to coldness. Christ said to the Christians at Ephesus: "You don't love Me like you used to". Then He commanded them to return to the point where they had fallen".

"There is no compassion without confrontation with the person causing the problem, the oppressor, otherwise it is empty sentimentality"

Author unknown.

Self-evidence of being a Christian – see Rom 8:16.

Someone has said: "Compassion is simply putting yourself in somebody else's place."

Someone has said: "If we are not mature in love, then we are not mature."

Someone has said: "A <u>fanatic</u> is someone who loves Jesus more than you do."

Love for God and others is not something we manufacture, it is something we receive, and the following Scriptures strongly suggest that the extent to which we are prepared to receive, desire and depend on God's love is the extent to which we can show God's love to others. See Rom 5:5; Gal 5:22; Eph 3:17-19; Phil 1:8-11; 1Thess 3:12; 1Tim 1:14; 2Tim 1:7; 1Jn 2:5; 1Jn 4:16-21.

<u>'The Friend Who Just Stands By'</u>
'When trouble comes your soul to try, you love the friend who just 'stands by'.
Perhaps there's nothing he can do - the thing is strictly up to you;
For there are troubles all your own, and paths the soul must tread alone;
Times when love can't smooth the road, nor friendship lift the heavy load.
But just to know you have a friend, who will 'stand by' until the end,
Whose sympathy through all endures, whose warm handclasp is always yours;
It helps, some way, to pull you through, although there's nothing he can do.
And so with fervent heart you cry, 'God bless the friend who just stands by!'

Poet unknown. Quoted from 'The Word for Today' Notes by Bob Gass.

OUR RESPONSE TO GOD - DISCIPLESHIP

-COMMITMENT TO TRUST AND LOVE-

Biblical Texts & Text References

Trust

In 1Pet 5:6-7 people are challenged to humble themselves before God, and leave all their anxieties with him because he cares for them.

5 Trust in the LORD with all your heart and lean not on your own understanding;
6 in all your ways acknowledge him, and he will make your paths straight.
7 Do not be wise in your own eyes; fear the LORD and shun evil.
8 This will bring health to your body and nourishment to your bones.

Prov 3:5-8

Additional Scripture references

Ex 14:13-14, Num 23:19, Deut 10:12-15, Jud 6:15-16, Neh 4:14-18, Ps 5:11; 18:1-2; 27:13-14; 31:22-24; 37:3-7; 46:1-3; 46:10-11; 84:11-12; 97:9-10; 112:6-8; 118:8-9; 145:19-20, Prov 16:3, Isa 43:1-2, Jer 17:5-8, Mat 6:25-34, Rom 4:16-22; 8:28, 2Tim 1:11-12, Jas 1:2-4; 1:12, 1Pet 1:6-9

Love for God and Others

34 "A new command I give you: Love one another. As I have loved you, so you must love one another.
35 By this all men will know that you are my disciples, if you love one another."

Jn 13:34-35

4 But because of his great love for us, God, who is rich in mercy,

5 made us alive with Christ even when we were dead in transgressions—it
is by grace you have been saved.

Eph 2:4-5

Additional Scripture references

Gen 29:20, Prov 10:12; 15:17; 16:6, Ps 33:18-21; 147:2-3, Jer 2:1-2, Lam 3:22-24; Mat 5:43-48, 22:36-40; Jn 15:10-12, Rom 5:17; 14:13-15; 14:21-24, Rom 3:8-10; 15:1-2, 1Cor 2:9; 13:1-7; 2Cor 5:14-15; 8:7-9, Gal 5:5-6 & 13-14; 5:22-23, Eph 3:18-19; 4:15-16; 5:1-2; 6:23-24, Phil 1:9-10, Col 3:12-14, 1Thess 1:2-3, Heb 10:23-24; 13:1-3, Jas 2:5, 1Pet 4:8-9, 1Jn 2:5-6; 3:16; 4:17-21; 5:1-3

E4

OUR RESPONSE TO GOD - DISCIPLESHIP

-GOSPEL PROCLAMATION - KNOWING THE HUMAN CONDITION-

Biblical Definitions

The Human Condition

When a person begins to think about God their first concern is often a consideration of their own character, the type of life they have lived, their present lifestyle, and perhaps a feeling of unworthiness to even approach God. However, God's first concern is whether or not a person knows Him and has a living relationship with Him. So whilst the nature and characteristics of people can vary from being kind, gentle, thoughtful, loving, etc., to being selfish, cruel, thoughtless, hateful, evil, etc., to one another, as far as God is concerned no person is good (see Ps 53:1-3, Rom 6:23,), because He sees goodness as putting Him first and walking with Him in trust and humility (Isa 66:1-2), and this is what we all fail to do.

The initial step in getting to know God is to be aware of how He sees us and the descriptions given in the Bible for the basic human condition, sadly, are not flattering, for it reveals that we all start out in life basically concerned about ourselves and what we want, and this means that we have ignored and/or disobeyed God's claim on our lives, and consequently we have failed to recognise Him as our creator and have not submitted our lives to Him nor worshipped Him only as God Almighty. This rebellious attitude towards God in the Bible is referred to as 'sin'. The word 'sin' is often confused with 'sins', but the word 'sins' refers to acts, attitudes and thoughts which are abhorrent to God and are the result of 'sin'.

The Biblical scholars state that the word 'sin' in the N.T. Greek as meaning 'a missing of the mark'. We have missed God's high standards, and cannot hope to even approach His standards, and a recognition of the above facts leaves all mankind in a position of dire need before God and therefore, it is absolutely necessary that we all repent, i.e. change our mind towards God, and then proceed to put our faith and trust in Jesus Christ as God's Son, confess our sin to Him, acknowledge that He died to pay the price for our sin (when He died on the cross), seek His forgiveness and receive the new life and power that He alone can give.

The following Scriptures are provided to help clarify and support the statements made above:see Rom 3:19-24, Jn 3:35-36, 1Thess 5:9-10, 1Jn 3:4

When a person has taken the above action then God initiates His second concern, that is, to begin the process of transforming the character to become more like His, and changing the person's aims and ambitions to fulfil His will and not theirs. This is a lifelong process and is the beginning of the person's salvation, which cannot be purchased by good works (Eph 2:8-9) but only through the grace (unmerited favour) of God.

Before the Good News the process of 'Conversion' is considered, the situation of people who follow a Formal Religion should be explained.

Formal Religion

Those who practice a 'Formal Religion', or those who follow a religion in a formal manner can be defined as those who follow rules, codes of behaviour, conventions and ceremonies that relate to any religious or Faith group, including Christianity, but do not have a personal interactive relationship with the author or originator of that Religion or Faith.

These people can be utterly sincere, zealous, and their motives honourable, but sadly they will not find a spiritual life that connects them into a source of power to change their character for the better and for the benefit of others, or be able to break an enslaving damaging addiction or lifestyle. In fact, these people may be able to achieve great areas of control in their lives and achieve great things through their endeavours, but their lack of a personal relationship with the central God of their Religion/Faith means that their Religion is lifeless. This is because the personal connection to God is missing.

Proclamation

The essential elements to be considered under this heading are to outline the message to be proclaimed, and state who should do this and how.

The Message to be Proclaimed - The 'GOOD NEWS' - The Gospel

This message is 'The Gospel Message' meaning 'The Good News' as taken from the Bible's New Testament, and the key details of this message and it's background are provided below.

To meet the above basic human needs, and much more, God has revealed Himself to us initially through the Jewish people as proclaimed in the Hebrew Scriptures (the Old Testament part of the Bible), and then gave us a fuller revelation of Himself through the Lord Jesus Christ, who, as God's Son is the source of the 'Good News', for in His life and character He showed us the very nature and heart of God, and to explain it briefly He:

- was miraculously born through a virgin Mary two thousand years ago;
- came and lived among ordinary people and became a carpenter, then called twelve disciples around him and started a preaching and teaching ministry;
- showed compassion through healing the sick and raising the dead;
- showed by His actions that he cared about and helped people whoever they were;
- showed that whilst He was concerned about the happiness of people's lives He was also concerned about their eternal destiny, and hence, provided a way whereby they could be eternally saved by believing that He was God's Son;
- taught His disciples, and later the apostles to call people to confess that they had led selfish lives, pleasing themselves and ignoring His rightful claim on their lives – (this lifestyle is referred to as 'sin' in the Bible);
- was crucified for the sin of everyone;

- rose from the grave and ascended back to heaven;
- did all this so that those who believed and repented could be forgiven, empowered to live a new life and be assured of a place in heaven with Him when they die.

All the above was prophesied many years before through the Old Testament prophets.

So from the above outline of the 'Good News' we can see that the Gospel message contains some 'bad or challenging news' and that to avail ourselves of the 'Good News' one has to acknowledge the 'bad news' concerning our need of God's forgiveness and of a new life.

The brief introduction to the Christian Gospel given above is followed now by a more detailed explanation of this message by looking at the important elements of: conversion; repentance; belief; confession; and becoming a Christian; that make up this message.

It is very important to realise that this intimate message comes from God who has shown His heart of love towards us and has made every provision for us, and this statement is supported by the fact that the Lord Jesus Christ whilst on earth was someone who showed a personal interest in people, and He has not changed because He still wishes to be in direct contact with us. Uniquely, this does not require an intermediary of a priest etc, because our God is a loving relational God and earnestly desires us to know Him personally, and hence, has done all that is necessary to provide for our personal salvation through the Lord Jesus being crucified for us. This means, however, to attain salvation we must first understand that in our 'natural' state we are estranged from Him and a miraculous interaction needs to take place between God and us, enabling us to come to know Him personally, and this divine process is known as 'CONVERSION'.

CONVERSION

The key distinguishing feature of the Christian Faith is that it operates through God's miraculous power and grace (undeserved love), and this requires our humble, thankful and repentant response.

The first thing to understand is that a person cannot be born a Christian, and someone is not found to be acceptable or unacceptable based on whether their parents or family were Christians or not. Another common misunderstanding is that a person can become a Christian through doing good deeds, unfortunately, this is not the way.

The fact is, that each person must always have a direct meeting with God – initially through recognition of the deity of the Lord Jesus Christ as God, coupled with confession and repentance, as explained below.

This process starts in a personal way when we first become aware of a need before God – a need to be forgiven for ignoring God's dying love and sacrifice for us – a need to know God's forgiveness for living just to please oneself – a need for a new start in life – a need to know God for myself. Becoming aware of these needs are indications of God's Spirit interacting with our spirit, when He is speaking to us and endeavouring to draw us to Himself in a love bond of salvation.

We begin to see our need to know God's forgiveness when we recognise that all we have wanted to do was to please ourselves how we lived, and in so doing have ignored and/or disobeyed Him and His loving claim on our lives, and this rebellion against God is referred to as our sin,- and the Bible states that we are all sinful. Accepting this, we appreciate what God has done to meet our need through the Lord Jesus Christ coming to earth and dying on a cross to pay the penalty for our sin. Hence, we confess and repent of our sin, ask for forgiveness and thank Him, the Lord Jesus Christ, God's Son, for all He has done for us, and so commit our life to Him. This response is known as Christian Conversion, and is also known as 'being born again', or 'being saved'.

When we have made this commitment to God with a sincere and humble attitude, and with a repentant spirit, then He responds by cleansing us from sin and the guilt of sin of our past life, and empowers us through the gift of His Holy Spirit that He gives to dwell within us, enabling us to start living a new life as we submit ourselves to God. We have now become a Christian, and start to live a new life in God's family.

So it can be said that unless we accept the Bad News (of our need before a Holy God to be forgiven and cleansed) then we are not in a position to receive or appreciate the 'Good News'.

Prior to making this 'commitment' we can see that we only wanted to live to please ourselves, and this, in essence, is the sin for which a penalty must be paid, either by us, or through accepting the penalty already paid by God's Son on our behalf.

There are many passages of Scripture that contain the conditions that have to be met for us to obtain personal salvation, and a few of these are given below:

"for all have sinned and fall short of the glory of God",

Rom 3:23

"For God so loved the world that he gave his one and only Son, that whoever believes in him shall not perish but have eternal life.
For God did not send his Son into the world to condemn the world, but to save the world through him.
Whoever believes in him is not condemned, but whoever does not believe stands condemned already because he has not believed in the name of God's one and only Son.

Jn 3:16-18

That if you confess with your mouth, "Jesus is Lord," and believe in your heart that God raised him from the dead, you will be saved.
For it is with your heart that you believe and are justified, and it is with your mouth that you confess and are saved.
As the Scripture says, "Anyone who trusts in him will never be put to shame."
For there is no difference between Jew and Gentile--the same Lord is Lord of all and richly blesses all who call on him, for, "Everyone who calls on the name of the Lord will be saved."

Rom 10:9-13

From the above three passages of Scripture we can see there are three basic conditions to be met by us to achieve personal salvation, namely: repentance, belief and confession. These elements or conditions are outlined below, and further reference is made to them in Sections E1 and E2 of the book.

It is to be noted that in the process of salvation the person receives forgiveness of sin, and the gift of the Person of the Holy Spirit to dwell within them providing the power to live for God.

Repentance:

In Christian terms this refers to a personal change of mind, regretting one's past lifestyle, seeking God's forgiveness for the fact that we have lived to please ourselves and ignored His claims on our lives', and confess that we need His power to start and continue a new life. Part of this process is recognising and accepting that God's Word, the Bible, is true and that we can rely on what it says, and be confident that we have received His forgiveness and salvation when we understand that The Lord Jesus Christ, the sinless Son of God, is the one who has made these things possible by dying to pay the price of our sin. Hence, this relates to what we truly believe concerning Him as outlined below:

Belief:

Personal salvation centres around what we believe concerning The Lord Jesus Christ, and the basic essential beliefs for someone seeking to come to God in repentance and faith is that they will initially acknowledge that He is God Almighty their only Saviour and Redeemer, and will go on to accept that:

- He is the eternal Son of God,
- He is part of the Godhead of Father, Son and Holy Spirit,
- He is Holy, All-knowing and All-powerful,
- He is the Creator of heaven and earth,
- He came from heaven to earth and was made man through a virgin birth by Mary,
- He was sinless, yet was crucified for the sin (rebellion) of His creation - mankind,
- He died, was buried and on the third day rose again in accordance with Scripture,
- He procured personal salvation, through His death and resurrection, for all who repent and believe on Him - become Christians,
- He will return to earth to judge the living and the dead,

- He sent the Person of the Holy Spirit to empower and guide Christians,
- He created The Church - the company of Christians.

<u>Confession:</u>
There are two aspects of confession: one informal and the other formal.

The informal aspect relates to our everyday conversations where we share openly about our Faith in a natural way, as opportunity presents itself and confining ourselves to answering only the point in question. Any further talk about the Faith should generally be by 'invitation only' from the other person(s). The words of 'confession' should be spoken in an attitude of humility, and backed up by appropriate actions and lifestyle.

The formal aspect of our confession relates to a public declaration of our Faith by giving a word of testimony, and by being baptised by immersion in a public place before a number of people.

Whilst baptism is not part of the process of personal salvation it is closely linked to it, and there is much evidence for this given in the Scriptures, particularly in the book of the Acts of the Apostles. The baptism referred to was by immersion in water, and according to Scripture is required of every Believer as an act of obedience to witness that they are a Christian. It is not an optional extra. Baptism has been described 'as an outward sign of an inner faith' in the Lord Jesus Christ and that the person has committed their life to Him.

Baptism is further likened to the death and burial of the old life when we go under the water, and rising to a new life as we come out of the water, and relates to Christ's death, burial and resurrection as shown by the following Scripture:

"We were therefore buried with him through baptism into death in order that, just as Christ was raised from the dead through the glory of the Father, we too may live a new life. If we have been united with him like this in his death, we will certainly also be united with him in his resurrection."

Rom 6:4-5

As our personal salvation is based on the supernatural actions and grace of God and His interaction with us through His Spirit, it follows that He has not required us to do anything to earn our salvation, because it cannot be earned - see the following passage of Scripture:

"For it is by grace you have been saved, through faith--and this not from yourselves, it is the gift of God-- not by works, so that no-one can boast."

Eph 2:8-9

It is after we have become Christians that God expects us to live for Him, serve Him and other people, and all this must come out of the love God gives us and not out of a sense of duty and self-will.

How to respond to God to become a Christian is further explained in this Section of the book.

Becoming a Christian

We have clear guidance from the Bible regarding this life-changing step as outline below: Jesus answered, "I am the way and the truth and the life. No-one comes to the Father except through me". See Jn 14:6

"For God so loved the world that he gave his one and only Son, that whoever believes in him shall not perish but have eternal life"

Jn 3:16

"All the prophets testify about him that everyone who believes in him receives forgiveness of sins through his name".

Acts 10:43

Using the authority of God's Word, The Bible, we can see the conditions that are laid down for becoming a Christian, namely, we need to recognise that our present lifestyle is lived for ourselves and others, but not God. The situation where God is not at the centre of our lives' is in fact a rejection of Him and is our chief sin. If therefore, we have reached this point then we need to continue on to the next steps as outlined below:

- repent of our sin, (change one's mind towards God - regretting our previous lifestyle),
- ask for forgiveness,

- believe on the Lord Jesus Christ as God's Son - the one who has paid the penalty for our sin,
- thank Him for what He has done for us,
- make a confession of our faith in the Lord Jesus Christ to others,
- thank Him for the gift of His Holy Spirit that He has given to live in us.

When we are prepared to take these steps with sincerity, humility and with a repentant spirit, then we need to pray to God in the way indicated above, or use a prayer like the one given below.

There is no exact set of words to make this commitment but remember, whatever words we use God does not only hear the expression of our lips but He reads the attitude of our hearts.

Lord Jesus Christ,
I know you died on the cross for my sin and
I want you to be the Lord of my life; now and forever.
Please forgive me for the way I have sinned against you by leaving you out of my life and living only as I wanted.
I submit my life to you and thank you for paying the penalty for my sin.
Thank you Lord for your forgiveness that I don't deserve, and for the person of your Holy Spirit to live in me.
With your help I will seek to love and obey you as Lord of my life.

Now – tell someone what you have done – see the Scripture below. And if you have prayed this, or a similar prayer containing the above essential truths with sincerity, then, based not on your feelings, but on the authority of the Bible you can state with confidence that:

God has saved you - see the Scripture below;

That if you confess with your mouth, "Jesus is Lord," and believe in your heart that God raised him from the dead, you will be saved.
For it is with your heart that you believe and are justified, and it is with your mouth that you confess and are saved.
As the Scripture says, "Anyone who trusts in him will never be put to shame."
For there is no difference between Jew and Gentile--the same Lord is

Lord of all and richly blesses all who call on him, for, "Everyone who calls on the name of the Lord will be saved." See Rom 10:9-13
He has made you into a new person with a fresh start - see the Scripture below;

"So from now on we regard no-one from a worldly point of view. Though we once regarded Christ in this way, we do so no longer. Therefore, if anyone is in Christ, he is a new creation; the old has gone, the new has come!"

2Cor 5:16-17

He has started a personal relationship with us, He knows us and we are just beginning to know Him - see the Scripture below;

"I am the good shepherd; I know my sheep and my sheep know me--just as the Father knows me and I know the Father--and I lay down my life for the sheep.

Jn 10:14-15

Evidence for those who claim to be Christians

After this 'conversion' experience has taken place our character begins to change little by little, to make us more and more like the character of The Lord Jesus Christ. Some of these miraculous changes are outlined below - given in no particular order.

We want others to know and experience what we have received from God - acceptance into God's Kingdom, forgiveness of sin, cleansing from guilt, joy, fellowship with God and other believers, a purpose in living and the power to live a new life.

We want to worship and praise God.

We want to share God's love with others.

We want to pray - to commune with our Father in heaven, and hear what He has to say to us.

We want to read His Word the Bible.

We want to meet together with other Christians to enjoy one another's friendship and fellowship.

We want to live pleasing to God - finding and fulfilling his will for our lives resulting in the fruit of God's Spirit being seen by positive changes in attitude and lifestyle - see Gal 5:22-24 as given under 'Scriptural Evidence' below.

We want to receive from God whatever spiritual gifts He has for us, and use these to bring honour to Him and benefit to others.

<u>Note:</u>
The extent to which the above changes take place will depend on a number of factors including; the person's walk of faith and obedience to the will of God. As the Christian matures more of the above changes will be realised.

It will be observed that none of the above characteristics are 'natural' but 'supernatural', and hence, it is not within our power or ability to effect these changes in attitude or lifestyle, nor can we take credit for them. We can only thank God for His love, grace and help for us and others.

<u>Scriptural Evidence</u>

The Lord Jesus Christ supplies further supporting evidence when He said:

"By their fruit you will recognise them. Do people pick grapes from thorn bushes, or figs from thistles? Likewise every good tree bears good fruit, but a bad tree bears bad fruit."

Mat 7:16-17

Also in 2Cor 5:17 it states that those who have submitted their lives' to the Lord Jesus Christ have become "a new creation"—as stated below:

> "Therefore, if anyone is in Christ, he is a new creation;
> the old has gone, the new has come!".

From the above statements it is clear that if the conversion experience has not really taken place, or the person is still a very immature Christian, then there will be little or no evidence of changes in attitude or lifestyle that would indicate that they have become or are becoming 'a new creation', as illustrated under the heading "Characteristics of the Christian Faith and its Historical Roots".

Also, these statements show that the distinguishing feature of the person who claims to be a Christian is the miraculous changes in character that have taken place, and are continuing to take place in the person's life. This will be observed by changes in attitude towards others and God. There will be increased love, care and concern for the welfare of others, Christians and non-believers, resulting in practical action for their benefit. There will also be a desire to live in a way that is pleasing to God, coupled with wanting to worship and serve Him. This can be summed up in the words of Scripture where it states that we become "a new creation" as given in 2Cor 5:17 above.

Opportunity and Freedom Offered

Another aspect of the 'Good News' is that we are all equal in His sight, all basically sinful and all in need of His salvation, and therefore, when we are called by God we have an opportunity of accepting or rejecting His offer of salvation, forgiveness and a fresh start in life. Also, the offer is such that it does not matter where a person was born, or into what family they were born, rich or poor, privileged or under privileged, fit or disabled or what were the religious beliefs of a person's parents, their tribe, race or nationality.

Our gracious God wants us to know Him, love Him and walk with Him in freedom and joy.

When we become Christians He provides freedom from the power of sin, and freedom from religious customs, practices and rituals devised by man - not ordained by God. In consequence, God has not placed any of the following conditions on us either as a means to attain personal salvation or to gain merit or approval and therefore, He has not requested us to:

- worship Him in a particular type of building;
- contact Him through an intermediary e.g. a priest;
- work for our personal salvation;
- fulfil any particular attainment (other than to obey Him and seek to fulfil His will for our lives) or ascetic lifestyle;

- worship any other person or thing besides Him;
- use icons, idols or statues of any kind;
- partake in elaborate ceremonies or processions;
- wear any special type of clothes;
- change or mutilate our body in any way;
- take up arms to defend the Bible or the Christian Faith;
- pray at any particular time, or frequency, day or night;
- pray using any particular form of words, except that we should include the model prayer that the Lord Jesus Christ gave us in Mat 6:5-13 - its frequency is not indicated.

<u>A few supporting Scriptures:</u>
In Jn 8:32 it says "you will know the truth, and the truth will set you free."

Live as free men, but do not use your freedom as a cover-up for evil; live as servants of God.

1Pet 2:16

Having read through this whole topic it should leave you to ask yourself one very important question: "am I just following a formal Religion, no Religion, or do I know the Living God and have a Living Faith and hence, am enjoying a useful and satisfying life here and looking forward to an assured, wonderful and everlasting future"?

In conclusion, any type of religion that is just a set of rules and regulations which seeks to please/appease a Deity where the ability and motivation to follow these codes is only provided through ardent desire, personal convictions, customs, traditions, family pressures, sincerity or fear etc, then, it is not a ***living*** faith, but a formal religion. Also, when Christianity is followed as a set of rules or codes, then again, it is not a ***living*** faith. But, when a person has a true Christian conversion experience, then they are changed 'within themselves' by God and are thus empowered and want to live for God. So whereas people following a religion are driven by many factors including traditions and fear etc., the truly converted Christian is motivated by love for God and others through a changed heart. This 'heart' change starts at conversion and should continue to develop throughout life, but the progress of change is determined by that person's obedience to God.

Another important and unique factor for the person who has come into this living faith in Christ is to know that whilst all the resources of God are made available to them through their relationship with Him, they must learn to trust and rely on Him to meet their needs.

When Christian's sin by going their own way instead of God's through disobedience, failing to trust or rely on Him, then they should not blame God because His resources are always available. The good news is that through confession and repentance the person can be forgiven and restored to fellowship with God.

To help confirm whether or not you are a Christian, then speak to a mature Christian.

The next important step is to join a Church, but, before doing so, look for one that has the following essential characteristics: a friendly welcome and acceptance; Bible-based teaching; a teaching programme for new Christians e.g. an Alpha Course; a place with the possibility of developing Christian friends; a place where you can grow as a Christian and go on to serve God in some way; and a Church that has a missionary outlook both local and overseas.

A note of caution - be wary of joining any Church where the leader or leaders demand absolute allegiance to them, and/or claim that they alone have the whole 'Truth' and the final say when interpreting the Bible.

God's Offer comes with a Caution

God's offer of being accepted by Him, knowing Him and receiving the gift of eternal life comes with the conditions of us recognising that there are first the matters of belief and repentance to be accepted and acted on by us. Many people would respond to this by saying: "what do I need to believe? and what do I need to repent about?" Basically we need to believe that Jesus Christ was and is God's Son and that He died on the cross to pay the penalty for the sin of the world, and that includes our sin.

Sin can be simply be explained as people just living to please themselves without reference to God, however, some erroneously think that following a religious code of rules will be acceptable to God. In the Scripture Rom 3:23 (given below) it states that we are all sinners in God's sight, and the solution to this problem is addressed in the Scripture 2Pet 3:9 (given below) by calling us to repent (to change our mind and direction of life), because this Scripture, among others, clearly shows us that God does not want anyone to perish. So in His kindness He warns us not to show contempt for His kindness, tolerance and patience, otherwise we are left only waiting for His judgment, (see Rom 2:4-5 below).

The death of the Lord Jesus Christ for the sin of all mankind provided the way to escape condemnation by people believing on Him as stated in the Scripture Jn 3:16-18 (given below).

True belief, however, is not just in the head, but starts with the action of repentance.

The Bible further states that He was the only one who could pay this penalty for sin because He alone was sinless. It is, therefore, everyone's responsibility to recognise the unparalleled sacrifice, the depth of mercy and the undeserved love shown by God and respond accordingly.

He also warns people who through their actions or inactions ignore the gracious call and offer of salvation by God who waits to grant them forgiveness and entry into His Kingdom. These are people who are presuming that their good works and kindly deeds will somehow be acceptable to God and give them a place in heaven, sadly however, they are mistaken. That is because firstly He wants to know us and have a Father/child relationship with us, and this comes about through us recognising Him as our creator God, confessing our failure of keeping Him out of a central place in our lives, and then thanking Him for dying to purchase our eternal salvation. The fact of God knowing us and we knowing Him is the very essence of being a true believer, a Christian, as borne out by the words of Jesus in Jn 10:14 given below.

Regarding our good works and kindly deeds, it's not that He does not want to see them, He welcomes them, but does not accept them as a means of earning eternal salvation, because it cannot be earned as stated in the Scripture Eph 2:8-9 given below.

It is clearly shown in the Scriptures that God does not want anyone to perish, (see 2Pet 3:9 below), but calls us to repent (to change our mind), and He warns us not to show contempt for His kindness, tolerance and patience, otherwise we are left only waiting for His judgment, (see Rom 2:4-5 below). Many people would respond to the statement above by saying: "what do I need to repent about"? The fact is, that when men and women just live to please themselves, without reference to God their creator, they are classified by Him as sinners and as He says in His Word the Bible in Rom 3:23, (given below) that we are ALL sinners, and all, therefore, in need of forgiveness and salvation.

God's solution to this situation was to send His Son, the Lord Jesus Christ, to die on a cross to pay the penalty for the sin of all mankind, thus providing the way to escape condemnation by repenting and believing as stated in the Scripture Jn 3:16-18 (given below). The Bible states that He was the only one who could pay this penalty for sin because He alone was sinless. It is, therefore, everyone's responsibility to recognise the unparalleled sacrifice, the depth of mercy and the undeserved love shown by God and respond accordingly.

He warns people who are sexually immoral, thieves, drunkards, slanderers or swindlers that they will not inherit the Kingdom of God, (see 1Cor 6:9-11 in E4 Texts). However, there is hope here because this text says: "and that is what some of you were", and that through repentance, mentioned in 2Pet 3:9, they were washed from sin (rejection of Him), sanctified and justified.

He also warns people who through their actions or inactions ignore the gracious call and offer of salvation by God who waits to grant them forgiveness and entry into His Kingdom. These are people who are presuming that their good works and kindly deeds will somehow be acceptable to God and give them a place in heaven, sadly however, they are mistaken. That is because firstly He wants to know us and have a Father/child relationship with us, and this comes about through us recognising Him as our creator God, confessing our failure of keeping Him out of a central place in our lives, and then thanking Him for dying to purchase our eternal salvation. The fact of God knowing us and we knowing Him is the very essence of being a true believer, a Christian, as borne out by the words of Jesus in Jn 10:14 given below.

Regarding our good works and kindly deeds, it's not that He does not want to see them, He welcomes them, but does not accept them as a means of earning eternal salvation, because it cannot be earned as stated in the Scripture Eph 2:8-9 given below.

"For God so loved the world that he gave his one and only Son, that whoever believes in him shall not <u>perish</u> but have eternal life.
For God did not send his Son into the world to condemn the world, but to save the world through him.
Whoever believes in him is not condemned, but whoever does not believe stands condemned already because he has not believed in the name of God's one and only Son.

Jn 3:16-18

<u>Note the word '*perish*'</u>
In verse 16 above this word is associated with God's Judgment and has great significance, - for explanation see Section B1 under the heading 'Judgment'

<u>Jesus said:</u>

14 "I am the good shepherd; I know my sheep and my sheep know me—

Jn 10:14

23 for all have sinned and fall short of the glory of God,
24 and are justified freely by his grace through the redemption that came by Christ Jesus.

Rom 3:23-24

8 For it is by grace you have been saved, through faith—and this not from yourselves, it is the gift of God—
9 not by works, so that no-one can boast.

Eph 2:8-9

9 The Lord is not slow in keeping his promise, as some understand slowness. He is patient with you, not wanting anyone to perish, but everyone to come to repentance.

2Pet 3:9

Methods of Proclaiming Scriptural Truths - See also Section D4

The following are notes taken from an article entitled: "Parabolic Preaching in the Context of Islam" published by 'Evangelical Review of Theology' Vol. 4 No 2 page 218.

"Why has the art of story telling remained an unexplored frontier in cross cultural evangelism? The author demonstrates his answer from his own experience of relating the message to the medium in a particular context.

Editor of the Evangelical Review.

The European mind is frequently accused of being unduly concerned on conceptual thinking, whereas Middle Eastern cultures tend generally to stress teaching through a more pictorial form, although the NT with the increasing influence of Gentile thought includes much of a more conceptual nature. God's revelation of Himself in the OT is fundamentally through His acts in history which are then recorded in verbal form. The language of the prophets is graphic, full of imagery and vibrant with activity – it is in form and character poles apart from our traditional works of conceptual systematic theology. Ezekiel in particular uses under the guidance of God acted visual forms.

In the NT also the message of the Word is taught not only with direct verbal communication, but also through signs and miracles. The structure of John's Gospel interweaves the visual sign and the preached word. The vital significance of the visual is further exemplified in the Book of Acts, also as a doctrinal treatise.

Jesus the Preacher and Teacher

Jesus Himself taught both by His deeds and also by His words. However, it is important to note that His words were again not merely conceptual, but also conjured up visual imagery and were often in the form of stories and parables. In the context of Asian and Middle Eastern peoples we may need to follow the teaching pattern of Jesus in speaking through pictorial language. In many Asian languages proverbs and stories form the basis of communication. In English too we use such expressions as "out of the frying pan into the fire" without the need to explain in detail the significance of such a proverb. In Asian languages there is liable to be a far greater use of such expressions and we need to learn to teach, preach and express ourselves in this way."

The above is just a short introduction to this article, - the whole article should be read to get a fuller explanation of the topic.

Definition of a Parable

The following definition is taken from "The Universal Bible Dictionary" edited by A.R. Buckland: "A parable is a narrative, imagined or true, told for the purpose of imparting a truth. It differs from a proverb in that the picture presented is not so concentrated, but contains more detail, and so requires less mental effort to its understanding."

In referring to the teaching of Jesus he further states: "The parable was an instrument of education for those who were children either in age or character. Thus the constant employment of parables in His ministry (Mk 4:34) served at once to illuminate His teaching by contact with common life and human interests, to set forth the nature of His kingdom, and to test the disposition of His hearers (Mat 21:45; Lk 20:19)."

Jamie Buckingham in the Introduction to his book, "Parables" states: "God has many ways of teaching us. Jesus taught by example. Men looked at how He lived and decided to walk that way also. He also taught by precept. By that I mean He often spoke directly to people. We might even call it preaching.

But his favourite way of teaching was through the use of the parable. He loved to tell stories – stories with spiritual meanings."

Preaching the Whole Gospel

Preachers are not at liberty to preach a partial Gospel, but only the 'whole' Gospel as outlined in the following Scriptures: Acts 20:25-27, Rom 15:14-19, Col 1:25-29.

Note also the warning given in Ezek 3:15-21, and the conviction of Paul in 1Cor 9:16.

It is also very important to understand that those who preach or proclaim the Gospel in various ways as outlined below, should always be aware that to be effective for God they must be the channel through whom His Holy Spirit flows in power.

God's Power in the Believer

One of the first things a new Christian should know is that they cannot live the Christian life in their own strength or ability, and God doesn't expect them to. Every true believer receives the Person of His Holy Spirit into their life, and He is the One whom they are expected to rely on for wisdom, power and timing for the right time and place to speak, so that His power is in the words and actions that follow.

God's power in the believer is also required to enable them to reach out in love and compassion to the needy and those who oppose them, and to act with mercy and grace toward the wayward, and graciously state a warning from Scripture to those who are intent on evil.

From the Scripture given here it is seen that it is the Holy Spirit that gives the fruit of the Spirit to the believer, also He provides gifts of power, and both these aspects are explained in Section D5.

But the fruit of the Spirit is love, joy, peace, patience, kindness, goodness, faithfulness, gentleness and self-control. Against such things there is no law.

Gal 5:22-23

Please see the Scriptures in the Biblical Texts in this Section that relate to this topic.

Those who '*Proclaim*' the Message of the Scriptures

There are very important conditions placed on all those who '*proclaim*', by any method, the truths of the Scriptures, that is, that they do this through the leading and power of God's Holy Spirit, coupled with prayer. This means that they will not depend on their own resources, but depend on His. When this does not occur, there can be little or much energy expended with no positive spiritual result.

The aspect of speaking through the power of the Spirit is supported by the apostle Paul when he says in Rom 15:18-19, 1Cor 1:17-19; 2:3-5; & 1Thess 1:5. and also, following his example, preachers should back up what they say by including an element of personal testimony, see Acts 22:17-21, 26:4-18, Rom 15;18-19, Gal 1:13-16, Phil 3:4-8.

It follows that Scriptures like 1Cor 1:17-19; 2:3-5; & 1Thess 1:5 refer to the power of the Holy Spirit working through people that enabled the miraculous happenings and the growth of the early Church to take place as reported throughout the Book of 'The Acts of the Apostles' – just a few of the many Scriptures that could be referred to being: Acts 2:1-41; 6:8; 8:14-17; 10:44-46; 13:9-11; 16:16-18.

The list, given below, of those involved in this exercise of *'proclamation'* is totally inclusive:

All Christians.
Evangelists.
Pastors and Teachers.

<u>The important twin factors in proclamation - Obedience and Compassion</u>

The secret of a God approved and Spirit led ministry is *obedience,* - not success, failure, Work done, achievements, people converted or discipled, but being obedient to that which God lays on the 'proclaimer's' heart – the results are in God's hands, not the one who proclaims.

A few pointers from the Scriptures:

'To obey is better than sacrifice' – 1Sam 15:22;

Jesus said: 'My sheep listen to my voice; I know them, and they follow me' Jn 10:27;

'Peter and the other apostles replied: "We must obey God rather than men! Acts 5:29;

'This is how we know that we love the children of God: by loving God and carrying out his commands' 1Jn 5:2;

Moses had to learn obedience to God before he could be used by Him – see Ex 3.

All Christians are meant to be involved in 'ongoing outreach' in everyday life and situations to those outside God's Kingdom, so they must not only learn to listen and obey, but should do so with compassion as Jesus Christ did, and as someone has so rightly said: "He loved to take the *lost*, the *last*, the *least* and the *lowest* and make something beautiful of them – see Mat 14:13-14, 15:32-38, 18:23-35; Lk 7:11-17, 10:25-37, 15:11-24; Jn 4:7-26, 5:1-9.

True Christian proclamation or witness is rewarded

The Scripture below clearly shows the reward offered:

"Whoever acknowledges me before men, I will also acknowledge him before my Father in heaven. But whoever disowns me before men, I will disown him before my Father in heaven.

Mat 10:32-33

The Message is Proclaimed by:

Christians - All Christians will *'proclaim'* a *'message'* to those around them, through their lifestyle, and this will show to others the reality or otherwise of their Christian Faith.

The 'truths' conveyed in this way will depend on the quality of the person's Christian character. It follows, therefore, that the Christian will range from being a Poor witness to a good witness, but they cannot escape from being a witness. A good witness is the testimony of a changed and more Godly life.

The Christian is also expected to explain aspects of the Christian Faith when asked, and this should be done without 'preaching' or answering questions that have not been asked.

The method that should be adopted by Christians when explaining their actions, attitude or aspects of the Faith, is to speak with humility and patience using a winsome manner, e.g. a manner which is winning, attractive and engages others with warmth.

A Christian can be given the privilege and responsibility to preach, usually when invited, to a number of assembled people.

<u>Evangelists</u> - The Evangelist according to the Biblical scholars is one who proclaims good news, where the 'good news' is the Gospel. From the Scripture Eph 4:11 we see that evangelists are gifted people that God has given to the Church. Thus evangelists will proclaim, or preach, the Gospel Message to individuals or crowds of people wherever and whenever they can and by any means at their disposal, e.g. at a meeting place, on radio, on television, on a website, or through a book. All missionaries are evangelists, and some of these are just preachers of the Gospel, and others 'proclaim' the Gospel through medical or educational roles.

<u>Pastor/Teachers</u> - Pastor/Teacher roles are often combined, and these people tend and teach those in their care, within a framework of discipline related to Biblical truth. Whilst they preach the Gospel they also teach to provide a deeper understanding of God and the Bible, and this teaching is related to how committed believers (Christians) should, with God's help, live.

The Pastor/Teacher(s), along with a group of elders and Christians within a church should provide the caring environment for each Christian to grow spirituality and enjoy mutual love and support. In Eph 4:1-13 it speaks about these issues and states, along with other matters, that Pastors /Teacher's are "to prepare God's people for works of service - - - - - - - and become mature."

<u>Effects of Proclaiming the Message</u>

It is always hoped that the effect of proclaiming the Gospel to non-Christians will be to bring about repentance from sin and faith in the Lord Jesus Christ for salvation, but it can receive a range of responses from apathy, indifference, arguments, hostility, to persecution and death.

When proclaiming/teaching to Christians concerning God, the Bible, and how these matters relate to a Christian lifestyle, there is also a range of responses from fully accepting what is taught and acting on it, to partially accepting it, indifference, arguments, to the breaking off of fellowship and the separation of one Christian or group from another. Some of these negative responses can be understood when the teaching is in error, but when it is true to the Scriptures, Christians are saddened and God's heart is grieved.

OUR RESPONSE TO GOD - DISCIPLESHIP

-GOSPEL PROCLAMATION – KNOWING THE HUMAN CONDITION

Notes and Quotations

The Human Condition

Someone has said: "A person has no more character than is revealed when they are in a crisis."

Philip Yancey in his book: "What's So Amazing About Grace" states: "People divide into two types: not the guilty and the "righteous," as many people think, but rather two different types of guilty people. There are guilty people who acknowledge their wrongs, and guilty ones who do not, two groups who converge in a scene recorded in John 8."

"The most damnable and pernicious heresy that ever entered the mind of man was the idea that somehow he could make himself good enough to deserve to live with an all-holy God." (See Rom 3:22-23 & 5:6-11).

Martin Luther

"The way we see God will govern the way we live and what we say about Him. We need a true and balanced view as is provided by the Holy Spirit's illumination of Scripture to obtain a balanced multi-faceted view of His character. This should give us a view of His nature revealing His warmth, beauty, loveliness, goodness, grandeur, power, justice and judgement etc." From "Every Day with Jesus" Notes by Selwyn Hughes.

'Pride' – It is better to <u>lose face</u> than:
Lose your soul,
Lose your way,
Lose His Way,

Lose His Joy,
Lose His Blessing.

The difference between:-
Image, Reputation (Acts 16:2) and Character (Phil 2:22)
Character – "Who we <u>are</u> when no one's looking" - Author unknown.

Bill Hybels picks out several elements that make a strong character which we see in Timothy's life:-

<u>Courage</u> – 2Tim 1:7-8; 2Tim 4:5; 1Tim 5:20
Courage is resistance to fear, mastery of fear, not absence of fear – (Mark Twain).
Courage is fear that has said its prayers.

<u>Discipline</u> – 1Tim 4:7; 2Tim 2:22; 2Tim 3:14-17; Heb 12:11-13
Short term pain for long term gain.

<u>Vision</u> – 2Tim 2:2; 1Tim 2:1-2; 1Tim 4:8
The ability to see things from God's point of view.

<u>Endurance</u> – 1Tim 6:14; 2Tim 2:3; 2Tim 3:14
'Blessed is the man who endures trials, for when he has stood the test he will receive the crown of life' Jas 1:12

<u>Character Consequences</u>
Sow a thought, reap a word
Sow a word, reap a deed
Sow a deed, reap a habit
Sow a habit, reap a character
Sow a character, reap a destiny. Author unknown

'Sin' – has been defined as: "The ego in the place where God wants to be."

Selwyn Hughes in his "Every Day with Jesus" Notes, commenting on Eph 2:14-15 has stated that Jesus has abolished not the moral law, but the ceremonial law by His death on the cross. He set aside the ceremonial law with all its rules and regulations.

v14 – God is our peace - He is working to unite men and women not by the reconstruction of human society but by the construction of an alternative society, as Paul shows so clearly in this passage.

A testing point for people of all Religions, including those who call themselves Christians, is to ask themselves whether their outward appearance and actions match their inner reality and desires.

Lk 6:45 states: "For out of the overflow of his heart his mouth speaks." – These words will show whether or not our lifestyle is counting for God, and to what extent we have been changed by Him.

Mc Cheyne has said: "Man is what he is on his knees, and no more."

Being a Witness and 'Proclaiming' The Gospel

For a very effective method of evangelism see Section E8 under the heading "Prayer/Spiritual Warfare – The First Tool of Evangelism."

Being a witness – Conveying Christ to others – with love.

Not merely in the words you say
Not only in your deeds confessed,
But in the most unconscious way
Is Christ expressed.

Is it a calm and peaceful smile?
A holy light upon the brow?
Oh no! I felt his presence while
You laughed just now.

For me 'twas not the truth you taught,
To you so clear, to me so dim,
But when you came to me you brought
A sense of Him.

And from your eyes He beckons me,
And from your heart His love is shed,
Till I lose sight of you, and see
The Christ instead.

Writer unknown.

Philip Yancey in his book: "What's So Amazing About Grace" quotes Dwight L. Moody saying: "Of one hundred men, one will read the Bible; the ninety-nine will read the Christian."

He further quotes: "Jesus reduced the mark of a Christian to one word. "By this all men will know that you are my disciples," he said: "if you *love* one another."

The Christian life that we live is the 'Gospel' that people see and perhaps it will be the only one they will 'read'. – 1Cor 11:1, 2Cor 3:2, Phil 4:9.

The Lord wants Christians to create an atmosphere not based on judgements, but on the anticipation of healing. – Mat 7:1-5

In "The Word for Today" Notes by Bob Gass he refers to Rom 1:16 and states:

"Be relevant.

Are you answering questions nobody's asking? Martin Luther said, "If you preach the gospel but do not address the issues of your time – you're not preaching the gospel at all." Strong words!

Chuck Swindoll writes, "The gospel is like a sword sharpened on the stone of scripture and tempered in the furnace of reality, relevance and need. Of all the reactions a person may have to it, I can think of none worse than a yawn, a sleepy 'so what?' or a bored 'who cares?'"

Do you want a new definition of failing the Lord? Here it is – using the gospel to bore people! His gospel is not some vague religious concept – it's an exciting relationship with God that works in everyday life. People need it, so go out and give it to them today!"

Jesus said: "out of the overflow of the heart the mouth speaks."

Mat 12:34.

The preacher's heart, the evangelist's and the Christian's heart, are seen in the following Scriptures: Ps 45:1, Jer 20:9, Acts 4:20, 1Cor 9:16.

"Effective preaching is a by-product of your life, as shown in your lifestyle, e.g. cannot effectively preach about love unless you show love in your lifestyle."- Author unknown.

"More flies are caught by honey, than by vinegar." - Author unknown.

When preaching the Good News, the Gospel, there should be a balance of saying what we are saved ***from,*** and what we are saved ***to***.

Outreach' should be preceded by 'Upreach'.
Evangelistic outreach and all work done in the Lord's service should come from the overflow, power and direction of the Holy Spirit through us, otherwise it has little or no effect, e.g. it is our 'work', not His.

Concerning the Gospel Jackie Pullinger has said: "Jesus heals, feeds, houses, delivers and forgives. And the people who carry the 'Good News' are the ones who have been, healed, fed, housed, delivered and forgiven."

"The Gospel is a fact; therefore tell it simply.
The Gospel is a joyful fact; therefore tell it cheerfully.
The Gospel is an entrusted fact; therefore tell it faithfully.
The Gospel is a fact of infinite moment; therefore tell it earnestly.
The Gospel is a fact of infinite love; therefore tell it feelingly.
The Gospel is a fact of difficult comprehension to many; therefore tell it with illustration
The Gospel is a fact about a person; therefore preach Christ," – Archibold Brown

Quoted from the book: "Why Revival Tarries" by Leonard Ravenhill

If you were arrested for being a Christian, would there be enough evidence to convict you? In Rev 3:1-6 we read of the church in Sardis which had a reputation for being alive as it had much activity, but was accused of being dead.

The 'Gospel' – We should be the 'Good News'.

"A '*fanatic*' is someone who loves Jesus more than you do."
Author unknown.

Charles Haddon Spurgeon said: "If we look for mercy in that day, we must show mercy in this day." – From "The Christian Book of Lists" by Randy Petersen.

"Until your misery factor exceeds your fear factor, you won't move." – From the "The Word for Today" Notes by Bob Gass.

"Life is not built on things, it's built on relationships. How's your relationship with God? How's your relationship with your family?" - From the "The Word for Today" Notes by Bob Gass.

"Without full disclosure of sin the Gospel of grace becomes impertinent, unnecessary and finally uninteresting." – From the book "Not the way it's supposed to be" by Cornelius Platinga.

In 'The Word for Today' Notes by Bob Gass he gives a caution regarding our attitude toward others by stating: "Your attitude will reach them long before your message does."

Jesus said He wants us to have life to the full, and this is experienced when it has as it's foundation a relationship with God – Jn 10:10.

Duncan Campbell said: "You must win people to yourself before you can win them to the Lord."

"Evangelism and service for God should come from an overflow of the Holy Spirit through us, otherwise it has little or no effect". Author unknown.

<u>Methods of Proclaiming Scriptural Truths – See also Section D4</u>

The greatest teacher and preacher of all time was Jesus Christ, therefore, we should note the methods He used. He mostly used a pictorial form of language, often associated with demonstration, where He wrapped the Truth, the issue, the morality teaching etc, in parables, stories, illustrations, proverbs, signs and miracles. In fact in Mat 13:34-35 Jesus says: "he did not say anything to them without using a parable" thus fulfilling the Scripture Ps 78:2. In Lk 8:9-10 Jesus says to his disciples: "The knowledge of the secrets of the kingdom of God has been given to you, but to others I speak in parables, so that, "'though seeing, they may not see, though hearing, they may not understand.' To help to throw light on this statement the NIV Study Bible referring to 'the secrets of the kingdom of God', states: "Truths that can be known only by revelation from God – Eph 3:2-5; 1Pet 1:10-12."

These methods of approach often did not tell people directly what to do, but let them make up their minds on the matter, without instantly losing face. The subject matter presented in this way held people's attention and was much easier to remember, and hence, according to the person's conviction, could be acted on at the time, or later, on recall.

Another consideration, regarding these methods is that they tend to make 'the issue' the focus of attention rather than the person preaching.

This form of preaching/teaching, however, is not generally used in the Western world, and is not a prominent feature of our culture. The preaching/teaching methods used in the West are generally a mix of concepts, straight talking, statements and plain facts, with perhaps the occasional illustration or story. With this approach the message may be understood at the time, but in reality it can be forgotten within minutes, and this frequently happens, and also for most people is difficult to recall. Another weakness, is that when the message takes a long time to deliver the listener's attention often wavers, and the early points of the message are rarely remembered at all.

The sermons preached in the Book of Acts are worthy of much study, to observe the material and methods used, e.g. the use of story and history material, the quoting of Scripture and prophetically fulfilled Scripture, and preaching that came from miracles.

Biblical preaching and teaching from preparation to delivery should be undertaken with humility and sensitivity to the leading of the Holy Spirit, and this can mean changing the preaching/teaching material on some occasion, bearing in mind that we should be on God's agenda not ours.

It should also be remembered that the N.T. Epistles (letters) are not direct preaching/ teaching material, but their substance needs breaking down into digestible pieces and illustrated in some way so that the listener can understand, remember, and act on the matter.

Parables

"The purpose of a parable is to create more time for an undecided people."

Author unknown.

"A gracious form of teaching to help keep the attention of his hearers awake until a more convenient time.""

John Calvin.

Preaching

"Preaching of the 'Good News' of the Gospel is the WHOLE task of the WHOLE church for the WHOLE age."

Author unknown.

Effective evangelism takes place when the lives of Christians overflow with the love, grace, wisdom and power that results from a close relationship with God and a dependency on Him. Always remembering, that any words of condemnation should be spoken with humility and grace, and offered with words of hope, thus providing a path of escape and reconciliation, not forgetting that we are also sinners that are only saved through the grace, the unmerited favour, of God.

"If there is no power, it is not preaching"

Dr Lloyd –Jones

"You must win people to yourself before you can win them to the Lord."

Duncan Campbell

"Our words will be largely ineffective if our body language is not one of love."

Author unknown.

The person who shares the Gospel with others must also share their life – see 1Thess 2:8. The effectiveness of a person's ministry depends on the fervency of their Love for God and others.

The power of Peter's preaching came out of a heart of one who had been forgiven much, - (he denied knowing Jesus) see Lk 22:34 & 54-62, and Jesus speaking about a sinful woman who came to Him, said:

"Therefore, I tell you, her many sins have been forgiven— for she loved much. But he who has been forgiven little loves little." Lk 7:47

Isn't it true though that all Christians have been forgiven much !!

From the Scriptures some key factors for effective preaching and evangelism are:

(1) Maintaining dependence on God.
(2) Avoiding professionalism.
(3) Operating in the power of the Holy Spirit through having a close relationship with God.

Various people have quoted the following regarding: preaching, teaching and training; by stating that:

We remember - 30% of what we hear,
- 60% of what we 'see' – through illustration or demonstration,
- 90% of what we do.

Dr R.T. Kendall in the book: "The Word and the Spirit" states, under the heading 'The Preaching of the Word and Spirit', "I stand between God and men either to intercept or to transmit what the Spirit wants to be and to do. If I do not block the Spirit he will be himself to my hearers." He then goes on to give seven ways in which the Spirit can be blocked, and the headings only of these are listed below:

Through:
Human wisdom.
Perverting the text.
Copying others.
Avoiding difficult Scriptures.
Personal feelings.
Grieving the Spirit.
Trying to keep the control.

Preachers of the Word of God should be those who firstly 'hear' the 'word' from God, and then proclaim what they have heard. See Jer 23:18-22

A Church Mission Statement

"Any local church that does not seek to equip its members for service and lead them towards spiritual maturity is not functioning in accordance with Biblical principles. I suggest every local church's mission statement should include wording along these lines: "We see our prime task as teaching our members to serve Christ and bring them to spiritual maturity." – From "Every Day with Jesus" Notes by Selwyn Hughes.

OUR RESPONSE TO GOD - DISCIPLESHIP

- GOSPEL PROCLAMATION - KNOWING THE HUMAN CONDITION-

Biblical Texts & Text References

The Human Condition

David in Ps 53:1-3 states 'that the fool says' "There is no God", and further states that there is no-one who does good.

8 For it is by grace you have been saved, through faith—and this not from yourselves, it is the gift of God—
9 not by works, so that no-one can boast.

Eph 2:8-9

In the last days people will be lovers of themselves, lovers of money, boastful, proud, abusive, disobedient to their parents, ungrateful, unholy,- and even more ungodliness – see 2Tim 3:1-5

26 If anyone considers himself religious and yet does not keep a tight rein on his tongue, he deceives himself and his religion is worthless.

Jas 1:26

Additional Scripture references

1Kg 8:46-50, Ps 10:2-4; 51:1-5, Isa 66:1-2; Jer 17:9-10, Mat 12:34-37; 16:13-17, Lk 6:43-45, 18:18-19; Rom 1:16-32; 3:10-12; & 19-24; 5:6-21; 6:21-23; 7:14-25; 8:1-5, 1Cor 6:9-11, Eph 2:13-15, 1Thess 5:9-10, Heb 3:7-8, Jas 1:13-15, 2Pet 2:10-14, 1Jn 3:4.

The Gospel to be Proclaimed

Repentance

Jesus said:" unless you repent, you too will all perish". See Lk 13:1-3

17 "Now, brothers, I know that you acted in ignorance, as did your leaders.
18 But this is how God fulfilled what he had foretold through all the prophets, saying that his Christ would suffer.
19 Repent, then, and turn to God, so that your sins may be wiped out, that times of refreshing may come from the Lord,

Acts 3:17-19

Additional Scripture references

Isa 50:20, Jer 15:19; Ezek 18:30; Mat 3:1-2; 21:32, Acts 2:36-38; 17:29-30

Belief

The words of Jesus:

35 The Father loves the Son and has placed everything in his hands.
36 Whoever believes in the Son has eternal life, but whoever rejects the Son will not see life, for God's wrath remains on him."

Jn 3:35-36

24 "I tell you the truth, whoever hears my word and believes him who sent me has eternal life and will not be condemned; he has crossed over from death to life.

Jn 5:24

Additional Scripture references

Mk 16:15-16; Jn 3:16-18; 5:37-46; 6:40; 11:25-26; 12:44-46, Acts 13:38-39, Rom 1:16-17, 1Jn 5:1-5

Confession

9 That if you confess with your mouth, "Jesus is Lord," and believe in your heart that God raised him from the dead, you will be saved.
10 For it is with your heart that you believe and are justified, and it is with your mouth that you confess and are saved.

Rom 10:9-10

11 It is written: "'As surely as I live,' says the Lord, 'Every knee will bow before me; every tongue will confess to God.'"
12 So then, each of us will give an account of himself to God.

Rom 14:11-12

<u>Additional Scripture references</u>
Ps 32:5; 38:18, Mat 10:32-33, Jn 5:22-23, Acts 4:7-12, 1Jn 1:8-9

<u>God's Offer of Salvation comes with words of Caution</u>

9 Do you not know that the wicked will not inherit the kingdom of God? Do not be deceived: Neither the sexually immoral nor idolaters nor adulterers nor male prostitutes nor homosexual offenders
10 nor thieves nor the greedy nor drunkards nor slanderers nor swindlers will inherit the kingdom of God.
11 And <u>that is what some of you were</u>. But you were washed, you were sanctified, you were justified in the name of the Lord Jesus Christ and by the Spirit of our God.

1Cor 6:9-11

16 know that a man is not justified by observing the law, but by faith in Jesus Christ. So we, too, have put our faith in Christ Jesus that we may be justified by faith in Christ and not by observing the law, because by observing the law no-one will be justified.

Gal 2:16

<u>Additional Scripture references</u>
Mat 7:21-23, Lk 12:1-5; 16:19-31, Acts 4:12, Rom 1:16-2:8, Gal 3:1-5, Heb 9:11-14, 2Pet 2:4-9

<u>Being a Witness and Proclaiming the Whole Gospel</u>

9 But if I say, "I will not mention him or speak any more in his name," his word is in my heart like a fire, a fire shut up in my bones. I am weary of holding it in; indeed, I cannot.

Jer 20:9

The apostle Paul said:

27 For I have not hesitated to proclaim to you the whole will of God.

Acts 20:27

<u>Additional Scripture references</u>
Ps 40:8-10; 45:1; 73:28; 145:5-12, Mat 7:1-5, Lk 10:1-12, Acts 4:19-20, 1Cor 9:16; 2Cor 3:2-3, Eph 4:22-25, Phil 4:8-9 ; Phm 1:6

Preaching the Whole Gospel

18 I will not venture to speak of anything except what Christ has accomplished through me in leading the Gentiles to obey God by what I have said and done—

19 by the power of signs and miracles, through the power of the Spirit. So from Jerusalem all the way round to Illyricum, I have fully proclaimed the gospel of Christ.

Rom 15:18-19

Additional Scripture reference

Prov 30:5-6; Jer 1:4-9; 15:19; 20:9, Ezek 3:15-21, Mat 10:7-8 & 14-15; 28:16-20; Mk 10:13-16; 16:14-16, Acts 2:14-21; 8:14-17; 8:29- 31; 10:44-46; 16:16-18; 20:25-27, Rom 10:17, 1Cor 1:17-19; 2:3-5; 9:16-18, Col1:25-29, 1 Thess 1:4-5, 2Tim 4:17

God's Power in the Believer

4 My message and my preaching were not with wise and persuasive words, but with a demonstration of the Spirit's power,

5 so that your faith might not rest on men's wisdom, but on God's power.

1Cor 2:4-5

Additional Scripture references

Mat 22:29, Lk 12:5; Jn 16:33, Acts 3:12, Rom 1:16; 15:13-19, 1Cor 4:20, 2Cor 10:4; 12:9, Eph 3:20; Col 1:10-11, 1Thess 1:5, 2Tim 1:7, 2 Pet 1:3

The Discipline of Preaching

The apostle Paul said that he had not hesitated from preaching anything that would be helpful, either taught publicly or from house to house. See Acts 20:20

2 Preach the Word; be prepared in season and out of season; correct, rebuke and encourage—with great patience and careful instruction.

2Tim 4:2

Additional Scripture references

Jer 23:18-22, Mat 10:7-8; 12:41; 13:33-34; 23:1-3, Mk 1:38; 16:14-16, Lk 7:47; 9:1-5; 22:34-35; 22:54-62, Acts 16:10, Rom 2:19-23, 10:14-15; 1Cor 1:17-23; 9:14-17, Eph 3:8; 1Thess 2:8, 1Tim 5:17-18

E5

OUR RESPONSE TO GOD - DISCIPLESHIP

-COMMISSION, SERVICE, LEADERSHIP & MATURITY-

Biblical Definitions

Commission

There are those who are directly commissioned/called by God for service in God's kingdom, and others who are commissioned/called by men to fill positions of responsibility as set out in the Scriptures for service in God's kingdom. In each case they should be especially appointed (anointed by God) for this service.

Leaders should:

- show in their lifestyle their faith in God – see Heb 13:7 & 17;
- have a servant heart – see Mat 20:25-28;
- speak with God's power – see 1Cor 2:4-5;
- speak the Word of God true to the Scriptures and in context – see 2Tim 2:15;
- remind others all Scripture is God breathed and they can always converse with the Living God – See 2Tim 3:16; 1Tim 3:15; & 1Tim 4:7-10;
- inspire others to follow them – see Mk 1:17-18

Given below is a typical warning to those who say they are speaking the words of God, but God says that He has not sent them:

Then the LORD said to me, "The prophets are prophesying lies in my name. I have not sent them or appointed them or spoken to them. They are prophesying to you false visions, divinations, idolatries and the delusions of their own minds. Therefore, this is what the LORD says about the prophets who are prophesying in my name: I did not send them, yet they are saying, 'No sword or famine will touch this land.' Those same prophets will perish by sword and famine.

Jer 14:14-15

Those commissioned by God

It is interesting to note that many of those called directly by God were reluctant to accept the calling and their responses ranged from: inability to speak well, inadequacy, fear, to being over confident. However, as these people submitted themselves to God and learned to put their trust in Him and not themselves, they proved God was able to achieve His purposes through them.

Listed below are some names of people in the Bible who were called directly by God:

Note: The Lord Jesus Christ was a unique 'calling' and He had no character defects.

Abraham – Gen 12:1-3
Moses -- Ex 3:1-10, 1Sam 12:6
David -- 1Sam 16:1 & 11-13, 1Sam 13:14
Jeremiah – Jer 1:4-8
Daniel -- Dan 5:11-12
Jonah -- Jon 1:1-3
The Lord Jesus Christ -- Mat 1:18-23, 3:11-17, Lk 1:26-56
Jesus' Disciples -- Mat 10:1-4, Mk 3:14-19, Lk 10:1, Jn 15:16
John the Baptist -- Lk 1:11-20 & 57-66
The Apostle Paul -- Acts 9:11-19, 13:2, 1Tim 1:12-14, 2:7, 2Tim 1:11
Apostles, Prophets, Evangelists, Pastors, Teachers – 1Cor 12:6-8, & 27-31, 1Cor 14:1-5, Eph 4:11-13

Those who serve, encourage, contribute to the needs of others – Rom 12:6-8

Those given spiritual gifts of wisdom, knowledge, faith, healing, miraculous powers, prophecy, discernment between spirits, speaking in tongues, administration -- 1Cor 12:4-11, & 27-31, 1Cor 13:1-3, Heb 13:7 & 17

Those commissioned by men

The men that carry out this function are led by the Holy Spirit to recognise those to be commissioned, and an indication of this is given in Acts 15:22 & 28 where it states: "it seemed good to us and the Holy Spirit", and this phrasing comes across as a good guiding principle when Church leaders or other decisions concerning believers are to be made.

This process of recognition of leaders is enacted by the 'laying on of hands', as stated in the Scriptures: Acts 9:17; & 13:3, 1Tim 4:14; & 5:22, Heb 6:2.

There are two specific church leadership positions recognised in the N.T. namely, elder and deacon, and the qualities of character expected in these people are given in the biblical references provided below:

Elder -- Acts 14:23, 1Tim 3:1-7, 2Tim 1:5-7, Tit 1:5-9
Deacon -- Acts 6:1-10, 1Tim 3:8-13

Service

Before considering the type of service, that as a Christian, they should be involved in, it is wise to first pay attention to making some progress at BEING the person God wants them to BE, and then, to concentrate on DOING what they feel God is calling them to DO.

The BEING aspect referred to is seen in the attitude the person has towards those they are seeking to serve, and the task to be done. Regarding a person's attitude Bob Gass points out: "your attitude will reach them long before your message does".

Also, when someone is considering undertaking any Christian service, they should carefully assess their gifting for that type of service. In a more rare case it maybe God calls someone to a field of service that they do not feel particularly suited to, and it becomes a faith and trust issue for that person.

Qualities looked for first in the server being: a servant heart; a right motive; humility; faith; love; grace; and THEN the use of the ability God has given.

Jesus Christ, above all others showed us the best example of a true servant – see the scripture below:

Your attitude should be the same as that of Christ Jesus:

Who, being in very nature God, did not consider equality with God something to be grasped, but made himself nothing, taking the very nature of a servant, being made in human likeness. And being found in appearance as a man, he humbled himself and became obedient to death—even death on a cross!

Phil 2:5-8

Good examples of those with a servant heart exist throughout the Bible, and there are many references, particularly in the N.T. to people referred to as servants:

The Lord Jesus Christ - Acts 3:26; 4:27;
David – Acts 4:25;
Christians – Acts 4:29; 2Tim 2:24;
Paul – Rom 1:1; Gal 1:10; Eph 3:7;
Phoebe – Rom 16:1;
Tychicus – Eph 6:21;
Epaphras – Col 1:7;
Moses – Heb 3:5.

We are called to serve God and one another in love, - see Mat 20:26-28

- We, as believers, are called to:
- serve Him without fear – Lk 1:74.
- serve only Him – Lk 4:8, 16:13.
- serve Him in humility, remembering that you have nothing "that you did not receive" – 1Cor 4:7; Acts 20:19; Col 3:12; 1Pet 5:5.
- serve constantly, with diligence – Lk 12:37.
- serve Him whole heartedly – Rom 1:9, Eph 6:7.
- serve Him through the Holy Spirit, and not through the old way of the written code – Rom 7:6.
- use our freedom to serve one another in love – Gal 5:13.
- serve the living God and not idols – 1Thess 1:9.
- have our service tested, if we are deacons – 1Tim 3:10.

- use our gifts to serve others, always remembering that without Him we "can do nothing" – Jn 15:5; 1Pet 4:10.
- be a holy priesthood serving God – 1Pet 2:5, Rev 1:5-6.

Our Weakness - His Strength

God wants us to use the gifting and talents we have been given, but to always act with humility and prepared to be led by the Holy Spirit, and so bringing praise to God, not ourselves.

Let us consider the Apostle Paul, the gifted writer of much of the New Testament, one that was greatly used to teach and establish many churches, and who was also used by God to effect miraculous healings – what did God have to say to him? God said: "my power is made perfect in weakness" (the full text 2Cor 12:9-10 is given below). This means that God's ability and authority will work through those believers who admit that they are not able to achieve the spiritual objective of a task or action, but are dependant on the Holy Spirit to do that through them or another channel.

Using Paul as an example, he could travel to a place and preach and teach, but he would be dependant on the guidance and power of the Holy Spirit to bring conversions to Christ and to cause people to respond positively to the teaching of the Bible.

But he said to me, "My grace is sufficient for you, for my power is made perfect in weakness." Therefore I will boast all the more gladly about my weaknesses, so that Christ's power may rest on me. That is why, for Christ's sake, I delight in weaknesses, in insults, in hardships, in persecutions, in difficulties. For when I am weak, then I am strong.

2Cor 12:9-10

Leadership

The leadership role is crucial in all spheres of activity, whether secular or religious, and is especially true for the Christian Church.

Over the years leadership role models have changed, and it is particularly important for present day Church leaders to note the changes that have occurred from O.T. days to now.

In the O.T. we have the leadership models of Moses, Judges, Kings and the Prophets where their word was authoritative and final, and covered all areas of judgement and direction from domestic to military affairs.

An example of the role and authority of the Prophet as God's spokesman who provides direction and leadership is seen in Deut 18:15-22. This Scripture also contains a warning to 'false prophets'.

When these leaders were obeying God they were submitting to His Lordship in all matters, but when they followed their own council they were not acknowledging Him as Lord.

The Jewish religious leaders of Jesus' day were severely criticised by Jesus (see Mat 23), and were accused by Him of hypocrisy, double standards and for teaching the precepts of men as the commandments of God, and also for failing to teach Scriptural truth.

The line of command of O.T. Kings and in present day governments is long, with officials at each level reporting to those above them right up to the top. However, the line of command for the N.T. Church, and that includes the present day Church, is short, as it has Christ as its head, and the only two Church offices mentioned in the N.T. are those of elder (overseer or bishop) and deacon, and these are only to represent local Churches.

The role of Christian leadership in a Church situation in different in some respects to the way in which leadership is carried out in industry and commerce. One of these differences is shown in the exercise and understanding of authority. In a company authority may be exercised with, or without, much concern for the people they manage. However, in a Church there must always be consideration of others and where people have a different view the situation must be explained with patience, love and grace. In Christian leadership authority is *given* not *taken.*

A common difficulty for Church leaders concerns the handling of 'a vision' of a way forward and its practical outworking, and this situation calls for it to be immersed in prayer and handled with humility, explaining with care and clear scriptural backing how the vision is to be fulfilled. Using this approach leaders should be able to take people with them, bearing in mind the adage, 'you are only a leader if others willingly follow you'.

In the Scriptures there are many aspects of leadership that can be taken note of: e.g. the humility of Moses, and the boldness, courage, faithfulness, suffering and obedience in the O.T. prophets, and some of the Judges and Kings (especially David), and in the N.T. there is the Lord Jesus Christ, the apostles and sometimes Jesus' disciples.

Let us remember that a key hallmark of biblical good leadership is humility, as denoted in Moses (Num 12:3), and he led a nation from captivity in Egypt, through a daunting wilderness to the 'Promised Land'. In that long journey, taking many years, he had many things to learn and that included, accepting his mission and leadership role (ref: Ex 3&4), accepting advice from his father-in-law, and how not to assume or act in arrogance, but to follow closely what God said (refs: Ex 17:5-7, Num 20:6-12, Deut 3:23-27)

The qualifications for elders and deacons are more to do with character, than formal scholarly qualifications, positions in society or through lineage, and these qualifications are given in 1Tim 3:1-13, Tit 1:5-9, 1Pet 5:1-4. W.E. Vine also states that the term "elder" indicates someone of 'mature spiritual experience.'

Elders and deacons are expected to use their appointed authority with love, humility, diligence and discipline as embodied in the Scriptures given above.

In the N.I.V. Study Bible notes referring to 1Tim 3:1 it states: "The duties of an overseer (or elder) were to teach and preach (3:2; 5:17), and to direct the affairs of the Church (3:5; 5:17), to shepherd the flock of God (Acts 20:28) and to guard the Church from error (Acts 20:28-31)."

It is clearly implied in the above Scriptures that elders should have a close relationship with God, know the Scriptures and how to apply them to, themselves, their family and to the members of His Church. Their remit of authority only extends to the people in their congregation, and only concerns their spiritual health, growth and lifestyle, and is not to be used in an overbearing or controlling fashion. The whole Church operates by consent with the people in the congregation being prepared to submit to the authority of the elders in matters of biblical teaching and spiritual direction.

In the N.T. it shows that elders were appointed in each Church, and not an elder, but elders, see Acts 14:23, 20:17, Phil 1:1, 1Tim 5:17, Tit 1:5, and this plurality of leadership provides an added safeguard against erroneous teaching and confirmation of spiritual direction.

In 1Tim 5:22 it states that the appointment of people to positions of authority within the Church should not be a hasty matter. Also in Tit 1:5-9 it points out that elders should be:

"blameless— not overbearing, not quick-tempered, not given to drunkenness, not violent, not pursuing dishonest gain", and in 1Pet 5:3 it says: "not lording it over those entrusted to you, but being examples to the flock".

Spiritual leaders should always remember, as quoted under 'Service', that they have nothing that they "did not receive" (1Cor 4:7), and hence should serve Him in humility, -Acts 20:19. Also, as they use 'their gifts' they should remember that without Him they "can do nothing" effective for God – Jn 15:5; 1Pet 4:10. Serving God in the ways outlined here will reveal that at the foundation of their actions there is the essential element of dependency on God.

As stated above there are two specific Church leadership positions recognised in the N.T. namely elder and deacon, and the qualities of character expected in these people are given in the biblical references provided below:

Elder -- Acts 14:23, 1Tim 3:1-7, 2Tim 1:5-7, Tit 1:5-9
Deacon – Acts 6:1-10, 1Tim 3:8-13

To those in Church leadership or others who contribute in any way in a service, e.g. to those who serve, encourage, contribute to the needs of others – see Rom 12:6-8;to those given spiritual gifts of wisdom, knowledge, faith, healing, miraculous powers, prophecy, discernment between spirits, speaking in tongues, administration – see 1Cor 12:4-11,

& 27-31, 1Cor 13:1-3. Bearing in mind that whatever spiritual gifts are given to people, they are to be used with humility and through the leading of the Holy Spirit, and they should also remember that the gifts outlined in 1Cor 12 with their use etc., outlined in 1Cor 14 has the chapter of 1Cor 13 between them which expresses that the motivation for the use of these is to be love.

When leaders are appointed they should be aware that they will have trials and difficulties as well as blessings. The difficult times can happen in various ways, either from internal or external factors. Difficult situations can come from our thoughts and actions, but when the leader is in the wrong they should quickly repent and show their repentance through appropriate actions. When difficulties come from external sources over which they have no influence then they can feel sorry for themselves, or take this as an opportunity to trust God more through the testing time. But wherever the troubles come from they provide an opportunity for the person to become a more mature Christian.

Christian Maturity and Leadership Characteristics

The common goal for those who aspire for Christian maturity or leadership is to seek to become more Christ-like in character. The maturing process, by its very nature, is never very quick and the person has to be: prepared to take knocks; patient; humble; gracious; always ready to forgive and to seek forgiveness; fully committed to follow the teaching of Scripture and the Holy Spirit's leading.

In the process of testing people are asked to, 'admonish one another' (Col 3:16). This subject is addressed below in 'The Word for Today' Notes by Bob Gass under the heading ' Try to be more open!' and uses Prov 27:17, but other references are: 1Thess 5:12-22, Heb 12:5-11.

Try to be more open

'As iron sharpens iron, so one man sharpens another: Prov 27:17.

"How do you handle correction? By taking offence? By hearing it as rejection? By getting defensive? All of us need people who'll be honest with us because we're easily blinded by our egos. When God sends somebody to correct you it is because He loves you. He only does that to those He values. Listen: 'If you are not disciplined.... then you are illegitimate children and not true sons' (Hebrews 12:8 NIV). Check your credentials!

So, how do you handle correction? By killing the messenger? By making sure he or she never gets to you again? By keeping score and saying, 'Look what I've accomplished; what have you accomplished?' By giving in to self-pity and saying, 'People do not understand or appreciate me?' Your mind needs to be sharpened constantly, so stay open to those whom God sends to do it.

Accountable people always exhibit four qualities: 1) *vulnerability.* They are capable of knowing when they are wrong and admitting it -even before they are confronted 2) *teachability.* They are willing to hear, quick to learn and always open to counsel 3) *availability.* They are accessible. They do not avoid you 4) *honesty.* They hate anything phoney and are committed to the truth regardless of how much it hurts. That is a high standard,' you say. You are right. It is a standard pride cannot handle and fragile egos won't tolerate. There's something in each of us that would rather look good than be good. So when God sends people into your life who love you enough to tell you the truth - try to be more open."

<u>Someone has attributed the following statements to indicate signs of maturity:</u>

- Not retaliating when wrongfully accused.
- Being calm in a crisis.
- Praising others, but not yourself.
- Putting the interests of others before your own. (Rom 12:10).
- Have no need among others to be 'FIRST', or to be 'PROVED RIGHT'.

This list could be added to by saying:

- Have a practical love for fellow believers.
- Always seeking a closer walk with God, but never considering that they 'HAVE ARRIVED'.
- Immediately committing all problems to prayer with thanksgiving. (Phil 4:6).

Self-Assessment topics for character and action

Are we teachable? – see Prov 12:15 – someone has said: 'If you are not teachable, you're not reachable'. Also learning requires submission and the admission that you do not know – see Prov 3:5-8; 13:14; 14:27; 15:1; 15:4; 15:33; 17:9-10; 17:27; 19:20.

Are we humble? In Isa 66:2 God says: "This is the one I esteem: he who is humble and contrite in spirit, and trembles at my word." See also Prov 22:4, Acts 20:18-19, Phil 2:3.

Do we have a tendency to domineer? – see 1Pet 5:1-3. Also the guidelines for the way to treat (or handle) others is given in 1Tim 5:1-2.

Do we always speak the truth in love? - see Eph 4:15. The business of speaking the truth in a loving manner can be difficult, but truth and love is a couplet that should never be separated.

So let us remember that - 'the heart reflects the person' – see Prov 27:19.

OUR RESPONSE TO GOD - DISCIPLESHIP

-COMMISSION, SERVICE, LEADERSHIP & MATURITY-

Notes and Quotations

Commission

Any perceived 'call' from God needs to be carefully weighed, as very few people it would seem receive a calling into service of some kind as clear as Moses (Ex 3:1-10), Samuel (1Sam 3:1-19), Jeremiah (Jer 1:5), the Disciples (Mat 4:18-22, Mk 2:13-14, Jn 1:35-51), or the Apostle Paul (Acts 9:1-20).

It is a more common experience that when God calls in a particular way that the subject becomes a burden, or conviction on the person's heart. This may occur, however, only after repeated 'calls' in various ways, perhaps, due to the fact that we are often 'dull' at hearing or interpreting the voice of God.

Service

Alan Redpath, after a stroke said: "I believe the Lord has taught me this lesson above all – to never undertake more Christian work than can be covered in believing prayer."

Bob Gass in his "The Word for Today" Notes reminds us that Jesus came to serve (Mk 10:45), and goes on to say:"Do not pray for a generous heart, practice being generous and your heart will follow. As long as you are a sower God will give you seed (see 2Cor 9:10). If He is not giving you all the seed you want at the moment, maybe you have not become a sower yet."

In another one of his 'Notes' he states: "The kind of assignments God gives in the Bible are always God-sized. They are always beyond what people can do, because He wants to demonstrate His nature, His strength....and His kindness....to a watching world." He also says: "Natural talent alone is not enough to honour a calling from God. You will need ideas, strength and creativity beyond your own resources to do what He asks of you. And it will have to be God and you doing it together. You are not just called to work for God, you are called to work with Him."

<u>Doing God's 'Work'</u>
He wants us to BE <u>before</u> we DO. To 'be' in a good relationship with Him, hearing and obeying His voice, then, our 'DOING' will come out of our 'BEING'.

God is more interested in who we are than what we can do for Him – for His sake lets start living as though we believed the Gospel, as many people don't think there are answers, so they don't ask the questions.

It is a common experience for Christians to give much more time and effort to a whole range of Christian activities and service for God, whilst spending little time in getting to know what He wants. The 'works' may be highly commendable but it is of utmost importance that they put 'knowing Him' FIRST so that the 'activities' are on His agenda and not theirs. See Ps 46:10; Phil 3:7-11.

When Christians are doing what they believe God has called them to do, they will encounter difficulties, and it is how they deal with these that is so important. The problems are meant to make them dependent on God for a solution, and the 'solution' may not always be to their liking. If we consider what happened to Daniel's three friends in Dan 3:8-30, - they were not delivered *from* the fiery furnace, but *through* it. There is a similar principle of 'deliverance' given in Isa 43:1-4 where it states: "*when* (not *if*) you pass through the waters" you need not be afraid because God loves you. This principle is given again in Jer 17:7-8 below:7 "But blessed is the man who trusts in the LORD, whose confidence is in him.

7 "But blessed is the man who trusts in the LORD, whose confidence is in him.
8 He will be like a tree planted by the water that sends out its roots by the stream. It does not fear when heat comes; its leaves are always

> green. It has no worries in a year of drought and never fails to bear fruit."

Note that what it says, the one who trusts and has confidence in the Lord will have no need to fear *when* (not *if*) the heat, or the drought comes.

There is again a similar thought in Ps 23:4 where it states: "Even though I walk through the valley of the shadow of death, I will fear no evil, for you are with me; your rod and your staff, they comfort me."

<u>Striving:</u> Christians should strive in *energy* but not in *attitude:* see Rom 15:30, 1Tim 4:9-10, Heb 4:11 & 12:14-15.

<u>Weakness:</u> God uses our *weakness* rather than our (puny) *strength* so that He can work through us in His power, then the glory is His: see Ex 4 10-17, Jud 6:15-16, 1Sam 2:8-9, Ps 84:5-7, Jer 17:5, <u>Zech 4:6</u>, 1Cor 1:26-31, <u>2Cor 12:9-10</u>, Eph 6:10-18, Heb 11:32-39.

Hudson Taylor, the great missionary to China once said, "Many Christians estimate difficulty in the light of their own resources, thus they attempt very little and always fail. The real giants have all been weak men who did great things for God, because they reckoned on <u>His power</u> and <u>His presence</u> to be with them."

He also said, "God is more concerned with our development than our mistakes – and that will happen if we learn from our mistakes." Quotations from "The Word for Today" Notes by Bob Gass.

"Jesus knew he had something that others needed, and He spent His life giving it to them. - - - - - - - - The people around you today want to change – they just don't know <u>how!</u> Jesus told his disciples He needed to go through Samaria. He went in order to meet a woman who'd been married and divorced five times. He talked. She listened and changed her life permanently. (Jn 4). He was <u>water</u> to the thirsty, <u>bread</u> to the hungry, a <u>road map</u> to the lost and a <u>companion</u> to the lonely." From "The Word for Today" Notes by Bob Gass.

"When God wants to use you, the first thing He looks for is <u>trustworthiness,</u> not talent." (Eph 4:25). From "The Word for Today" Notes by Bob Gass. In another one of his Notes he refers to Martha in Lk 10:38-42, and states:

"God values your attitude more than your service," and "Do everything without complaining" (Phil 2:14).

Thornton Wilder has said: "In love's service, only the wounded soldiers can serve"

The above is a quotation from Rob Parsons' book: "Bringing Home the Prodigals."

If we get concerned about what others are doing or not doing in God's work, let us see what Jesus said about such a situation recorded in Jn 21:21-22 where Peter said: "Lord what about him?" and Jesus answered, "what is that to you? You must follow me." Let us be sure what God has called us to 'be' or 'do', and do not get diverted from it as the anointing goes with the assignment.

Someone has said: "God doesn't bless hard work, He blesses commanded work." So have we discovered His purpose/vision for our lives? And does His purpose align with ours?

Jim Elliot, a missionary who was killed whilst trying to reach people in South America for God said: "He is no fool who gives what he cannot keep to gain what he cannot lose."

Qualities that will keep Christians from being ineffective and unproductive are given in 2Pet 1:5-8.

There is an example of people and leaders giving willingly of their substance to God as part of their service in 1Chron 29, and this brought great rejoicing.

In the Scripture 1Pet 4:8-11 given below, it refers to various forms of 'service' that we are to give to others, and this should include; love; hospitality; and the gifts we have received from God, remembering that they were given freely to us to be used.

Above all, love each other deeply, because love covers over a multitude of sins.

Offer hospitality to one another without grumbling.

Each one should use whatever gift he has received to serve others, faithfully administering God's grace in its various forms.

If anyone speaks, he should do it as one speaking the very words of God. If anyone serves, he should do it with the strength God provides, so that in all things God may be praised through Jesus Christ. To him be the glory and the power for ever and ever. Amen.

1Pet 4:8-11

Regarding Christian service and activities, someone has stated that they can be considered to be 'dead works', where they are engaged in things not initiated by God, and hence, will achieve nothing. Please see 1Cor 3:13-15.

The study of the Bible without acting on what it says produces pride and judgmental attitudes. Jas 1:22-25

Leadership

In Numbers 11:14-17 God said to Moses: "Bring me seventy of Israel's elders who are known to you as leaders . . . ." and He would put His Spirit on them. We see from this passage of Scripture that it is God who ordains – we only recognise leaders (elders).

We can ordain a man only to be what he already is.

"Jesus first called His disciples to Him, then He sent them out from Him. Until you learn to spend time with Him, you'll never accomplish much for Him." Jeremiah said, "The shepherds…..do not enquire of the Lord; so they do not prosper……" (Jer 10:21). - From the "The Word for Today" Notes by Bob Gass.

Bob Gass in his "The Word for Today" Notes states: A good leader has two important characteristics: he or she knows where they're going, and can show others the value of going with them. There are talented people who'll never be effective leaders because they are more interested in themselves than in those they lead.

A.W.Tozer wrote:' A true a safe leader is likely to be one who has no desire to lead, but is forced into a position of leadership by the inward pressure of the Holy Spirit, and the press of the external situation. A person who is ambitious to lead is disqualified as a leader. The true leader will have no desire to lord it over God's heritage, but will be humble, gentle, self-sacrificing and altogether as ready to follow as to lead, when the Spirit makes it clear that a wiser and more talented man than himself has appeared'. This is an extract from "The Word for Today" Notes by Bob Gass. See 1Pet 5:1-5

"God doesn't call the qualified, He qualifies the called"

Author unknown.

Someone has suggested a way to assess a person's, or leader's character by checking their: Strengths, Weaknesses, Opportunities and Threats – the S.W.O.T. test.

Let the word of Christ dwell in you richly as you teach and admonish one another with all wisdom, and as you sing psalms, hymns and spiritual songs with gratitude in your hearts to God. Col 3:16.

In the context of this verse we are asked to *admonish one another*, which means to give a warning based on the instruction of Scripture. This should be done with a gracious attitude remembering our own weaknesses, and only when someone is straying away from the clear teaching of Scripture. This term *admonish* is used again in 1Thess 5:12 in the context of discipline over the flock, where that may be necessary. A church leader can only use his 'authority' in matters of sin and disobedience to the Scriptures, and, in a gracious way as previously stated. In a dispute, if the actions of the leader are right but their attitude is ungracious, the argument may have been won, but the leader runs the risk of losing the person's respect and also of not complying with Scripture when it says we should be, "speaking the truth in love." – Eph 4:15, 2Tim 2:24-25.

There are some more general Scriptures that apply to all Christians given in Ps 141:5, Prov 27:6 & 28:23.

<u>The five basic ingredients of spiritual leadership</u>

In the book "A Way Through the Wilderness" by Jamie Buckingham he refers to a key statement said by Jethro, the father-in-law of Moses, when Moses was finding leading the people at this time a heavy burden and

Jethro says: "Listen now to me and I will give you some advice." "Then he quickly outlined the five basic ingredients of spiritual leadership – things Moses needed to incorporate into his life if he were to minister effectively and not in his own strength.

You must be a priest – the people's representative before God.

You must be a teacher, teaching them the decrees and laws.

You must be an example, showing them the way to live and the duties they are to perform.

You must be an administrator, selecting capable men from all the people and appointing them as officials over thousands, hundreds, fifties and tens.

You must be a judge, having them bring the difficult cases to you but letting them decide the simple cases for themselves."

"If you do this and God so commands," Jethro finished, "you will be able to stand the strain, and all these people will go home satisfied." (Exodus 18:19-26).

The potential quality of spiritual leadership in a person is often seen in their characteristics and lifestyle long before it is recognised in some official way. Many of the qualities of a Christian leader can be observed in the following Scriptures: Ex 4:10-17; 1Sam 16:1-13; Jer 1:4-8; 1Tim 3; 1Tim 5; Tit 1; 1Pet 5:1-11.

As the Christian leader follows the words and principles of Scripture in their lifestyle, preaching, teaching and pastoral work they will encounter at some point differences of view and perhaps opposition, as well as some encouragement, and in these situations they will need, as always, to rely on the Lord for; the Holy Spirit's guidance, wisdom, patience, a good knowledge of the Scriptures and Biblical principles, love, grace, humility, a strong resolve, spiritual insight and boldness of faith.

It is interesting to note that the *authority* of the Christian, (especially a leader), is fundamentally depended upon *character* and not *age,* e.g. Jer 1:4-6; Lk 2:41-49; 1Tim 4:12.

The following is a list of headings on leadership given by Bob Gass in his "The Word for Today" Notes:

Qualities looked for: "(1) Compassion, (2) Creativity, (3) Commitment."

Questions a leader should ask:

(1) Is my personal walk with God up to-date?
(2) Are my priorities in order?
(3) Am I accountable to anybody?
(4) Am I asking myself the difficult questions?
(5) Am I overly concerned with image building?
(6) Am I sensitive to what God says through others in the Body of Christ?
(7) Am I a loner in my service to the Lord?
(8) Am I honest about my weaknesses?
(9) Is my commitment to God constantly before me?"

Someone has said: "Power is the ability to complete a task given by God, and Authority is the right to use the power of God." (Acts 1:8).

There are guidance principles given in 2Chron 20:1-24 that applies to church leaders and all Christians when faced with a difficult situation like King Jehoshaphat in this passage, that firstly he calls people to fast and pray, and then prays (in v12) 'For we have no power to face this vast army that is attacking us. We do not know what to do, but our eyes are upon you'.

In this particular situation the Lord provided guidance through someone led by God's Spirit, and this is just one way that guidance is given.

<u>Humility:</u> Someone has stated that: "Humility is the recognition of the limitations of our abilities and the realisation that what we have comes from God."

The attitude of 'servanthood' is an integral part of Christian leadership, as shown in the following Scriptures: Lk 22:24-27; Acts 5:31; Phil 2:7-8.

<u>Note:</u> There are no celebrities, but only servants in the Kingdom of God,

- Dan 4:28-34, Mat 5:1-16, 20:25-28, Lk 7:24-28, Phil 2:5-11, Col 3:23-24.

Samuel shows the characteristics of good leadership in that he: heard God; obeyed God; spoke God's words; and others recognised him as God's spokesman and as their leader. See 1Sam 3:10-21.

It is important to note the attitude of humility and dependency shown by the apostle Paul in 2Cor 3:4-6.

Boldness

It says in Acts 4:13 "When they saw the *boldness* of Peter and John . . . . ." and referring to this Scripture Bob Gass in his "The Word for Today Notes states: "You can't walk with God and be timid. You can be gentle, but you can't be timid! You can be compassionate, but you can't be coerced by the opinions of those around you. Paul wrote, ". . . . .be strong in the Lord, and in the power of His might" (Eph 6:10). That kind of strength is not arrogance, it's *resilience!* It means refusing to budge when God tells you to stand firm."

Characteristics in leaders to be wary of:

The following is an outline of these characteristics taken from "The Word for Today" Notes by Bob Gass where he refers to 'blind guides' in Mat 15:14 and says: "Here are some signs to help you to identify them:

- Inflexibility! A true leader has a teachable spirit and a servant's heart. He rejoices in your growth and isn't threatened by your development. . . . . . .
- Elitism! Look out for the 'We-alone-are-right' types. When you can't acknowledge and fellowship with the members of God's larger family, there's something wrong. . . . . . .
- Money-grubbing! Here's God standard for leadership: "…… not greedy for money, but eager to serve" (1Pet 5:2). . . . . . .
- Accountability! Beware of the untouchable, 'I-am-God's-anointed' types. No matter how gifted we are, we all have blind spots and we all need to be counselled and confronted. . . . ."

If a person, however godly in lifestyle, has been appointed to a position of Church leadership and they fail to provide a clear lead that others are willingly prepared to follow then their leadership is called into question. If, however, the person shows leadership qualities that call people to follow them unquestioningly then, this is dangerous form of leadership, a common feature of Sects. If, on the other hand, the leader leads by example, is sound in the principles of Scripture, is humble, has an attitude of servanthood, is open to question and the 'lead direction' is not for the leader's benefit, but for those that would follow – this then, is an example of good leadership.

Another situation to be wary of is when a person puts themselves forward as a leader without the recognition and confirmation of other mature Christians.

<u>Aids to Spiritual Maturity</u>

The sort of aids to spiritual maturity we might expect would be situations and circumstances that are largely the result of our own endeavours, e.g. hard work, study, using our talents etc., but the Bible states quite a different path to maturity, one that we would not readily choose of hardship, trials, difficulties, and of discovering that we are of ourselves inadequate for the task required. This path causes us to depend more and more on God, and this is reflected in the James 1:2-4 Scripture below that when it says our faith is tested through difficulties as they develop our perseverance and so our maturity. This means that we are expected to listen, obey and act on what God says, trusting Him to guide and provide for us through the difficulties.

This Scripture is referred to by Selwyn Hughes in his "Every Day with Jesus" Notes where he states: "When all kinds of trials and temptations crowd into your lives . . . . don't resent them as intruders, but welcome them as friends!" . . . . . Why? Because: "Perseverance must finish its work so that you may be mature and complete, not lacking anything"(v.3). "One of the greatest discoveries I have made in my Christian life is that God has a wonderful way of disguising opportunities as problems. Every problem provides us with the opportunity to know God better and grow in dependence on Him." He further states: "The point of all trials is that God uses them to deepen our character and draw us closer to Him."

Consider it pure joy, my brothers, whenever you face trials of many kinds, because you know that the testing of your faith develops perseverance. Perseverance must finish its work so that you may be mature and complete, not lacking anything.

Jas 1:2-4

Referring again to the above Scripture someone has written:
"Jesus can make,
Music out of misery,
A song out of sorrow,
Achievement out of an accident.

See Acts 16:19-40, 1Pet 1:6-7, Job 23:10, Isa 48:10.

Under the heading, "UNTIL WE ALL……BECOME MATURE……" Eph 4:13, Bob Gass in his, "The Word for Today" Notes writes: "When God saves you, your spirit is immediately changed, but your *emotions,* your *appetites,* and your *attitudes* still need working on. In each of us there are things that need to be healed, and until they are, we struggle with them. What are those areas in *your* life? Are you dealing with them? ……

The answer cannot be found in people or things, *it can only be found in a relationship with God!* Real peace comes when you turn to Him in your weakness and allow Him to do for you what nobody else can. Only *He* can regenerate your spirit. Only *He* can satisfy your emotions. Only *He* can bring you to a place of maturity and wholeness. Why don't you come to Him today?

<u>"Maturity does not come with the years for the Christian, but with obedience"</u>

Author unknown.

Be careful how you think; your life is shaped by your thoughts – see Prov 4:23, & Mat 12:34

Christian maturity is seen by the amount of spiritual growth we have achieved in a period of time, and Bob Gass has stated in his "The Word for Today" Notes: "The formula for spiritual growth is simple: rate multiplied by time equals distance. The degree to which you use your time to pursue

God will determine the speed at which you arrive at your destination of maturity."

In other words, the 'rate' is determined by your hunger for God to know Him better, and the 'time' relates to the time we spend pursuing God.

OUR RESPONSE TO GOD - DISCIPLESHIP

-COMMISSION, SERVICE, LEADERSHIP & MATURITY-

Biblical Texts & Text References

Commission

In verse 11 it is referring to Jesus Christ 'who gave',

11 It was he who gave some to be apostles, some to be prophets, some to be evangelists, and some to be pastors and teachers,
12 to prepare God's people for works of service, so that the body of Christ may be built up
13 until we all reach unity in the faith and in the knowledge of the Son of God and become mature, attaining to the whole measure of the fulness of Christ.

Eph 4:11-13

Additional Scripture references

Gen 12:1-3; 1Sam 12:6; 16:1 & 11-13, Jer 1:4-8, Dan 5:11-12, Jon 1:1-3, Mat 3:11-17; 10:1-4, Mk 2:13-14; 16:14-20, Lk 24:44-49, Acts 13:1-3; 14 :23, 1Cor 9:16-18, 12:27-31; 1Tim 1:12-14; 3:1-13

Service

58 Therefore, my dear brothers, stand firm. Let nothing move you. Always give yourselves fully to the work of the Lord, because you know that your labour in the Lord is not in vain.

1Cor 15:58

10 Each one should use whatever gift he has received to serve others, faithfully administering God's grace in its various forms.

1Pet 4:10

Additional Scripture references

Ps 46:10, Ezek 33:1-4, Lk 4:8; 12:37, Acts 4:25-29, Gal 1:10; Eph 3:7; 6:7; Phil 3:7-11, 1Thess 1:8-9, 1Pet 2:4-5, 2Pet 1:5-8

Our Weakness - His Strength

27 But God chose the foolish things of the world to shame the wise; God chose the weak things of the world to shame the strong.
28 He chose the lowly things of this world and the despised things—and the things that are not—to nullify the things that are,
29 so that no-one may boast before him.

1Cor 1:27-29

Additional Scripture references

Ex 4:10-17, Jud 6:15-16, 1Sam 2:8-10; Ps 84:5-7, Jer 17:5, Zech 4:6; 2Cor 12:9-10, Eph 6:10-18, Heb 11:32-39

Leadership

16 Paul and Barnabas appointed elders for them in each church and, with prayer and fasting, committed them to the Lord, in whom they had put their trust.

Acts 14:23

1 To the elders among you, I appeal as a fellow-elder, a witness of Christ's sufferings and one who also will share in the glory to be revealed:
2 Be shepherds of God's flock that is under your care, serving as overseers—not because you must, but because you are willing, as God wants you to be; not greedy for money, but eager to serve;

1Pet 5:1-2

Additional Scriptures references

Ex 4:10-17; 18:19-26, Num 11:16-17, 1Sam 16:1-13, 2Sam 23:1-5, Ps 141:5, Jer 1:4-8; 10:21, Mat 10:1-4, 20:25-28; Mk 3:13-19, Acts 9:10-20; 20:28-31, Rom 12:6-8, 1Cor 4:1-2; 12:27-31, 2Cor 3:4-6; Col 3:23-24, 1Thess 5:12-15, 1Tim 3:1-13, Tit 1:5-9

Maturity

13 until we all reach unity in the faith and in the knowledge of the Son of God and become mature, attaining to the whole measure of the fulness of Christ.
14 Then we will no longer be infants, tossed back and forth by the waves, and blown here and there by every wind of teaching and by the cunning and craftiness of men in their deceitful scheming.
15 Instead, speaking the truth in love, we will in all things grow up into him who is the Head, that is, Christ.

Eph 4:13-15

2 Consider it pure joy, my brothers, whenever you face trials of many kinds,
3 because you know that the testing of your faith develops perseverance.
4 Perseverance must finish its work so that you may be mature and complete, not lacking anything.

Jas 1:2-4

Additional Scriptures references

Job 23:10; Isa 48:10, Rom 12:10-16; Phil 4:6-7, 1Pet 1:6-7

E6

OUR RESPONSE TO GOD - DISCIPLESHIP

-SANCTIFICATION-

Biblical Definitions

Sanctification

When a person recognises their need to be forgiven and get right with God, and become a Christian (as explained in Section E4), they start their new life with vibrancy and joy, but as an immature Christian. At the beginning of this new relationship between God and the person, God begins to change the person's motives and aims in life and their character. God's purpose in all this change is to make the person more Christ like in their character, and this process of change is referred to as 'sanctification' and lasts a lifetime.

The amount of character change and spiritual maturity that occurs, however, depends on their response to see their need to go on changing and learn lessons through the mistakes that they make in life, and also learn to trust God through events and experiences over which they had no control.

When Christians fail to learn from their mistakes and experiences they will be quite immature at the end of their lives and will have forfeited much of the joy and peace that God intended them to have.

So, basically it can be said that the process of sanctification begins at the time when a person first puts their faith in the Lord Jesus Christ alone for forgiveness and salvation, and the process continues throughout life.

Given below are short extracts taken from Wayne Grudem's book "Bible Doctrine", and at the outset of the chapter headed "Sanctification (Growth in Likeness to Christ)" he gives here a brief outline of the following terms:

'Conversion' as the process, "in which we repent of sins and trust in Christ for salvation"

'Regeneration' as the process, "by which God imparts new life to us"

'Justification' as the act, "by which God gives us right legal standing before him"

'Adoption' as the process, "in which God makes us members of his family"

'Sanctification' as, "a progressive work of God and man that makes us more and more free from sin and like Christ in our actual lives".

In this chapter he states that: "Sanctification has a definite beginning at regeneration.

A definite moral change occurs in our lives at the point of regeneration, for Paul talks about the 'washing of regeneration and renewal in the Holy Spirit' (Titus 3:5). Once we have been born again, we cannot deliberately continue to sin as a habit or a pattern of life (1John 3:9), because the power of new spiritual life within us keeps us from yielding to a life of sin.

This initial moral change is the first stage in sanctification."

He further states:"The initial step in sanctification involves a definite break from the ruling power and love of sin, so that the believer is no longer ruled or dominated by sin and no longer loves to sin. Paul says, 'So you also must consider yourselves dead to sin and alive to God in Christ Jesus . . . . . . For sin will have no dominion over you' (Rom 6:11, 14). Paul says that Christians have been 'set free from sin' (Rom 6:18)."

In a further extract from a detailed explanation of this subject he says: "Sanctification increases throughout life. Even though the New Testament speaks about a definite beginning to sanctification, it also sees it as a process that continues throughout our Christian lives."

In the extracts quoted below W.E.Vine in his "Expository Dictionary of Bible Words" makes the following statements:

"Sanctification is used of (a) separation to God, 1Cor 1:30; 2Thess 2:13; 1Pet 1:2; (b) the course of life befitting those so separated, 1Thess 4:3, 4, 7; Rom 6:19, 22; 1Tim 2:15; Heb 12:14. Sanctification is that relationship with God into which men enter by faith in Christ, Acts 26:18; 1Cor 6:11, and to which their sole title is the death of Christ, Eph 5:25, 26; Col 1:22; Heb 10:10, 29; 13:12.

<u>How can we be sanctified?</u>

Through the Word	Jn 17:17, Eph 5:26
Through a closer relationship with Christ	1Cor 1:30, Heb 13:12
Through striving against sin	2Tim 2:19-21
Through the indwelling of the Spirit	1Pet 1:2

The above extract has been taken from the book "Principles Of Christian Faith" by Harold McDougal and expository [illegible] W. E. Vine in his "Expository Dictionary of Bible Words," makes the following statements:

Sanctification is used of (a) separation to God, 1 Cor 1:30; 2 Thess 2:13; 1 Pet 1:2; (b) the course of life befitting those so separated, 1 Thess 4:3, [illegible] Rom 6:19, [illegible] Sanctification is that relationship with God into which [illegible] Christ, Acts 26:18; 1 Cor 1:30, [illegible] to which [illegible] the death of Christ, [illegible] Heb 10:10, [illegible]

How can we be sanctified?

[illegible]

[illegible] Heb 13:12

[illegible]

[illegible]

[illegible]

[illegible]

OUR RESPONSE TO GOD - DISCIPLESHIP

-SANCTIFICATION-

Notes and Quotations

Sanctification

In simple terms 'sanctification' may be defined as: "Growth in character likeness to the Lord Jesus Christ." This term has been sub-divided here into 'Spirituality' and 'Practical Holiness'.

Spirituality

"Spirituality can be measured by the time gap between when we sin and when we repent – we need to close the time gap – so is it years, months, weeks, days, hours, minutes, seconds, or do we reach a point where we can see the impending danger just before we would have sinned.." (2Sam 24:10)

By Dr R.T. Kendall

"Spirituality is what you are in the dark."

Unknown source.

"Bitterness always seems right at the time."

By R.T. Kendall

The more I allow the Lord to do IN me, the more He will be able to do THROUGH me.

See 2Pet 1:3

Leo Tolstoy said: "Everybody thinks of changing *humanity* and nobody thinks of changing *himself*."

"He is no fool who gives what he cannot keep to gain what he cannot lose."
By Jim Elliot – a missionary martyred in South America.

Supernatural and Sacrificial – 1Chron 21:18-24; 1Chron 21:26 - 22:1
Having the supernatural without the sacrificial is DANGEROUS,
Having the sacrificial without the supernatural is DRUDGERY,
Having the supernatural and the sacrificial is DYNAMITE.

Source unknown.

Practical Holiness

Let us be mindful of the winnowing fork of the Lord Jesus Christ in Mat 3:11-12 and let us be winsome (attractive of manner, engaging, bright, winning), and also follow what God requires of us as stated in Mic 6:8.

A well known preacher had been spoken about in an untruthful way, and he felt bitter about it. A friend came to see him who, after a brief condolence, said: "unless you utterly forgive those people, the bitterness and unforgiveness in you will act as a blockage and you will be prevented from going on with God".

He did forgive, and the weight lifted from his spirit.

Questions to ask ourselves when confronted with a difficult situation or decision:

"What would Jesus do - WWJD"
"Would it please Him - WIPH."

"Holiness is making sure that God is comfortable in my life."

Alex Buchanan

Selwyn Hughes in his "Every Day with Jesus" Notes, states: "The word "sanctified" means "set apart", or "to be made holy". As justification implies deliverance from the penalty of sin, sanctification implies deliverance from the power and pollution of sin."

He also states: "In Him (Jesus Christ) sanctification is a dynamic, outside of Him it is merely a doctrine. Sanctification is, of course, an important doctrine, but the teaching must not be separated from our relationship to Christ. It is an experience which comes about as we surrender to Him, and remains as long as we continue in Christ."

He further states: "Sanctification is not achieved by human effort, but by divine effort – by Christ working in us."

The whole process of sanctification will involve being disciplined. Being prepared to discipline ourselves in our daily Christian life as we seek to listen and obey the things God is saying to us in various ways, e.g. through: the Word of God; circumstances; events etc.

Also, we must be prepared to accept God's discipline in our lives, and this aspect is referred to in Heb 12:5-15.

Those who came into direct contact with His moral majesty and purity were overwhelmed as is shown for example in the passage Isa 6:1-13.

Recognition of and submission to His holiness are the divine prerequisites for admission to the inner heart of God and the most important requirements for knowing Him and fulfilling His Will for us, and is also the most important qualification for learning from Him.

Make every effort to live in peace with all men and to be holy; without holiness no-one will see the Lord.

See Heb 12:14

"The most damnable and pernicious heresy that ever plagued the mind of man was the idea that somehow he could make himself good enough to deserve to live with an All-Holy God".

Martin Luther

See Rom 3:22-23 below:

"22 This righteousness from God comes through faith in Jesus Christ to all who believe. There is no difference,
23 for all have sinned and fall short of the glory of God,"

The fear of the LORD is the beginning of wisdom; all who follow his precepts have good understanding. To him belongs eternal praise.

Ps 111:10

The above verse and other passages like Ps 99 show that we should be overawed by His holiness. Hence, all Christian activities should be rooted in this 'fear'. The word 'fear' meaning to 'revere' Him. It is considered that we are not likely to be much affected by the Doctrines of love and grace unless we are first aware of His holiness.

Therefore, prepare your minds for action; be self-controlled; set your hope fully on the grace to be given you when Jesus Christ is revealed.

As obedient children, do not conform to the evil desires you had when you lived in ignorance.

But just as he who called you is holy, so be holy in all you do; for it is written: "Be holy, because I am holy."

1Pet 1:13-16

OUR RESPONSE TO GOD - DISCIPLESHIP

-SANCTIFICATION-

Biblical Texts & Text References

Sanctification

3 It is God's will that you should be sanctified: that you should avoid sexual immorality;
4 that each of you should learn to control his own body in a way that is holy and honourable,
5 not in passionate lust like the heathen, who do not know God;

1Thess 4:3-5

Additional Scripture references

Ps 17:3-5, 119:9-10; Mat 3:11-12, Jn 17:15-19; Acts 20:32; 26:17-18, Rom 6:11-14; 19-22; 15:15-16, 1Cor 1:30; 6:9-11; Gal 5:22-25, Eph 5:25-26, Phil 3:12-14, Col 1:21-22, 1Thess 5:23-24, 2Thess 2:13, 2Tim 2:19-21, Tit 3:4-6, Heb 10:9-10; 12:14; 13:12, 1Pet 1:1-2; 2:9-10, 1Jn 1:8-9; 3:9

E7

OUR RESPONSE TO GOD - DISCIPLESHIP

-SUBMISSION, FAITH & ASSURANCE-

Biblical Definitions

Submission to God

Overcoming the clash of wills

The very word 'submission' does not sit easily with most people because it goes against a person's natural instincts of wanting to be in control of every aspect of their life. So the thought of having to 'submit' to somebody else's will and lead often brings about a clash of wills.

However, when God asks us to 'submit' our lives to Him, the situation changes when the person knows something of the character of God and that He has their best interests at heart. So whilst the initial act of submission to God may be difficult, the person will soon realise His goodness and grace and will learn to trust Him more and continue to submit their life to Him.

As we consider the whole act of 'submission' let us remember that although God is our creator He does not wish to dominate and control us like puppets, but He invites us to submit to Him as a loving Father and we become His sons and daughters. When this occurs we will discover the practical outworking of 'His and our best' for our lives.

It should be borne in mind that submission to God is not weakness, but wisdom.

Ongoing Submission – the key to being effective for God

When the believer overcomes the potential clash of wills for the first time and submits to the will of God, as explained above, they become a Christian. However, this step of faith initiates an ongoing internal struggle where they will often be tempted to go their own way, so that many re-submissions will be required throughout life.

It is as this process of ongoing submission continues that the person becomes more and more convinced of God's goodness and graciousness, discovered initially for forgiveness and salvation, and further realised in all aspects of their life.

The whole process of submission is always a voluntary action on the part of the believer, see the following Scriptures: Rom 8:6-7; 10:1-3; 13:1-5; Eph 5:21-24; Jas 4:6-7.

The above is accomplished in practice by the believer being prepared to be led by the Holy Spirit, - see: Acts 4:8; 10:19; 13:2; Rom 8:13-14; Gal 5:18.

L.O. Richards in his book "Expository Dictionary of Bible Words" under the heading "Servanthood for the believer" states: "The believer is to submit his will to the will of God, acknowledging Jesus as Lord. The lordship of Jesus in our lives is worked out as we remain faithful to him, doing the work he has delivered to us (Mt 24:45-47; Lk 12:35-48).

<u>Submission to Spiritual Leaders</u>

The believer, as a matter of discipline, should be prepared to be subject to the spiritual leaders in their own Church, particularly with regard to the believers' lifestyle, that is, as long as the direction and teaching given by the leadership is in line with the principles of Scripture. See the following Scriptures: Heb 13:7;:17.

Believers in a congregation should not be subjected to any form of 'heavy shepherding', as the leaders should have the characteristics and lifestyle as given in Section E5, namely, as those who rely on the Lord for wisdom and patience, having a good knowledge of the Scriptures and Biblical principles, coupled with love, grace, humility, a strong resolve, spiritual insight and boldness of faith. It follows, therefore, that if these qualities of leadership exist there would be no need to resort to any type of heavy guidance.

Submission to Others

The Scriptures state that believers should also "submit to one another" (Eph 5:21), and be "competent to instruct one another", (Rom 15:14). These aspects of the believers' life should develop through relationships and proven trust over time. See the following Scriptures: Mat 20:25-28; Rom 12:4-5;:10; 1Cor 16:15-16; Gal 6:1-2; Phil 2:3-4; 1Pet 5:5.

We are also asked to submit ourselves to the governing authorities, see: Rom 13:1; 1Pet 2:13-14.

Faith

People use faith/trust everyday when they take a ride on a train, for example, they put their faith in the driver to take them safely to their destination. They do not know or see the driver, but they trust him. This analogy has some similarity with a person taking an initial step of faith in Christ, where they do not know and have not seen the Lord Jesus Christ, but they are invited to put their faith in Him for forgiveness and a new start in life with eternal life as their destination.

After the person has taken this initial step of faith they receive in themselves a confirmation and inner witness that they have entered into a relationship with God. From this initial step the person is expected to continue to place their faith in Him throughout life, and so develop an increasingly intimate relationship with Him.

It follows that the basic requirement for everybody is that they must have faith, trust, in the Lord Jesus Christ if they want to please God, for the Scripture states: " . . . . without faith it is impossible to please God . . . . . . "Heb 11:6.

Abraham demonstrated complete faith in God and total availability to Him when he said to God: "Here I am" Gen 22:1, and he showed that he meant it by being prepared to offer up his only son to God as a sacrifice – see Gen 22:1-19.

The whole of chapter eleven of the Book of Hebrews is particularly significant on this subject of faith as verse one provides a definition for it and the following verses give us a list of heroes of faith in the pre-Christian era. These verses present us with demonstrations of, and exhortations to, faith.

Verse six of this chapter shows us the absolute necessity for faith in the Lord Jesus Christ as God if our lives are going to count for Him.

1 Now faith is being sure of what we hope for and certain of what we do not see.
2 This is what the ancients were commended for.
3 By faith we understand that the universe was formed at God's command, so that what is seen was not made out of what was visible. (see Col 1:16).
4 By faith Abel offered God a better sacrifice than Cain did. By faith he was commended as a righteous man, when God spoke well of his offerings. And by faith he still speaks, even though he is dead.
5 By faith Enoch was taken from this life, so that he did not experience death; he could not be found, because God had taken him away. For before he was taken, he was commended as one who pleased God.
6 And without faith it is impossible to please God, because anyone who comes to him must believe that he exists and that he rewards those who earnestly seek him.

Heb 11:1-6

There are numerous references to 'Faith' in the New Testament and someone has produced the listing below that shows the importance of placing our 'faith' (trust, confidence) in the Lord Jesus Christ for all our true needs for this life and eternity. <u>Note</u> here the various important preconditions to faith and resulting life changing effects:

<u>Precondition</u>	<u>Results of Faith</u>	<u>Ref.</u>
Jesus saw their faith	Man's sin forgiven and paralysis healed.	Mat 9:2
Jesus saw her faith	Excessive bleeding healed	Mat 9:22
Jesus given no honour in home town	Not many miracles due to lack of faith	Mat 13:58
Jesus commended mother for her faith	Demons cast out of daughter	Mat 15:28

Jesus said to disciples they must have faith and not doubt	Unfruitful fig tree died	Mat 21:21
Jesus saw the man's faith	Instantly healed of blindness	Mk 10:52
When disciples saw Jesus' actions	They asked for an increase in faith	Lk 17:5
Jesus saw the blind beggar's faith	Instantly healed of blindness	Lk 18:42
As Jesus spoke	Many put their faith in Him	Jn 8:30
God opened the door of faith to the Gentiles	Gentiles accepted into God's kingdom	Acts 14:27 Acts 15:8-9
Paul gives message of salvation to jailer	Jailer believed and was baptised	Acts 16:31-33
Paul gives salvation requirements	Jews and Greeks must repent and have faith in the Lord Jesus	Acts 20:21
Paul extolling faith in Jesus	To encourage each other's faith	Rom 1:12
Faith in Jesus Christ	Gives imputed righteousness	Rom 3:22
Message came with the Holy Spirit's power	People's faith to rest on God's power, not on man's wisdom	1Cor 2:4-5
Living by faith, not by sight	Increases confidence in God	2Cor 5:7-8
As faith grows	God's work expands	2Cor 10:15
Faith in Jesus Christ	Provides justification, that cannot be given through keeping the law	Gal 2:16
Faith in Jesus Christ	Brings blessing	Gal 3:9

Through faith in Jesus Christ	Become sons of God	Gal 3:25-26
Through faith in Jesus Christ	Saved by grace, not by works	Eph 2:8-9
Through faith in Jesus Christ	Can approach God with freedom and confidence	Eph 3:12
Taking up the shield of faith	Can extinguish all flaming arrows of the evil one	Eph 6:16
Faith in Jesus Christ	Gives progress and joy in the faith	Phil 1:25
Holding the deep truths of the faith	Aids Christian character development	1Tim 3:9
Those who have served well	Gain great assurance of faith	1Tim 3:13
Those who wander from the faith	Pierce themselves with many grief's	1Tim 6:10-11
Knowing the holy Scriptures	Makes us wise for salvation through faith in Jesus Christ	2Tim 3:15
Drawing near to God with a sincere heart	Acquires full assurance of faith in Jesus Christ	Heb 10:22
Fixing our focus on Jesus	Perfects our faith	Heb 12:2
The testing of faith	Develops perseverance	Jas 1:2-3
Faith without deeds. Faith with deeds	Achieves nothing for God. Produces righteousness	Jas 2:17-24
Prayer offered in faith	Provides healing	Jas 5:15
Belief in Jesus as the Son of God	Overcomes the world	1Jn 5:4-5

Faith is primarily defined by W.E. Vine in his "Expository Dictionary of Bible Words" as: "firm persuasion, a conviction based upon hearing, is used in the N.T. as always of faith in God or Christ, or things spiritual." See; Acts 6:7; 14:22; Rom 3:25; 4:20-21; 1Cor 2:5; 15:14-17; 2Cor 1:24; Gal 1:23; 3:23-25; Phil 1:25; 2:17; 1Thess 3:10; - - - - - - - - -.

A short extract from the "Expository Dictionary" by L.O. Richards on this subject states: "John sees 'believing' as an active, continuing trust in Jesus. The act of believing draws an individual across the dividing line between death and eternal life.

He further states: "It recognises Jesus as the Son of God and trusts completely in him as he is unveiled in God's Word. Saving faith demonstrates belief by acting on the words Jesus has spoken (Jn 8:30-31)."

Supernatural Faith

The unique characteristic about the Christian Faith is that it is concerned with people having a living trusting relationship with the One True and Only God and He operates supernaturally, often on His own, and at times through people, especially Christians. However, as we look at the history of the Church we can see from its many shortcomings that too often Christians are not living close enough to God to hear what He is saying and lack the utter dependency required, coupled with the necessary obedience to provide the evidence for a 'supernatural' faith. The following Scripture typically portrays Paul as having the necessary characteristics for this type of faith.

I came to you in weakness and fear, and with much trembling.

My message and my preaching were not with wise and persuasive words, but with a demonstration of the Spirit's power, so that your faith might not rest on men's wisdom, but on God's power.

1Cor 2:3-5

Hence, it can be seen from this Scripture that the one who has faith in God is not trusting in their own ability or strength to live the Christian life, but they are trusting in God's power.

Assurance

Assurance in the Christian life is gained through living a life trusting God, accepting the guidance of God's Holy Spirit and obeying the Word of God – the Bible.

As the Christian continues to live in this way, their confidence grows as they see more of His wisdom, and understand and experience more of His goodness, grace and love.

All this experience in life provides the foundation for being assured of things that they have not yet experienced like eternal life and heaven.

Wayne Grudem in his book, "Bible Doctrine" refers in some detail to the very important subject of 'personal salvation' under the following headings:

<u>"The Perseverance of the Saints (Remaining a Christian)"</u> Where he asks the following two questions: 'Can true Christians lose their salvation? and, 'How can we know if we are truly born again? and provides an explanation and Scriptural basis.

<u>"All Who Are Truly Born Again Will Persevere to the End"</u>
He commences by saying: "Many passages teach that those who are truly born again, who are genuinely Christians, will continue in the Christian life until death and will then go to be with Christ in heaven. - - - - - - - - -" He continues by referring to a number of Scriptures including: Jn 3:16-17; 3:36; 5:24; 6:4-7; 6:38-40; 10:27-29; Rom 8:1, 30; 1Jn 5:13.

<u>"Only Those Who Persevere to the End Have Been Truly Born Again"</u>
He states: "While Scripture repeatedly emphasizes that those who are truly born again will persevere to the end and will certainly have eternal life in heaven with God, there are other passages that speak of the necessity of continuing in faith throughout life. - - - - - - -" and he makes reference to the following, with explanation:

"who ***by God's power*** are guarded ***through faith"*** 1Pet 1:5.
"***If you continue in my word"*** Jn 8:31-32.
"***He who endures to the end"*** Mat 10:22.
"***provided that you continue in the faith,*** stable and steadfast, not shifting from the hope of the gospel which you heard" Col 1:22-23.
"For we have become partakers of Christ, ***if we hold fast the beginning of our assurance firm to the end."*** Heb 3:14.

Having 'assurance' is an integral part of our faith in Christ which is shown by a confidence in the attitudes and actions that follow from these, and so demonstrate the outworking of that faith in a positive manner. When this confidence is lacking there are doubts, and these have serious consequences as outlined below:

- people put limits on what God can do; see Mat 14:31, 21:21,
- people lose direction in their life; see Lk 24:38,
- people are uncertain of what to do; see Rom 14:23,
- there is a loss of blessings and benefits from God; see Jas 1:6,
- believers are expected to be merciful to those who doubt; see Jude 1:22.

and to demonstrate the power of that dominant-positive manner. When that influence is lacking [illegible] and [illegible] have serious consequences, as outlined below:

[illegible] people [illegible] what [illegible] [illegible]

[illegible] in the [illegible]

people [illegible] what to do [illegible]

[illegible] loss of [illegible]

[illegible] period [illegible] to those [illegible]

[illegible]

OUR RESPONSE TO GOD - DISCIPLESHIP

-SUBMISSION, FAITH & ASSURANCE-

Notes and Quotations

Submission

Submission is closely linked with humility, and humility has been defined as, "an attitude of mind that regards the interests of others as more important than one's own", Phil 2:1-11.

Living in the *'Will of God'* is fulfilling the *'Word of God'* as it is revealed to you personally and obeying Him as He speaks to you.

God has a number of ways in which he 'speaks' to us, including the following:

Through: reading the Bible; Biblical preaching; personal and wider circumstances; Biblical meditation; inner convictions of the Holy Spirit.

"True happiness comes only when we are in submission to God, and to one another." A statement from the book, "A Way Through the Wilderness" by Jamie Buckingham.

Something to consider – The thing that a person continually submits to becomes their life, so the more we submit to God the more closely will be our fellowship with Him and guidance from Him.

Submission and Healing

God can't heal what you won't reveal to Him, of cleanse what you won't confess to Him. See Mat 26:33-34 & 69-75, Jn 18:15-17 & 25-27, Heb 4:11-13

Submission – Surrender – Self-Discipline.

"Self-discipline, is not so much your responsibility as *your response* to *His ability.* Self-discipline for a Christian is not a matter of striving; it is a matter of surrender. It all hinges on the closeness of our relationship to Jesus Christ. The closer we are to Him, the more power we are able to draw from Him. It is as simple as that." From "Every Day with Jesus" Notes by Selwyn Hughes.

Bob Gass refers to the Scripture text James 4:7, given below:

"Submit yourselves, then, to God. Resist the devil, and he will flee from you." and states under the heading: "The reality of the spirit realm"

"The devil constantly searches for an entry point into your life. Listen, "We wrestle .... against powers, against the rulers of the darkness of this world .... "(Eph 6:12)

Your enemy will study you to see which doors he can come in through; like your temper, your lust, tour attitudes, your moods, your background or your past hurts. His first goal is to dominate you; his next is to destroy the purposes of God that are meant to be fulfilled through you. Then he can say to God, "He's mine not yours! He'll obey me, not you!" That's what the battle is all about!

But the good news is that Jesus defeated him – and He's given you the power to do it too. Listen, "Behold I give you power .... over all the power of the enemy ... (Lk 10:19) That means the only power the enemy has over you is the power you give him."

From "The Word for Today" Notes.

People need to obey from the heart, and not just follow the written word like a code hoping that this will please God – see the Scripture below:

The Lord says: "These people come near to me with their mouth and honour me with their lips, but their hearts are far from me. Their worship of me is made up only of rules taught by men.

Isa 29:13

Faith

"Faith is a walk in the dark with your hand firmly planted in the hand of God who you cannot see. It is asking Him to do what you can't do, and being able to smile in the storm, because you know – ABSOLUTELY know – He's going to do it." Prov 3:4-8; Phil 1:6. From "The Word for Today" Notes by Bob Gass.

He also writes again and refers to the angel coming to Mary, a virgin, to tell her that she was going to miraculously have a child who would be the Son of God, as recorded in Lk 1:35-38, and then states with reference to verse 45: "Mary not only believed God, she staked her reputation and her future on it. ***Faith always precedes fulfilment.***"

"Unbelief puts our circumstances between us and God. But faith puts God between us and our circumstances" – a quote by F.B. Mayer given in "The Word for Today" Notes by Bob Gass.

If you want to 'walk on water' then you must get out of the 'boat' (your safe, or comfort zone) and fix your eyes on the lord Jesus Christ. But before any faith undertaking we need to ask the question: "Lord is it YOU asking me"? See Mat 14:28-29

"Faith is hearing what God says, believing it, and acting on it."

Author unknown.

"Faith hears the inaudible, believes the incredible, and receives the impossible".

Author unknown.

"The only saving faith is that which casts itself on God for life or death"

Martin Luther

Faith and Fear

Faith and fear are enemies – when one is embraced the other retreats.

"Faith only grows by using it – going out into the unknown with God".
"Faith = expectation. Its what we believe, not what we feel".

Author unknown.

"Three hundred and sixty-five times your Bible says, "Fear not." That's one for each day. Why? Because each time you do the thing you fear most, fear loses its hold over you, and you become a little stronger, and a little more dependent on God." From "The Word for Today" Notes by Bob Gass. He has also said:

"Here are 3 reasons why you should not be afraid today:

First, fear is not from God – "For God hath not give us a spirit of fear . . . ."(2Tim 1:7).

Fear is a spirit – don't yield to it, resist it! - - - - - - Second, fear is like a magnet. Job said, "For the thing which I greatly feared is come upon me . . . . (Job 3:25). The more you fear something, the more you give it <u>access</u> into your life. You see, fear activates the enemy, just like faith activates God, so don't give it an inch, or it'll take a mile.

Third, God is greater than your fear. David said, "In my anguish I cried to the Lord, and He answered by setting me free. The Lord is with me; I will not be afraid. What can man do to me?" (Ps 118:5-6). - - - - - - -"

<u>Faith or Fear</u>

Fear is the faith for bad things. Job, in the Bible, discovered what happened when he succumbed to fear, and he said: "What I feared has come upon me; what I dreaded has happened to me."

Job 3:25.

Jesus put out unbelievers from a prayer meeting, -
See Mk 5:35-42.

Fear opens the door for the enemy to attack us.
We choose what we invest our faith in – the word of man, or the Word of God.

"Faith only grows by using it – going out into the unknown with God."
Author unknown.

"Faith *means* Expectation. It's what we believe, not what we feel."
Author unknown.

Faith or Worry

"Worry is the darkroom in which we develop all our negatives."

Author unknown.

Free from Fear

Someone has said, "Patience is just FAITH taking its time."

Faith enables us to 'see' – "Then Jesus said, "Did I not tell you that if you believed, you would see the glory of God?" (Jn 11:40). We 'see' not with the natural eye, but with the spiritual eye in the future, "Now faith is being sure of what we hope for and certain of what we do not see." (Heb 11:1).

Walk of Faith

Our chief aim before any service or work we may do for God, is to '*know Him'*, and

This entails hearing, obeying and submitting to Him out of love for Him, not duty: see Jer 31:34; Jn 10:14; Phil 3:8-11; 2Tim 2:19; Heb 8:11; 1Jn 4:8.

"God is not as interested in ends as he is in means. In fact, how we do a thing seems more important to God than whether we succeed. The means are not only more important than the end; the means are an end in themselves. It was a truth Jesus also taught: God does not require men to succeed, He just requires them to be faithful." From the book "A Way Through the Wilderness" by Jamie Buckingham.

"Good works/deeds are the fruit and evidence of our salvation. We have not been saved BY good works, but have been saved FOR good works. Eph 1:12; 5:8-10."

From Every Day with Jesus" Notes by Selwyn Hughes.

The world says, *"seeing is believing"* but the Christian concept is *"believing is seeing" – seeing* the true character, worth, love, grace, power, and works of God in the Lord Jesus Christ. Barriers to an active faith in the Lord Jesus Christ will include: unbelief; ignorance; sin; unforgiveness; bitterness; anger.

"If failure is not a possibility, then success doesn't mean anything. When Abraham decided to follow God and leave home, he had no idea where that journey would take him; neither will you, when you leave your comfort zone.

It begins with God stirring up your nest (Deut 32:11). *Until your misery factor exceeds your fear factor,* you won't move." From "The Word for Today" Notes by Bob Gass.

Referring to the early Christians, J.B. Phillips said:

"If we believed what they believed, we might achieve what they achieved."

Sayings concerning faith:
"Faith only grows by using it."
"Faith is going out into the unknown with God."
"Faith is what we believe, not what we feel."
"Faith is rooted in action" – see Heb 11:1-40.

<u>The fight of faith</u>
David, through his trust in the Lord was delivered from and killed a lion, a bear, and the giant Goliath. See 1Sam 17:36-47.

Daniel was delivered from the lions den. See Dan 6:11-24.

In New Testament times there is a much stronger emphasis on spiritual warfare. See Eph 6:10-18, and Section E8.

<u>Assurance</u>

"The doctrine of eternal security has been disputed in the Church for close on 2,000 years now, and in the nature of things there will be opponents of the doctrine as long as the Church remains here on earth. I lean very much towards the idea that once saved we are always saved, although I still struggle with the problem of those who, having shown some evidence of being saved, then return to the old life "as a dog returns to its vomit"(2Pet 2:22).

Can it be that in these people there was only outward change but no inner change – that they were not saved in the real sense of that word? One thing I am certain of having considered this issue for many years – we can become so caught up with doctrine that we miss the gripping assurance given to us by statements such as these: "He who began a good work in you will carry it on to completion until the day of Christ Jesus" (Phil 1:6). "My sheep listen to my voice; I know them, and they follow me. I give them eternal life, and they shall never perish; no-one can snatch them out of my hand" (Jn 10:27-28)."

This statement is an extract taken from the "Every Day with Jesus" Notes by Selwyn Hughes.

<u>Who Am I?</u>

In the book "Victory over the Darkness" by Dr Neal Anderson, he relates in first-person language who every believer really is and what they possess as a child of God, and reminds them that these qualities cannot be earned or bought.

He then provides two lists of these qualities and a selection from these is given below:

I am a child of God (Jn 1:12).
I am chosen and appointed by Christ to bear His fruit (Jn 15:16).
I am a joint heir with Christ, sharing His inheritance with Him (Rom 8:17).
I am a new creation (2Cor 5:17).
I am chosen of God, holy and dearly loved (Col 3:12; 1Thess 1:4).

<u>Since I am in Christ, by the grace of God . . . .</u>

I have been justified – completely forgiven and made righteous (Rom 5:1).
I am free forever from condemnation (Rom 8:1).
I have been bought with a price; I am not my own; I belong to God (1Cor 6:19-20
I have direct access to God through the Spirit (Eph 2:18).
I have been saved and set apart according to God's doing (2Tim 1:9; Tit 3:5).

OUR RESPONSE TO GOD - DISCIPLESHIP

-SUBMISSION, FAITH & ASSURANCE-

Biblical Texts & Text References

Submission

6 But he gives us more grace. That is why Scripture says: "God opposes the proud but gives grace to the humble."
7 Submit yourselves, then, to God. Resist the devil, and he will flee from you.

Jas 4:6-7

Additional Scripture references

Mat 20:27, 24:45-47; Lk 12:35-48, Acts 4:8; 10:19; 13:2, Rom 8:6-7; 13-14; 10:1-3; 13:1-5, Gal 5:18, Eph 5:21-24; 1Pet 4:10-11

Submission to Spiritual Leaders

7 Remember your leaders, who spoke the word of God to you. Consider the outcome of their way of life and imitate their faith.
17 Obey your leaders and submit to their authority. They keep watch over you as men who must give an account. Obey them so that their work will be a joy, not a burden, for that would be of no advantage to you.

Heb 13:7 &, 17

Submission to Others

25 Jesus called them together and said, "You know that the rulers of the Gentiles lord it over them, and their high officials exercise authority over them.
26 Not so with you. Instead, whoever wants to become great among you must be your servant,

Mat 20:25-26

17 Submit to one another out of reverence for Christ.

Eph 5:21

Additional Scripture references

Rom 12:4-5; 12:10; 15:14, 1Cor 16:15-16, Gal 6:1-2; Phil 2:3-4, 1Pet 2:13-14; 5:5

Faith

Jesus Christ said to a sick woman;" your faith has healed you". See Mat 9:22

On another occasion it says that Jesus;" did not do many miracles there because of their lack of faith". See Mat 13:58

The Apostle Paul speaking to Jews anf Greeks said:" that they must turn to God in repentance and have faith in our Lord Jesus. See Acts 20:21

4 My message and my preaching were not with wise and persuasive words, but with a demonstration of the Spirit's power,
5 so that your faith might not rest on men's wisdom, but on God's power.

1Cor 2:4-5

16 know that a man is not justified by observing the law, but by faith in Jesus Christ. So we, too, have put our faith in Christ Jesus that we may be justified by faith in Christ and not by observing the law, because by observing the law no-one will be justified.

Gal 2:16

Saved through faith in Christ – see Eph 2:8-9

Additional Scripture references

Gen 22:1-19, Mat 9:2; 9:22; 15:28; 21:21, Mk 10:52, Lk 17:5; 18:42, Jn 1:12; 6:35; 8:30, 20:29 Acts 6:7; 14:22-27; 15:8-9; 16:31-33, Rom 1:12; 3:22-25; 4:20-21, 1Cor 15:14-17, 2Cor 1:24; 5:7; 10:15, Gal 1:23; 3:9; 3:25-26, Eph 3:12; 6:16, Phil 1:25, Col 1:16, 1Tim 3:9; 3:13; 6:10-11, 2Tim 3:15, Heb 10:22; 11:1-6 & 16; 12:2, Jas 1:2-3; 2:17-24, 5:15; 1Jn 4:19; 5:4-5

Assurance

36 Whoever believes in the Son has eternal life, but whoever rejects the Son will not see life, for God's wrath remains on him."

Jn 3:36

18 "I tell you the truth, whoever hears my word and believes him who sent me has eternal life and will not be condemned; he has crossed over from death to life.

Jn 5:24

Additional Scripture references

Mat 10:22, Jn 3:16-18; 6:4-7; 6:38-40; 8:31-32; 10:27-29, Acts 17:31' Rom 8:1 & 30, Col 1:22-23, Heb 3:14, 10:22; 1Pet 1:5, 1Jn 5:13

SALVATION

36 Whoever believes in the Son has eternal life, but whoever rejects the Son will not see life, for God's wrath remains on him.

Jn 3:36

24 I tell you the truth, whoever hears my word and believes him who sent me has eternal life and will not be condemned; he has crossed over from death to life.

Jn 5:24

Scripture

[illegible]

E8

OUR RESPONSE TO GOD - DISCIPLESHIP

-PRAYER, SATAN, SPIRITUAL WARFARE & BIBLICAL MEDITATION-

Biblical Definitions

Prayer

A basic definition of prayer would be: 'Prayer is communication with God'.

God always wants us to communicate with Him – whether we feel like or not. This involves talking and listening to Him, remembering that He is the living God – see 1Tim 4:9-10.

A depressing or discouraging situation, or one of great difficulty may cause us to worry rather than pray. One place to look for encouragement is to read the biblical book of Psalms. It is here that we find the writers like David and others express freely how they feel towards God – their anger, frustration, trouble – they pour it all out. They ask for His help and understanding and thank and praise Him that they can trust Him.

It is in prayer that people make commitments or requests to Him and He is always listening, and by one way or another answers, unless the person is insincere or has a wrong motive or attitude. It is always to be remembered that God reads peoples hearts rather than their lips.

The definitions of prayer given below have been taken from the book "A Body of Practical Divinity" by John Gill.

"Prayer is one part of the saints' spiritual armour, and a principal one, though mentioned last, Eph 6:18. It has been often of use against temporal enemies, and for obtaining victory over them; as the prayers of Asa,

Jehoshaphat, and others, show, 2Ch 14:11,12 20:3-5,22. It is reported of Mary, queen of Scots, that she dreaded the prayer of John Knox, an eminent minister, more than an army of twenty thousand men. And it is of use against the spiritual enemies of God's people, and for the vanquishing of them. Satan has often felt the force of this weapon; resist the devil, by faith in prayer, and he will flee from you. When the apostle Paul was buffeted and distressed by him, he had recourse to it; he besought the Lord thrice that the trial might depart from him; and had for answer, "My grace is sufficient for thee!" and indeed, as this part of the Christian armour is managed, so it goes with the saint, for or against him. In the war between Israel and Amalek, when Moses held up his hands, an emblem of vigorous prayer, then Israel prevailed; but when he let down his hands, a token of remissness in prayer, Amalek prevailed. Prayer has great power and prevalence with God, for the removal or prevention of evil things, and for the obtaining of blessings. - - - - - - - - -

1. Take notice of the various sorts of prayer, which will lead on to that; for there is a praying with all prayer, which denotes many sorts and kinds of prayer.

   1a. There is mental prayer, or prayer in the heart; and, indeed, here prayer should first begin; so David found in his heart to pray, 2Sa 7:27 and it is "the effectual fervent", or energoumenh, "the inwrought prayer of the righteous man that availeth much"; which is wrought and formed in the heart by the Spirit of God, Jas 5:16. Such sort of prayer was that of Moses, at the Red Sea, when the Lord said to him, "Wherefore criest thou unto me?" and yet we read not of a word that was spoken by him; and of this kind was the prayer of Hannah; "She spake in her heart", 1Sa 1:13 and this may be performed even without the motion of the lips, and is what we call an ejaculatory prayer, from the suddenness and swiftness of its being put up to God, like a dart shot from a bow; and which may be done in the midst of business the most public, and in the midst of, public company, and not discerned; as was the prayer of Nehemiah in the presence of the king, Ne 2:4,5 and such prayer God takes notice of, and hears; and, as an ancient writer observes,

"Though we whisper, not opening our lips, but pray in silence, cry inwardly, God incessantly hears that inward discourse," or prayer to him, conceived in the mind

1b. There is prayer which is audible and vocal. Some prayer is audible, yet not articulate and intelligible, or it is expressed by inarticulate sounds; as, "with groanings which cannot be uttered"; but God knows and understands perfectly the language of a groan, and hears and answers. But there is vocal prayer, expressed by articulate words, in language to be heard and understood by men, as well as by the Lord; "I cried unto the Lord with my voice", &c. Ps 3:4 5:2,3 and to this kind of prayer the church is directed by the Lord himself, Ho 14:2.

1c. There is private prayer, in which a man is alone by himself; to which our Lord directs, Mt 6:6 an instance and example of this we have in Christ, Mt 14:23 see also an instance of this in Peter, Ac 10:9.

1d. There is social prayer, in which few or more join together, concerning which, and to encourage it, our Lord says, "Where two or three are gathered together in my name, there am I in the midst of them", Mt 18:19,20 an instance of this social prayer with men is in Ac 20:36 and it is this social prayer with fewer or more the apostle Jude has respect unto, Jude 1:20.

1e. There is family prayer, performed by the head and master of the family in it, and with it. Joshua set a noble example of family worship, Jos 24:15 and an instance we have in David, 2Sa 6:20 and even Cornelius, the Roman centurion, before he was acquainted with Christianity, was in the practice of it, Ac 10:2,30 and the contrary behaviour is resented, and the wrath and fury of God may be expected to fall upon the families that call not on his name, Jer 10:25 and it is but reasonable service, since family mercies are daily needed, and therefore should be prayed for; and family mercies are daily received, and therefore thanks should be every day returned for them.

1f. There is public prayer, which is performed in bodies and

> communities of men, who meet in public, unite and join together in divine worship, and particularly in this branch of it; for prayer always was made a part of public worship. - - - - - - - - -

Given below are a few extracts from the book "Expository Dictionary of Bible Words" by L.O. Richards:

"Prayer remains one of the mysteries of our faith. Yet prayer is a simple act and a comfort to believers, who from the beginning have turned with confidence and faith to God. - - - - - -

The Bible emphasizes the simplicity of prayer. Believers are to pray about everything, confident that God hears prayers, cares, and is able to act.

<u>The foundations of NT prayer.</u>
The basic elements of OT prayer are carried over into the NT, where they are given even richer expression. In the NT, prayer is related to the intimate relationship that the believer sustains with the Father, the Son, and the Holy Spirit.

<u>Prayer and the Father.</u> Jesus condemns a ritualistic, hypocritical approach to prayer and presents true prayer as an intimate expression of relationship with a God who is one's Father (Mat 6:5-8). Jesus' model prayer, known to us as the Lord's Prayer, sums up the beautiful relationship we have with God. - - - - - We approach him as we would a father.

<u>Prayer and the Son.</u> Jesus is seen in the NT as the key to that personal relationship with God that is central to prayer.

He further relates to Jn 14:6 where it says: "No one comes to the Father except through me" - - - - Through Jesus, and because of his cross, we can "approach the throne of grace with confidence," sure that he will "receive mercy and find grace to help us in our time of need"(Heb 4:16). - - - - - - -

<u>Prayer and the Holy Spirit.</u> The Holy Spirit lives within believers. He has a unique role in this intimate exchange known as prayer. "The Spirit himself intercedes for us with groans that words cannot express" (Rom 8:26), and "the Spirit intercedes for the saints in accordance with God's will" (v. 27). While the Spirit may assist us in prayer without our conscious awareness,

our understanding clearly must be involved (1Cor 14:13-15). Jesus told the apostles that the Spirit would take from what belonged to Jesus and make it known (Jn 16:15). - - - - - - -

Prayer conditions.

"Those who seek, knock, and ask receive what they request (Mat 7:7-11). Jesus told the apostles that when two agreed regarding a matter, it would be done by God (Mat 18:19). To pray "in Jesus' name" means to identify with his character and purposes (Jn 14:13-14; 15:16; 16:23). The trust that we have in God, which calms our doubts and uncertainties, also testifies to us that God's answer will come.--------As we obey the Lord, we are assured that we live in a relationship with him in which our prayers are heard and answered (1Jn 3:22). - - - - - -"

The Scriptural passage below shows us 'The Lord's Prayer' that Jesus taught his disciples to pray, together with His surrounding conditions. You will also observe that the prayer is in two basic parts:

A) Declaration to God – v9-10.
B) Dependency of man – v11-13.

5 "And when you pray, do not be like the hypocrites, for they love to pray standing in the synagogues and on the street corners to be seen by men. I tell you the truth, they have received their reward in full.
6 But when you pray, go into your room, close the door and pray to your Father, who is unseen. Then your Father, who sees what is done in secret, will reward you.
7 And when you pray, do not keep on babbling like pagans, for they think they will be heard because of their many words.
8 Do not be like them, for your Father knows what you need before you ask him.
9 "This, then, is how you should pray: "'Our Father in heaven, hallowed be your name,
10 your kingdom come, your will be done on earth as it is in heaven.
11 Give us today our daily bread.
12 Forgive us our debts, as we also have forgiven our debtors.
13 And lead us not into temptation, but deliver us from the evil one.' *{Or from evil; some late manuscripts one, for yours is the kingdom and the power and the glory for ever. Amen.}*

14 For if you forgive men when they sin against you, your heavenly Father will also forgive you.
15 But if you do not forgive men their sins, your Father will not forgive your sins.

Mat 6:5-15

Introduction to Spirits and Satan

To many people talk of Satan, demons or evil spirits is the speech of myths, legends or fantasy. There are, however, many references to these terms used in most, if not all, religions.

Also, concerning people there are common terms used to describe them such as: having a buoyant spirit; being spirited; etc., and a human being is described as consisting of body, mind and spirit. Indeed a key factor that makes a huge difference between people is the amount of driving force, determination, the energy, the ambition, and a whole range of character features that define the type of spirit a person possesses.

So it can be seen that the type of non-physical 'spirit' a person possesses is the element that best describes their character, and is the fundamental initiator that uses the mind and body to fulfil its desired actions.

As people are thus led by the spirit element within them, it means that they are sensitive to, and could be influenced by, 'other spirits' around them – the spirits that emanate from the personalities of other people and from other spirits, both good and evil. The good Spirit coming from the good God – the Lord Jesus Christ, and the evil spirits coming from the Devil (Satan) and his agents (demons).

The following are a few Biblical facts taken from the book "Principles of Christian Faith" by Harold McDougal concerning Satan and demons.

Satan

His origin Isa 14:12-15, Eze 28:12-19.

His names (they express his character): accuser Rev:12:10; adversary (enemy) 1Pet 5:8; devil Mat 4:1; wicked (evil) one Mat 13:19; the god of this world (age) 2Cor 4:4; prince (ruler) of the power of the air Eph 2:2.

His opposition to the work of God includes: tempting, afflicting, destroying, condemning.

Other characteristics: Disguises himself as an angel of light 2Cor 11:14; Is a liar and the father of lies Jn 8:44; Is limited in his ability to act Job 1:9-12, Jn 12:31; He must be resisted Eph 4:26-27, Jas 4:7, 1Pet 5:8-9, Rev 12:11; He has an end Rev 12:9, Rev 20:10.

Demons
Their origin 2Pet 2:4, Jude 6.
Their characteristics are spirits Mat 12:43-45; are Satan's emissaries Mat 12:26; are numerous Mk 5:9; can enter into and control men and animals Mk 5:13, Acts 16:16; cause mental problems Mk 5:4-5; afflict the sick Mat 12:22, 17:15, Lk 13:11-16; are unclean Mat 10:1, 12:43; have an eternal destiny Mat 25:41; know their end Mat 8:29, Lk 8:31; appear religious at times 1Tim 4:1; know Jesus and recognise His authority Mat 8:29, Jas 2:19; are all subject to Him Mat 4:24, 8:16, 9:32-33, 12:22; were cast out by early Christians Acts 8:7, 16:16; are also subject to Christians today Mk 16:17, Lk 10:17, Acts 16:18, 19:12, 1Jn 4:4.

Spiritual Warfare

When a person becomes a believer in the Lord Jesus Christ and trusts in Him as their only and all sufficient God for their personal salvation they soon find out that they have entered into an area of spiritual warfare. The reason for having been put into a war zone is the fact that Satan has lost one of his people to God, his sworn enemy, and so he will seek every opportunity to make life difficult for that person and try to cause them to disobey God by any means possible.

This warfare shows itself in a variety of ways, direct or subtle, through: conflicts in the mind concerning moral standards; relationship difficulties; adverse or challenging changes in circumstances; personal opposition to your views; lifestyle challenges; feeling weak in the face of temptations; find it difficult to pray; doubts concerning the security of our salvation, etc.

In view of the above set of difficulties we need to assess our own personal situation and lifestyle, and as we do this let us remember that God is on our side and we are not left alone or without help. We can see from the following Scriptures our position of power and authority, and who is against us:

Jesus gave his disciples "power and authority to drive out all demons and to cure diseases,"

(Lk 9:1), and He further told them that "I have given you authority to trample on snakes and scorpions and to overcome all the power of the enemy; nothing will harm you." (Lk 10:19).

Later, in the times of the apostles and the Early Church we read how the apostle Paul used the spiritual authority he had been given to cast demons out of a soothsaying girl (Acts 16:18). Paul writing under the influence of the Holy Spirit says: "For though we live in the world, we do not wage war as the world does.

The weapons we fight with are not the weapons of the world. On the contrary, they have divine power to demolish strongholds."(2Cor 10:3-5). Every controlling habit that does not please God is a demonic stronghold.

In 1Pet 5:8-9 we are called on to be self-controlled and alert because our enemy the devil prowls around like a roaring lion seeking for someone to devour, and we are told to resist him, and stand firm in the faith. It should be remembered that Satan (the devil) has many agents, known as demons. With this in mind, there is a warning given in 1Cor 10:19-21 that sacrifice/worship given to any god or idol, except to the one true and living God (as revealed in the Bible), is in fact being offered to demons, and this invites the entrance of demons into the locality. One result from this is that it is much harder to pray, so their presence should be prayed against in the name of Jesus.

In Eph 6:10-18 Paul states clearly the realm of the conflict that every believer is involved in as shown in verse 12 of this passage: "For our struggle is not against flesh and blood, but against the rulers, against the authorities, against the powers of this dark world and against the spiritual forces of evil in the heavenly realms." He then continues by urging us to "put on the full (whole) armour of God," and states that the 'armour' consists of:

"*the belt of truth*" – we should walk in truth, and live by the Word of Truth, aware that the '*belt*' holds the other parts of the 'armour' together;

"*the breastplate of righteousness*" – this piece of armour made of metal plates covered the body front and so protects the heart, symbolising the believer's imputed righteousness (i.e. righteousness attributed to them) in Christ (1Cor 1:30, 2Cor 5:21, Phil 3:9). As we have received Christ's 'righteousness' we are protected against Satan's accusations and attacks, whilst we are living a life that is dependent on Him, in the knowledge that our salvation is secure;

"*the shoes of the Gospel*"–the soldier's shoes were to protect their feet from obstacles placed in their way by the enemy, and "*the readiness that comes from the gospel of peace*" signifies a prepared and resolved frame of heart, to adhere to the gospel as it brings peace with God and others;

"*the shield of faith*" – placing and keeping our faith in the Lord Jesus Christ will act as a shield against the 'darts' of temptations that Satan will shoot at us. These darts are unexpected, and shot at a fast speed with the intention of wounding and inflaming our spirit, so that we will be deflected from following Christ's way;

"*the helmet of salvation*" – as the helmet protects the head, so in this case the mind is controlled and protected by God from Satan's lies;

"*the sword of the Spirit*" – is the offensive weapon God provides us with, and is described in the text as 'the word of God', the Bible. It is by knowing and using Scripture and Scriptural principles, that we can repel and refute Satan's temptations, as Christ resisted his temptations with, "*It is written*" (Mt 4:1-11). The Psalmist states that he has hidden God's word in his heart so that he might not sin against Him (Ps 119:11). In Heb 4:12 it describes the word of God thus: "For the word of God is living and active. Sharper than any double - edged sword, it penetrates even to the dividing soul and spirit, joints and marrow; it judges the thoughts and attitudes of the heart." As this 'Word' is living and active it has its own power, which just the words of people do not possess. A physical sword wounds to hurt and kill, while the sword of the Spirit wounds to heal and give life.

"*pray in the Spirit*" – Whilst we are asked not to be anxious about anything, but to pray with intercession and thanksgiving for everyone (Phil 4:6; 1Tim 2:1), we are particularly asked to pray 'in the Spirit' (Eph 6:18; Jude 1:20; Rev 1:10), as this is prayer led by the Holy Spirit – i.e. where our relationship with God is close enough to receive something of God's heart and desires when we pray, so that we not on our agenda, but His. It follows that the closer our relationship is with Him, the more His thoughts and desires become ours, hence, the more we shall find that our requests are answered in a positive way as they are in accordance with His will.

Some thoughts in the Eph 6:10-18 passage referred to above have been taken from Matthew Henry's Bible Commentary.

Biblical Meditation

Biblical meditation should not be confused with other types of 'meditation' as practiced by other religions because these practices can place the person under some form of possession, oppression or dominance by the 'spirits' associated with those religions. When this occurs the person is not fully responsible for their own actions because they are being influenced to take actions which were not originally their idea. It follows that as a person subjects themselves to more and more of these' influences' they run the risk of becoming 'possessed' and under the dominance of these spirits, and this can lead to a person suffering from various mental illnesses. On the other hand these meditation practices are portrayed as being helpful to people in a whole variety of ways, and many of those who advocate them are not aware of their associated dangers.

The good news is that, if the above problems occur people can be offered special deliverance ministry. By contrast, biblical meditation has only positive outcomes and relates to a person quietly and thoughtfully reading the Bible, considering the message it presents to them, and then praying to God and making their response to the message received.

The following are extracts taken from the book "Bible Meditation" by Alex Buchanan.

"<u>Bible Meditation and Prayer</u> - These two disciplines belong together; they are both important to the development of our life with God. Meditation and quietness help us to understand the mind, will and feelings of God. Prayer leads us on from here to sense more accurately what he feels and what he wants us to do for and with him. - - - - - - Prayer without Biblical meditation can be a waste of time if we pour out our requests without pondering his word. Ps 66:18 warns us: 'If I regard (cherish) wickedness in my heart, the Lord will not hear.' However, there is a remedy as David found: 'Thy word I have treasured in my heart, that I may not sin against Thee.' (Ps 119:11). If we often meditate on the word, we are likely to pray effectively, because our hearts are pure enough for God to listen to us.

Prayer without Biblical meditation can be unscriptural. If we do not pray in the name of Jesus (Jn 15:16) [see Prayer Section above] we will not receive any answers to our prayers.– - - - - - - - - -. The Holy Spirit is the inspirer and illuminator of the Scriptures and when we study them together with him and ponder them in his company, he is more able to lead us into effective prayer. Paul says that we must 'pray at all times in the Spirit'(Eph 6:18), which means praying for that which conforms to God's will and desires. We can know the will of God, otherwise Paul would not have prayed for the Colossians 'that [they] may be filled with the knowledge of his will' (Col 1:9). - - - - - - - - - - We often talk about our 'quiet times', or periods of prayer and Bible study. It is very important that they actually do include time to be quiet before the Lord so that he can speak to us, and time for the Holy Spirit to enable us to digest the word so that it becomes part of our daily life, as in George Mueller's case."

OUR RESPONSE TO GOD - DISCIPLESHIP

-PRAYER, SATAN, SPIRITUAL WARFARE & BIBLICAL MEDITATION-

Notes and Quotations

Prayer

In the book "Don't just stand there . . . . .Pray Something" by Ronald Dunn, he shows the importance of prayer when he says: "The book of Acts is filled with prayer meetings; every forward thrust the first church made was immersed in prayer. Take another look at the church at Pentecost. They prayed ten days and preached ten minutes and three thousand souls were saved. Today we pray ten minutes and preach ten days and are ecstatic if anyone is saved."

The hymn shown below, written on the topic of prayer by J. Montgomery, (1771-1854) illustrates the essential characteristics of this subject:

1 Prayer is the soul's sincere desire,
Uttered or unexpressed,
The motion of a hidden fire
That trembles in the breast.

2 Prayer is the burden of a sigh,
The falling of a tear,
The upward glancing of an eye,
When none but God is near.

3 Prayer is the simplest form of speech,
That infant lips can try;
Prayer, the sublimest strains that reach,
The Majesty on high.

4 Prayer is the Christian's vital breath,
The Christian's native air,
His watchword at the gate of death;
He enters heaven with prayer.

5 Prayer is the contrite sinner's voice,
Returning from his ways;
While angels in their songs rejoice,
And cry, "Behold, he prays!"

6 O Thou by whom we come to God,
The Life, the Truth, the Way!
The path of prayer Thyself hast trod;
Lord, teach us how to pray.

Prayer not only changes our circumstances, but also changes us.

In Leonard Ravenhill's book "Why Revival Tarries" he makes a number of observations including the following:

"No man is greater than his prayer life. The pastor who is not praying is playing; the people who are not praying are straying. The pulpit can be a shop window to display one's talents; the prayer closet allows no showing off. Poverty-stricken as the Church is today in many things, she is most stricken here, in the place of prayer.

We have many organisers, but few agonizers;
many players and payers, few pray-ers;
many singers, few clingers;
lots of pastors, few wrestlers;
many fears, few tears;
much fashion, little passion;
many interferers, few intercessors;
many writers, but few fighters.
Failing here, we fail everywhere.

The two prerequisites to successful living are vision and passion, both of which are born in and maintained by prayer. The ministry of preaching is open to few; the ministry of prayer -- the highest ministry of all human offices – is open to all."

Prayer is more an activity of the spirit than of the mind, see 1Chron 16:11, 2Chron 7:1-3, Jer 33:2-3, Lk 11:2-4, 18:1, Eph 6:18, Jude 20.

Pray – not <u>for</u> the Work, but prayer <u>is</u> the Work. See Ps 27:7-8.

<u>Prayer/Work</u>
Work heartily (Col 3:23) <u>but,</u> don't get so involved with the work of God, that you neglect the God of the work. – see Mat 11:28-30

Pray within your faith – not what He CAN but what you believe He WILL do, be specific.

When praying with another person, be agreed about the matter, see Mat 18:19.

Note: Our prayers reveal our concerns.

"Thou art coming to a king,
large petitions with thee bring."

John Newton

Persistence is required in prayer
Jesus told His disciples that they should always pray and not give up – see Lk 18:1-8.

A type of prayer that is heard and received by God
An example of such a prayer is given in Neh 9:6-15, & 32-38, - this prayer is one that is focused on God, reminded Him of his faithfulness to them, was thankful, was repentant in attitude and grounded in Scripture.

In Lk 11:1 Jesus' disciples asked him: "Lord teach us to pray" and he responded by the prayer known as 'The Lords prayer' –see Mat 6:9-15 and Lk 11:1-4.

Prayer should follow this pattern and should have the following characteristics of being: passionate, scriptural, intimate, unhurried, faith-filled and Spirit led – see Eph 6:18, 1Thess 5:19, and Jude 20.

Sometimes prayer will be accompanied by fasting – see Mat 6:16-18.

Urgent prayer is characterised by intensive impassioned crying out to God for help – see Mat 27:46, Lk 18:7-8 and Rom 8:15

Someone has provided an anagram for prayer – 'PUSH' meaning, Pray Until Something Happens.

Supplying your needs
When faced with the need to feed 5000 people the first response of Jesus' disciples was to send the people away, but Jesus said: "You give them something to eat", so they found five loaves and two fish – not enough they thought. But when they obeyed and placed it into the hands of Jesus it became enough. So let us use this principle to meet needs. See Mk 6:36-44, Phil 4:19.

Prayer and the power of lament (passionate expression of grief).
David's prayer in Ps 55 gives us an example of a person telling God how he feels and makes his requests along with passionate expressions of grief. This type of prayer can be a model for us, and we can mourn personal loss, or the loss of integrity, truth, righteousness and love as we cry out to God to act and change these situations. Selwyn Hughes in his "Every Day with Jesus" Notes writes: "Another matter we must face as participants in God's big story is this: we must be willing to lament. I am aware that this theme is not popular with the majority of Christians today, who seem to think that whenever a negative feeling arises, it is best to pretend it isn't there. Do you realise that 70 per cent of the psalms are laments? These laments arose from the disappointments, losses, and tragedies the psalmists faced, because they did not avoid these issues or deny that things were as they were."

The writer also says: "Listen to David's words in the psalm before us today. He faces everything, and prays through everything. Eugene Peterson claims that "The craggy majesty and towering dignity of David's life are a product of David's laments." I agree."

He also states: "Lament is a cry of agony. Psalm 80 has several examples. Here is one: "How long will your anger smoulder against the prayers of your people?" (v.4). Lament, properly understood, is more entering the agony of loss than attempting to get an answer."

In the light of these comments, how should we pray when we are in difficult circumstances? Perhaps a helpful framework for prayer should be along the following lines: Tell God how we feel – admit we do not understand the situation – confess any failures / sin on our part – seek the mercy and grace of God for these circumstances – seek God's guidance – continually re-assert, even through tears, our trust in God.

The following are quotes from the book "The Christian Book of Lists" by Randy Petersen:

Archbishop Trench: "We must not conceive of prayer as an overcoming of God's reluctance, but as a laying hold of his highest willingness."

Dwight L. Moody: "The Christian on his knees sees more than the philosopher on tiptoe."

John Bunyan: "Prayer is a shield to the soul, a sacrifice to God, and a scourge to Satan."

Thomas a Kempis: "It is a great art to commune with God."

Bob Gass in his "The Word for Today" Notes quotes Richard Forster who says: "To pray is to change. It is the central avenue God uses to transform us. If we are not willing to change, we will soon abandon prayer."

In a another note Bob Gass states: "Your life will never be balanced if all you do is <u>ask,</u> but never <u>adore</u>, <u>petition</u>, but never praise Him. If you want to get to God, enter His gates with thanksgiving, cross his courtyard with praise and you'll find Him waiting for you. (Ps 100:4).

In yet another quotation concerning prayer he states: "Listen: . . . . 'we do not ask because we deserve help, but because you are so merciful' (Daniel 9:18).

He also refers to '...The prayer of the righteous is powerful...' James 5:16 and states:

"Why pray? Because nothing lies beyond the reach of prayer, except that which lies outside the will of God".

Bob Gass in his "The Word for Today" Notes writes concerning having a prayer strategy:

"<u>God always has a strategy.</u>

For every battle, God has a strategy, so stop praying about the problem and start praying for a strategy." See Jud 6:15-16, &:25-27; Mat 18:19-20.

In the book "A Prayer for Today" by Bob Gass he refers to the Scripture below and states, with reference to a man named Jabez: "Here are four things he prayed for, (as stated in the New King James Version of the Bible):

- Greater success: "Oh that you would bless me indeed."
- Greater influence: " . . . . and enlarge my territory."

- Greater power: " . . . . that your hand be with me."
- Greater protection: " . . . . and that you would keep me from evil, that I may not cause pain."

And the Bible says, "So God granted him what he requested."

He then points out that God's promises come with conditions, and further states: "It's a four-line prayer, *backed up by a lifestyle* that pleases God!" (Heb 10:35-36).

10 Jabez cried out to the God of Israel, "Oh, that you would bless me and enlarge my territory! Let your hand be with me, and keep me from harm so that I will be free from pain." And God granted his request.
1Chron 4:10

Selwyn Hughes in his "Every Day with Jesus" Notes writes: "Prayer, of course, has many elements, but fundamentally there are just two: communion and commission. All the other elements belong to these two. Someone has described communion and commission as the two heart-beats of the prayer life. A heart has to keep beating or death sets in. All communion without commission results in death. All commission without communion also results in death. When the two beat in proper rhythm – that is life."

As God knows what's in our hearts, it follows that He will listen more to the INNER desire of our hearts, than to the OUTER expression of our words. See Isa 29:13, Mk 7:5-7.

Selwyn Hughes in his "Every Day with Jesus Notes" quotes a definition of prayer that he likes: "Prayer is not overcoming God's reluctance, but laying hold on His highest willingness."

We are invited to take *all* our concerns to God in prayer coupled with thanksgiving, leave them with Him, and then experience His peace in our hearts and minds –see Phil 4:6-7.

Prayer for Healing

In the area of praying for healing there has been much confusion and disappointment, and a way to minimise these effects is firstly to spend time waiting on God in prayer to discover His will in these matters so that we can then pray in accordance with His will, and not ours.

The following Scriptures relate to this area: Mat 20:29-34 (Note v32), Mk 10:46-51 (Note v51), Jas 1:5-8, Jas 5:13-16.

<u>A Method of having a Daily Quiet Time (A time with God)</u>

1. Find a quiet place, and choose a time when you will not be interrupted, e.g. early morning.

2. Allow a minimum of twenty minutes if you can.

3. Consider some aspects of God's character, confess sin, and worship/praise Him.

4. Read Bible – perhaps a set portion, but most importantly LISTEN for God to speak, and if you are not 'spoken to' in this portion then keep on reading until you are. You may find Scripture Notes helpful.

5. Respond to God – "If you had responded to my rebuke, I would have poured out my heart to you and made my thoughts known to you." Prov 1:23 It may be a challenge to faith or trust. "We know that God does not listen to sinners. He listens to the godly man who does His will. Jn 9:31

6. Record the response, Biblical reference and date in a note book.

7. Pray for the people within your sphere of influence, and others the Lord lays on your heart.

8. Thank Him for His love and grace.

<u>Biblical Conditions</u> for receiving answers to prayer are given in Ps 91:9-16, Mat 6:15, 1Pet 3:7-12, and these include: trusting God; loving God; freely acknowledging His name; forgiving others; putting wrong relationships right.

<u>Prayer of St Francis</u> (Accredited to him)
Lord make me a channel of your peace,

that where there is hatred, I may bring love,
where there is discord, I may bring harmony,
where there is doubt, I may bring faith,
where there is despair, I may bring hope,
where there is sadness, I may bring joy.

The prayer given below is by an Anonymous Confederate soldier, and is quoted from 'The Oxford Book of Prayer'

'I asked God for strength, that I might achieve,
I was made weak,
that I might learn humbly to obey.
I asked for health, that I might do greater things,
I was given infirmity,
that I might do better things.
I asked for riches, that I might be happy,
I was given poverty,
that I might be wise.
I asked for power, that I might have the praise of men,
I was given weakness,
that I might feel the need of God.
I asked for all things that I might enjoy life,
I was given life
that I might enjoy all things.
I got nothing that I asked for –
but everything that I had hoped for.
Almost, despite myself, my
unspoken prayers were answered.
I am among all men,
most richly blessed.'

A prayer from an anonymous writer:
And God said "No"
I asked God to take away my pride, and God said "No",
he said "it was not for Him to take away, but for me to give up."

I asked God to make my handicap child whole, and God said "No,
. . . . . her spirit is whole, her body is temporary."

I asked God to give me patience, and God said "No",
he said that "patience is a by-product of tribulation. It isn't granted, it is earned."

I asked God to give me happiness, and God said "No",
he said "he gives me blessings, and happiness is an attitude up to me."

I asked God to spare my pain, and God said "No",
he said "suffering will draw you apart from the worldly cares and bring you closer to me."

I asked God to make my spirit grow, and God said "No,
. . . . . it will grow on its own, but I will prune you to make you fruitful."

I asked God if he loved me and God said "Yes",
he said "he gave his only son to die for me to prove it and I will be with him in heaven someday because I believe that."

I asked God to help me love others as much as he loves me, ... he said "At last you finally have the idea."

Prayer from Kenya
"From the cowardice that dare not face the truth,
from the laziness that is contented with half truth,
from the arrogance that thinks that it knows all truth -
Good Lord, deliver me."

Bob Gass in his "The Word for Today" Notes relates a story of answered prayer, as follows:

"God answers prayer

In the summer of 1876, grasshoppers nearly destroyed all the crops in Minnesota. The following spring, farmers were worried that the plague would come back again and bring financial ruin to the State. The situation got so serious that Governor Pillsbury proclaimed a day of prayer and fasting. All the schools, stores and offices closed, and men, women and children gathered to pray.

The next day, temperatures soared to mid-summer levels, even though it was only April. Suddenly, they were devastated to discover billions of grasshopper larvae, wriggling to life. For three days the unusual heat persisted and the larvae hatched. It appeared it wouldn't be long before they started feeding, which meant they'd again destroy the State's entire wheat crop. But on the forth day, the temperature suddenly dropped and a heavy frost covered the earth, killing everyone of those creeping, crawling pests, just as surely as if poison or fire had been used. Grateful farmers never forgot that day. It went down in the history of Minnesota as the day God answered the prayers of the people."

In "The Word for Today" Notes by Bob Gass he quotes some words from Francois Fenelon a 17th Century Frenchman on how to improve your prayer life, and he says:

"Tell God all that is in your heart, as one unloads one's heart, it pleasures and its pains, to a dear friend. Tell Him your ***troubles*** that He may comfort you; tell Him your ***longings*** that He may purify them; tell Him your ***dislikes*** that He may help you conquer them; tell Him your ***temptations*** that He may shield you from them; show Him the ***wounds*** of your soul that He may heal them; lay bare your indifference to good, your ***depraved*** taste for evil, your ***instability.*** Tell Him how ***self-love*** makes you unjust to others, how ***vanity*** tempts you to be insincere, how ***pride*** hides you from yourself and from others. If you thus pour out all your weaknesses, needs and troubles, there will be no lack of what to say. You will never exhaust the subject, for it is continually being renewed."

Spiritual Warfare

The following are short extracts from the book "Discipleship" by David Watson. Under the heading of 'Spiritual Warfare' he writes: "Every Christian knows that discipleship is a struggle." He then refers to the following difficulties we often have: a reluctance to pray; finding it hard to love and forgive; shrink from keeping our hearts open to God and other Christians; reluctance to witness; continue to be proud, selfish, angry, jealous, covetous; are easily defeated; have difficulties with relationships; have difficulties in understanding why there is such oppression, injustice and frustration? The questions are endless.

He then states: "Two main answers are given in the Bible. First, in our rebellion against God, we have become captive to sin: 'I do not understand my own actions,' wrote Paul. 'For I do not do what I want, but I do the very thing I hate.' (Rom 7:15). Second, we are involved in a spiritual battle, in which Satan seeks constantly to frustrate God's will for our lives."

He continues under the heading 'The Biblical witness' by stating: "Those who find the whole concept of Satan's activity difficult to take seriously, tending to dismiss it as fanciful or medieval, should note carefully the volume of biblical teaching on this subject. Leaving on one side the numerous passages in the Old Testament, it is significant that as soon as Jesus began his public ministry he 'was led up by the Spirit into the wilderness to be tempted by the devil (Mat 4:1)."

Prayer/Spiritual Warfare - The First Tool of Evangelism

This truth is clearly illustrated on the video tapes entitled "Transformations" produced by "The Sentinel Group" – made available in the UK through: Gateway Christian Media Ltd.

In these tapes is seen a few dedicated and united Christians coming together firstly, to identify the particular spiritual forces that are preventing people from coming into the kingdom of God in their area, and secondly, to pray and enter into spiritual warfare (Eph 6:12) until they see a spiritual 'breakthrough' and people wanting to get right with God. The results that these Christian groups enjoy are amazing and very encouraging.

Bob Gass in his "The Word for Today" Notes, gives a word of warning to Christians when he writes:

"The danger of past victories!

The time to be careful is when you reach your goals! There are three periods in every battle: the easiest period is usually the battle itself. The most difficult period is the period of indecision just before it – whether to fight or run away. But by far the most dangerous period is the aftermath. It's then, with all your resources spent and your guard down, that you have to watch out for .....discouragement or overconfidence ......dulled reactions or faulty judgment. - - - - - - - - -

Don't fall prey to the peril of past victories! Remember your H.A.L.T.

sign. When you're Hungry, Angry, Lonely or Tired, you're in a vulnerable place; do something about it!

Resting on your laurels is just a synonym for 'flirting with disaster'. Danger awaits the man or woman who dwells in the comfortable land of accomplished dreams. Think about it."

On a separate occasion Bob Gass refers to Jeremiah 17:7 "But blessed is the man who Trusts in the LORD, whose confidence is in him." and writes: "Paul says we go ".... from faith to faith ....."(Rom 1:17). In those (early) days, I went from faith to doubt, then back to faith. I discovered that when you give the devil a foothold, he'll turn it into a stronghold. But gradually I learned (yes, you have to learn it and it takes time) how to be confident consistently confident in God!"

Biblical Meditation

Discerning the voice of God

Bob Gass in his "The Word for Today" Notes referring to the life of Moses, says: "It was during that time that he encountered God at the burning bush and discovered a fire that wasn't dependent on him, because God started it and God sustained it. It was there that he learned to discern the voice of the Lord from every other voice. Imagine the value of that when 101 different people are giving you their opinions! It was there that he built a relationship with God that would enable him to believe God for manna from heaven, water from a rock, and even a way through the Red Sea.

Alex Buchanan in his book "Bible Meditation" describes this topic as: "the art of being still before God, and allowing the Spirit to speak to us through the Scriptures, as we think them over slowly and carefully.' It involves 'chewing and digesting the Word until it gets from our head to our heart, thus affecting our will and conduct.' It has a clear purpose – it is what I call the 'thoughtful contemplation of God's Word in order to obey it.'"

This book provides a valuable in-depth study into this subject.

The following are a few extracts of statements taken from a Paper headed "Hearing from God" by Alex Buchanan:

Why bother?
If you love someone, you want to hear their voice and be close enough to do so. Our love for God is measured by the time we make, and the effort we give in order to hear Him.

It's so hard!
Of course it is. It is God we are speaking about. Our enemy Satan will do anything to prevent us from being close to God.

And costly!

It demands time and sacrifice. Our sacrifice may be the TV, hobbies, a night out, or even Christian fellowship if it prevents us from listening to God.

It demands silence. The spirit of the world creeps into the Church and makes us nervous of silence. We are not used to being quiet, either in our private prayer times or public meetings.

He continues with a number of headings including: We need to focus; It requires waiting on God; It needs practice; and many more helpful headings.

OUR RESPONSE TO GOD - DISCIPLESHIP

-PRAYER, SATAN, SPIRITUAL WARFARE & BIBLICAL MEDITATION-

Biblical Texts & Text References

Prayer

The Apostle Paul asks the believers to pray 'in the Spirit' on all occasions with all kinds of prayers and requests. See Eph 6:18

The words of Jesus:

13 And I will do whatever you ask in my name, so that the Son may bring glory to the Father.
14 You may ask me for anything in my name, and I will do it.

Jn 14:13-14

A prayer for a sick person is given in Jas 5:14-16 that calls for the elders of the church to pray over the person and anoint them with oil in the name of the Lord. And the prayer offered in faith will make the sick person well.

Additional Scripture references

Jud 6:15-16, 1Sam 1:13, 2 Sam 7:27-28, 2Chron 14:11-12; 20:3-6 & 20-22, Neh 2:4-5; Ps 3:4; 5:2-3; 27:7-10; 34:4-6, Jer 10:25; 33:2-3, Hos 14:2, Mat 6:5-13; 7:7-11; 14:23; 18:19-20, Mk 11:24, Jn 9:31; 14:6, Acts 10:9, Rom 8:26-27, 1Cor 14:13-15, Phil 4:6-7, Heb 4:16, Jas 1:5, 1Jn 3:21-22, Jude 20

Satan

12 How you have fallen from heaven, O morning star, son of the dawn! You have been cast down to the earth, you who once laid low the nations!

13 You said in your heart, "I will ascend to heaven; I will raise my throne above the stars of God; I will sit enthroned on the mount of assembly, on the utmost heights of the sacred mountain.
14 I will ascend above the tops of the clouds; I will make myself like the Most High."

Isa 14:12-14

6 When the crowds heard Philip and saw the miraculous signs he did, they all paid close attention to what he said.
7 With shrieks, evil *{Greek unclean}* spirits came out of many, and many paralytics and cripples were healed.

Acts 8:6-7

The devil and the false prophet will be thrown into the lake of burning sulphur and they will be tormented day and night for ever and ever. See Rev 20:10

Additional Scripture references

Job 1:9-12, Isa 14:12-15; Ezek 28:12-19, Mat 4:1; 8:29; 9:32-33; 12:26; 12:43-45; 13:19; 17:15; 25:41, Mk 5:4-8; Lk 8:31, Jn 8:44, Acts 16:16, 2Cor 4:4; 11:14, Eph 2:2, Jas 4:7, 1Pet 5:8-9, 2Pet 2:4, 1Jn 4:4; Jude 6; Rev 12:9-10

Spiritual Warfare

1 When Jesus had called the Twelve together, he gave them power and authority to drive out all demons and to cure diseases,
2 and he sent them out to preach the kingdom of God and to heal the sick.

Lk 9:1-2

There is an example of a spirit being commanded by the apostle Paul to come out of a girl who was following him, and at that moment of command the spirit left her. See Acts 16:17-18

Additional Scripture references

Ps 119:11, Mat 13:39, Mk 9:25, Jn 17:15, Rom 1:17; 7:15, 1Cor 10:19-20; 12:10, 2 Cor 5:21, Eph 4:26-27; 6:10-18, Phil 4:6-7, 1Jn 4:1-3

Biblical Meditation

18 If I had cherished sin in my heart, the Lord would not have listened;
19 but God has surely listened and heard my voice in prayer.
20 Praise be to God, who has not rejected my prayer or withheld his love from me!

Ps 66:18-20

16 And pray in the Spirit on all occasions with all kinds of prayers and requests. With this in mind, be alert and always keep on praying for all the saints.

Eph 6:18

Additional Scripture references

Josh 1:8, 2Chron 7:14; Job 23:4-5, Ps 46:10; 77:12; 119:11; 15 & 27; 139:17, Isa 30:21; 50:4, Jn 2:5; 15:15-16, 1Cor 2:9-16, Col 1:9-10, 1Thess 5:16-21; Jas 1:22, Jude 1:20

Biblical Meditation

18 If I had cherished sin in my heart, the Lord would not have listened;
19 but God has surely listened and heard my voice in prayer.
20 Praise be to God, who has not rejected my prayer or withheld his love from me!

[illegible]

18 And pray in the Spirit on all occasions with all kinds of prayers and
requests. With this in mind, be alert and always keep on praying
[illegible]

[illegible]

Additional [illegible]

[illegible]

[illegible]

E9

OUR RESPONSE TO GOD - DISCIPLESHIP

-FORGIVENESS, UNITY & FELLOWSHIP-

Biblical Definitions

Forgiveness - To one another

One of the greatest hindrances to the work of God within the life of a Christian is pride.

Pride comes in many guises, like, the attitude of holding to the fact that that you are right and they are wrong, so that even if you are right the attitude adopted has helped to destroy any relationship you had with the other person.

Another attitude that is destructive to relationships is to refuse to forgive someone, even if they have said, and meant, sorry. When this occurs they not only hurt the other person, but they hinder their own spirit, and from this point they stop the process of maturing further into the person God wants them to be. By contrast, if the person truly forgives, then they will experience relief, peace of mind and ongoing blessing from God.

In the Scriptures there is a common theme of forgiveness from God (referred to in Section D3), requiring from all people repentance in word, attitude and action, and particularly in the N.T. we see that we can personally ask for forgiveness on the basis that when the Lord Jesus Christ died on the cross, He died to pay the penalty for the sin of the world, and this includes us if we repent and thank Him for dying for us personally.

When we have taken this step we should begin to have a more tolerant and forgiving view of those who sin against us.

We are exhorted by God to forgive others, "***Forgive as the Lord forgave you***"(Col 3:13) with the condition that, unless we forgive others He will not forgive us, - see the Scripture below:

For if you forgive men when they sin against you, your heavenly Father will also forgive you.

But if you do not forgive men their sins, your Father will not forgive your sins.
Mat 6:14-15

W.E. Vine in his: "Expository Dictionary of Bible Words" states the meaning of forgiveness as: "to send forth, send away, denotes besides its other meanings, to remit or forgive debts, Mat 6:12; 18:27, 32; these being completely cancelled".

We should also note that no exceptions are made. If anyone could have made an exception it would have been Jesus Christ, but He showed us that even when he was being crucified His inherent character was to forgive, and in this extreme situation He said: "Father, forgive them, for they do not know what they are doing." (Lk 23:34). We can see, therefore, that God is not asking us to do something that He was not willing to do, and His was the greatest test of character where He was wrongfully accused and put to death.

If we are not willing to forgive others, then apart from the serious consequences mentioned above, there are many other effects that can result as outlined below:

- blessings withheld from God;
- loss of hearing God's voice;
- loss of spiritual fervour;
- breakdown of relationships;
- loss of support to and from others;
- exclusion/separation through pride of spirit;
- fail to experience release, freedom and a fresh start in life;
- suffer from depression;
- cast a depressive atmosphere around yourself, affecting others;
- others suffer as they know they are not forgiven or accepted;
- etc.

The dangers of the above effects usually increase with the passage of time, unless the issue is resolved. But God wants us to enjoy the release of experiencing a life freed from the oppressive and disheartening situations given above as gained through forgiving others and thereby knowing His forgiveness and all that that implies.

Unity - With God and one another

When there is a sense of oneness of purpose and cooperation much progress is made and people are mutually helped and encouraged. Attitudes that destroy unity are the lack of honesty, humility and love. Another unhelpful attitude is that of obstinate pride.

All the above unhelpful and counterproductive attitudes apply not only between people, but also between each Christian and God.

Now let us consider the many aspects of unity that God requires Christians to observe and heed, and a number of these are listed below:

He desires us to be united:

- in Christ – Rom 6:5, Phil 2:1
- in the worship of God the Father and the Lord Jesus Christ – Mat 15:9, Lk 4:8, -Jn 4:23-24, 1Tim 3:15, Heb 12:28
- in the Holy Spirit – Eph 4:3
- in Biblical Truth – Ps 25:5, 26:3, Jn 1:17, 14:6, 16:13, Rom 2:8, Eph 1:13, 4:14-15, 2Thess 2:10-12, 1Tim 4:16, Tit 1:9
- in faith and knowledge – Eph 4:13
- in purpose – Ps 133:1-3, Eph 4:2
- in love for one another – Col 1:5, 2:2, 3:14, 1Pet 1:22
- in mind, thought and deed – 2Chron 30:12, 1Cor 1:10, 1Jn 3:18
- in prayer – Mat 6:5:13, Acts 4:24, 12:12-17, Jas 5:14
- in marriage – Mat 19:5, Eph 5:31, 1Tim 4:3
- in Holy Communion – 1Cor 11:23-29

It is important to note that God does not require us to be united in the following aspects:

the type, format or timing of church services,
the type of dress to be worn,

the type of food we eat, or do not eat,
the type of jobs we do, unless it is immoral, illegal or in a criminal activity.

Fellowship

When a person becomes a Christian they are brought into a common family relationship with God and other Christian believers, and this friendship relationship is referred to as Christian fellowship. This results in giving the Christians a common purpose as ordained by God. In this respect Christian fellowship is unique, as these special characteristics of friendship and purpose unite Christians throughout the world.

This common bond, which is birthed by God when a person becomes a Christian, means that He plants the desire in them to want friendship with others and an ever-closer union with Himself.

When people become Christians they usually recognise the characteristics of other Christians, and this enables friendships to form relatively quickly between people who did not previously know one another.

W.E. Vine in his "Expository Dictionary of Bible Words" defines 'fellowship' from the original Greek as meaning 'communion, sharing in common' (koinonia).

"We become part of the 'Body of Christ' – part of the collective body of those with a common relationship by faith in the Lord Jesus Christ." See 1Cor 1:9, 2Cor 13:14, Phil 2:1, 1Jn 1:3.

For the Christian, fellowship with other like-minded believers is very important, and has been a source of strength, encouragement and practical help in the past, as it is today.

A number of Scriptures are given below that refer to fellowship between Christians and what this means: The Early Church, "devoted themselves to the apostles' teaching and to the fellowship, to the breaking of bread and to prayer." Acts 2:42

This 'fellowship' involves:

–	loving one another	Jn 13:34-35, 1Pet 1:22
–	walking in the light	1Jn 1:5-7
–	confessing sins to each other	Jas 5:16
–	praying for one another	Jas 5:16
–	fulfilling our part in the body of Christ	1Cor 12:20-27
–	encouraging one another	1Thess 5:11
–	spurring one another on towards love and good deeds	Heb 10:23-24
–	regularly meeting together	Heb 10:25

OUR RESPONSE TO GOD - DISCIPLESHIP

-FORGIVENESS, UNITY & FELLOWSHIP-

Notes and Quotations

Forgiveness

A key aspect in the process of forgiveness is related to the attitude we adopt in judging others. The Scriptures below provide guidance in this matter, so when there is a problem with a person, let us approach it with prayer, grace and humility, remembering that the Lord wants us to create an atmosphere not based on judgements but on the anticipation of healing.

"Forgiving others isn't an option – it's an order." From the "The Word for Today"

Notes by Bob Gass. See the Scripture below:

For if you forgive men when they sin against you, your heavenly Father will also forgive you.

But if you do not forgive men their sins, your Father will not forgive your sins.

Mat 6:14-15

A Prayer of Forgiveness
(found on a body at Ravensbruck Concentration Camp)

O Lord,
Remember not only the men and women of goodwill,
but also those of ill will.
But do not only remember the suffering they have inflicted on us,
remember the fruits we bore, thanks to this suffering,

our comradeship, our loyalty, our humility,
the courage, the generosity,
the greatness of heart which has grown out of all this,
and when they come to judgment,
let all the fruits that we have borne be their forgiveness.

Unity

The Lord wants His Church to have unity in variety, not unity in conformity. – See the following Scriptures: 1Cor 12:4-7, & 14-20, Col 3:14-17.

The following statements are taken from a few "Every Day with Jesus" Notes by Selwyn Hughes:

Unity is this – the bonding of one believer to another, an overriding sense of belonging to the same family, a disposition of oneness that is so deeply ingrained that it brings its influence to bear on all thinking, all decisions, and all actions. We are going much deeper than denominational affiliation now – we are talking about the same kind of unity that the Son has with the Father. Does that kind of unity characterise the relationships of the Church of today?

Christian unity begins with understanding what it means to be a Christian. Notice before our Lord prayed for the unity of all His people He made clear in His prayer just what was involved in being one of His disciples. (Jn 17:20-21). A Christian is someone who knows that his or her salvation was planned in eternity, has entered into it through faith in Christ, is utterly different from the world, and enjoys a continuing relationship with the Lord Jesus Christ.

One of the reasons why many of the ecumenical movements of our day come to nought in their efforts to bring about unity is because a significant number of the leading proponents are religious but do not appear to have a clear testimony of being converted. Unity is not something that can be imposed upon the Church by simply getting together; unity is something that has to be exposed from within the Body of those who know without any shadow of doubt they belong to Christ. (Eph 4:11-13, Phil 1:27, 1Pet 3:8).

The first unity to get straight is our unity with God. For if there is disunity here then disharmony spreads itself all down the line. One of the central difficulties in the Church of today is that we are trying to relate to one another without relating to God. When we live in unity with God then we take on the significance of the One to whom we are united.

There is another unity, however, of which Paul speaks Ephesians 4 – the unity of the Spirit. "Make every effort to keep the unity of the Spirit through the bond of peace" (Eph 4:3). The unity being spoken about here is a spiritual unity – the kind of unity our Lord was thinking of in His prayer in John 17. The moment we come into the Church we become part of a Body that is united by the power and energy of the Holy Spirit. Our task then is not to "make" unity, but simply to maintain it.

In a further statement he quotes our Lord when He says: -- "something I think you must admit is quite staggering: "*that the world may believe that you have sent me*" (Jn 17:21). Our Lord says it is the unity of believers that will convince men and women of His mission to this world. *The visible unity of believers is then the greatest form of evangelism.* What a rebuke this is to the groundless and often bitter divisions among Christians." (Rom 15:1-7).

Christians are exhorted in Eph 6:16 to "take up the shield of faith," and Bob Gass in his "The Word for Today" Notes states: "The large shields used by Roman soldiers in battle could be locked together in such a way that an entire row could move forward as one single unit, each soldier fully protected. They looked like a moving wall! Their protection was multiplied because of their unity! Their power was increased, because of their ability to work together." This is a relevant call to unity for us today.

The practical implications of Christian unity is well illustrated by the following collection of <u>"The One Another"</u> Scriptural statements given below:

Love one another	Jn 13:34-35
Mutually depend on one another	Rom 12:5
Be devoted to one another	Rom 12:10
Outdo one another in showing favour	Rom 12:10

Rejoice with one another	Rom 12:15
Have the same mind to one another	Rom 12:16
Do not judge one another	Rom 14:13
Build one another up	Rom 14:19
Accept one another	Rom 15:7
Counsel one another	Rom 15:14
Wait for one another	1Cor 11:33
Care for one another	1Cor 12:25
Serve one another	Gal 5:13
Bear one another's burdens	Gal 6:2
Be kind to one another	Eph 4:32
Forgive one another	Eph 4:32
Submit to one another	Eph 5:21
Forbear one another	Col 3:13
Admonish one another with all wisdom	Col 3:16
Encourage one another	1Thess 5:11
Live in peace with one another	1Thess 5:13
Stir up one another	Heb 10:24
Do not speak evil against one another	Jas 4:11
Do not grumble against one another	Jas 5:9
Confess your faults to one another	Jas 5:16
Pray for one another	Jas 5:16
Offer hospitality to one another	1Pet 4:9
Fellowship with one another	1Jn 1:7

OUR RESPONSE TO GOD - DISCIPLESHIP

-FORGIVENESS, UNITY & FELLOWSHIP-

Biblical Texts & Text References

Forgiveness – From God - (see also Section B1)

14 if my people, who are called by my name, will humble themselves and pray and seek my face and turn from their wicked ways, then will I hear from heaven and will forgive their sin and will heal their land.

2Chron 7:14

Believers have redemption through his blood, the forgiveness of sins. See Eph 1:7-8

Additional Scripture references

Ps 79:8-9, Jer 31:33-34, Lk 23:33-34, Rom 4:25, 5:8-10; Gal 1:3-4, Heb 9:12-14, 1Pet 1:18-21, 1Jn 1:6-8; 2:1-2

Forgiveness - To one another

19 And when you stand praying, if you hold anything against anyone, forgive him, so that your Father in heaven may forgive you your sins."

Mk 11:25

Jesus said:" Forgive, and you will be forgiven." See Lk 6:36-37

Additional Scriptures references

Gen 50:15-17; Mat 6:12-15; 18:23-35. Lk 17:3-4; Rom 13:7-8, Col 3:12-14

Unity

Jesus said:" Love one another. As I have loved you, so you must love one another. By this all men will know that you are my disciples." See Jn 13:34-35

9 I appeal to you, brothers, in the name of our Lord Jesus Christ, that all of you agree with one another so that there may be no divisions among you and that you may be perfectly united in mind and thought.

1Cor 1:9

Additional Scripture references

2Chron 30:12, Ps 25:4-5, 133:1-3; Mat 15:8-9, Lk 4:8, Jn 4:23-24; 14:6; 16:13; 17:20-21, Acts 4:24, Rom 2:7-8; 6:4-5; 12:10; 12:15-16; 15:1-2 &7, Eph 1:13, 4:2-3 & 13-15; Phil 1:27, 2:1-2; Col 1:4-5; 2:2, 1Tim 4:2-3; 4:16, Heb 12:28, 1Pet 1:22, 1Jn 3:18

Fellowship

See Jn 13:34-35 and 1Cor 1:9 given in 'Unity' above

6 If we claim to have fellowship with him yet walk in the darkness, we lie and do not live by the truth.
7 But if we walk in the light, as he is in the light, we have fellowship with one another, and the blood of Jesus, his Son, purifies us from all *{Or every}* sin.

1Jn 1:6-7

Additional Scripture references

1Cor 12:20-27; 2Cor 13:14, 1Thess 5:11, Heb 10:23-25, Jas 5:14-16; 1Pet 1:22

E10

OUR RESPONSE TO GOD - DISCIPLESHIP

-THIRSTING FOR GOD & HIS PRESENCE-

Biblical Definitions

Thirsting for God

In a world where life for many is an unending rush to meet all the daily needs of work, home life and leisure, there are those at the other end of the spectrum whose life is a daily struggle for survival amidst many needs and poverty.

With these thoughts in mind the subject of 'thirsting for God' may be considered a strange subject to contemplate. However, whether people are wealthy or poor, in good or poor health, or whatever their circumstances or position in society they all need to initially seek and find God for themselves. When people have 'found God' by becoming Christians there is always a need to know Him better, to hear 'His voice' more clearly and to learn to follow His lead more closely.

There is a basic human desire to seek after God, and this pursuit can occur in various ways. It can come out of a desperate need to hear God and make contact with Him, or out of a desire to know Him better.

The statements below describe in outline the passage of Scripture, given as a reference, and relates to thirsting for God. They reveal something about the intent of the seeker(s) and their surrounding circumstances:

Moses sought the favour of the Lord.
See Ex 32:11

Those who seek God will find Him.
See Deut 4:29, Ps 9:10

Due to a famine, David sought the Lord.
See 2Sam 21:1

A repentant king sought the Lord's favour.
See 2Kgs 13:4

Let the hearts of those who seek the Lord rejoice.
See 1Chron 16:10-11, Ps 105:3

When people humble themselves and pray and seek God's face, He hears and answers them.
See 2Chron 7:14

The people sought God and He gave them rest from their enemies.
See 2Chron 14:7

People in distress, sought and found God.
See 2Chron 15:3-5, 20:3-7

Whilst the king sought God, He gave him success.
See 2Chron 26:5

When Hezekiah the king sought God and worked wholeheartedly, he prospered.
See 2Chron 31:20-21

People separated themselves from unclean practices in order to seek the Lord.
See Ezra 6:21

David's key priority in life was seeking God and gazing on His beauty.
See Ps 27:4

David sought the Lord, He answered and brought him deliverance.
See Ps 34:4

David's experience was that those who sought the Lord lacked nothing good.
See Ps 34:10

There is an urgency to seek the Lord while He may be found.
See Isa 55:6

People will find God when they seek Him with all their heart.
See Jer 29:13

People will find God when they firstly admit their guilt.
See Hos 5:15

There are times of famine of hearing the words of the Lord.
See Amos 8:11-13

Happiness comes to those who thirst for righteousness.
See Mat 5:6

Those who seek will find.
See Mat 7:7

Those who believe in the Lord Jesus Christ will never be thirsty.
See Jn 6:35, 7:37

God waits for people to seek Him, because He is near us.
See Acts 17:27

God rewards those who earnestly seek Him.
See Heb 11:6

To those who are thirsty for God, He will freely give the water of life.
See Rev 21:6

The Presence of God

A Christian by themselves or in a group of Christians can know something of 'the Presence of God' in an almost tangible way, and know within themselves that they are in a special place near to God. At this time they sense the awe of the occasion and feel the acceptance and pleasure of this privileged position that brings in its wake, joy, confidence, peace and harmony. Many of the experiences referred to above can be seen in the Scriptures quoted below. The range of the Scriptures referred to that relate to this subject vary from a general overall sense of His Presence to that which is of a more intimate nature, and this should be borne in mind as the following Biblical references are considered. The statements below describe in outline the passage of Scripture, given as a reference, and relates to the Presence of God. They reveal something of the effects of 'His Presence' and the accompanying circumstances surrounding them.

After Cain had killed his brother we read: "Cain went out from the Lord's presence" Gen 4

A situation of harmony and sacrifices happened in the presence of God. See Ex 18:12

Moses was not prepared to lead the people on their journey towards the "Promised Land" unless he was assured of God's Presence with them.
See Ex 33:14-19

When Moses came out from the presence of the Lord his face was radiant, but he did not know it.
See Ex 34: 30-35

The Israelite leaders and people stood in the presence of the Lord to enter into a covenant with Him.
See Deut 29:10-15

God revealed Himself to Elijah when he was in His presence.
See 1Kgs 19:9-13

The Israelites forsook all the commands of the Lord, worshipped idols, practised divination and sorcery, so the Lord removed them from His presence.
See 2Kgs 17:16-20

The people praised the Lord, made sacrifices and feasted with great joy in the Lord's presence.
See 1Chron 29:20-22

Praying in God's presence.
See 2Chron 6:19

Confident of having prayers heard and answered in God's presence even when troubles come.
See 2Chron 20:9

The king of Judah's prayer was heard when he humbled himself and repented in the Lord's presence.
See 2Chron 34:27

Because of guilt people could not stand in God's presence.
See Ezra 9:15

The arrogant cannot stand in God's presence.
See Ps 5:5

People are granted eternal blessings and joy in the presence of the Lord.
See Ps 21:6

God's presence provides a shelter to those who take refuge in Him.
See Ps 31:19-20

God's presence is a gateway to spiritual restoration.
See Ps 51:9-12

God's presence is everlasting.
See Ps 61:5-7

They are blessed who walk in the light of God's presence.
See Ps 89:15

Those who speak falsely will not stand in God's presence.
See Ps 101:7

Those who oppose God will one day tremble in His presence.
See Ezek 38:20

The Lord Jesus Christ enjoyed the presence of God the Father.
See Jn 17:3-5

There is joy in God's presence.
See Acts 2:28

People hear from God when in His presence.
See Acts 10:32-33

Believers in the Lord Jesus Christ will spend eternity in His presence.
See 2Cor 4:13-14

Believers will be blameless and joyful in God's presence.
See 1Thess 3:9-13

Those who do not know God will suffer eternally and be shut out from His presence.
See 2Thess 1:8-9

There is rest in God's presence.
See 1Jn 3:18-20

God is able to keep His own people and present them in His glorious presence.
See Jude 1:24-25

OUR RESPONSE TO GOD - DISCIPLESHIP

-THIRSTING FOR GOD & HIS PRESENCE-

Notes and Quotations

Thirsting for God

One aspect of people thirsting for God is to want to know Him better. In this pursuit we often spend most of our thought, time and energy on issues such as Christian principles, doctrine and lifestyle etc., important as they are, rather than spending time with getting to know God better. Selwyn Hughes relates to this issue in his "Every Day with Jesus" Notes when he states: "We all find it easier to ***do*** than to ***be***; we prefer a plan to follow rather than a Person to trust. What our carnal nature hates to be faced with is the challenge of throwing ourselves in utter dependency on a God who is invisible and intangible. Yet this is what a relationship with God entails."

"Human beings must be known to be loved; but the Divine must be loved to be known." Quote by Blaise Pascal from the book "The Christian Book of Lists" by Randy Petersen.

John 14 in the Bible has much to say about 'knowing God and the Holy Spirit', and in the "Every Day with Jesus" Notes by Selwyn Hughes, he states with special reference to Jn 14:17: "The word "know" signifies a true and close relationship between the person knowing and the person known. Hence it is more than knowing about – it is *knowing* in a deep and intimate way. When the Holy Spirit is received He is also perceived. To know Him is to be swayed by His truth, inspired by His love, kept by His grace, led by His hand, sustained by His presence, cheered by His promise and used in His service."

The book, "The Heart of a God Chaser" by Tommy Tenney, contains a rich source of quotations and Biblical texts for those who engage in the pursuit of God. Given below is a quotation from this book:

What is a God Chaser? – "A God chaser is an individual whose hunger exceeds his reach."

Tommy Tenny

David said: "My soul followeth hard after thee."

Ps 63:8 KJV

Who is chasing whom? – "We pursue God because, and only because, He has first put an urge within us that spurs us to the pursuit."

A.W. Tozer

It is very important to know the characteristics that God is looking for in those who would want to follow him and the Scripture Isa 66:2 provides some key answers when it says the person he esteems will be humble and contrite in spirit, and trembles at his word.

He is no fool who gives what he cannot keep to gain what he cannot lose.

Jim Elliot

We must put away all effort to impress and come with the guileless candour of childhood.

A.W. Tozer

He who makes God's glory the one and only aim before which all other things bow themselves is the man to bring honour to his Lord.

Charles H. Spurgeon

To have found God and still to pursue Him is the soul's paradox of love.

A.W.Tozer

In the Psalm of David below we see him earnestly thirsting after God. Many people experience a sense of dryness in their Christian life, and this can be caused through many things such as: mental, physical, emotional or spiritual exhaustion; sin; business pressures etc. It should be recognised and confessed, and time spent on refocusing on God, seeking Him afresh and meditating on Him through His Word. See Biblical Meditation in Section 8.

(A psalm of David. When he was in the Desert of Judah.)
O God, you are my God, earnestly I seek you; my soul thirsts for you, my body longs for you, in a dry and weary land where there is no water.
I have seen you in the sanctuary and beheld your power and your glory.
Because your love is better than life, my lips will glorify you.
I will praise you as long as I live, and in your name I will lift up my hands.
My soul will be satisfied as with the richest of foods; with singing lips my mouth will praise you.
On my bed I remember you; I think of you through the watches of the night.

Ps 63:1-6

In Ps 107:8-9 we see God meeting the need of those who are hungry and thirsty for Him: This Psalm also shows how people sought the Lord for a variety of other needs, Conditions and circumstances, and how He heard, delivered and healed them.

The Presence of God

Repentance precedes coming into His presence, - see Isa 59:1-3

King David having sinned and repented wanted to be reassured that he had not been cast out of God's presence, - see Ps 51:9-12

We can come into a worship service, but still not enter His presence because there is a blockage in our personal relationship with God, due to the fact that there is sin in our life that we have not confessed and repented of.

Someone has said: "The measure to which we have the presence of God with us will be the measure with which we cause people to become aware of God." - See Acts 4:8-14

The psalmist in Ps 73:23-28, affirms his nearness to God, and verse 28 can be seen as a conscious act to fulfil a divine purpose through a spontaneous response.

Because we're so easily distracted by what's around us, we can't see that "fullness of joy" comes from ***within.*** It can only be found in God's presence. Time alone with Him; meditating on where he's brought you from; personalising His promises to you; <u>that's</u> what will cause you to soar to heights that no human achievement, relationship or mood-altering substance can bring. Why do you constantly run after the world's pleasures? They're temporary at best and addictive at worst. In your Father's presence, you'll find pleasure without guilt and joy without pain. So let's regroup and stay on (or get back on) the path that leads to real life, for everything you're seeking is already in His presence. Think about it!

The above statement was written by Sarah Utterbach and taken from "The Word for Today" Notes by Bob Gass.

We are each encouraged to seek God's face –see 1Chron 16:10-11.
His presence is known in the congregation -- see 2Chron 5:11-14.

St Augustine used to ask his students: "Which would you prefer: to have all your questions answered and be bereft of God's presence or to have God's presence and none of your questioned answered?" "(words paraphrased)." From the "Every Day with Jesus "Notes by Selwyn Hughes. See Ex 33:14-19

When the people were praising God in the temple it was filled with a cloud, and it says that the glory of the Lord filled the temple – see 2Chron 5:13-6:2, & 7:1-3. In the N.I.V. Study Bible it states: "The glory cloud represented the presence of God."

In 1Kgs 19:9-13 we read how Elijah, God's prophet, flees in fear of his life and goes into a cave. It was here, in the presence of the Lord, that God spoke to him.

When we are in God's presence and He 'speaks' to us who have a relationship with Him, that 'word' must be received with faith and acted on with grace and humility. For these 'words' are given for the common good of believers, for their strengthening, encouragement, comfort and edification. 1Cor 12:7, 13:1-2, 14:1-4, 2Pet 1:19-21.

In Jonah 1:1-17 we see the story of how Jonah, a man of God, who intended to flee from the presence of the Lord because he did not want to do what God had asked him, and the subsequent problems he caused for himself and others. After God had disciplined him, He brought blessing to others through him. A lesson here is that we should seek to remain in His will, and so in His presence.

<u>God's Presence is a place:</u>

– to find rest,	Ex 33:14; 1Jn 3:18-20
– to converse with God and become radiant	Ex 34:30-34
– to hear God's voice,	1Kgs 19:11-13; Acts 10:32-33
– to pray,	2Chron 6:19
– to find protection,	2Chron 20:9
– where people humbled themselves and	
– wept in prayer,	2Chron 34:27
– to find joy,	Ps 16:11; 21:6; Acts 2:28; 1Thess 3:9
– for those who have confessed all to God,	
– and find blessing	Ps 24:3-5
– to find shelter from those who would accuse you	Ps 31: 19-20
– of confession and restoration,	Ps 51:9-12
– of refuge,	Ps 73:28
– of enlightenment,	Ps 89:15
– where we will be kept from falling and finally presented to God without fault and with great joy,	Jude 1:24-25

<u>Actions and attitudes that will exclude people from God's Presence:</u>

– murder,	Gen 4:16
– idolatry and ignoring God's commands,	2Kgs 17:16-20
– guilt,	Ezra 9:15
– arrogance,	Ps 5:5
– the practice of deceit,	Ps 101: 7
– unconfessed sin,	Isa 59:1-3
– those who refuse to obey the gospel of the Lord Jesus Christ,	2Thess 1:8-9

Through him, ... [illegible] ... we should seek to remain in His will and ... in His presence.

[illegible]

Ex 33:14

[illegible]

OUR RESPONSE TO GOD - DISCIPLESHIP

-THIRSTING FOR GOD & HIS PRESENCE-

Biblical Texts & Text References

Thirsting for God

6 Seek the LORD while he may be found; call on him while he is near.

Isa 55:6

6 Blessed are those who hunger and thirst for righteousness, for they will be filled.

Mat 5:6

Additional Scripture references

Ex 32:11, Deut 4:29; 2Sam 21:1, 2Kgs 13:4, 1Chron 16:10-11, 2Chron 7:14; 14:7; 15:3-5; 26:5; 31:20-21, Ezra 6:21, Ps 27:4; 34:4; 42:1-4; 51:9-12; 84:10; 107:8-9, Prov 2:1-6, Jer 28:13, Hos 5:15, Mat 6:31-33; 7:7, Jn 4:13-14; 6:33-35; 7:37-39, Acts 17:27, Heb 11:6, Rev 21:6-7

The Presence of God

A prayer of King David – after he had committed adultery:

9 Hide your face from my sins and blot out all my iniquity.
10 Create in me a pure heart, O God, and renew a steadfast spirit within me.
11 Do not cast me from your presence or take your Holy Spirit from me.
12 Restore to me the joy of your salvation and grant me a willing spirit, to sustain me.

Ps 51:9-12

7 No-one who practices deceit will dwell in my house; no-one who speaks falsely will stand in my presence.

Ps 101:7

24 To him who is able to keep you from falling and to present you before
his glorious presence without fault and with great joy—
20 to the only God our Saviour be glory, majesty, power and authority,
through Jesus Christ our Lord, before all ages, now and for evermore!
Amen.

Jude 1:24-25

Additional Scripture references

Gen 4:13-16, Ex 18:12; 33:14-19; 34:30-35, Deut 29:10-15, 1Kg 19:9-13, 2Kg 17:16-20, 1Chron 29:20-22, 2Chr 5:11-14; 6:19, 20:9; 34:27, Ezra 9:15, Ps 5:5; 16:11; 21:6; 24:3-5; 31:19-20; 61:5-7; 73:23-28; 89:15, Isa 59:1-3, Ezek 38:20, Jn 17:3-5, Acts 2:28; 4:8-14; 10:32-33, 1Cor 12:7; 13:1-2; 14:1-4, 2Cor 4:13-14, 1Thess 3:9-13, 2Thess 1:8-9, 2Pet 1:19-21, 1Jn 3:18-20

ACKNOWLEDGMENTS

The author has made every effort to trace the copyright holders to secure permission for quotations used in this book. Should any have been inadvertently missed, copyright holders are asked to contact the publishers.

John Gill DD. from his *"A Body of Doctrinal Divinity"*
John Gill DD. from his *"A Body of Practical Divinity"*
NIV Bible Text used via 'Access Code'

The above items have permission through "The Word from Online Bible" software Copyright 2000, Timnathserah Inc, Canada, from John Ritchie Ltd, UK.

Anderson, Dr Neil T., *Victory Over the Darkness, p.51.*Copyright 2000, Gospel Light/Regal Books, Ventura, CA 93003. Used by permission.

Berkhof, Louis., *Systematic Theology,* Page 318, The Banner of Truth Trust.

Brown, Colin., General Editor, Dictionary of New Testament Theology Vol 2, 1986, Zondervan, USA.

Buckland, A., Editor, *Universal Bible Dictionary,* 1960, The Lutterworth Press.

Campbell, Murdoch., *In All their Affliction,* 1987, Presbyterian Publishing Corporation.

Dunn, Ronald., *Don't just stand there……Pray Something,* 1992, Tyndale House Publishers, Inc.

Gass, Bob., *The Word for Today,* United Christian Broadcasters Ltd.

Grudem, Wayne., *Bible Doctrine,* 1999, Zondervan, USA.

Henry, Matthew., *Bible Commentary,* 2001, Marshall and Pickering.

Hession, Roy., *The Calvary Road – Be Filled Now,* 1988, Publisher CLC USA.

Hughes, Selwyn., *Every Day with Jesus,* copyright CWR. Used with permission.

Jones, Dr E. Stanley., *The Seven R's,* Every Day with Jesus notes (Selwyn Hughes).

Kendrick, Graham., Quotations on worship, Make Way Music, PO Box 320, Kent, UK.

McDougal, Harold., *Principles of the Christian Faith,* 1986, McDougal Publishing.

Nicene Creed.,As printed in the Alternate Service Book 1980 is C 1970, 1971, 1975

International Consultation on English Texts (ICET).

The Open Bible – New King James Version, Copyright C 1982 by Thomas Nelson, Inc.

Parsons, Rob., *Bringing Home the Prodigals,* 2008, Hodder and Stoughton.

Petersen, Randy., *The Christian Book of Lists,* 1997, Tyndale House Publishers, Inc.

Platinga, Cornelius., *Not the way it's supposed to be,* 1996, Wm B Eerdmans Publishing.

Pratney, Winkie., *Revival,* 1983, Whitaker House publishers.

Pullinger, Jackie., Quotation on the Gospel, St Stephens Society.

The Protestant Dictionary, 1933 Edited by Charles Carter, Harrison Trust publishers.

Ravenhill, Leonard., *Why Revival Tarries,* 1959, Baker Publishing Group.

Richards, Lawrence. O., *Expository Dictionary of Bible Words,* 1988, Zondervan, USA.

SASRA "Ready" magazine Volume 1997-2002 No 13 Jan-June 2001, *The Bible.*

Schirrmacher, Dr Thomas., *Evangelical Review of Theology,* World Evangelical Commission.

Swindoll, Chuck., Quotations on the Gospel, Zondervan, USA.

Tenney, Tommy., *The God Chasers,* 1998, Destiny Image Publishers, USA.

Tozer, A.W., *The Pursuit of God,* 1948, Gospel Light / Regal Books, Ventura, CA 93003, USA.

Verwer, George., Quotation on grace. USA.

Virgo, Terry., Quotation relating to Neh 1:1-9, New Frontiers, UK.

Willmington, H.L., *Willmingtons Book of Bible Lists,* 1988, Tyndale House Publishers, Inc. USA.

Yancey, Philip., *What's So Amazing About Grace,* 1997, Zondervan, USA.

Bullinger, [illegible] of the Gospel, St Stephens [illegible]

The Protestant Dictionary, 1933, [illegible] Charles Carter, Harrison Trust Publisher.

[illegible] 1998, Baker Publishing Group.

[illegible] Lawrence, [illegible] Dictionary of Bible Words, 1958, [illegible] Zondervan, USA.

[illegible] No 13 [illegible] June 2001, The [illegible]

[illegible]

[illegible]

[illegible] Publishers, [illegible]

[illegible]

[illegible]

[illegible] House, [illegible] USA.

[illegible] Zondervan, USA.

CITATIONS

The author has made every effort to cite the authors of the quotations used in this book, but should any have been inadvertently missed, they are asked to contact the publishers.

The author is very grateful for the use of statements made by authors listed below through the generosity of their 'Fair Use' policies.

Bruce, F.F., Quotation, InterVarsity Press, USA.

Buckingham, Jamie., *A Way Through the Wilderness,* 1985, Zondervan, USA.

Buchanan, Alex., *Bible Meditation,* 1987, Kingsway Publications, UK

Campbell, Duncan., Two short quotations, sermonaudio.com.

Cassidy, Michael., *Bursting the Wine Skins,* 1983, Hodder, UK.

Clair, Colin., *Word Abiding, 1963,* Bruce & Gawthorn, UK.

Crabb Dr, Larry., Quotation-*Warning about having a lightweight view of God.* New Way Ministries. USA.

Hybels, Bill., Quotation-*Defines elements for a strong Christian character,* Willow Creek organisation, USA.

Kendall, R.T., *The Word and the Spirit,* 1996, Struik Christian Books, South Africa.

Lockridge, Dr S.M. Quotation entitled *'My King Is',* San Diego, CA, USA.

Oxford University Press, Prayer by an *'Anonymous Confederate Soldier'*, UK.

Redpath, Alan., Quotation about Christian work and prayer, sermonindex@gmail.com

Thompson, F.C., *Thompson Chain Reference Bible (NIV)*, 1986, Hodder, UK.

Vine, W.E., *The Expository Dictionary of Bible Words*, 1981, HarperCollins publishers.

Watson, David., *Discipleship*, 1983, Hodder, UK.

THE USE OF THE BOOK

The book could be used for a number of purposes including those set out below. To provide some guidance, the book is divided into two parts with different purposes. Part One is designed for those people particularly outlined in (a) to (c) below, and Part Two is for those outlined in (d) to (k).

a) Is principally written for those who are searching for: the meaning to life; security, purpose and hope; and for those wanting to get the best out of life.

   It provides a step-by-step approach, avoiding jargon, to understanding the essential aspects of the Christian Faith, and outlines its unique claims.

   It assumes the reader will have little or no prior knowledge of the Christian Faith, or the Bible. Also, it does not assume the person possesses a Bible or has access to one.

b) For those seeking to come to know God in a personal way and be assured of eternal security.

c) For those who want to know more why not chat now at www.Groundwire.org.uk - they are available 24/7

d) To act as a guidebook to those seeking to understand and look into the Christian Faith in depth for themselves, even if they have little or no prior knowledge of it. Also, to provide the teaching contained in the Faith. The book contains the essential biblical texts related to the topics covered, and hence, does not assume the reader either possesses a Bible, or has access to one.

e) To act as a reference book or manual for new and young Christians and Churches by providing the foundational building blocks of biblical principles and teaching materials for them to refer to.

f) To act as a reference book or manual for established Churches by comparing their teaching with the materials and Scriptures provided.

g) For those wishing to deepen their knowledge of the Bible and to understand and experience more of God in their lives.

h) To act as a reference book for those undertaking private or group Bible study.

j) To act as an aid in sermon preparation.

k) For those wishing to compare the Christian Faith with other Faiths.

ABBREVIATIONS FOR BOOKS OF THE BIBLE

The Canon of the Old Testament

Book Name	Abbreviation
Genesis	Gen
Exodus	Ex
Leviticus	Lev
Numbers	Num
Deuteronomy	Deut
Jushua	Josh
Judges	Jud
Ruth	Ru
Samuel (1 & 2)	1Sam & 2Sam
Kings (1 & 2)	1Kg & 2Kg
Chronicles (1 & 2)	1Chron & 2Chron
Ezra	Ezr
Nehemiah	Neh
Esther	Est
Job	Job
Psalms	Ps
Proverbs	Prov
Ecclesiastes	Ecc
Song of Solomon	Ss
Isaiah	Isa

Jeremiah	Jer
Lamentations	Lam
Ezekiel	Ezek
Daniel	Dan
Hosea	Hos
Joel	Joel
Amos	Am
Obadiah	Ob
Jonah	Jon
Micah	Mic
Nahum	Nah
Habakkuk	Hab
Zephaniah	Zep
Haggai	Hag
Zechariah	Zec
Malachi	Mal

The Canon of the New Testament

Book Name	Abbreviation
Matthew	Mat
Mark	Mk
Luke	Lk
John	Jn
Acts of the Apostles	Acts
Romans	Rom
1Corinthians	1Cor
2Corinthians	2Cor
Galatians	Gal
Ephesians	Eph
Philippians	Phil
Colossians	Col

1Thessalonians	1Thess
2Thessalonians	2Thess
1Timothy	1Tim
2Timothy	2Tim
Titus	Tit
Philemon	Phm
Hebrews	Heb
James	Jas
1Peter	1Pet
2Peter	2Pet
1John	1Jn
2John	2Jn
3John	3Jn
Jude	Jude
Revelation	Rev